THE MUKTEŚVARA TEMPLE IN BHUBANESWAR

WALTER SMITH

MOTILAL BANARSIDASS PUBLISHERS
PRIVATE LIMITED • DELHI

First Edition: Delhi, 1994

ISBN: 81-208-0793-6

Also available at:

MOTILAL BANARSIDASS
41 U.A., Bungalow Road, Jawahar Nagar, Delhi 110 007
120 Royapettah High Road, Mylapore, Madras 600 004
16 St. Mark's Road, Bangalore 560 001
Ashok Rajpath, Patna 800 004
Chowk, Varanasi 221 001

PRINTED IN INDIA
BY JAINENDRA PRAKASH JAIN AT SHRI JAINENDRA PRESS,
A-45 NARAINA, PHASE I, NEW DELHI 110 028 AND PUBLISHED BY
NARENDRA PRAKASH JAIN FOR MOTILAL BANARSIDASS PUBLISHERS
PVT. LTD., BUNGALOW ROAD, DELHI 110 007

TO MY PARENTS

ACKNOWLEDGEMENTS

An Earlier Version of this study was completed as a doctoral thesis at the University of Iowa, under the direction of Professor Wayne Begley, to whom I must express great thanks. I am grateful also to M. A. Dhaky, Associate Director of Research at the American Institute of Indian Studies, Center for Art and Archaeology, Varanasi, who has shown great interest in this study, and has provided much encouragement. Thanks also to Krishna Deva, formerly of the A.I.I.S. Center in Varanasi, and to D. R. Das, Calcutta University for their advice and suggestions. I am greatly indebted to Nancy Kipp Smith, who has provided drawings for this study, and has read and criticized several drafts.

Financial assistance for this study was given by the American Institute of Indian Studies in the form of a Junior Research Fellowship in 1982-83; and by the University of Iowa, School of Art and Art History. For permission to illustrate works from various archives I must thank the American Institute of Indian Studies, the Archaeological Survey of India, and the Asian Art Archive, University of Michigan.

CONTENTS

LIST OF FIGURES

31. Enclosure wall, Sarasvatī.
32. Enclosure wall, composite figure.
33. Enclosure wall, Vārāhī.
34. Enclosure wall, Sarasvatī/celestial musician.
35. Enclosure wall, Kārttikeya.
36. Enclosure wall, Gaṇeśa.
37. Enclosure wall, Śiva Gajāsurasaṁhāramūrti.
38. Enclosure wall, *yogin* (Lakulīśa?).
39. Enclosure wall, goddess.
40. Enclosure wall, composite figure.
41. *Toraṇa,* from west.
42. *Toraṇa*, detail of base.
43. *Toraṇa,* detail of capital.
44. *Toraṇa,* arch from west.
45. *Toraṇa,* arch from east.
46. *Maṇḍapa,* entrance (AIIS).
47. Entrance, left *dvārapāla.*
48. Entrance, right *dvārapāla.*
49. Entrance, detail of lintel.
50. West wall, detail of *ratha.*
51. South wall, lattice window.
52. Lattice window, Gajalakṣmī.
53. Lattice window, *gaṇa.*
54. Lattice window, left side, *gandharva* couple.
55. Lattice window, right side, *gandharva* couple.
56. Entrance, left pilaster, female figure.
57. Entrance projection, north side, *vyāla* and male figure.
58. West wall (left of entrance), *nāga*-pilaster and *karṇa* figure.
59. West wall (left of entrance), *nāga*-pilasters.
60. Entrance, right pilaster, *śālabhañjikā.*
61. Entrance projection, south side, *śālabhañjikā* and *vyāla.*
62. West wall (right of entrance), *nāga*-pilasters and *karṇa* figure.
63. North wall, *karṇa* figure (*śālabhañjikā)* and *nāga*-pilaster.
64. North wall, *nāga*-pilasters.
65. North wall, right side of projecting lattice window, *vyāla* and *karṇa* figure.
66. North wall, lattice window, right pilaster, *śālabhañjikā.*
67. North wall, female figures above lattice windows.
68. North wall, lattice window, left pilaster, *śālabhañjikā.*
69. North wall, left side of projecting lattice window, *karṇa* figure and *vyāla.*
70. North wall, *nāga*-pilasters.

ABBREVIATIONS

AA	*Artibus Asiae*
ARB	K. C. Panigrahi. *Archaeological Remains at Bhubaneswar.* Calcutta, 1961.
CJRTO	A. Eschmann. *et al.*, eds. *The Cult of Jagannatha and the Regional Tradition of Orissa.* New Delhi, 1978.
HCIP	R. C. Mazumdar. ed. *History and Culture of the Indian People.* Bombay, 1951-69.
HTAO	T. Donaldson. *Hindu Temple Art of Orissa.* Leiden, 1985-87.
IHQ	*Indian Historical Quarterly.*
JAOS	*Journal of the American Oriental Society.*
JAS	*Journal of Asian Studies.*
JBORS	*Journal of the Bihar and Orissa Research Society.*
JIH	*Journal of Indian History.*
JISOA	*Journal of the Indian Society of Oriental Art.*
MASI	*Memoirs of the Archaeological Survey of India.*
OHRJ	*Orissa Historical Research Journal.*

INTRODUCTION

The Mukteśvara temple in Bhubaneswar, a Śaivite shrine dating to ca. 970 A.D., is a monument of singular importance in the study of the development of the Hindu temples in Orissa. In this stylistic development the Mukteśvara plays a pivotal role; it marks the culmination of all earlier developments, and initiates a period of experiment which continues for an entire century, as seen in such temples as the Rājarāni and Liṅgarāja, also in Bhubaneswar.

While the history of Orissan temple architecture has been outlined in several general works,[1] there exists at present no exhaustive monograph on any Orissan temple. Yet such studies are greatly needed in order not only to clarify the relative chronological position of particular monuments within an overall formal development, but also to fully document their individual features. The Mukteśvara temple is taken up for study here because of its importance in the stylistic development of the Orissan Hindu temple, as well as for its unique iconographical interest.

Aside from being of a highly general nature, previous scholarship has made little attempt to deal in depth with any of the more complex and problematic issues of Orissan architecture. Reference is made particularly to issues concerning context, whether on the historical, artistic, or religious levels. One of the most basic issues in regard to the artistic context of Orissan temple architecture is chronology, yet this issue has not been systematically dealt with by any scholar. To be valid, such a chronology must consider various types of evidence together, such as the development of the plan and elevation, the development of various architectural elements and sculptural motifs, and whatever inscriptional evidence that may survive (unfortunately, little inscriptional material is of direct relevance to Orissan architecture). Most previous scholarship, however, has taken the opposite approach. Rather than dealing with the temples as cohesive entities, they have emphasized instead the study of individual sculptural motifs and isolated iconographical elements, usually surveying the entire history of Orissan architecture.[2] These studies attempt to present a general stylistic development, of the particular motif under study, and by extension of the temples on which the motifs appear. For the most part, however, these studies have simply surveyed the various motifs, and moreover, have been relatively unconcerned with chronology as an art historical issue.

These same studies have also attempted to deal with the meaning (religious, metaphysical, symbolic) of Orissan temple. But by considering only the meaning of particular motifs, they have contributed little to an understanding of the meaning of the temples as the summation of many symbols and motifs, as unified conceptual statements.

This monograph will attempt to address both the problems of formal development and symbolic meaning in relation to the Mukteśvara temple. It is divided into five chapters. Chapter 1 is a review of the literature on the Hindu temple in Orissa; it will place this study within its scholarly context, and indicate the various approaches to the subject yet to be taken. Chapter 2 is a detailed description of the Mukteśvara temple and its sculptural program. Chapter 3 is an interpretation of the temple and its iconography. The sculpture of the temple is seen as constituting a cohesive, unified program that can be read on a variety of levels, rather than as a generalized arrangement of various sculptural motifs. The Mukteśvara temple's symbolic meaning can be interpreted more fully if a functional context is kept in mind. Two major ritual activities were practised in ancient Hindu temples and continue to the present-day; *pradakṣinā,* a ritual clockwise circling of the temple, and *pūjā*, worship of the divinity within the *garbhagṛha* (inner shrine) with oblations, lights, the chanting of *mantras* and so forth. These rituals are primarily performed by individuals, and little is known about the purpose served by the large *maṇḍapa* (usually translated "audience hall"), placed before the *prāsāda* (shrine proper). From the evidence assembled here, we can with some confidence suggest that the *maṇḍapa* was used as a meditation hall, and perhaps as a place for private initiation ceremonies which excluded the general public. In addition to providing a locus for religious rituals, the Mukteśvara may have also served a very different function. The images of kings placed prominently on the *śikhara* (superstructure) and in conjunction with imagery connected to the god Śiva, to whom the temple is dedicated, the Mukteśvara may also have served as a monument glorifying the early kings of the Somavaṃśī dynasty, perhaps also proclaiming their divine legitimacy as the rulers of Orissa.

Chapter 5 presents a chronological sequence for temples preceding, contemporary with, and following the Mukteśvara, tracing the development of the "mature" style, and indicating the place of the Mukteśvara within this development. It establishes the Mukteśvara as the temple which makes a major shift from earlier styles, also introducing various non-Orissan elements which came to have a lasting impact on the Orissan temple.

A final note should be added here about the use of technical Sanskrit terminology in describing Orissan temple architecture. An attempt is made to reach a balance between the use of Sanskrit terms for every part of the temple down to the smallest moulding, and a total substitution of these terms with Western "equivalents", which are often not equivalents at all, and can often be very misleading.[3] The use of Sanskrit architectural terms here is modified, primarily for the major parts of the temples which have no obvious Western equivalents. Sources include the various Purāṇas which have sections on architecture,[4] and the glossary of terms found in the first volume of the American Institute of Indian Studies' *Encyclopaedia of Indian Temple*

Architecture.[5] The terms will be clearly defined upon their initial use, and a glossary is included for further reference.

NOTES

1. For example ARB, and HTAO. For detailed discussions of these and other general works, see Chapter 1.

2. I refer in particular to studies on various sculptural motifs by T. Donaldson, and the iconographical studies of K. C. Panigrahi. These will be fully discussed in the following chapter.

3. I am in basic agreement, then, with M. M. Ganguly, *Orissa and Her Remains* (Calcutta, 1912). See below, Chapter 1, note 14.

4. See T. Singh, "Some Reflections on Temple Architecture from Garuḍa Purāṇa", *Purāṇa,* (July, 1980), p. 186; "Bhaviṣya Purāṇa and Bṛhat Saṁhitā on Temple Architecture: A Collative Study", *Purāṇa,* "An Appraisal of the Data Regarding Temple Architecture Gleaned from Agni Purāṇa", *Purāṇa,* 23.2 (July, 1981), pp. 188-200.

5. See M. W. Meister, ed., *Encyclopaedia of Indian Temple Architecture, South India, Lower Draviḍadeśa* (Delhi, 1983), vol. 1, part 2, pp. 285-95; and A. K. Coomaraswamy, "Indian Architectural Terms", JAOS 48 (1928), pp. 250-75. My reasons for rejecting the data compiled in A. Boner and S. R. Śarmā, trans. *Śilpa Prakāśa* (Leiden, 1966), and for using less extensively than previous scholars the work of N. K. Bose, *Canons of Orissan Architecture* (Calcutta, 1932), are given in the following chapter.

CHAPTER 1

REVIEW OF THE LITERATURE

The earliest systematic overview of the temples of Orissa is in James Fergusson's *History of Indian and Eastern Architecture* (1876).[1] As the first attempt, it is a solid assessment of the general characteristics of the Orissan temple form. At the end of the brief essay, Fergusson presents a tentative chronology of about thirty major temples. He chooses not to describe each one; rather since the scope of his work is so vast, he presents a selection of those monuments which he ascertained to be the most significant. He discusses the major temples in and around Bhubaneswar, mentioning also the temples at Mukhaliṅgam (Andhra Pradesh), thus taking into account the spread of the Orissan style beyond the major center of Bhubaneswar.

Fergusson's chronology is by his own admission tentative, but certain statements are particularly amiss.[2] For example, he assigns the Mukteśvara and the Paraśurāmeśvara to the same general date, between 500 and 600, and sees them as contemporary. The Liṅgarāja is placed specifically to 657. This date is based upon Sterling's account of the history of Orissa that appeared in *Asiatic Researches* in 1825. This history is based upon an uncritical acceptance of local legend, and Fergusson is at fault for accepting it. Giving the date of the Mukteśvara an upper limit of 600 implies that it may have been built only fifty years before the Liṅgarāja. This close correlation, however, is at variance with Fergusson's textual commentary. At one point he states that the Mukteśvara represents in its "porch" (*maṇḍapa*) "at least the germ of what we find in the porches of the Great Temple at Bhubaneswar (the Liṅgarāja),[3] and so should be placed much earlier. Such unclearness indicates that Fergusson did not have a clear conception of the chronological sequence of Orissa's temples, and was able only to point out the general features of the major examples.

Fergusson characterizes the Orissan temple as a pure and homogeneous expression of the "Indo-Aryan" (now usually referred to as the Northern or Nāgara style),[4] and states that from the earliest to the latest examples, "the style steadily progresses without admixture of foreign elements."[5] At certain points, however, he seems to realize that there are exceptions to this generalization. In discussing, for example the Paraśurāmeśvara temple, "he states that its style is certainly different from the other early temples here, and more like what we find in other places outside the province,"[6] pointing specifically to the temples of Aihole and Badami. Later, he makes the contradictory assertion that there are *two* styles of Orissan architecture, one represented by the Paraśurāmeśvara and Mukteśvara, the other by the Liṅgarāja, which he felt to be totally indigenous. In his view the two groups constitute "sister styles", which seem to have "at least partially different origins".[7] Fergusson states that these two styles "ran side by side during the whole course" of development,[8] perhaps to rationalize his highly tentative chronology.

The lack of refinement in Fergusson's chronology marks it as a pioneering attempt, and it must be said that his sense of sequence was fairly accurate. A more important issue is Fergusson's insistence on the "purity" of the Orissan style, for this seems to have caused subsequent scholars to ignore or gloss over the many obvious affinities between Orissan architecture and other regional expressions of the Nāgara style. Fergusson mentions the possibility of the early temples being related to temples of the southern Deccan, and makes the vague assertion that the Rājarāni is related to the Khajuraho group, but these comments are lost in his overall insistence on the separateness of the Orissan style.

A monograph concerned solely with Orissan architecture was attempted by R. L. Mitra in his two-volume work *Antiquities of Orissa* (1875-80), undertaken by order of the Government of India.[9] James Fergusson had little faith in Mitra's abilities as an art historian, and went so far as to express the opinion that Mitra's researches were not likely "to be worth much more than the value of the paper on which they may be written."[10] This frank and perhaps biased assessment has a certain validity, for Mitra's two volumes are burdened with mass of material only remotely, if at all related to the topic at hand. These include a lengthy summary of Indian religion (from the Vedas to Sufism), a discussion of the origins of Indian architecture, and historical background, and for the most part have been superseded by subsequent scholarship. Much effort is also put into defending Indian art against the disparaging attitudes held by many of Mitra's contemporaries, and he refutes the then current idea that anything showing exceptional merit in Indian art must be of a foreign, i.e. classical Greek origin. In his own discussion of Orissan sculpture, however, Mitra is a rather poor apologist, for in his view, the best works are those showing the highest degree of naturalism, while anything showing conventionalized or stylized forms is inferior. These highly westernized and classically oriented aesthetic values show up even more strongly in Mitra's attitudes toward Egyptian and Assyrian art, which he uses rather ill-advisedly in comparison with the sculpture of Orissa.[11]

Art historically, Mitra's discussion of Orissan architecture is far too generalized and ahistorical to generate any understanding of origin and formal development. In his discussions of the temples of Bhubaneswar, there is no consideration of stylistic development or chronological sequence. The order of discussion is determined, rather, by the pilgrims' itinerary found in the *Ekāmra Candrikā*, a late Sanskrit text (ca. sixteenth century) of Orissan origin. Mitra gives more attention to temple's settings, physical conditions and to anecdotes connected with them, rather than to a treatment of architecture and sculpture.

Mitra cites passages from several other late Orissan Sanskrit texts which relate the legendary origins of the temples of Bhubaneswar, which, while interesting as mythology, tell us nothing about such historical concerns as dating and patronage. Mitra makes almost no use, however, of the body of texts which could have been immensely useful in the analysis of architecture—the *śilpa śāstras.* While briefly mentioning several of these works, Mitra was unable, because of their corrupt nature, and the unavailability of *paṇḍits* sufficiently familiar with the texts, to extract any meaning from them.[12] He apparently did not attempt, moreover, to locate local craftsmen still versed in the terminology of the Orissan *śilpa śāstras.* Had he done this, a greater clarity and precision might have been present in his descriptive treatment of the temples.

In this later respect, M. M. Ganguly in *Orissa and Her Remains* (1912), was much more successful.[13] By consulting local craftsmen, he assembled a fairly useful set of terms, which he rightly felt would help him describe various parts of the temple with a greater degree of accuracy than would English equivalents.[14] His terminology, however, which was derived from oral informants rather than from texts,[15] is greatly lacking in accuracy, and was superseded by the later textual studies of N. K. Bose.[16] But in his general discussion of the Orissan temple, Ganguly gives a much clearer idea of its salient characteristics, with the aid of an Indian vocabulary, than does Mitra, with his adaptation of Classical Greek terms. Further clarity is added by the use of plans and elevations, their various parts labeled with the proper terms.

In his use of religious texts, Ganguly brings into discussion only those which were of particular relevance. In his study of the *Agni Purāṇa*, for example, Ganguly found that its iconographical sections, such as the one dealing with the placement and iconography of the *dikpālas,* bore significant correspondence to the placement of images on the temples themselves.[17] This demonstration of the *Agni Purāṇa's* relevance to Orissan architecture was further substantiated by his observation that some of the ritual procedures recommended during the construction of a temple in this text were still being observed in the building of new shrines in Orissa.[18] By citing further textual references to various other images typically found on Orissan temples, such as *nāgas* and *nāginīs,* the *navagrahas* and the female figures, Ganguly took the first step toward detailed and fully explored iconographical studies.

In setting forth the general characteristics of the Orissan temple, then, Ganguly made considerable advances on his predecessors. In dealing with the development of temple architecture in Orissa as a historical phenomenon, however, he succeeds less well. His descriptions of individual temples tend to get lost in florid prose, which often lapses into philosophical and aesthetic rambling. Further, he does not attempt to trace the stylistic development of the temples; instead, he takes each example as the reflection of an *archetype* discussing it in terms of how it adheres or deviates from the norm.[19] This lack of historical sensibility is seen very clearly in the following statement: "Both Mukteśvara and Paraśurāmeśvara are obvious departures from the established type, of which the great Liṅgarāja is a typical example."[20] As a result of such an approach, Ganguly's subsequent attempt at dating the temples appears very unsystematic.[21]

The next major treatment of Orissan temples is a chapter on "Medieval Architecture" in R. D. Banerji's two-volume *History of Orissa* (1931).[22] One of Banerji's major goals, apparently, was to supersede the work of Ganguly, whom he criticizes, often disdainfully, throughout his discussion. Banerji himself, however, makes only a few new contributions to the scholarship of Orissan temple architecture, for in spite of bringing together some new archaeological material, he does not give analytical assessment of the monuments that leads to any conclusions significantly more advanced than those of his predecessors. Banerji's major contribution was his documentation of the temples at Baudh and Gandharadi.[23] As previous studies had focused almost solely on the major temples of Bhubaneswar (Puri and Koṇārka were also given much attention), Banerji's discoveries extended the corpus of monuments, contributing to the formation of a more complete body of material with which to assess the development of Orissan architecture.

In dealing with chronology, Banerji alters a few dates, but not the basic sequence as proposed by Ganguly. Banerji arranges the temples into three groups, having as his single criterion the shapes of the temples' *śikharas* (shrine towers), believing, "the constant principle in the evolution of Indian temples is the shape and outline of the *śikhara*."[24] The first group includes the Paraśurāmeśvara, the "twin temples" at Gandharadi, and the Mukteśvara. These he dates to the eighth century, with the Mukteśvara being the latest in the group. This refutation of Ganguly's sixth century date for the Paraśurāmeśvara is argued for by citing the inscription on that temple's *navagraha* lintel, which, according to Banerji, could not have been written earlier than the eighth century.[25] These four temples are grouped together solely on the grounds of the similarity of their *śikharas*, being, according to Banerji, of "the same type as the Dasāvatāra at Deogadh."[26] The second group, comprising the three Śiva temples at Baudh, the temples of Khiching,[27] and "certain temples at Bhubaneswar", Banerji never specifically dates, but groups together for one reason—they lack *maṇḍapas*, or forehalls. The third group, dated to the tenth century, includes the Liṅgarāja, Ananta-Vāsudeva and Brahmeśvara temples, the connecting factor here being their tall *śikharas*, which "curve suddenly toward the end, near the *āmalaka*, and their pyramidal-roofed *maṇḍapas*."[28]

Such a limited criterion for chronology is obviously inadequate, especially in the case of Banerji's discussion, where they are so vaguely and incompletely described. And in spite of the many pages of pure description of temples, Banerji brings no other evidence, such as wall articulation, decorative motifs or the character of base mouldings, into the consideration of chronology. This ultimately leads to some rather startling statements, such as, that the *maṇḍapa* of the Mukteśvara is a twelfth century addition,[29] and that the Rājarāni, because its *śikhara* is seen to be similar to that of the Jagannātha temple at Puri (a rather unfathomable statement in itself), dates also to the twelfth century.[30]

Rather ironic in light of the fact that Banerji was writing a history of Orissa, is that he fails to convey any sense that the monuments are part of a historical context, especially since evidence for connecting particular monuments with specific rulers and dynasties was not totally non-existent. Citing the *Mādalā Pāñji*, the chronicle of the Jagannātha temple at Puri, Banerji notes that the Liṅgarāja temple is ascribed to "a mythical king named Yayāti Keśarī, probably the same as Mahāśivagupta Yayāti, son of Mahābhavagupta Janmejaya."[31] And in discussing the Brahmeśvara temple inscription, he states that "it is quite possible that Uddyota Keśarī (son of Kolāvatī Devī, the temple's builder) was a lineal descendent of Mahābhavagupta Janmejaya."[32] Banerji fails to mention, however, that the inscription contains a genealogy which, in fact, begins with the name Janmejaya, which makes the identification of Uddyota Keśarī and Mahābhavagupta I Janmejaya very plausible.[33]

Earlier in his book, Banerji refutes the assertion of the epigraphist B. C. Mazumdar that the Somavaṃśī rulers were "the makers of Orissa"[34] Banerji felt that they were not much more than petty chieftains who never had any control over Orissa proper, and so had little role in Orissa's cultural development. Banerji fails to assess the evidence of the Brahmeśvara inscription and of the *Mādalā Pāñji* together, which indicates that the Somavaṃśīs were much more than petty chieftains, and that by the eleventh century they had control over the central part of Orissa, including the Bhubaneswar-Puri area, and were great patrons of art. Ganguly took the first successful steps in discussing the religious (if not the historical) content and context of Orissan temples. Banerji, in spite of his knowledge of the historical records, fails to make similar advancements.

Appearing shortly after Banerji's *History* was N. K. Bose's *Canons of Orissan Architecture* (1932).[35] This work constitutes an extensive analysis of the *Bhubanapradīpa*, a late medieval *śilpa śāstra*. Bose does not give a translation of the entire text, nor even a complete critical edition (which could have been done, since there were several manuscripts at his disposal). Instead, he has arranged the material according to specific topics, such as classifications of soils (upon which the temple is to be built), auspicious ceremonies, and the classification of temple types and their constituent parts, while not necessarily following precisely the order presented in the text itself.

Bose's work sets forth what was to become for art historians the standardized set of terms for the various parts of the Orissan temple. It also presents the text's analysis of the systems of proportions for various temple types, which can be applied to the study of individual monuments (something that Bose himself, however, does not do extensively). Aided in his study by the practising *śilpins* of Orissa, Bose was able to clearly interpret the text, and advanced the work of Ganguly by concerning himself with a text primarily, not depending solely upon the craftsmen for information.

Canons of Orissan Architecture would have been more useful had Bose prepared a critical edition and English translation of the text. This would have presented a clearer idea of the nature of *śilpa śāstras* in general and the *Bhuvanapradīpa* in particular, as important sources for the study of Orissan architecture. Even if many of its parts were corrupted beyond intelligibility,[36] a critical edition would have provided a foundation for future study of Orissan *śilpa śāstras*, and would have allowed scholars to reinterpret the *Bhuvanapradīpa* in the light of subsequently discovered knowledge.

In view of the corrupt nature of the *Bhuvanapradīpa*, however, the value of its architectural terminology comes into question. Many of the terms are of Oriya origin (*ganḍi* for *śikhara, bho* for *śukanāsā/Candraśālā*), or are Oriya corruptions of Sanskrit terms (*raha* for *ratha*, *piṣṭa* for *pītha*), and it does not seem likely that the former were used at the time the temples were built.[37] They are in use by modern craftsmen (at least in Bose's and M. M. Ganguly's time), but do not seem to come out of the northern Indian Sanskrit tradition of *śilpa* texts. The complete adaptation of the *Bhuvanapradīpa's* terminology by art historians, then, was perhaps ill-advised.[38]

The works discussed up until now (except for Bose's study and the parts of Ganguly's book which deal with iconography) have considered the Orissan temple from a purely archaeological point of view. A totally different approach was taken by Stella Kramrisch in two articles published in the *Journal of the Indian Society of Oriental Art*, one in 1934 and the other in 1947.[39] The approach taken here is emphatically art historical, focusing primarily on the visual properties of the temples. In her analysis Kramrisch minutely describes the various parts of selected monuments, how they work together to produce a cohesive artistic statement, and discusses the nature of the Orissan temple's stylistic development through several centuries.

Though published several years apart, these articles should be considered as a single unit, the later piece being a revised and somewhat expanded version of the previous one. In both articles, the temple is conceived as a metaphysical statement, this idea being conveyed by two distinct sets of terminology, one Jungian, the other philosophical. The earlier article relies on the notion that each Orissan temple (and indeed any temple of the Nāgara class), is the expression of a single "archetype". According to Kramrisch, the archetype seeking expression here is that of "dynamic mass. . . shot across by the upward surge"[40] In other words, an inherent sense of massive bulk, resulting in large part from the nature of the material (stone), is qualified by the builder's desire for verticality. Contained within this "archetype", furthermore, is the "indissoluble connection of architecture and sculpture."[41] Kramrisch reaches this conclusion through a painstaking visual analysis, where, for example, the squat, squarish images of the seventh century Paraśurāmeśvara temple, confined to their rectangular frames, are compared to those of the tenth century Mukteśvara, which are three-dimensionally conceived and advance from the body of the temple in much the same way as the "pilasters" (*rathas*) against which they stand.[42]

This observation of the close interrelation of sculpture and architecture (which has now become axiomatic in any discussion of Hindu temples), is given further treatment in the article of 1947. Here the archetype concept has been set aside in favor of a vocabulary based on Hindu metaphysics. The exterior of the temple form is now seen as "the progression from the center: it is a raiment whose texture adheres to the (divine) presence within and clothes it."[43] Images, moreover, are extensions of this progression, they are "bodied forth", and the architectural members against which they stand are their monumental equivalents.[44]

Kramrisch does not, however, concern herself with the specific problem of chronology. Rather than using her various observations as criteria for a chronological sequence, she instead simply accepts and works within the sequence put forth by previous authors.[45] Further, Kramrisch does not analyze a large body of Orissan monuments, but only selected temples, precluding even further a detailed study of stylistic development. She also discusses rather too briefly the problem of the influence of monuments from other regions and the origins of the decorative elements like scroll work and the *gavākṣa* motif.[46] While these statements could have been developed further, they do, however, at least begin to consider a broader stylistic perspective than had been taken in any previous study.

The major contribution of Kramrisch's articles is that they invoke both the visual dynamism and metaphysical profundity of the temples. In that they do not concern themselves deeply with precise chronology and specific sources, the articles may be classified as "appreciations", or "interpretations". However, no previous description of Orissan temple architecture had been so fully concerned with its visual concepts.

Percy Brown's *Indian Architecture: Buddhist and Hindu* (1942) was the first comprehensive study of Indian architecture using standard art historical methodology. It is singularly concerned with just those aspects of the history of the Hindu temple that Kramrisch neglected, i.e. chronology, stylistic development and inter-regional influences.[47] The chapter on Orissa is a concise survey of the major monuments, yet is substantial enough to convey a clear impression of the broad stylistic development of the temples.

One of Brown's most important suggestions is that certain outside influences played a role in the development of the Orissan temple. He points specifically to the early Cālukyan monuments at Aihole, which he feels had an impact upon the earliest phases of temple architecture in Orissa.[48] A separate study would have been needed in order to deal more fully with all the specific historical considerations concerning Cālukyan influence, but he at least begins to make a departure from the view prevalent since Fergusson of the "purity" of the "Indo-Aryan" style in Orissa.

Brown's chronology, while improving upon earlier ones, lacks, however, conceptual clarity.[49] The temples are grouped into three different periods: early (750-900), middle (900-1100), and later (1100-1250). These groupings, however, fail to reflect accurately the conceptual phases within the development of the Orissan temple. For example, the Mukteśvara (ca. 975) is grouped together with the Liṅgarāja (ca. 1000), the Brahmeśvara (1075), and the Jagannātha temple, Puri (ca. 1100). Brown includes within the later period the Rājarāni, and gives it the same date as the Ananta-Vāsudeva temple, 1100-1200. Brown thus groups together, quite arbitrarily, temples at obviously different stages of development. Further, he does not take into account several important monuments which could have conveyed more clearly the idea of a "middle period", such as the temples at Baudh and Gandharadi, documented by Banerji, and the Gaurī temple at Bhubaneswar.

Another survey of the temples of Orissa, by S. K. Sarasvati, appeared in 1953.[50] The article amplifies Brown's essay in that it gives a much more thorough description of the general form of the Orissan temple and its various parts, and is more clear and illuminating than any such description preceding it. The survey, however, is very selective, and like Brown's, neglects several temples that would shed more light on the development of the mature Orissan temple form. In its general disconcern with chronology, Sarasvati's essay is less historical than Brown's. Neither scholar presents information on the cultural background against which the temples were produced, nor are they concerned with symbolic meaning or iconography.

Sarasvati's views differ from Brown's on the important question of the role of external influence. Sarasvati is of the opinion that the Orissan temple is indeed a pure reflection of the "original archetype" of the Nāgara or Northern style. He theorizes that the prominent *śikhara*-clusters of the Rājarāni are not a product of Central Indian influence, but rather, originated in Orissa, developing logically from the rounding of the *karṇa* and *bhadra* projections, seen in an early stage on the Muktešvara temple.[51] Sarasvati, however, does not attempt to prove his ideas by presenting a detailed argument. But it is an intriguing notion, and will be given further consideration in chapter 5 of this study.

The first comprehensive study of Orissan architecture was published by K. C. Panigrahi in 1961, *Archaeological Remains at Bhubaneswar*.[52] This study surpasses all previous writings on Orissan architecture. It is not merely a descriptive inventory, but attempts to place the monuments within their historical context; for the first time a carefully considered chronology for the temples of Bhubaneswar is proposed. In its detailed discussions of the temples it also provides much factual information concerning iconography annd religious and political history. While often not relevant to the argument at hand, this information cannot be found elsewhere, and so Panigrahi's work has become an indispensable source book on Orissan art.[53]

The sources upon which Panigrahi depends most heavily in formulating his chronology are the inscriptions found on a few of the temples. He also gives considered attention to various historical sources, which help us to associate particular temples with specific dynasties and even rulers. The most important and reliable of these sources are various epigraphical records, interpreted by Panigrahi himself and in several articles by D. C. Sircar.[54] Panigrahi enlarges upon the often sketchy findings from these sources by carefully considering passages from traditional Orissan Sanskrit texts which seem to preserve at least a germ of historical material.[55]

Panigrahi's emphasis upon paleographic sources was instrumental in clarifying several misconceptions about the entire chronological development of Orissan architecture. The Paraśurāmeśvara temple had been dated by R. D. Banerji to the late eighth-early-ninth century on the basis of the inscription on the lintel of the *maṇḍapa*, and this date and since been widely accepted.[56] By noting several inaccuracies in Banerji's reading, however, and by analysis of letter-forms and comparisons with inscriptions of known dates, Panigrahi convincingly assigned it to ca. 600-50. This established the development of the early form of the Orissan temple during the seventh century, and allowed comparison of the Paraśurāmeśvara and related monuments to the Daśāvatāra temple at Deogarh and to the Early Cālukyan monuments at Badami and Aihole, as a way of dealing with the ongoing problem of the origin of the Hindu temple in Orissa.[57] In addition, Panigrahi's account of the Brahmeśvara temple's dedicatory inscription, which contains an extensive genealogy of the Somavaṃśī dynasty, and his consideration of other sources, clarified the role of this dynasty as the major cultural patron during the tenth and eleventh centuries,[58] a role which Banerji chose to ignore.

As a result of Panigrahi's interest in historical records, however, the monuments themselves tend to assume a secondary importance as evidence for a chronology. Panigrahi discusses too summarily the temples' architectural elements, usually mentioning only their general form, and is relatively unconcerned with stylistic changes in the sculpture. More attention is paid to "iconographical development", that is, to the various changes in attributes, animal vehicles, etc. associated with the various images on the temples. The contribution of this analysis to chronology, however, is minimal. While documenting a great number of images and their attributes, Panigrahi finally can only divide them and the temples upon which they occur into two stylistic groups, early and late, with the Mukteśvara temple at the beginning of the second group.

Panigrahi concludes his arguments on chronology by placing the temples into several cognate groups, formed on the basis of epigraphical evidence, focused around the Paraśurāmeśvara, Vaitāl Deul, Brahmeśvara, and Ananta-Vāsudeva.[59] These basic groupings should be accepted. However, within the groups, the chronological sequence remains vague, with very few monuments being assigned even an approximate date. This stems from Panigrahi's failure to consider stylistic changes in various architectural elements, such as mouldings, *rathas* (the prominent vertical "pilasters"), etc., as indicators of chronological sequence. Panigrahi limits his approach further by generally excluding temples outside of Bhubaneswar from discussion, and by neglecting some of the more unassuming, yet art historically important temples within that city. In discussing the Mukteśvara temple, for example, which he dates to 966 (on the basis of a somewhat questionable palm-leaf manuscript),[60] Panigrahi cites only briefly the three Śiva temples at Baudh and the Gaurī temple at Bhubaneswar as having general similarities.[61] Further, he makes no mention of the temples at Gandharadi and Ganeswarpur, which help to clarify the innovative character of the Mukteśvara, which had always been treated as if it had sprung from nowhere.

Panigrahi's discussion of the Rājarāni temple is similar for its lack of attention to formal aspects of architecture. Panigrahi compares this temple to the Mukteśvara, noting certain common sculptural motifs and pointing out that the *maṇḍapas* of both are "undeveloped *pidha* temples;"[62] that is, their pyramidal roofs lack the more elaborate *mastaka* or crowning elements to be found on the later Liṅgarāja temple (ca. 1050). On the basis of these comments, Panigrahi gives the Rājarāni an unspecified date between the Mukteśvara and the Liṅgarāja. Panigrahi also quickly glosses over the interesting problems of the Rājarāni's *śikhara*-clusters, which had previously been either ignored, or explained with simplistic or undeveloped theories. While noting one temple with a generally similar *śikhara*, the Dākrā Bhīmeśvara,[63] he presents no discussion of several temples which would help to explain the development of the *śikhara*-cluster within Orissa. It is this failure to consider formal developments on all relevant monuments that prevents Panigrahi from establishing a more definitive chronology.

Debala Mitra's *Bhubaneswar*,[64] one of many sight guides published by the Archaeological Survey of India, basically provides a highly condensed summary of Panigrahi's findings, along with concise, yet thorough general descriptions of the major temples. Because it is condensed, clear, and carefully organized, however, Mitra's work serves as a useful reference book. The first part consists of general chapters on historical background, basic architectural characteristics, important sculptural motifs, and iconography. The second part contains brief descriptions of the temples, formed into two large groups, early and late. The book ends with a glossary of terms based on N. K. Bose's *Canons of Orissan Architecture*, and contains diagrams illustrating the major terms as they occur on the temples, making their meaning even more clear. Also published here is a site map of Bhubaneswar, which shows the location of all the major temples.[65]

After a thirty year lapse, the study of Orissan Śilpa Śāstras began by N. K. Bose was again taken up by Alice Boner and Pandit S. R. Śarmā, whose critical edition and translation of the *Śilpa Prakāśa* was published in 1966.[66] Upon its publication, the *Śilpa Prakāśa* was hailed as a landmark discovery of unpralleled importance to the study of Indian temple architecture.[67] The text was thought to be most remarkable for its uniqueness, for no other known text gives such a detailed description of a specific type of temple. The *Śilpa Prakāśa* is almost exclusively concerned with a detailed, technical description of the *vimānamālinī* temple type, which in almost every aspect is identical with the Vārāhī temple at Chaurasi. In addition, it contains iconographical descriptions of prominent images and motifs on Orissan temples, for example Śiva dancing (here called Nāṭāmbara, "clothed in dance"), gurus with disciples, female figures (here called *alasā kanyās*, "indolent-maidens"), and the *śukanāsā/Candraśālā* (here called *vajra-mastaka*). The *Śilpa Prakāśa* is also unique in its use of *yantras* (geometric diagrams) as the conceptual basis of the temple. In the *Śilpa Prakāśa*, *yantras* replace the classic *vāstu-puruṣamaṇḍala* (a diagram of sixty-four or eight-one squares populated by the Vedic gods, with Brahmā in the center) as the temple's symbolic "plan", and seemed to indicate that a rather Tantric ideology was at work during the period at which this text was produced, which in Alice Boner's opinion was between the ninth and twelfth centuries.[68] Other purely compositional *yantras* seem to show that a particular system of visual organization was being used by ancient Indian craftsmen, and were taken to lend credence to Boner's earlier formulated theories of composition in Indian sculpture.[69] Perhaps the most unusual feature of the text is the inclusion of drawings in one of the palm-leaf manuscripts utilized for the printed edition.

Boner was highly praised by critics for her scholarly presentation of the text. From the accuracy of the translation, to the insightful introduction, through notes, detailed glossary and correlation of photographs of actual monuments with relevant textual passages, her work was cited as an exemplary piece of scholarship.

There are, however, serious questions regarding the authenticity of the *Śilpa Prakāśa*. According to D. R. Das, the language seems to be very late, particularly in regard to the Oriya elements, which are not thought to have been developed by the twelfth century.[70] It was further pointed out by Kramrisch in a book review (although her opinion of the text and translation as a whole was completely favorable), that the drawing of human figures and architectural elements and elevations in one of the palm-leaf manuscripts, "seem to presuppose exposure to Western drawings".[71]

Doubts to authenticity have also arisen regarding the basic content of the *Śilpa Prakāśa*. In its concern with describing in detail a single temple type, the *Śilpa*

Prakāśa deviates from the much more encyclopedic nature of other *śilpa* texts. What, one wonders, was the need for such a specialized text? For, as D. R. Das has pointed out,

> Striking similarity in the constructional and other features of different types of temple is against the possibility of creating specialists in the line the *Śilpa Prakāśa* suggests. Was it possible for an architect to sustain himself with expert knowledge of a single temple of a very limited demand?[72]

One could argue, however, that the *Śilpa Prakāśa* is encyclopedic in its own way, and its love of detail is certainly characteristic of much technical Indian literature. And after all, the surface has barely been scratched in regard to the discovery and study of *śilpa* texts, particularly Orissan ones. Perhaps specialized texts were prepared for all the major temple types, and were meant for all architects, not just "specialists". Surely the manuscripts themselves, their condition, the style of the script, that of the drawings, and the language are better indications of authenticity than unusual content.

In this connection it should be pointed out that Alice Boner, again in collaboration with S. R. Śarmā, brought out another elaborate publication based on the study of newly discovered palm-leaf manuscripts, *New Light on the Sun Temple of Koṇārka*.[73] It has been established by K. S. Behera that the manuscripts used in this study date to the twentieth century, not to the seventeenth, as stated in their colophons. Some of the descriptive statements, as well as the drawings, are apparently based on a post-restoration view of the temple.[74] The doubtful antiquity of the Koṇārka manuscripts unfortunately casts doubt upon the reliability of Boner's sources for the *Śilpa Prakāśa* as well.

At present, it seems that the *Śilpa Prakāśa* is a late compilation, and however remarkable in its detail and depth, does not reflect the technical vocabulary in use when the temples it describes were built.

Vidya Dehejia's *Early Stone Temples of Orissa* (1979) is a history of Orissan architecture from the period ca. 600-1000, and discusses the earliest known examples through those in the early mature style, the latter exemplified by the Mukteśvara.[75] A brief introduction to the historical and religious background of the period is followed by a general presentation of the basic components of the typical Orissan temple, and a survey of the various types of sculptural imagery found on its walls. The following chapters group the temples into three broad categories or phases: Formative (with two sub-divisions), Transitional, and Culminative. The final chapter puts forth speculations on the origins of the Hindu temple in Orissa, and assigns dates to the three formulated periods; 600-750, 700-850 and 850-950 respectively.[76]

While presenting the findings of an extensive period of field-work, bringing together a large number of early temples, and giving a description of the standard Orissan temple type perhaps more accessible to the general reader than that of

S. K. Sarasvati,[77] Dehejia's discussion of many topics—such as iconography and historical and religious background—is simply too brief to add significantly to the present body of knowledge. Even in her discussion of the three chronological phases, Dehejia's brief descriptions of individual temples, with comparative statements often no more detailed than that one shrine is similar to another, give the reader little faith in the analytical depth of the study.

In discussing the origins of the early Orissan temple and their *śikharas*, Dehejia limits herself mainly to a comparison with the Daśāvatāra temple at Deogarh. This limited comparative base does not result in informative conclusions. She avoids, moreover, a group of monuments which form a more significant comparison, the early Cālukyan temples at Aihole and Badami. She dismisses as "far fetched", Panigrahi's theory of Orissan contact with early Cālukyan art, based on an observation of iconographical similarities between an early Orissan Naṭeśa and one from Badami,[78] and ignores Brown's speculations on the possibility of contacts between the two regions.[79] In so doing, Dehejia avoids a line of enquiry that could shed more light on the problem of the temple's origin in Orissa than do her general comparisons with Gupta architecture. Further, Dehejia gives no consideration to outside influences in the "Transitional" and "Culminative" groups, carrying on the simplistic notion of the "purity" of the Nāgara style in Orissa.

Dehejia's chronology mainly reiterates that of Panigrahi.[80] Only her three periods are given dates and monuments within the groups are not arranged in a specific sequence. The Vārāhī temple at Chaurasi, for example, is the first temple discussed in Chapter 6 (Transitional Phase), yet it is described as "advanced transitional"[81] Thus, in terms of the problems of chronology and stylistic sequence, Dehejia only repeats the findings of previous scholars, rather than refining them.

An extremely ambitious study of Orissan architecture was realized in 1985-87 with the publication of Thomas Donaldson's *Hindu Temple Art of Orissa*.[82] This massive three-volume work, with over 4,500 illustrations, is virtually the only one of its kind in the field of Indian art—a detailed, encyclopedic catalog of almost every surviving Orissan Temple and detached sculpture dating from the sixth to the fifteenth century. The first two volumes are essentially a survey of Orissan temples, arranged in a chronological sequence based largely upon that of Panigrahi. The third volume primarily concerns sculpture, and as such is a unique and valuable reference to almost every image-type and motif occurring in Orissan sculpture.

Donaldson has also written on the symbolic aspects of Orissan scultpure. He has generally concluded that the most prominent imagery on the temple—the "*vajra-mastaka*",[83] scroll work, and above all, the various erotic images—primarily served a propitious-apotropaic function.[84] Donaldson has demonstrated through cross-cultural comparisons and scattered textual references a certain validity to his theory, especially in regard to erotic imagery. By his insistence on only the propitious-apotropaic symbolism of these motifs, however, Donaldson somewhat obscures other, perhaps deeper levels of meaning.

Recent studies by D. R. Das deal primarily with the analysis of temples in western Orissa, a 1976 article on the Kośaleśvara temple at Baidyanath (Bolangir district), and a short book, *Temples of Orissa (Study of a Sub-Style)* (1982).[85] The book discusses the temple at Baidyanath, the nearby Kapileśvara temple at Charda (Bolangir district), the Someśvara temple at Ranipur Jharial (Bolangir district), and the Narasiṃhanātha temple near Paikanal (Sambalpur district). Das is concerned primarily with analysis of *maṇḍapas*. The temples seem to be unique in Orissa in that they exhibit projecting balconied porches and raised central platforms marked by four columns, both features common to temples of central and western India.

Das gives detailed descriptions of the temples, pointing out that iron beams are used to support architraves and ceiling slabs, a feature previously noted only in temples dating to the tenth century or later. He also makes general comparisons of the temples with similarly planned *maṇḍapas* in various parts of India, but feels that Khajuraho provides the closest parallel.

In spite of his painstaking visual analysis, Das does not come to any solid conclusions. In regard to the temples at Baidyanath and Charda, he gives a tentative date of ca. ninth century. Das states that the temples exhibit "contradictory evidence", that is, they have both early and late iconographical elements. Sculptural style, however, seems later than the seventh or eighth century, and the base mouldings are similar to those of the Mukteśvara. These are difficult art historical problems that need to be solved in order to understand the dynamics of these western Orissan sites. The major question to be answered, however, is whether these western Orissan temples relate directly to the stylistic "mainstream" of coastal Orissa, to schools of Central Indian architecture, or are a provincial mixture of both.

It is apparent from this survey of the literature on Orissan temple architecture that most studies so far have been broad and general; a continuation in this direction will only produce work that is repetitive and unoriginal.[86] What is needed at this point are monographic studies of single temples, focusing upon a given monument's individual character, its iconography and its relationship to other works of the same period. Such studies would elucidate the individual statement of style and meaning of a single important monument, while also demonstrating its role within an overall trend.

NOTES

1. James Fergusson, *History of Indian and Eastern Architecture* (London, 1876). An earlier account, though hardly to be described as systematic or art historical is found in A. Sterling, "An Account, Geographical, Statistical and Historical of Orissa Proper, or Cuttack (Part III; Religion, Antiquities, Temple and Civil Architecture)", *Asiatic Researches*, 15 (1825), pp. 305-38 (especially

pp. 305-16). Here the general environs of Bhubaneswar are described, with brief appreciatory comments upon the Liṅgarāja temple, which Sterling felt to be "...the finest monument of antiquity which the province contains and likewise indisputably the most ancient" (p. 310). Although Sterling is generally enthusiastic about the aesthetic quality of Indian architecture, his essay is more interesting for its description of the neglected state of Bhubaneswar and its temples in the early 19th century than for any sort of art historical insights.

A later document of the temples of Bhubaneswar, documenting the pre-restoration condition of some of the temples is M. H. Arnot, *Report with Photographs of the Repairs Executed to some of the Principle Temples at Bhubaneswar and Caves in the Khandagiri and Udaygiri Hills, Orissa, India, between 1898 and 1903* (London, 1903). Arnot includes some interesting "before and after" views of the key temples, but these are far too few and unsystematic (the comparative shots are always taken from very different viewpoints, and only two plates are included for each temple), to be of more than basic use in determining how much the temples may have suffered from over-zealous restoration. Arnot assures us, however, that an "attempt has been made simply to restore, with reworking of damaged scultpural elements being kept to a minimum" (where they do exist the results are disastrous enough). The text is perhaps more valuable than the photographs as a document of restoration, stating exactly the previous condition of the temple, the causes of dilapidation (usually uneven land settlement and growth of trees), and what measures were taken to correct the situation.

2. Fergusson gives the following rough chronology for the principal temples of Orissa: 500-600, Paraśurāmeśvara, Mukteśvara; 600-700, Sarī Deul, Maitrī Serāī, Ananta-Vāsudeva, Liṅgarāja (657, based on the legends recorded by Sterling); 700-850, Vaitāl Deul, Mārkaṇḍayeśvara at Puri, Brahmeśvara; 873, Sun Temple at Koṇārka; 900-1000, Kedāreśvara, Rājarāni; 1105, Naṭamandira of the Liṅgarāja; 1198, Jagannātha temple at Puri. A second edition of Fergusson's *History* appeared in 1910, revised and edited by James Burgess. Burgess expanded and revised Fergusson's chronology, later dates to the Liṅgarāja and Ananta-Vāsudeva temples. Burgess's revised chronology is as follows: 650-900, Paraśurāmeśvara, Śiśireśvara, Kapālinī,Uttareśvara, Someśvara at Mukhaliṅgam; 900-1000, Sarī Deul, Mukteśvara, Liṅgarāja, Kedāreśvara, Siddheśvara, Bhagavati, Someśvara, Brahmeśvara, Mukhaliṅgeśvara at Mukhaliṅgam, Viraja and Varanātha at Jajpur, Mārkaṇḍayeśvara at Puri; 11th century, Rāmeśvara, Yameśvara, Maitreśvara, Jagannātha at Puri, Megheśvara; 13th century, Ananta-Vāsudeva, Sun Temple at Koṇārka, Naṭamandira of the Liṅgarāja, Viṣṇu at Madab (Cuttack district), Gopināth at Remuna.

3. Fergusson, *History*, p. 414.

4. *Ibid.*, p. 414.

5. *Ibid.*, p. 435.

6. *Ibid.*, p. 417.

7. *Ibid.*, p. 425.

8. *Ibid.*, p. 425.

9. R. L. Mitra, *Antiquities of Orissa*, 2 vols. (Calcutta, 1875-80, reprint Calcutta, 1961).

10. Mitra, *Antiquities*, vol. 2, p. 19, note 11, quoting Fergusson from an unidentified source.

11. The style of the line drawing illustrating this work is highly westernized—the treatment of the anatomy and faces reflects observation of casts of classical Greek sculpture, with only the details (jewellery, costume), evoking the Orissan works.

12. Mitra, *Antiquities*, vol. 1, pp. 26-27.

13. M. M. Ganguly, *Orissa and Her Remains: Ancient and Medieval* (Calcutta, 1912).

14. "The students of Indian history and literature are well aware of the difficulties the author has to labor under, he cannot but stick to Indian terms which invariably connote more or less than what their English equivalents do. There are many terms, again, which do not admit of being expressed by English terms at all" (Ganguly, Orissa, p. viii).

15. *Ibid.*, pp. 170-74.

16. N. K. Bose, *canons of Orissan Architecture* (Calcutta, 1932).

17. Ganguly, *Orissa*, pp. 170-74.

18. *Ibid.*, p. 175.

19. *Ibid.*, pp. 295-307.

20. *Ibid.*, p. 307.

21. Ganguly's dates for the major temples in Bhubaneswar: Paraśurāmeśvara, 5th or 6th century; Mukteśvara, 6th or 7th century; Liṅgarāja, early 9th century; Ananta-Vāsudeva, 12th century (Ganguly, *Orissa*, p. 273). While the sequence is accurate, the proposed intervals between the monuments obviously show little consideration of the notion of architectural development through time.

22. R. D. Banerji, *History of Orissa*, vol. 2. (Calcutta, 1931), pp. 333-83.

23. R. D. Banerji, "Antiquities of the Baudh State", JBORS, 5 (1929), pp. 64-86.

24. Banerji, *Orissa*, vol. 2, p. 374.

25. *Ibid.*, p. 338.

26. *Ibid.*, p. 336.

27. See R. P. Chandra, "Note on the Ancient Monuments of Mayurbhanj", JBORS, 13 (1927), pp. 131-36.

28. Banerji, *Orissa*, vol. 2, p. 357.

29. *Ibid.*, pp. 147, 358.

30. *Ibid.*, pp. 343, 374.

31. *Ibid.*, p. 356.

32. *Ibid.*, p. 366.

33. For translations of the inscription see R. L. Mitra, *Antiquities of Orissa*, 150-52; and P.P. Acharya, "Geneology of the Somakulī Kings of Kosala and Utkala", *Studies in Orissan History, Archaeology and Archives* (Cuttack, 1969), pp. 77-79.

34. Banerji, *Orissa*, vol. 1, p. 204.

35. N. K. Bose, *Canons.*

36. See for example *Ibid.*, p. 165.

37. At least one term, *mastaka*, is of Bose's own coinage, and is used to designate the area of the temple between he *śikhara* and *kalaśa* (*ibid.*, pp. 115, 183 and diagram, p. 21).

38. A Sanskritic terminology is preserved in texts like the *Manasara* (see P. K. Acharya, *Indian Architecture According to the Manasaraśilpaśāstra* and *A Dictionary of Hindu Architecture* (Allahabad, n.d., 1927-28); and A. K. Coomaraswamy, "Indian Architectural Terms", JAOS, 48 (1928), pp. 250-75).

39. S. Kramrisch, "Kalinga Temples", JISOA 2.1 (1934), pp. 43-60; and "The Walls of Orissan Temples", JISOA 15 (1947), pp. 178-96.

40. Kramrisch, "Kalinga Temples", p. 59.

41. *Ibid.*, p. 59.

42. *Ibid.*, pp. 46, 47, 52.

43. Kramrisch, *Walls*, p. 189.

44. *Ibid.*, p. 181. See also p. 189.

45. Kramrisch uses the chronology put forth in R. P. Chanda, "The Liṅgarāja or Great Temple of Bhubaneswar", *Archaeological Survey of India Annual Report*, 1922-24, pp. 119-22: Paraśurāmeśvara, c. 750; Rājarāni, 1100-1175; Liṅgarāja, ca. 1000; Brahmeśvara, late 11th century. Chanda's short article is primarily of a descriptive nature. He bases his dates on readings (after Banerji), of the inscriptions on the Paraśurāmeśvara and Brahmeśvara temples.

46. *Walls*, p. 178. "New elements. . . were assimilated from the more western branches of the tradition as practised in the Central Provinces and Central India." The origin of scroll work and the creeper motif are briefly traced from their nomadic Aryan origins to their transformation in Gupta art and finally to their diffusion in Orissa (*Walls*, pp. 192-93).

47. P. Brown, *Indian Architecture: Buddhist and Hindu Periods*, 2nd ed. (Bombay, 7th reprint, 1976). The first edition was published in 1942.

48. Brown, *Indian Architecture*, p. 101. Yet, strangely, a logical conclusion of a date of ca. 650 for the Paraśurāmeśvara is not reached in making these comparisons.

49. *Ibid.*, p. 102; Early Period (ca. 750-900), Paraśurāmeśvara, Vaitāl Deul, Uttareśvara, Īśvareśvara, Śatrughneśvara, Bhārateśvara, Lakṣmaṇeśvara; Middle Period (ca. 900-1100), Mukteśvara (ca. 975), Liṅgarāja (ca. 1000), Brahmeśvara (ca. 1070), Rāmeśvara (1075), Jagannātha, Puri (ca. 1100); Later Period (ca. 1100-1250), Ananta-Vāsudeva, Siddheśvara, Kedareśvara, Yameśvara, Megheśvara, Sarī, Deul, Someśvara, Rājarāni, Sun temple, Koṇārka (ca. 1250).

50. S. K. Sarasvati, "Temples of Orissa", OHRJ, 1.4 (1953), pp. 233-53. The same essential essay appears in HCIP vol. 4, pp. 530-56.

51. Sarasvati, "Temples of Orissa", pp. 240, 243, 244.

52. K. C. Panigrahi, ARB (Calcutta, 1961).

53. See in particular, Chapter 8, "Chronology of the Cult Images: Development of Hindu Iconography" (pp. 124-45), and Chapter 10, "A Short Political and Cultural History of Bhubaneswar" (pp. 177-262).

54. D. C. Sircar, "Ancient Orissa", OHRJ 4.3.4 (1955-56), pp. 51-57; "A Note on the Later Somavaṃśīs", IHQ 22 (1946), pp. 300-07; "The Later Somavaṃśīs", OHRJ 1.4 (1935), pp. 289-300; "Some Minor Dynasties of Orissa", OHRJ 2 (1935) 1, pp. 13-20; *Review of Chronology of the Bhaumakaras and Somavaṃśīs*, by K. C. Panigrahi, JIH 40.1 (1962), pp. 208-10.

55. Panigrahi, ARB, pp. 26, 27. See also R. D. Banerji, *History*, vol. 2, p. 340.

56. *Ibid.*, pp. 50, 56, 114, 138, 139, 178, 223, 224. For Panigrahi's discussion of the Paraśurāmeśvara's inscription, see, pp. 56-58.

57. *Ibid.*, pp. 21-24 and *passim.*

58. See Chapter 2.

59. ARB, Chapter 9 (pp. 146-76): Śatrughneśvara, ca. 575; Paraśurāmeśvara and its group, ca. 650; Vaitāl Deul, Śiśireśvara and their group, ca. 700-900; Mukteśvara, 966; Brahmeśvara and its group, ca. 1075-1176: Megheśvara, Ananta-Vāsudeva and their group, ca. 1195-1425.

60. See *ibid.*, pp. 159-60.

61. *Ibid.*, p. 162.

62. *Ibid.*, p. 163.

63. *Ibid.*, p. 164.

64. D. Mitra, *Bhubaneswar*, 7th ed. (New Delhi, 1977). (1st ed., 1958).

65. Several other books appearing in the last twenty years on Orissan architecture have contributed little or no new information or ideas and tend to be of a popular rather than scholarly nature, basing what factual information they do contain on Panigrahi or D. Mitra. Such works include C. Fabri, *History of the Art of Orissa* (Calcutta, 1974), and K. Lal, *Temples and Sculpture of Bhubaneswar* (Delhi, 1970 useful illustrations). Other works which provide good illustrations are O. C. Gangooly, *Orissan Sculpture and Architecture* (Calcutta, 1956); and D. P. Ghose, "The History of Orissan Hindu Temples", *Marg* 8.4 (1955), pp. 34-46.

66. A. Boner and S. R. Śarmā, trans., *Śilpa Prakāśa: Medieval Orissan Sanskrit Text on Temple Architecture* (Leiden, 1966).

67. For reviews of the *Śilpa Prakāśa* see H. G., JAOS 88.2 (June 1968), pp. 381-82; S. Kramrisch, JAS 27.2 (Feb. 1968), pp. 408-09; J. R. Marr, *Bulletin of the School of Oriental and African Studies* 31.2 (1968), p. 406.

68. A. Boner, *Śilpa Prakāśa*, pp. xvii-xix.

69. See A. Boner, *Principles of Composition in Hindu Sculpture* (Leiden, 1962).

70. This has been pointed out to me by Dr. D. R. Das of Calcutta University. I would like to thank Dr. Das for discussing with me various problems regarding the *Śilpa Prakāśa's* authenticity.

71. Kramrisch, rev. of *SP*, p. 409.

72. In a letter to the author dated Nov. 11, 1983.

73. A. Boner and S. R. Śarmā, *New Light on the Sun Temple at Koṇārka* (Varanasi, 1972).

74. K. S. Behera, "Palm Leaf Manuscript on the Architecture of Konarka Temple", *Annals of the Bandharkar Oriental Research Institute*, 57 (1976), pp. 175-80. See also review of *New Light on the Sun Temple*, South Asia 6 (1976), pp. 127-29.

75. V. Dehejia, *Early Stone Temples of Orissa* (New Delhi, 1979).

76. Dehejia deals with inscriptions in Chapter 8 (pp. 154-72), but not in a way having relevance to the chronology of the temples. Rather, she presents the development of the Oriya script.

77. See above, note 48.

78. Dehejia, *Temples*, p. 87. See also ARB, pp. 137ff.

79. See Brown, *Indian Architecture*, pp. 101-02.

80. Formative Phase (650-750); Group A—Bhavānī-Śaṅkar, Paraśurāmeśvara, Śatrughneśvara group, Svarnajaleśvara, Taleśvara, Paścimeśvara at Kulao, Madhukeśvara at Mukhaliṅgam, Ruins at Jajpur, Īśvara temple at Paikapada, Amangai temple, Jain temple at Subei; Group B—Mārkaṇḍayeśvara, Śiśireśvara, Vaitāl Deul, Monastery at Ratnagiri, Bhringeśvara temple at Bajrakot, Simhanātha temple at Baramba, Śiva temple at Borogram. The following temples, while discussed in Chapter 5, "Formative Phase", are listed as "transitional" in the Conclusion; Manikeśvara temples at Sukleśvara, Śiva temple at Mohanagiri. Transitional Phase (700-850); Vārāhī temple at Chaurasi, Tīrtheśvara, Temples at Gandharadi, temples at Baidyanatha and Charda, temples at Jogāmunda and Paikapada (Potaleśvara temple), Shrine at Sarapali. Culmination Phase (830-950); Mukteśvara, Gaurī temple, Kiñcakeśvarī at Khiching, Pañcayatana temple at Ganeśwarpur, three temples at Baudh.

81. Dehejia, *ibid.*, p. 128.

82. HTAO. For reviews see M. Meister, JAS, 46.2 (1987), pp. 428-30 (for vol. 1); and W. Smith, JAS 47.4 (1988), pp. 916-17 (for vols. 2, 3).

83. In all his writings, Donaldson uses the terms found in Bose, *Canons*, and Boner, *Śilpa Prakāśa*.

84. See T. Donaldson, "Propitious-Apotropaic Eroticism in the Art of Orissa", AA, 37.1/2 (1975), pp. 75-100.

85. D. R. Das, "Kosaleśvara Temple at Baidyanatha (Bolangir District, Orissa)", AA 38.4 (1976), pp. 297-307; and *Temples of Orissa* (Delhi, 1982).

86. A recent general work on the subject is P. R. Ramachandra Rao, *Bhubaneswar: Kalinga Temple Architecture* (Hyderabad, 1980).

CHAPTER 2

HISTORICAL AND RELIGIOUS BACKGROUND

The history of Orissa during the great period of temple building is obscure. While broad genealogies and chronologies of Orissan dynasties have been worked out, little can be said with certainty about such particulars as where these ruling families came from, how they came to power, or the exact circumstances of their declines. Almost all historical information has been gleaned by various scholars from copper plate land grants, which document royal donations of villages to Brahmins.[1] These copper plate inscriptions sometimes give brief genealogies and laudatory descriptions of rulers, but with such hyperbole as to give us little idea of their true abilities and accomplishments. Neither can a vivid picture of cultural patronage be made. In terms of royal patronage of temple architecture, very little inscriptional material exists. Only one temple, the Brahmeśvara in Bhubaneswar, has a dedicatory inscription.[2] This temple was built by Kolāvatī Devī, the mother of the Somavaṃśī king Uddyotakeśarī (reigned c. 1040-65). The inscription is of great importance, for it gives the complete genealogy and regnal years of the Somavaṃśī dynasty up to the reign of Uddyotakeśarī, while also, of course, being undeniable evidence for royal support of temple building in Orissa.

In relation to the Mukteśvara, which was built around 970, two particular dynasties figure prominently—the Bhauma-karas and the Somavaṃśīs, the latter apparently wresting control of coastal Orissa from the former around the middle of the tenth century. In fact, as the discussion in Chapter 4 will suggest, the Mukteśvara temple itself may have been a statement by the Somavaṃśī dynasty which declared their supremacy over Bhauma-kara territory in coastal Orissa. Such a statement could be part of the overall meaning of the temple, which was built in the important pilgrimage center of Ekāmra (Bhubaneswar), and very possibly bears images of the Somavaṃśī kings upon it.

THE BHAUMA-KARAS

The Bhuma-kara dynasty, which dated its inscribed land grants with its own era, most probably began c. 736 A.D.[3] The dynasty consisted of eighteen rulers. The approximate lengths of most of their reigns can be determined through their various copper plate inscriptions, which contain not only regnal years and dates in the Bhauma era, but also refer to conflicts with various powers outside Orissa, such as the Rāṣṭrakūṭas and the Pālas. The records of these outside powers, as well as those of the Somavaṃśīs, help to further corroborate certain dates.[4]

A list of the most important Bhauma-kara rulers is as follows:

1. Kṣemaṅkaradeva (c. 736)
2. Śivakaradeva I (c. 756 or 786)
3. Śubhākaradeva I (c. 790 ?)
4. Śivakaradeva II (c. 809 ?)
5. Śāntikaradeva I
6. Śubhākaradeva II (c. 836)
7. Śubhākaradeva III (c. 839)
8. Tribhuvana Mahādevī I (c. 846, queen of Śāntikaradeva I)
9. Śāntikaradeva II
10. Śubhākaradeva IV (c. 881)
11. Śivakaradeva III (c. 885)
12. Tribhuvana Mahādevī II (c. 894, queen of Śubhākaradeva IV)
13. Śāntikaradeva III
14. Śubhākaradeva V
15. Gaurī (queen of Śubhākaradeva V)
16. Daṇḍī Mahādevī (c. 916 or 923, daughter of Śubhākaradeva V)
17. Vakula Mahādevī (queen of Śubhākaradeva V)
18. Dharma Mahādevī (queen of Śāntikaradeva III)

Non-Aryan origins have been suggested for the Bhauma-karas, specifically, that they descended, "perhaps from the Bhumij tribe of northern Orissa and Chota Nagpur."[6] The Bhauma-karas seem to have held control over most of coastal Orissa by the time of their second king, Śivakaradeva I, and by 850 certainly ruled over most of what is now modern Orissa.[7]

The first three rulers of the Bhauma-kara dynasty were Buddhist, although the queen of Śubhākaradeva I is known to have built a temple to Mādhaveśvara Śiva and appointed a Śaiva *ācārya* for conducting the worship.[8] The first Bhauma king to declare himself Paramamaheśvara, or a devotee of Śiva was Śubhākaradeva IV.[9] The records of all subsequent Bhauma rulers bear this same Śaivite affiliation, and virtually every temple built during the period of Bhauma-kara rule (the Vaitāl Deul, dedicated to the horrific goddess Cāmuṇḍā being an exception) is dedicated to Śiva.

Between 810 and 850, a series of invasions by the Rāṣṭrakūṭas and the Pālas left the Bhauma kingdom in a state of weakness and disorder.[10] The kingdom was later reunified by Queen Tribhuvana Mahādevī I,[11] but previous strength was probably never regained.

Around 880, various internal troubles within the Bhauma dynasty began, which led to its gradual extinction by around the middle of the tenth century. The reign of Śubhākaradeva IV was extremely short (c. 881-84). He was succeeded by a brother, Śivakaradeva III, who after about nine years was succeeded by Śubhākaradeva IV's wife, Tribhuvana Mahādevī II. Most scholars believe that she acquired the throne through the intervention of her father, Janmeyjaya I, Mahābhavagupta I, the second king of the Somavaṃśī dynasty, and that this intervention was part of an overall drive toward a gradual takeover of the Bhauma-kara holdings.[12] Exactly when Tribhuvana's reign ended is not known, although it was probably quite short, her accession may never have been fully acknowledged by various court factions.

Between 894 and 923, at least five rulers claimed the Bhauma-kara throne, indicating considerable instability.[13] Tribhuvana Mahādevī II was succeeded by a nephew, Śāntikaradeva III, followed by his brother Śubhākaradeva V. His queen, Gaurī, probably acted as regent until the accession of their daughter, Daṇḍī Mahādevī. After c. 923 two more queens acceded to the throne, Vakula Mahādevī (another queen of Śubhākaradeva II and Daṇḍī Mahādevī's step-mother), and Dharma Mahādevī, who as the queen of Śāntikaradeva III was probably fairly advanced in years at the time of her succession. We have no information on their regnal years.

From this sequence of rulers it becomes obvious that a lack of male heirs was a major factor in the downfall of the Bhauma kingdom. But there were also certainly various internal dissensions and intrigues. Panigrahi suggests that much of these internal conflicts were brought about by members of the Bhañja dynasty of Khiñjali. This dynasty, which ruled in the area of Baudh and Sonepur,[14] through intermarriage placed two of their princesses as the last two rulers of the Bhauma-kara kingdom.[15] In any event, with the Bhauma-kara kingdom in such a state of upheaval, yet still in nominal command of their territories, a newly rising power, such as the Somavaṃśīs, would be most anxious to firmly establish their growing power and assume supremacy over the region.

The Somavaṃśīs

The Somavaṃśīs have their origins in the ancient area of Mahākośala or South Kośala (northwest Orissa and eastern Madhya Pradesh), and during the eighth century had their capital in Śrīpura (modern Sirpur, Madhya Pradesh). They were driven from this area in the ninth century by the kings of the Kalacuri dynasty, and settled further east in Vinitapura (modern Binka, Sambalpur district). Within a few generations the Somavaṃśīs consolidated their power in this area and made further attempts at penetrating into eastern Orissa. While dates cannot be assigned to any of the rulers of this "early" Somavaṃśī dynasty, a genealogical sequence can be worked out. This sequence ends with the name of Mahāśivagupta Bālārjuna, who was most likely the father of the earliest known ruler of the "later" Somavaṃśīs, Mahābhavagupta Janmejaya.[16]

Panigrahi formulates the chronology of the "later" Somavaṃśīs as follows:[17]

1. Janmejaya I Mahābhavagupta (c. 882-922)
2. Yayāti I, Mahāśivagupta (c. 922-55)

3. Bhīmaratha, Mahābhavagupta II (c. 955-80)
4. Dharmaratha, Mahāśivagupta II (c. 980-1005)
5. Nahusa, Mahābhavagupta III (c. 1005-21)
6. Yayāti II, Caṇḍīhara Mahāśivagupta II (c. 1025-40)
7. Uddyotakeśarī, Mahābhavagupta IV (c. 1040-65)
8. Janmejaya II, Mahāśivagupta IV (c. 1065-85)
9. Purañjaya, Mahābhavagupta V (c. 1085-1100)
10. Karṇadeva, Mahāśivagupta IV (c. 1100-1110)

It cannot be said with certainty exactly when the Somavaṃśīs gained control of most of Orissa, though various evidences suggest that this control may have been accomplished by the time of Yayāti I Mahāśivagupta. It is clear, however, that the Somavaṃśīs were beginning to make inroads into the Bhauma kingdom even during the reign of Yayāti I's predecessor, Janmejaya I, who may have had partial control of coastal Orissa. Mention has already been made of his daughter, Tribhuvana Mahādevī and the possibility that Janmejaya was instrumental in placing her on the Bhauma throne.[18] Janmejaya had an extremely long reign of at least thirty-four years, during which he "solidly organized the kingdom of the Somavaṃśīs in western Orissa, and his earlier copper plate grants issued from various 'victorious camps' suggest that he was busy moving from place to place in his task of consolidation."[19] Three of these grants, from his thirty-first regnal year, were issued from "Kaṭaka", which has been identified by various scholars with Chaudhwar, near modern Cuttack,[20] indicating that his influence moved quite far east.

Much has been made of the statement in the Brahmeśvara temple inscription that "the king of the Oḍra country. . . was killed by his (Janmejaya's) *kunta* (spear) in battle."[21] Panigrahi takes it to mean that Janmejaya killed Śivakaradeva III (his son-in-law's brother) and placed his own daughter on the throne, paving the way to his family's supremacy.[22] Other scholars have stated, however, that "Oḍra" indicates not the whole of Orissa, but only a territory (*viṣaya),* specifically, that comprising modern Dhenkanal district, and that the "king of Oḍra" was probably a rebel monarch of the Bhañja dynasty.[23] But even in this light, we can see that Janmejaya did much to extend the power of the Somavaṃśīs.

Janmejaya's son and successor Yayāti Mahāśivagupta apparently continued the expansionist policies of his father and appears to have consolidated the Somavaṃśīs holdings even further. A larger number of his inscribed charters grant villages in the Kośala area, the Somavaṃśī's traditional stronghold. These charters were issued from Yayātinagara, which was probably the older Somavaṃśī capital of Vinitapura on the Mahanadi River (modern Bikna), renamed by Yayāti I. But Yayāti I also granted several villages within previously foreign territories.[24] Candgrama (modern Changan, thirty-two miles southeast of Cuttack) was part of the Bhauma kingdom;[25] and Gandaṭapāti (modern Gandharadi), was within the Bhañja territories.[26] It has also been argued fairly convincingly that Yayāti I was responsible for re-establishing the image of Puruṣottama (Jagannātha) and building a new temple at Puri, after it had been removed during the Rāṣṭrakūṭa invasion which occurred around the year 800.[27] If this is true, then Yayāti I was certainly in control of coastal Orissa; specifically the important cultural areas surrounding Puri and Bhubaneswar, and was probably at least something of the cultural patron that the Orissan tradition considers him to be.[28] The monuments themselves support this tradition, for it is during this time that we see the beginnings of the "Somavaṃśī's style" in temple architecture. Striking changes begins to occur both in the temple's form, decoration, and iconography, and there seems to be a new awareness of artistic traditions from outside Orissa, this perhaps owing something to the Somavaṃśī's central Indian origins.

Little is known about the next Somavaṃśī king, Bhīmaratha Mahābhavagupta II.[29] His son, Dharmaratha Mahāshivagupta II is to also obscure. He died without issue and was succeeded by Nahuṣa Mahābhavagupta III, who was possibly his brother. During their reigns the Somavaṃśī kingdom was plagued by several foreign invasions, the most well-known being that of the Colas on the capital Yayātinagara (modern Jajpur?) in c. 1021.[30] There is also evidence of invasions into the Somavaṃśī kingdom by the Paramāras of Malwa and the Kalacuris.[31]

According to the Brahmeśvara temple inscription, order was restored to the kingdom by Yayāti II Caṇḍīhara. He was ". . . son of Abhimanyu and grandson of Vicitravīrya, a lineal descendant of the celebrated Janmejaya . . . made king by the ministers."[32] Other inscriptions corroborate. One states that Nahuṣa was succeeded by his *anuja* (younger cousin) Yayāti Caṇḍīhara ". . . who freed both the *rāṣṭras* of Kośala and Utkala which had been seized by combatant chiefs."[33] And one of Caṇḍīhara's own charters states that he was "the chosen lords of Kaliṅga, Utkala and Kośala."[34] If it is unclear how exactly the Somavaṃśīs gained control of the regions previously associated with the Bhauma-karas, it is evident, nonetheless, that these lands had passed into Somavaṃśī hands by the time of Dharmaratha, were overrun with enemies after this king's death,[35] and subsequently regained by Yayāti Caṇḍīhara. This king is attributed with defeating the kings of many northern Indian kingdoms (e.g. Gurjara and Laṭa),[36] though this is not proven by inscriptions from these regions. While the claims of defeating these kingdoms are probably poetic hyperbole, they do indicate that these areas were known to the Somavaṃśīs, and so indicate cultural contacts with them.

Caṇḍīhara was succeeded by his son Uddyotakeśarī Mahābhavagupta IV. His reign was "comparatively peaceful", and he retained hold of the vast territories consolidated by his predecessor.[37] He is considered a great champion of Brahmanism, having restored many tanks and temples, while also patronizing the Jain establishment of Udayagiri.[38] He assumes a greater importance, however, in that during his eighteenth regnal year his mother, Kolāvatī Devī, dedicated the Brahmeśvara temple at Bhubaneswar.[39] This information on cultural patronage, while scanty, is at least unambiguous on the point that the Somavaṃśīs did indeed support religious establishments, and that they were responsible for the Brahmeśvara temple, one of the most monumental structure in Bhubaneswar. In the later part of Uddyotakeśarī's reign work must have begun on the greatest monumental structure in Bhubaneswar, the Liṅgarāja temple, which was possibly not finished until the time of his successor, Janmejaya II.[40]

The subsequent history of the Somavaṃśīs is not relevant to the subject of this monograph. After the reign of Uddyotakeśarī, with wars involving the Nāga kings to the northwest and the Gaṅgas to the south, the Somavaṃśī's territories began to dwindle considerably, so that by the time of their last known ruler, Karṇadeva, "the Somavaṃśī kingdom was confined only to the coastal tract comprising the present districts of Puri, Cuttack and Balasor."[41] By ca. 1114 the Gaṅga king Anantavarman Coḍagaṅga had taken over the remains of the Somavaṃśī kingdom.[42]

As cultural patrons, the Somavaṃśīs are generally credited with being great contributors to the propagation of Hindu *dharma* in general, and particularly in regard to temple building.[43] Yet there is little inscriptional evidence pointing to the Somavaṃśīs as temple builders. As mentioned earlier, only one Orissan temple from this period, the Brahmeśvara, is known to have had a dedicatory inscription, recording the donor as Kolāvatī Devī. In many local legends and those preserved in the *Mādalā Pāñji,* the chronicle of the Jagannātha temple at Puri, almost all the temples of Bhubaneswar are attributed to Yayāti I.[44] No modern scholar takes the *Mādalā Pāñji* as an unimpeachable, or even semi-reliable source for historical data. Panigrahi is of the opinion, however, that the legends built around the Somavaṃśīs, while bearing much exaggeration and historical inaccuracy, have at least some bases in fact. Supporting this stand is the fact that many of the names of the legendary Keśarī kings of the *Mādalā Pāñji* are obvious corruptions or variations of those of Somavaṃśī rulers.[45] Be this as it may, there is very little direct evidence relating specific temples to individual monarchs, although it is assumed here that many of the temples we are considering, particularly those of great monumentality and decorative complexity, resulted from royal or aristocratic patronage.

From their inscription, we know that all the Somavaṃśī kings were devotees of Śiva.[45] Inscriptions, however, give us no real indication as to what particular cult they followed. It is generally held that the Paśupata cult was widely prevalent from at least the seventh century, as many temples dating from this period, and continuing into the tenth and eleventh centuries, display prominent images of Lakulīśa, the legendary founder of this cult.[46] It seems, however, that the Śaivism of the Somavaṃśī period was essentially eclectic, and it is probably incorrect to associate any single cult and its doctrine and philosophy with this time.

One particular group which was highly influential during the Somavaṃśī period is known as the Maṭṭamayūra line, or spiritual clan of Śivācāryas. The Maṭṭamayūras were adherents to the so-called "Śaiva" sect, one of medieval India's four major schools of Śaivism.[48] The theology of the Śaiva school is dualistic and can be thought of as a kind of theistic Sāṃkhya. Simply stated, through a breaking down of the bonds of material existence, the soul eventually comes to a realization of its oneness in nature with the Supreme Lord, Śiva.[49] The Maṭṭamayūras (like the Paśupatis) had a strong tradition of Yoga and asceticism, and are closely associated with several monastic sites in central India.[50] One of the Maṭṭamayūra's Ācāryas, Vyomaśiva, has been firmly associated through inscription with the Orissan temple site of Ranipur Jharial, and can be placed within the period of the mid-ninth century. This indicates that the Śaiva school, probably along with the Paśupata, enjoyed wide popularity in Orissa, and both indeed have strong doctrinal affinities.[51]

Inscriptions bear further evidence of the Maṭṭamayūra's eclecticism. V. V. Mirashi states that they were familiar with "various orthodox and even heterodox systems", referring particularly to the Maṭṭamayūra's familiarity with Buddhist philosophy,[52] while they engaged also in theological discussions with the Paśupatas.

We must consider also the prevalence of Tantrism throughout central and northern India at this time. Tantric Śaivism was in a well developed state long before the tenth century, and most of its elements — secret rituals, emphasis on ideational meditation, the Śiva-Śakti/Puruṣa-Prakṛti concept, complex *mantra* symbolism, etc.,[53] are not such separate concerns from "orthodox Hinduism" as it so often assumed. Inscriptional evidence points concretely to Tantric practices in northern India during the tenth and eleventh centuries,[54] as well as do various aspects of temple imagery. The ceiling of the Mukteśvara temple's *maṇḍapa* is a case in point. The ceiling has the form of one of Tantrism's most well-known symbolic/ritual devices—a *maṇḍala*, consisting of an exposition of *mantra* symbolism, where Śiva is identified with *nāda*, primordial, unheard sound.[55] Various temples of this period are dedicated to aspects of the Goddess, the Vaitāl Deul and Gaurī temple in Bhubaneswar, the Vārāhī temple at Chaurasi, and particularly the Cauṃsat Yoginī temples at Hirapur and Ranipur Jharial, point to the prominence at this time of Śākta Tantrism, which given the emphasis in Śaivism on the role of the Goddess in both myth and doctrine, was extremely influential on the cult of Śiva.

A means by which these various religious ideas were transmitted is undoubtedly the phenomenon of Brahmanical migrations from various parts of India, and the donations to them of tax-free villages. This practice of donating whole villages to Brahmins began as early as the fifth century and was a standard practice by the sixth.[56] Inscriptions recording the grants of villages to Brahmins often mention the place of origin of the priests. While most of these name places cannot be precisely identified, they can at least tentatively be associated with parts of Uttar Pradesh, particularly Kanauj.[57] A famous legend tells that Yayāti Keśarī (Yayāti I Mahāśivagupta ?) brought 10,000 Brahmins from Kānya Kubja (Kanauj) to conduct an *āśvamedha* sacrifice at Jajpur.[58] Hermann Kulke states that the presence of Brahmin communities both in the royal centers and in outlaying villages, influenced Orissa's integration into "an all-Indian sphere of Sanskritic learning . . . and temple architecture, both indispensable paraphernalia of . . . Hindu Kingship."[59] Brahmin migrations were a primary means by which Orissa established and maintained a strong connection with the mainstream of north Indian culture, and accounts, indirectly, for the presence of many borrowed architectural elements in the temples of the Somavaṃśī period, particularly the Mukteśvara (ca. 970) and the Rājarāni (ca. 1000). The various borrowings seen in the Mukteśvara temple may also be partly accounted for in that Ekāmra/Bhubaneswar was a major pilgrimage center, as indicated by the large number of temples surviving here, which date from the seventh to the fourteenth century.[60]

It was in this culturally rich and dynamic period that the Mukteśvara temple was built. It is to this temple that we now turn.

NOTES

1. See S. Rajaguru, *Inscriptions of Orissa,* 4 vols. (Bhubaneswar, 1958-60).

2. The Brahmeśvara temple inscription (now lost) was published by John Princep in *Journal of the Asiatic Society of Bengal,* 7 (1838), p. 557, plate 24. For translations see R. L. Mitra, *Antiquities of Orissa* (Calcutta, 1875-80), (reprint Calcutta, 1961), vol. 2, pp. 150-52.

3. This date is arrived at through rather complicated calculations and not a few basic assumptions. First of all, we must consider the Somavaṃśī king Janmejaya I to be contemporary with the Kalacuri king Saṅkaragana Mugdhatunda, who, according to V. V. Mirashi ruled c. 878-910 (HCIP, vol. 4 (Bombay, 1955), pp. 87-88). Janmejaya was involved in the Bhauma-kara succession dispute which occurred between the Bhauma years 145 and 158, when Śivakaradeva III and Pṛthvī Mahādevī (Śivakaradeva's sister-in-law and Janmejaya's daughter) were ruling. Panigrahi takes the year of Janmejaya's intervention to be the Bhauma year 155; and from this surmises that the Bhauma era began between 723 and 755. The year 736 as the initial date of the Bhauma era is found through astronomical calculations. The Dasapala copper plate grant, dated to the Bhauma year 198 "was issued on the day of Viṣṇu-Saṁkrāntī, Pañcamī, Ravi-dina, Mṛgaśirasnakṣatra [S. N. Rajaguru, "The Dasapala Copper Plate Grant of Ranaka Satrubhañja Deva, Saṃvat 198", OHRJ, 1.3 (1952), pp. 208ff. and D. C. Sircar, "Two Grants from Daspalla", *Epigraphica Indica,* 29.6 (1952), pp. 189ff.]. This is a combination of solar and lunar reckoning, and it has been ascertained that this combination occurred three times between 700 and 1100 A.D.; March 21, 812, March 23, 934, and March 23, 1029. By subtracting 198 from 934, the year 736 is obtained (K. C. Panigrahi, *Chronology of the Bhauma-karas and the Somavaṃśīs of Orissa* (Madras, n.d., 1961?), pp. 3-9.

4. See Panigrahi, *Chronology,* pp. 6-10 and 21-31.

5. *Ibid.,* p. 18.

6. Hermann Kulke, "Early State Formation and Royal Legitimation in Late Ancient Orissa", M. N. Das, ed., *Sidelights on the History and Culture of Orissa* (Cuttack, 1977), p. 110. See also HCIP, vol. 4, pp. 62-63; and H. Mahtab, *History of Orissa,* vol. 1 (Cuttack, 1959), p. 131. Panigrahi, *Chronology,* pp. 20-21 and Biswarup Das, *The Bhauma-karas: Bhuddhist Kings of Orissa and Their*

Times (New Delhi, 1978), pp. 25ff. believe that the Bhauma-karas descended from a non-Aryan tribe from Assam.

7. Panigrahi, *Chronology,* p. 22.

8. J. K. Sahu, "Śaivism in Orissa", Das, ed., *Sidelights*' p. 329 (citing *Epigraphica Indica,* 28.4 (1949), p. 183). See also HCIP, vol. 4, pp. 66-67.

9. Sahu, "Śaivism", p. 330.

10. Panigrahi, *Chronology,* p. 27.

11. Tribhuvana Mahādevī I was probably the daughter of Rajamalla I of the Western Gaṅgā dynasty of Mysore (reigned c. 817-35). Panigrahi feels that it was through his aid that this queen "retrieved the lost position of the Bhauma kingdom" (*Chronology,* p. 22).

12. Panigrahi, *Chronology,* pp. 7, 9.30; and Das, *The Bhauma-karas,* pp. 81-82, 192-93.

13. See the genealogy above, and Panigrahi, *Chronology,* pp. 20-31. See also HCIP, vol. 4, p. 67; and Das, *Bhauma-karas,* pp. 190-94.

14. HCIP, p. 69.

15. Panigrahi, *ibid.,* p. 31. That Vakula Mahādevī was a member of the Bhañja family is strongly implied by one of her copper plate grants, describing her as an "ornament . . . in the family of the Bhañja kings" (Panigrahi, *ibid.,* p. 31, citing G. Das and K. C. Panigrahi, "Taltali Plate of Dharma Mahādevī", IHQ, 21 (1945), pp. 218-21. Panigrahi cites no evidence, however, for Dharma Mahādevaī's family ties.

16. N. K. Sahu, "History of Kośala and the Somavaṃśīs of Utkala", OHRJ, 3.8 (1954), pp. 127-32; Majumdar, HCIP, vol. 3, pp. 220-22; K. C. Panigrahi, *History of Orissa* (Cuttack, 1981), pp. 96-97.

17. Panigrahi, *Chronology,* p. 17. B. K. Sarma, *The History of Somavaṃśī Rule in Orissa* (Calcutta, 1983), pp. 9-16, follows the same basic sequence as Panigrahi, but dates the beginning of the dynasty about four years later. While much of her chronology is based on a more critical assessment of various records than Panigrahi's—particularly those of dynasties like the Kalacuris and Colas, with whom the Somavaṃśīs were in conflict—she fails to relate the probable beginning of the previous Bhauma-kara dynasty (736 A.D.) to her chronological sequence, which would give the Somavaṃśī dynasty an earlier beginning than she allows.

18. See above.

19. Sahu, *History of Kośala,* p. 132.

20. P. B. Misra, *Dynasties of Medieval Orissa* (Calcutta, 1933), p. 75; Mahtab, *History of Orissa,* p. 60. Sahu, *History of Kośala,* p. 132, appears to agree with this identification.

21. P. P. Acharya, "Genealogy of the Somakulī Kings of Kośala and Utkala", *Studies in Orissan History,* p. 77.

22. Panigrahi, *Chronology,* pp. 6, 7.

23. See S. R. Nema, *Political History of the Somavaṃśī Kings of South Kośala and Orissa* (New Delhi, 1978), p. 201. See also Rajaguru, *Inscriptions of Orissa,* vol. 4, 364-65; and Das, *Bhauma-karas,* p. 195-96.

24. HCIP, vol. 4, pp. 146-47.

25. Panigrahi, *Chronology,* p. 9.

26. One land grant states that king Silabhañja occupied Gandhaṭpāti (modern Gandharadi) by force, which was "being enjoyed by force" by the Somavaṃśīs. Panigrahi, *History,* p. 137.

27. According to the *Mādalā Pāñji*, the chronicle of the Jagannātha temple in Puri, Jagannātha was re-established by "Yayāti Keśarī 146 years after the Raktavahu invasion". Panigrahi identifies Yayāti Keśarī with Yayāti I on the basis that his reign (c. 922-55) fits into chronological position with the reign of the Rāṣṭrakūṭa emperor Govinda III (c. 793-814), who invaded Orissa during that time. Panigrahi feels that the elements of the tradition recorded in the *Mādalā Pāñji* and actual facts recorded by inscription justify the identifications of Raktavahu-Rāṣṭrakūṭa and Yayāti Keśarī-Yayāti I. (See Panigrahi, *Chronology*, pp. 26-27 and 32-33; and K. C. Panigrahi, ARB, p. 248n.).

28. ARB, pp. 236-52.

29. It is known from two copper plate grants which mention Bhīmaratha that he ruled for at least thirteen years [Mahtab, *History of Orissa*, vol. 1, p. 182; and Majumdar, HCIP, vol. 5, p. 209. Panigrahi assigns him a much longer reign (955-80) on the basis that he may have been a contemporary of the Kalacuri King Lakṣmaṇarāja, who ruled from 945-70, and who came into conflict with "the Prince of Oḍra" Panigrahi, *Chronology*, p. 33. The date assigned to Bhīmaratha by Panigrahi obviously needs more evidence.

30. It is generally believed by scholars that by the time of Dharmaratha there were two Somavaṃśī capitals called Yayātinagara—the older city in Kośala and Abhinavayayātinagara ("New Yayātinagara", a usage found only in the *Mādalā Pāñji*), identified with modern Jajpur. See Panigrahi, *Chronology*, pp. 9-13. D. C. Sircar also believes in the existence of a "second capital" at Jajpur. See HCIP, vol. 5, p. 212.

31. Panigrahi, *ibid.*, pp. 34-35; and HCIP, vol. 5, pp. 66-67.

32. From the Brahmeśvara temple inscription, cited in Panigrahi, *ibid.*, p. 35. See also the Somavaṃśī genealogy above.

33. The Balijhari Inscription, cited in HCIP, vol 5, p. 210.

34. Panigrahi, *Chronology*, p. 35, citing B. C. Majumdar, "Maranjamura Charter of Mahāśivagupta *alias* Yayāti", JBORS, 2.1 (1916), p. 53.

35. HCIP, vol. 5, p. 210.

36. Panigrahi, *ibid.*, p. 37; Mahtab, *History of Orissa*, pp. 188-89; HCIP, vol. 5, pp. 211-12.

37. Panigrahi, *Chronology*, pp. 36, 62, 64-68.

38. HCIP, p. 189.

39. *Ibid.*, pp. 189-90; and ARB, pp. 41-47.

40. On stylistic grounds it is impossible to accept Panigrahi's belief that the Liṅgarāja temple was begun by Caṇḍīhara and finished by Uddyotakeśarī (thus preceding the Brahmeśvara). See Chapter 5. Panigrahi's ideas are based entirely on the legends "current in Bhubaneswar" that the Liṅgarāja was begun by Yayāti Keśarī and finished by Lalatendu Keśarī (see ARB, p. 265). These identifications have absolutely no supporting evidence from inscriptions. Furthermore, Panigrahi's identification of Yayāti Keśarī with Yayāti Caṇḍīhara is inconsistent with his previous identification of the legendary king with Yayāti I (see above, note 24).

41. Panigrahi, *Chronology*, p. 38.

42. B. Masthanaiah, *The Temples of Mukhaliṅgam* (New Delhi, 1978), p. 20.

43. ARB, pp. 236-52.

44. Panigrahi, *History*, p. 106.

45. See B. Das, "Śaivism in Ancient Orissa", Das, ed., *Sidelights*, p. 342 for references to Somavaṃśī inscriptions referring to the kings as Paramaheśvara, or devotees of Śiva.

46. Temples in Bhubaneswar with images of Lakulīśa include the Bhārateśvara, Paraśurāmeśvara, Vaitāl Deul, Śiśireśvara, Mukteśvara (enclosure wall), Marīci Kuṇḍa, and Rājarāni.

47. For genealogies of the Maṭṭamayūra clan and summaries of their beliefs and practices see J. K. Sahu, "Śaivism in Orissa", *Sidelights*, pp. 330-32; Panigrahi, *History*, p. 319; J. N. Banerjea, *Paurāṇic and Tāntric Religion*, (Calcutta, 1966), pp. 104-06; V. V. Mirashi, "The Śaivācāryas of the Maṭṭamayūra Clan", IHQ, 26.1 (1950) pp. 1-16.

48. These four sects are the Śaiva, Paśupata, Karuka (or Karunika Siddhāntin) and Kapālika. They are referred to by the commentators on Śaṅkarācārya's works, Ramānuja and Keśani Kaśmiri. See Mirashi, "Ācāryas", p. 14; and V. S. Pathak, *History of Śaiva Cults in Northern India from Inscriptions (700 to 1200 A.D.)* (Varanasi, 1960), p. 2.

49. Banerjea, *Religion*, p. 103. See also E. B. Cowell and A. E. Gough, trans., *Sarvadarśanasaṃgraha by Madhvācārya* (Varanasi, 1978 reprint), pp. 112-27.

50. See Mirashi, "Ācāryas"; and V. V. Mirashi, ed., *Inscriptions of the Kalachuri-Chedi Era*, Corpus Inscriptionum Indicarum, vol. 4 (Ootacamund, 1955), pp. cli-clx.

51. Cowell and Gough, *Sarvadarśana*, pp. 103-11 ("The Śaiva System"), and pp. 112-27 ("The Lakulīśa-Pāśupata System").

52. Mirashi, "Ācāryas", p. 15. See also F. Kielhorn, "Ratnapur Stone Inscription of Jajalladepa", *Epigraphica Indica*, 1 (1892), p. 39 (vs. 28).

53. Tantric Śaivism was in a well developed state long before the 10th century. For a general history see S. Gupta, *et al.*, *Hindu Tantrism* (Leiden, 1979).

54. For inscriptional evidence of Tantric practices in northern India see Pathak, *Śaiva Cults*, pp. 13, 16, 22, 25 and *passim*.

55. See Chapter 4.

56. Kulke, "Early State Formation", p. 107.

57. Das and Panigrahi, "Taltali Plate", pp. 213-22. Kalancha, the home of the Brahmin grantee of this inscription was "famous in the early medieval period as the seat of orthodox Brahmins, and the Brahmins of Bengal and Orissa used to feel proud of connecting their origin with it" (p. 216). B. Das, *The Bhauma-karas*, pp. 160-61, discusses several Bhauma-kara and Somavaṃśī grants which mention the origins of Brahmin grantees, e.g. Takari (situated in the limits of Śrāvastī and identified with modern Sahet-Mahet, Bahraich district, Uttar Pradesh), and Kolancha (Kanauj area). See also A. H. Sah, *Life in Medieval Orissa* (Varanasi, 1976, p. 121).

58. Mahtab, *History of Orissa*, p. 178; ARB, p. 250.

59. Kulke, "Early State Formation", p. 107.

60. Ekāmra is mentioned as a *tīrtha* in the *Garuḍa Purāṇa* (ca. 800-1100 A.D.), the *Matsya Purāṇa* (6th?-13th century) and the *Brahmā Purāṇa* (ca. 900-1350). See S. M. Bhardwaj, *Places of Pilgrimage in India* (Berkeley, 1973), pp. 62-66.

CHAPTER 3

DESCRIPTION OF THE MUKTEŚVARA TEMPLE

The origin of the name of the Mukteśvara temple is not known. Mukteśvara, "Lord of the spiritually liberated", is a general epithet of Śiva (as are all compound names ending in *īśvara*, such as Brahmeśvara, Tīrtheśvara, etc.), used in the names of his temples. The name Mukteśvara is used in the *Ekāmra Candrikā,* a pilgrim's guide to the temples of Bhubaneswar, but this is generally considered a very late text (the latest temples of Bhubaneswar are included in it). The temple's original name, if not Mukteśvara, is not known, although it was undeniably conceived as a Śiva temple, as are most of the temples of Bhubaneswar.[1]

In many ways, the Mukteśvara temple (figs. 7, 8, 12) is a unique monument. Its most unusual features are its low decorated enclosure wall and *toraṇa*; these have no precedent or subsequent use in Orissa. Also unusual is the carved ceiling of its *maṇḍapa*, with its formal, narrative and iconographic complexity (fig. 87). And on the temple's overall exterior, various new or recently developed architectural elements and motifs are arranged with an exquisite sense of composition and pattern, and we are presented with a monument of exceptional finish.

The following descriptive analysis of the Mukteśvara temple attempts to clearly delineate each individual architectural element and sculptural motif. The purpose of this extensive description is to provide a clear image of the form and imagery of the monument. The data compiled here will be used further in the following chapter as evidence for interpreting the meaning of the temple as a whole.

THE COMPOUND

The Mukteśvara, Siddheśvara, and various small shrines are set within a garden-like enclosure popularly called Siddhāraṇya, or Forest of the Perfected Ones.[2] While its present state resembles more a well-manicured park than an ascetic grove, the spacious setting is very pleasant, with various flowing plants and shady trees providing color and shelter from the activity beyond the walls (figs. 2, 9, 11). A modern enclosure wall (quadrangular in appearance, but actually an irregular octagon) encompasses an area 250 by 200 feet and spaciously surrounds the various temples. The entire enclosure rests upon what originally was a low mound.[3] The southwestern section of the compound is empty, but for a modern sundial. Across the well tended lawn, at the northern end of the compound, is the eleventh-century Siddheśvara temple. The western part of the compound constitutes a raised terrace, while the southeast contains a recessed courtyard, which holds the Mukteśvara, its tank, and several miniature shrines. The courtyard is accessible by two short flights of steps to the north and south.

Just a few feet west of the center of the compound, at the edge of the raised terrace just before it drops into the courtyard, is a north-south alignment of six miniature temples (fig. 10). Their entrances face east, and so face inward toward the entrance of the Mukteśvara itself. The shrines are arranged in two groups of three, with the space left between the groups aligned with the east-west axis leading to the Mukteśvara's doorway.

In the southeastern area of the compound is a group of four miniature temples roughly contemporary in style to the Siddheśvara (fig. 11). All have entrances at the west (as does the Mukteśvara). The shrines are set in a strict north-south alignment. The two farthest south and the one farthest north are quite small, rising to a height of only about fifteen feet. The third temple from the south, however, is much larger, only a little less tall (though much more simple in decoration) than the Mukteśvara. On the *bhadra* of its *śikhara,* above the entrance, is an elaborate *śukanāsā* design, and the doorway is flanked by two *dvārapālas* on either side. A fairly wide space separating this temple from the small shrine flanking it to the north suggests that another small temple was to have been placed there, thus completing the symmetry of the line of temples.

The Mukteśvara temple itself and its low enclosure wall command the space of the stone-paved quadrangular courtyard, with four miniature shrines also placed therein. Two are just north of the Mukteśvara's *prāsāda* (fig. 12) and two others are placed along the northern side of the quadrangle, next to a row of steps leading up toward the Siddheśvara (fig. 13).

South and slightly east of the enclosure wall's entrance is a small enclosed well or tank. According to Debala Mitra it is locally known as the Marīci Kuṇḍa, and its water is renowned for its curative properties (figs. 14, 15).[4] The doorframe leading to it is carved. Represented at the center of its lintel is a seated figure of Lakulīśa surrounded by four disciples. The remainder of the lintel is carved with figures of seated ascetics facing toward the central figures.

Facing the eastern (back) end of the Mukteśvara is a large rectangular tank stretching almost the entire length of the east enclosure wall. It is fed by a natural spring, which may have been a contributing factor to the temple's being built on this site. In combination with the other elements of the setting a truly serene, almost idyllic environment is completed for the temple, which fits into its surroundings perfectly, because of its non-monumental scale and elegant proportions.

THE ENCLOSURE WALL

The Mukteśvara temple rests upon a stone pavement which serves as a circumambulatory path. This pathway is further defined by a low (fifty and one-half inches high) enclosure wall (see figs. 3, 16, 17). The enclosure wall is constructed out of the same red, warm-hued sandstone as the temple. Its outlines echo the shape of the temple, the central *rathas* of which create a kind of truncated cruciform ground plan. This cruciform-shaped wall contains a series of corners, which on the exterior hold several relief sculptures.

The lowest course of the wall's exterior takes the form of a simple *khura*, or "hoof-shaped" moulding, as seen on the lower portions of the *rathas* of the temple itself (fig. 94). On the wall, however, the shape is continuous rather than being divided up into pilaster-like *rathas*. The course is decorated with small long and narrow crest-like motifs resembling stylized *gavākṣa* windows. They mostly contain floral patterns or scroll work, while several of them hold standing figures, some resembling naked Jain Tīrthaṅkaras. The second course, slightly recessed, contains a series of niches along its entire length, one being superimposed above each of the small crest-like designs. The niches consist of two flanking pilasters decorated with scroll work and capped by *gavākṣa* windows which contain at the center either a male face, lotus emblems, or *kīrtti mukhas* (see fig. 16). The niche spaces themselves are filled (except those at the corners) with round *cakra*-like designs, lotus medallions or *kalaśa* motifs.

The thirty corner niche-panels all bear (or once did) images of various deities and the well-known "enigmatic figures" that have frequently been pointed out. Beginning with the first corner to the west (directly to the left of the main entrance), the niche imagery is as follows (see also wall diagram, fig. 3):

1. (fig. 18). Central standing male figure with tall crown holding a long stalked lotus in his left hand. The right hand hangs down, with the palm turned outward. The figure is flanked by two dwarfish attendants. The panel is badly worn and damaged, and very little detail survives. Because of the lotus stalk, Panigrahi identifies this figure as the Bodhisattva Avalokiteśvara.[5]

2. (Fig. 19). Single male figure of dwarfish proportions seated in *lalitāsana* upon a lotus platform. The right hand rests upon the right knee and holds an indistinct object, possibly a cup. The image is eroded, but otherwise undamaged. This dwarfish figure may represent a *yakṣa*.

3. (Fig. 20). Lakulīśa. The figure sits frontally in *yogāsana* upon a lotus platform. The right hand is in the earth-touching gesture (*bhūmisparṣa mudrā*). The left holds the identifying attribute of the club (*lakula*). The ears are distended and the hair rendered as a cap of curls. These elements show how the Lakulīśa figure derives from that of the Buddha. The image is quite eroded and slightly damaged.

4. (Fig. 21). Male figure seated in *yogāsana*, with hands folded across the lap in the meditative gesture (*dhyānamudrā*). He sits on a lotus platform before which is placed a low stool or bench. The figure has distended ear lobes and the hair is rendered as a smooth cap, recalling the standard treatment of Buddha figures. Two stylized leaves flank the head of the figure. Panigrahi identifies the figure as the

Buddha under the Bodhi tree,[6] but given the profusion of yogic figures on the Mukteśvara temple, and their Buddhist derived iconography, this figure was probably conceived as a meditating yogin.

5. (Fig. 22). Female figure, four armed, seated on a lotus in *lalitāsana*. She wears a tall crown and has distended ear lobes. Attributes are indistinct, the upper right hand holds a discus or possibly a *mālā* (rosary), the upper left, a lotus stalk. On the left knee and supported by the left hand are the badly worn and damaged remains possibly of a child figure. The image may represent one of the Sapta Mātṛkās, perhaps Maheśvarī or Vaiṣṇavī.

6. Empty.

7. (Fig. 23). Male figure in *lalitāsana* on a lotus platform. The figure wears an elaborate headdress, necklace and sacred thread. His attributes are badly eroded. They are possibly the animal attributes (peacock and rooster) of Kārttikeya (Skanda).

8. (Fig. 24). Sūrya. The figure sits cross-legged on a stylized chariot (looking more like a low table) with his seven mares before it. He holds two lotuses and wears a tall crown. Detail survives well in this panel, although the face has been slightly damaged.

9. (Fig. 25). King with attendants. In this badly damaged panel, the main figure, with hair tied into a chignon, sits in an easy posture upon a low table. He holds an indistinct object in his right hand. He is flanked by attendant figures (the right one is completely obliterated) and before him sits a miniature figure.

10. (Fig. 26). Yogin. This single, headless figure sits in *yogāsana* upon a lotus pedestal. The damaged hands are held in the gesture *kapota* (dove), with the palms joined at the thumbs and opening outward. Though badly damaged, the carving here is fine and detailed, with little erosion.

11, 12. Empty.

13. (Fig. 27). Sūrya. The figure sits in *padmāsana* upon a chariot resembling a low dias. Before the chariot are seven rearing miniature horses, those on the left being quite worn down. The god holds a large lotus in each hand, and wears an elaborate hair style and crown. Hands, feet and face are damaged.

14. (Fig. 28). Gaṇeśa. The right side of the panel is totally destroyed. The finely carved, corpulent figure is shown in a squatting or possibly dancing position.

15-18. Empty.

19. (Fig. 29). Viṣṇu (?). The four-armed figure sits in yogic pose with the two main hands in *dhyānamudrā*. The upper right hand holds a *cakra* (discus), the upper left is demolished. The rest of the figure is largely intact and there is very little erosion.

20. (Fig. 30). In this well preserved panel, a portly male figure with an elaborate chignon, jewellery,. and holding a sword (?) sits comfortably on a low mound. He is flanked by two female attendants with a small figure seated at his feet. This scene may represent a guru with disciples, or may possibly depict a royal figure with attendants.

21. (Fig. 31). Sarasvatī. The goddess sits in *lalitāsana* upon a lotus pedestal, flanked by female attendants. She holds a standard attribute, the *vīṇā*. The panel is badly damaged, particularly around the face.

22. (Fig. 32). Composite figure. This panel depicts four interlaced human figures arranged so that they have only two heads. The panel is well-preserved.

23. (Fig. 33). Vārāhī. The boar-headed goddess is seated with one knee on the ground, the other raised upward. The panel is badly damaged and little detail survives.

24. (Fig. 34). Sarasvatī/celestial musician. The figure sits cross-legged on a low lotus pedestal. She has no attendants. She plays the *vīṇā* and the face, though slightly damaged, bears a meditative cast.

25. (Fig. 35). Kārttikeya. The frontally posed and hieratic god sits upon his peacock. He wears a crown, ear-rings and holds a staff or weapon. The panel is slightly damaged and the details worn down.

26. (Fig. 36). Gaṇeśa. Less damaged than the previous Gaṇeśa image (though eroded), the fat, dwarfish figure sits in an easy pose on the flat ground. Four-armed, he holds an axe and other indistinct objects.

27. (Fig. 37). Śiva Gajāsurasaṁhāramūrti. The figure is four-armed and extremely emaciated, with exposed rib cage and sunken abdomen. The details are badly worn down. He holds a weapon or a staff in his upper right arm. His lower left hand holds a knife. A dog or jackal is seen to the right. To the left, behind the figure, is the head of an elephant, alluding to Śiva's battle with the elephant demon.[7]

28. (Fig. 38). Yogin (Lakulīśa). The figure sits with his legs tied with a *yogabandha*. The hands are in a meditative gesture. The head is smooth and ear lobes distended. The two lotus stalks flank the figure, and upon the lotuses, at the top corners of the panel, sit two attendant figures. The details are quite worn down.

29. (Fig. 39). Goddess. The four-armed figure sits in *lalitāsana* upon a lotus pedestal. The objects she holds are indistinct. To the left of the pedestal sits a deer, to the right, a lion (?).

30. (Fig. 40). Composite figure. Less well-preserved than the previous composite image (number 22, fig. 32). Four bodies share two heads in an intricate puzzle image.

The top two courses of the wall are quite plain. Above the recessed niches is a continuous *khura*-shaped course. Its curving portion is shorter than the one on the lowest level, and is decorated only occasionally with miniature *gavākṣa* patterns. Above it is a plain course. Its curving portion is shorter than the one on the lowest level, and is decorated only occasionally with miniature *gavākṣa* patterns. Above it is a plain square course, faced with half oval shaped stone slabs.

TORAṆA

A ten-inch high and eleven-inch wide basement juts out fifty-three and one-half inches from the enclosure wall's entrance, and at its end is erected the temple's celebrated *toraṇa* or ornamental gateway (figs. 41-45). It consists of two massive columns, thirty-one inches square and forty-six and one-half inches apart, which rise to a height of about 106 inches. Spanning the distance above is a massive rounded arch. The bases of the columns (twenty-two and one quarter inches high) consist of two square stone courses. Each side is decorated identically, but for those facing inward, which are left plain. At the center of each side is a relief carving resembling a miniature temple. Its lowest portion consists of a low base moulding. Above it is a kind of triptych, the central panel consisting of a female figure flanked by panels depicting *vyālas*, images of rearing leogryphs mounted by a male or female figure, and pouncing on an elephant. The upper part of the shrine motif consists of five horizontal courses. The lower two are of the *khura* shape, their lower portions decorated horizontally with scroll work, the upper part with vertical lotus petals. They have an outward jutting *bhadra* (as do the lower "triptych" panels and the courses above them). The upper three courses are flat and decorated respectively with animal carvings, upward pointing lotus petals and a row of small "rosettes". The whole design is capped by a fluted *āmalaka* stone surmounted by a *kalaśa*.

The shafts of the columns contain sixteen facets and consist of five stone courses. Only the top and bottom ones contain ornamentation. The bottom courses, upon which the *āmalaka* of the miniature shrine is placed, contain at the corners, high relief figures of crouching elephants being attacked by lions. The uppermost course is surrounded by a series of *kīrtti mukhas* spewing forth ropes of pearls from their mouths. The continuous motifs form looping garlands all around the upper circumference.

Above the *kīrtti mukhas* is a narrow band covered with an undulating creeper motif. Jutting out from this band, and facing each of the cardinal directions, are half-circular protuberances, looking almost like bowls attached to the column's surface. They are deeply carved with rounded scroll work and their "rims", with narrow bands of rosettes.

The "capitals" of the columns are much more organically conceived than the simply articulated shafts below. The lowest portion consists of a squat, cushion-shaped stone with ribbing, similar to an *āmalaka*. Above it is a similarly shaped, but non-ribbed course, which corresponds closely to the Western Classical abacus. The uppermost part of the capital consists of a strange, undulating mushroom-like form, appearing to grow outwards and curling under at its outer rim. This rim is decorated with thirty-two incised, downward pointing lotus petals, each of which is in turn bordered by incised circular patterns.

The massive, rounded arch is by far the most highly decorated part of the *toraṇa*. The imagery is identical on both sides. Jutting outward (north and south) on the lower part of the arch are two *makara* heads, composite crocodile monsters with parted jaws and upward curling snouts. The face of the arch itself is completely symmetrical. Along its lower edge is a border consisting of a narrow band of scroll work.

At the lower parts and at the apex of this arched band are three elaborate *gavākṣa* windows, similar in composition and ornamentation to the window motifs on the *candraśālās* (large heraldic window motifs) of the *śikhara*. Within each window is a male face. These window motifs are similar to those at various Buddhist sites, which house images of meditating Buddhas.[8] The face within the left window on the west (outer) side of the archway is destroyed.

To the side and slightly above the two lower windows are dwarfish male figures in meditation. Their hands are placed in various *mudrās* or hold *mālās*, and their legs are held into the meditative posture by *yogabandhas*. These figures are modern restorations.[9]

The entire semi-circular arch is divided by the miniature *gavākṣas* into two curving bands. The lower part of each band contains a narrow frieze sparsely decorated with figures of frolicking monkeys. Above this is a wider band holding reclining female figures. Four in all, they are of the voluptuous *yankṣiṇī* type, their breasts are round, their hips swelling and their poses seductive. They wear ornaments around their waists, ankles, wrists, necks, and in their hair (the face of the right, inward facing or eastern figure and the left, outward or western one have been poorly restored. The two others are intact). The female figures are framed above by a narrow border of rosettes.

The upper portion of the arch, barely visible from the ground, is decorated all over with a rich swirling pattern of scroll work. At the very top is a raised, slightly crenellated rib, extending lengthwise over the entire arch. Surmounting the whole structure is an *amṛta kalaśa*.

THE TEMPLE

The Mukteśvara temple consists of two basic units, the *maṇḍapa* (forehall, audience chamber), and the *prāsāda* (the "temple proper", which houses the sacred *liṅga*). They are connected by a narrow buffer wall, which recedes inward, thus preserving a sense of separateness to the two structures (see figs. 4 and 8). The temple rests upon a low plinth, thirteen inches high.

The ground plan (fig. 4) gives a general view of proportionate relationships. Broadly speaking, the *maṇḍapa* is twice as long as the *prāsāda*, if the farthest projection of the entrance way is included. The proportion of interior space is also approximately two to one; the *garbhagṛha* (square interior of the *prāsāda*) is ninety by ninety inches, the *maṇḍapa* 183 by 144 inches. The *maṇḍapa* interior is punctuated by several pilasters, at the exit, entrance to the *garbhagṛha*, corners, and before the deep openings of the lattice-windows (see also fig. 88). These doorways and window openings resemble transcepts (the window spaces less so because of their raised floor areas).

The exterior surface of the temple is articulated with multiple vertical salients (*rathas*) jutting out from the wall at various levels, creating strong patterns of light and dark. The central portions of the walls of both the *maṇḍapa* and *prāsāda*, the central projecting element *(bhadra)* consists of a niche elaborately framed by pilasters. The *prāsāda's bhadra* continues onto the *śikhara* (tower), which on its lower section contains a large heraldic *gavākṣa* window.

Three *rathas* flank each side of the *maṇḍapa's* lattice window, with narrow *nāga*-pilasters placed between them. On either side of the *prāsāda's bhadra* are three vertical elements, the *karṇa, nāga*-pilaster and *pratibhadra.*

The pyramidal roof of the *maṇḍapa* is made up of twelve narrow stone terraces, progressively receding, though not in a perfect pyramidal recession, and surmounted by an *amṛta kalaśa.* The total height of the *maṇḍapa* is twenty feet, six and one-half inches.[10] The *prāsāda* is surmounted by a tall curvilinear *śikhara,* capped by a large ribbed *āmalaka* stone, crowned again by an *amṛta kalaśa.* The total height of the *prāsāda* is thirty-four feet, four inches.[11]

Lengthwise, both structures measure forty-eight feet (*maṇḍapa*), twenty-six feet, eight inches, *prāsāda,* twenty-one feet, four inches, buffer wall, sixteen inches. The width of the *maṇḍapa* is twenty-four feet, eight inches (thirty feet, eight inches including the projecting windows), and of the *prāsāda* (at its widest, central point), twenty-two feet, eight inches. The proportions, then, are non-monumental, and further, there is not the somewhat unsettling visual discrepancy between the height of the *maṇḍapa* and *prāsāda* seen in earlier temples. The terraced, rather than flat roof of the forehall is in a harmonious formal relationship to the taller *śikhara,* and together they form a completely unified compositional unit. The temple is made from a "fine grained sandstone, locally called *lāl rājarāṇiya,* with a reddish tinge and small particles of mica."[12]

The lower *rathas* of the temple bear sculpted figures (male and female) in high relief. In brief, these, as well as the *nāga* figures are typified stylistically by a kind of earthy naturalism, a sense that is heightened by the warm, reddish-brown sandstone. Even the most elegant figures have a full, it not stocky appearance, contrasting both with the archaic style of the images on the Paraśurāmeśvara temple and the more stylized and attenuated figures from later monuments such as the Rājarāni and Liṅgarāja. Unfortunately, most of the figures have been systematically mutilated, especially around the faces. The hands, holding particular attributes and held in specific gestures have also been damaged, making identification of each particular female type difficult.

The ceiling of the *maṇḍapa* is elaborately sculpted, its dome-like shape created by the overlapping of stone courses, forming progressively receding octagons and squares (figs. 5, 87). At the center of the ceiling is a round, *maṇḍala*-like composition with figures of the Seven Mother Goddesses and Vīrabhadra-Vīṇādhara.

The *garbhagṛha* is approached by a narrow corridor or vestibule (twenty-eight and one-half by thirty inches). Its walls and ceiling are absolutely plain. At the center of its floor space is a solid stone *liṅga* in a *yoni*-shaped base, and this appears to be the original icon of the temple.

In the description which follows, architecture and sculpture will be discussed separately. The placement of the various architectural elements is for the most part consistent on all sides of the *maṇḍapa* and *prāsāda.* The figures differ, however, and a separate discussion will give a clearer idea of their placement around the body of the temple.

MAṆḌAPA

DOORWAY

In front of the doorway (fig. 46) is placed a semi-circular stone step (forty-seven by twenty and one-half inches), just before the low platform upon which the temple rests. The doorway itself is recessed eighteen and one-half inches from the front of the platform. The door space is raised twelve inches from the surface of the platform and is faced by another semi-circular stepping stone; this one, however, is decorated with a wide horizontal band of scroll work edged with a single line of bead work above and below.

The doorframe is decorated in the traditionally elaborate manner. At the bottom, flanking the decorated steps are two crouching lions. Above them are placed two *dvārapālas,* each with a female *cauri*-bearing attendant (figs. 47 and 48). They stand upon lotus pedestals within a summarily carved niche with a narrow pilaster facing outward and a round arch-shaped curve overhead. Panigrahi identifies these male figures as the "Śaivite *dvārapālas* Caṇḍa and Pracaṇḍa".[13] The figures are four-armed, hold various attributes (trident, bowl, club, noose), and have matted hair and horrific expressions. In the group to the right, a small dwarf figure stands to the right of the *dvārapāla.*

The doorway is bordered all around by three decorative bands. The outer- and inner-most bands contain vegetal designs. The other band contains repetitions of a single motif. Rather like an acanthus leaf, it consists of a large central leaf, flanked by mirror images of itself, cut vertically in half. The leaves are incised with vertical lines. Repeated all along the outer band, they have something of a garlanding effect. The inner band contains rounded scroll work which is rather flatly articulated when compared to the band of leaves. The middle band contains an undulating vine motif, along which are located small dwarf figures. The lintel formed by these decorative borders contains a plaque, at the center of which is a figure of a divinity seated upon a lotus pedestal in a cross-legged pose (fig. 49). The badly mutilated figure has four arms. The lower right hand is in *varada mudrā* (the boon-bestowing gesture), the lower left is placed palm upward upon the knee and perhaps held a now missing object. The attributes in the upper hands are indistinct (the left arm is completely missing, although the right hand seems to hold a rosary). The face has been virtually obliterated. The figure appears to have had either a conical headdress, a pile of matted hair, or both. The ears are distended from heavy ear-rings. The deity wears an elaborate necklace, arm ornaments and a sacred thread. Two flying *gandharvas* are placed at the upper corners of the plaque, while at the lower corners, flanking the deity, are two ascetic figures paying obeisance (the figure to the right is badly damaged).

With the lack of clear attributes, it is impossible to say exactly who is represented here, but given the Śaivite affiliation of the temple and the abundance of ascetic/yogic figures elsewhere on the temple we can tentatively say the image represents Śiva in his aspect of Yogeśvara (lord of yoga). More specifically, because of the presence of images of Lakulīśa on the enclosure wall and on the lintel of the Marīci Kuṇḍa, the figure here may well have represented Lakulīśa. Since Lakulīśa images are often accompanied by ascetic figures, this identification is all the more likely.

The wall space above this lintel has been left unfinished. Only roughly carved in are six vertical panels containing one of the motifs most often repeated on the temple, a panel of scroll work with a *kīrtti mukha* at the top center, emitting strands of pearls which go off in two directions in the form of a "V" (compare with the motifs on the *toraṇa,* fig. 43, and those on the pilasters flanking the doorway).

Flanking the recessed doorway are two "pilasters" (*rathas*), here perhaps more properly called engaged columns, identical in structure and decorative details to all the *rathas* placed at various corners of the temple (the *karṇas*). The base mouldings consist of a *khura*-base bearing a small *gavākṣa* housing on the left a lotus motif, and on the right a demonic face. Above this is the *kuṃbha* element, faced with a narrow vertical leaf. This is surmounted by two *kapotāli* mouldings.

Above the double *kapotāli* is the central portion of the *rathas.* Here, against a background of scroll work is placed a female figure in high relief. Indeed, it is virtually carved in the round, and is only slightly attached to the wall from behind. These *ratha* figures are the major sculptural images found on the temple. The figures stand on full lotus pedestals, placed above a kind of miniature double *kapotāli,* which is faced by a miniature female figure in relief. The main figures are placed just in the center of the *ratha.* The scroll work background is densely packed into an almost carpet-like pattern, and its deep, sharp carving creates a dynamic pattern of light and dark. The panel is bordered on either side by a single row of rosettes.

At the top of each panel, several inches above the female figures' heads, is the repeated motif of *kīrtti mukhas* with pearl strands. Above the panel are two additional courses of mouldings, topped by square relief panels of atlantid dwarfs, squat figures appearing to hold up the heavy cornice above them.

The inner sides of these *rathas* are plain. The outer sides, however, are articulated in exactly the same way as the fronts, each bearing a figure in high relief upon the scroll panel. The north side carries a male figure, standing in a slight *tribhaṅga* and holding a flower in his right hand (fig. 57). The south side bears, as is more usual, a female figure (fig. 61), standing next to a tree and holding a fly whisk.

The doorway in its entirety almost constitutes a small structure conceptually separate from the temple wall to which it is attached (fig. 46). The north and south walls of the entrance are treated in much the same way as the walls connecting the *maṇḍapa* and the *prāsāda*. They are left quite plain; the mouldings are not broken up into *khura, kuṃbha*, etc., but are long and horizontal. The wall above them is blank, but for a high relief carving of a *vyāla,* a rearing leogryph with garlands of pearls pouring from its mouth, pouncing on an elephant. On the north wall it is mounted by a male warrior, on the south by a female (figs. 57 and 61).

The columnar *rathas* of the doorway support a cornice which is in turn capped by a *gavākṣa* pediment, of a type never seen before or since in Orissa. The cornice is flat and narrow, and hangs over the doorway in a way reminiscent of an awning. Its top-most part is lined with ribs. Standing at the entrance, one sees the "faces" of these ribs, which terminate in miniature *gavākṣa* designs. The face of the cornice is also decorated all around by rosettes, and below this, a recessed portion is carved with a simple pattern of vertical bands.

The triangular pediment is divided into three parts. The stone course serving as its base bears three horizontal decorative patterns. The lowest consists of an undulating creeper band. Above the creeper band is a narrow row of horizontal bead work, with deep shadows on either side. This is capped by a roof-like element decorated with downward pointing lotus petals.

The two-leveled pediment proper rests upon this moulding. Here is the *gavākṣa*-type pediment seen throughout this period in Central India, Rajasthan and Gujarat.[14] Highly stylized and consisting of flat, ribbon-like patterning, the central portions jut out from their adjacent sides. Embedded within the intricate linear pattern is the arch-window shape deriving ultimately from the *gavākṣa* window.[15]

The upper central portion contains, in addition to the linear patterning, two circular areas, vertically aligned in the exact center, containing traditional Orissan scroll work. A *makara* head is placed at the lower (corner) portions of both levels. The entire pediment is capped by a lion, carved fully in the round and standing on all fours. With jaws parted, it has a ferocious expression. This cornice-pediment is repeated almost exactly above the large grilled windows on the north and south walls of the *maṇḍapa*.

WEST (FRONT) WALL

The wall sections flanking the doorway are identical and vertically articulated into five *rathas* (figs. 7 and 46). These *rathas* all stand upon the conventionally articulated five-part base mouldings, except those of the *karṇas,* which are quadrapartite. The *karṇas* are also identical in articulation to the two outer *rathas* flanking the doorway, and like them, they each bear a female figure in high relief.

Adjacent to the *karṇa* is a narrow *nāga*-pilaster, the main sculptural motif of which is a *nāga,* or serpent deity. Next to this is a wide pilaster having the shape of a miniature shrine. Another *nāga*-pilaster flanks its other side, and at the end of the wall, adjacent to the side wall of the doorway, is another miniature shrine pilaster.

The *nāga*-pilasters consist, from the bottom up, of *khura* and *kuṃbha* base mouldings, a miniature relief of a female figure (usually shown at a door, sometimes also with a parrot), three marrow horizontal mouldings, and a high relief rendering of two elephants being pounced upon by lions. Above this is the image of the *nāga* (male) or *nāginī* (female) itself. These figures are always of the same basic type. They have human torsos (however with a multi-headed serpent hood behind their heads) and serpentine tails. They are shown in a way indicating descending movement; the torsos are at the lower parts of the shafts, with their tails wrapped around the upper parts. Like the female figures, the *nāgas* wear heavy necklaces, jewelled girdles, arm bands and sometimes, crowns on their heads. Some hold fly whisks, and others, garlands of flowers or jewels. Their faces (on the whole not as systematically damaged as those of the female figures), have sweet, gentle expressions, slightly smiling and with eyes lowered.

The top of the shaft is decorated with series of *kīrtti mukhas* with pearl strands. Above it is a moulding in the shape of a *khura* and *kuṃbha,* while above it is a miniature *candraśālā.* The male and female *nāgas* are placed on the front wall in a deliberate pattern; *nāginīs* are next to each *karṇa,* while their male counterparts are placed between the miniature shrine-shaped pilasters.

The lower parts of these pilasters consist, at the bottom, of two narrow five-part base mouldings. Placed upon both are two drum-shaped mouldings, which serve as bases for two narrow scroll panels, again superimposed by the *kīrtti mukha* motifs. These panels create a niche, which has placed over it a miniature canopy. Every one of the niches thus formed on the temple is empty; they originally held free standing statues, rather than figures carved as an integral part of the wall.

Above each niche is a series of horizontal courses of a modified *khura* shape, being much more squat than those of the bases of the *rathas.* The lowest one is decorated with a horizontal band of scroll work. Eight identical courses placed above take the form of a miniature *śikhara.* The faces of these courses are each decorated with three miniature *gavākṣa* motifs (figs. 46 and 50). Each is a linear simplification of the small *gavākṣas* found on various parts of the temple. The overall pattern, while beginning to produce the "lace-net" effect seen on the miniature shrines on the *prāsāda* and on the *śikhara* itself, are not as highly abstracted, and each individual motif retains its readability. These miniature *śikharas* are surmounted with a slightly smaller capping stone, again in a modified *khura* shape. Its upper portion is sometimes left plain, other times decorated at the center by a small figure of a squatting dwarf or meditating ascetic.

NORTH AND SOUTH (SIDE) WALLS

The side walls of the *maṇḍapa* measure eight feet, eight and one-quarter inches, up to a terminating roll cornice, decorated with a narrow band of scroll work and a pattern of downward pointing lotus petals, above which rises the multi-terraced pyramidal roof. But for minor details and differences in preservation, the north and south walls are identical. At the centre of the wall, below the cornice, is a large canopy-like construction, jutting considerably from the rest of the wall (figs. 4 and 8). It consists of two standard *rathas* which support a cornice and pediment, both identical to those above the entry wall. The pilasters frame a recessed stone lattice window, which is itself framed by various bands of relief sculpture. Symmetrically flanking this canopied window construction are *pratibhadras* (two on each side) and *karṇas* bearing high relief female figures, at the wall's end. Alternating with these elements, and immediately flanking the window pilasters, are *nāga*-pilasters (three on each side).

The grille window (fig. 51), with its pattern of squares at a diagonal, creates a diamond-like pattern. Three bands of scroll work surround the window. The inner band consists of a narrow border of undulating scroll work, the middle one a simple rosette pattern, and the slightly wider outer one the "acanthus leaf" border, as seen on the entrance's door frame. At the center of these bands are placed four relief carvings. The upper one depicts Gajalakṣmī (fig. 52). She is seated upon a lotus pedestal, under which is a rectangular panel of vegetal designs, from which rise lotus stalks. The flowers of these flanking stalks bear elephants, which bathe the goddess. Lakṣmī carries a lotus in her left hand, with her right in *varadamudrā*. The lower relief figure is a squatting *gaṇa* (fig. 53). Of the corpulent *yakṣa* type, he wears an elaborate curly wig and holds a club over his knees. To the left and right are reliefs of flying *gandharva* couples (figs. 54 and 55). To conform with the square format, the female is depicted as much smaller than the male and rides on his angularly upturned leg.

Further decorating the recessed window is a wider relief border on all sides but the bottom. This contains the celebrated "frolicking monkeys" reliefs (fig. 50). Undulating creepers form large rondels within which the monkeys are involved in various activities, grooming each other, hanging from trees by their tails, or encountering other animals. Small portions of the relief have been weathered, but not enough to detract from the integrity of the overall composition.

An additional horizontal relief is placed above the monkey composition. In the center is a *kīrtti mukha*, with two thick vines coming from either side of its mouth (the *kīrtti mukha* on the south wall has been defaced). The vines form rondels similar to those on the relief below; which are, however, populated by flying *gandharva* couples. At either end of the panel are inward facing *makara* heads, with open mouths, appearing to swallow up the figures.

Above this lintel is a rectangular wall section, faced with a vertical relief panel only partially finished. Three architectural motifs, in the form of miniature *śikharas,* consist of five stone courses, each with a projecting central portion. They alternate with two panels depicting female figures standing at a door, a motif that is seen repeatedly on the *prāsāda* and the main *śikhara.*

EAST WALLS AND BUFFER WALLS

The eastern face of the *maṇḍapa* is divided into two sections by plain buffer walls (facing north and south), which are on an axis with the outer sides of the *rathas* flanking the main entrance, and which, indeed, are the outer walls of a narrow corridor leading from the interior of the *maṇḍapa* to that of the inner shrine. These outer corridor walls divide the east wall into two parts, which are articulated in precisely the same way as the walls flanking the western entrance. A *ratha* with double base mouldings, a niche framed by scroll panels and a flat miniature *śikhara* decorated with *gavākṣa* motifs abutts each buffer wall. To its side is an identical shrine-shaped *ratha* flanked by *nāga*-pilasters. At the wall's end is a *karṇa* bearing a high relief female figure. The warrior mounted on the leogryph is female on the south buffer wall, male on the north wall (see figs. 71 and 83).

MAṆḌAPA SCULPTURES

WEST SIDE

(Fig. 56). Entrance, left pilaster, female figure. The figure stands in *tribhaṅga* (or *contrapposto*) stance, the left hip being slightly exaggerated. The relaxed left arm and the right arm raised behind the head are mostly broken off. The upper torso, face, and top of the head are smashed. The figure wears ear-rings, necklace, jewelled girdle, and scarves trail from her arms.

(Fig. 57). Entrance projection, north side, male figure. Wearing a jewelled girdle, the figure stands in equipoise. The left arm hangs freely, the right is raised toward the chest, the broken hand once possibly held a flower or made a particular gesture. The top portion of the slightly tilted head is broken off. To the left of the figure is a *vyāla* mounted by a warrior. The animal consists of a lion head and a horse body with clawed feet. The *vyāla* emits strands of pearls from its mouth and is about to pounce on a miniature elephant. The image is largely intact, but for the top of the warrior's head.

(Figs. 58, 59). West wall (left of entrance), *nāga*-pilasters and *karṇa* figure. The *nāga* figures (left female, right male) hold a jewel-offering and a garland respectively. Their faces and serpent hoods are mutilated. The *karṇa* figure is a *śālabhañjikā* (girl at a tree). She holds an intricate pose; the legs are in profile, with the right foot raised upon a low mound-like object. The left arm, originally held above the head and clutching the tree's top branches, is broken off, as is the right forearm. The face, however, is largely intact, rare for the Mukteśvara's sculptptures, although the nose is broken off.

(Fig. 60). Entrance, right pilaster, *śālabhañjikā*. The figure stands in a kind of scissor-step, with her left hand raised at an angle toward the branches above her. Both arms are slightly damaged, as is the entire top of the head. The figure's ornaments are sparse, she wears scarves around her waist rather than a jewelled girdle. Two monkeys are at play in the branches at upper left side of the composition.

(Fig. 61). Entrance projection, south side, *śālabhañjikā and vyāla*. The *śālabhañjikā* stands in slight *contrapposto* with arms raised in a circular composition toward the branches above her. The feet and lower legs are broken away, as is most of the left side of her torso. The nose and mouth are damaged, and the overall detailing is not as fine as in most other figures on the temple. The *vyāla* rearing above an elephant is similar to that on the opposite position, however, the beast here is mounted by a female warrior.

(Fig. 62). West wall (right of entrance), *nāga*-pilasters and *karṇa* figure. The well preserved *nāga* figure holds an open garland. The *nāginī* figure is damaged at the face and the hands are missing. The female figure is also highly damaged; both arms are broken, the face is almost completely obliterated. The lower torso is largely intact.

NORTH WALL (WEST TO EAST)

(Fig. 63). *Karṇa* figure (*śālabhañjikā*) and *nāga*-pilaster. In a simple composition the female figure reaches only to chin level towards the branches curving round her head. Standing in subtle *contrapposto*, her right hip is slightly exaggerated. Although there is damage to the face, the sweetness of the expression survives. The *nāga* holds an open garland. The face has been slightly damaged, but the typically sweet smile remains.

(Fig. 64). *Nāga*-pilasters. The male figure (left) holds an open garland. The female figure holds a fly whisk. The faces of both figures are damaged.

(Fig. 65). Right side of projecting lattice window, *vyāla* and *karṇa* figure. The warrior on the leogryph is worn and damaged. The leogryph again rears above a crouching elephant. The female figure stands in equipoise with an exaggerated left hip. The face, hands and one breast are broken away. The figure as a whole is quite worn.

(Fig. 66). Lattice window, right pilaster, *śālabhañjikā*. The figure, in simple equipoise, is badly eroded. She does not clasp the tree but originally held something in her hands, possibly a baby.

(Fig. 67). Female figures above lattice window. These figures (ladies at the doorway) alternate with three unfinished shrine motifs. The right side figure stands within a beaded frame. The door is on the left side of the composition. The whole composition is obscured by whitewash. The left side figure is also disfigured with paint. The door is to the right of the composition. The enclosing frame is unfinished.

(Fig. 68). Lattice window, left pilaster, *śālabhañjikā*. Almost all detail has been worn away. The figure stands with legs crossed, reaching toward the tree branches with her left hand.

(Fig. 69). Left side of projecting lattice window, *karṇa* figure and *vyāla*. The *karṇa śālabhañjikā* is broken away at the face, upraised hands, and left leg. The figure was originally posed with the left leg raised and bent; the left foot placed alongside the right knee still survives. The *vyāla* group shows a male warrior and leogryph rearing above an elephant. The warrior's left arm and face are broken away.

(Fig. 70). *Nāga*-pilasters. Both figures are badly eroded. The right figure is a *nāga*, the left, a *nāginī*.

(Fig. 71). *Karṇa* figure (music playing *śālabhañjikā*) and *nāga*-pilaster. The female figure leans against a tree bracing herself with her left foot. She holds a long-necked *vīṇā*. To the left sits a dwarf figure. The figure is damaged only at the head, which is broken off above the eyebrows. The *nāga* figure is well-preserved but for some breakage around the left side of the face and shoulder. He holds an open garland. The typical surface treatment of faces on the Mukteśvara can be seen well here. The carving is sharp and crisp.

EAST WALL NORTH (SIDE)

(Figs. 72, 73). *Karṇa* figure (*śālabhañjikā) and nāga*-pilasters. The *śālabhañjikā* is heavily damaged and worn. Chisel marks show it to be unfinished. Between the *karṇa* and the *ratha* niche is a *nāginī*, well-preserved, wearing the usual jewellery and carrying a mace and a lotus. A *nāga* figure is to the left of the niche (fig. 73). Holding a jar and lotus, the nose is broken, but otherwise the figure is well-preserved.

NORTTH BUFFER WALL

(Fig. 74). *Vyāla*. The form of the *vyāla* here differs from the examples previously discussed. The leogryph mounted by a male warrior, here has an elephant's trunk. It pounces not on an elephant but on a demonic dwarf.

SOUTH WALL (WEST TO EAST)

(Fig. 75). *Karṇa* figure (*śālabhañjikā*) and *nāga*-pilaster. The female figure, reaching upwards with her right hand, is broken at the face, hands, arms, and right leg. The *nāga*, slightly damaged at the face, holds a lotus in his right hand.

(Fig. 76). *Nāga*-pilasters. To the left, a *nāginī* is holding a lotus. The figure is broken only at the face. The *nāga* figure to the right is more heavily damaged (face, hands). He holds his hands in *añjali*, the prayer-like gesture of greeting.

(Fig. 77). Left side of projecting lattice window, *vyāla* and *karṇa* figure. The lion-headed composite animal is mounted by a male warrior and rears over a crouching elephant. The *karṇa* figure (male), wearing a girdle, arm bands, and necklace, has its head and lower arms missing.

(Fig. 78). Lattice window, left pilaster, female figure. The figure stands in slight *contrapposto* with left hip exaggerated. The figure is badly damaged, the breasts, face, and most of the left arm are broken off.

(Fig. 79). Female figures above lattice window. The composition of women standing at a door here echoes that above the north window. These figures are also marred by whitewash, but are otherwise intact.

(Fig. 80). Lattice window, right pilaster, male figure. The figure stands in slight *contrapposto*, the weight on his left leg. The head and lower arms are missing.

(Fig. 81). Right side of projecting lattice window, female figure and *vyāla*. Only the upper torso and feet of the female figure survive. The leogryph bears a female warrior, the face of which is eroded, and rears above an elephant.

(Fig. 82). *Nāga*-pilasters. The *nāga* (left) holds an open garland and is well-preserved but for gouge marks on the torso. The *nāginī* (right) holds a conch and a lotus. Breasts and face are moderately damaged.

(Fig. 83). *Karṇa* figure and *nāga*-pilaster. The *nāga* is badly damaged. The head and torso are completely effaced. The *karṇa's* female figure is also damaged; face, breasts, and left arm are obliterated. She stands in slight *contrapposto* with the left hip exaggerated. To her left stands a child, his height reaching up to her hips. The head of this figure is broken off.

EAST WALL (SOUTH SIDE)

(Figs. 84, 85). *Karṇa* figure and *nāga*-pilasters. The *karṇa* figure stands on one foot, her bent right leg supporting a baby. With her right hand she makes some gesture at the child. Her face is destroyed, most of her right leg is broken away. Only the lower torso of the infant survives. The *nāginī* holds a jar with her left hand, the right one is broken off. The face is badly damaged. The *nāga* holds an open garland. The lower part of the face is broken away.

SOUTH BUFFER WALL

(Fig. 86). *Vyāla*. This image corresponds to its counterpart on the north buffer wall, with its elephantine leogryph and crouching demon below. The whole composition is very well-preserved. The warrior here is female.

INTERIOR OF THE MAṆḌAPA

CEILING

The ceiling of the Mukteśvara's *maṇḍapa* (figs. 6, 87)[16] consists of an elaborate system of five progressively receding stone courses. The first (that is, the central, innermost one), is square, the next three octagonal, and the fifth (the outermost) is rectangular. They are elaborately carved with various decorative motifs and narrative relief scenes within the triangular and trapezoidal panels formed at their corners. At the center of the ceiling, within the innermost course, is a fairly deep "dome", having the shape of an eight-petaled lotus. These lotus petals are actually cusped niches within which are placed images of the Sapta Mātṛkās (Seven Mother Goddesses), and their attendant, Vīrabhadra. These images seem to emanate from the absolute center of the ceiling, a multi-petaled lotus medallion. Surrounding this whole central composition are six relief panels. Those within the second course depict the gods Kārttikeya and Gaṇeśa.

Within the third course are two scenes of musicians and dancers, and two narrative panels depicting women in meditation. Beneath these panels are attached very high relief images of garland-bearing *nāga* couples, which have the illusion of being supporting elements. The fourth stone course has at its four corners nearly identical triangular relief panels, each representing a solitary woman seated in meditative posture. The fifth and lowest stone course is rectangular, and bears images of *kīrtti mukhas* at the corners. These corner reliefs take the form of triangular braces and are placed at the juncture between the wall and ceiling proper. The ceiling is bordered with a wide panel decorated with large, flat lotus petals. Attached to them, at the center of the north and south walls, are high relief flying *gandharva* couples.

At the very center of the lotus-shaped "dome" is a circular disk, circumscribed by three rings, each consisting of sixteen lotus petals. The disk is incised with a crescent moon, one of the most prominent symbols of Śiva. The eight lotus-form cusped niches surrounding this central medallion each contain an image of a Mātṛkā or Vīrabhadra. All the figures sit cross-legged with one leg hanging down *(lalitāsana)* upon elaborate lotus pedestals, and behind them, carved in flat relief, are upside-down lotuses on stalks, which appear to grow out from the central lotus. All the Mother images (except the horrific Cāmuṇḍā) hold a baby within the crook of the left arm.

Discussing the images in the order in which they are usually found on horizontal relief slabs, we begin with that of Vīrabhadra (southwest), and move counter-clockwise.

Vīrabhadra here is four-armed (as are all the deities in this circular composition). His upper right hand holds a flower, while with his upper right hand he plays a *vīṇā*. At his feet is the bull Nandin, marking Vīrabhadra as an aspect of Śiva. Six of the Seven Mothers are conceived as the female energies (*śaktis*) of major male deities, as is indicated by their names; Brahmāṇī has at the foot of her pedestal two facing swans, the vehicle of her counterpart, Brahmā. Her two upper hands hold indistinct object. Śiva's counterpart, Maheśvarī, like Vīrabhadra, has a bull at her feet. Her upper hands hold a *mālā* (rosary) and possibly a *ḍamarū* (hourglass-shaped drum). Kaumārī, Skanda's counterpart, has that god's animal vehicle, the peacock at her feet. Her upper right hand holds a weapon. Vaiṣṇavī holds a conch and a discus. She wears the tall conical crown characteristic of Viṣṇu. Vārāhī has the head of a boar and is pot-bellied. At her feet is a cow, an allusion to her counterpart Varāha's rescue of the Earth Goddess from the subterranean regions. She holds two indistinct object in her upper hands. Indrāṇī (Indra's counterpart) has an elephant at her feet. She holds a mace in her upper left hand and a *vajra* (thunderbolt) in her right. Cāmuṇḍā is the only Mother not conceived as the counterpart of a male deity, and the only one not depicted with a child. She is a skeletal figure, and her emaciated left leg reaches down toward the figure of a corpse placed below her lotus-seat. Her upper left hand carries a spear-like weapon.

The trapezoidal relief panel to the west of the central composition depicts Gaṇeśa, the elephant-headed son of Śiva and Pārvatī, who with Vīrabhadra, usually figures as an attendant of the Seven Mothers. The six-armed figure holds a cobra above his head with his two upper hands, and with his others holds an axe, *mālā*, and his broken tusk (the lowest left hand is broken off). He dances, imitating the dance of Śiva (which is depicted on the outside of the temple, on the four sides of the *śikhara*), upon a low lotus platform. Flanking Gaṇeśa on the lower side of the trapezoid are two musician figures, playing drums and cymbals, while at the feet of the drummer is a rat, the god's animal vehicle (*vāhana*). Above the musicians are two larger *gaṇas* who stand upon open lotuses, the stalks of which grow from behind the musicians.

On the opposite (eastern) side of the ceiling is a depiction of Kārttikeya, Śiva's other son, and the general of the army of the gods. The youthful, two-armed figure sits on a low lotus pedestal, holding a long spear in his left hand. To his right is placed a peacock, his usual *vāhana*, and to his left, a rooster, another animal often associated with him. The upper levels of the composition contain three celestial figures (one to the god's right, two to his left), holding weapons and lotuses.[17]

Two long narrow relief panels flank both the Gaṇeśa and Kārttikeya reliefs. To the left of the Gaṇeśa panel is a scene of a woman in meditation. She sits cross-legged, with her hands in her lap (*dhyānamudrā*), and is flanked by four attending maid-servants, who offer gifts of food. Stylistically and iconographically, all five figures are of the same type as those on the outer walls of the temple, that is, they are voluptuously proportioned figures beautifully adorned with bracelets, anklets, necklaces, and jewelled girdles. The central figure, however, is slightly larger than her attendants, denoting a special rank. This relief (as well as a similar one flanking the Kārttikeya relief) will be discussed further in the next chapter as a depiction of the Penance of Pārvatī.

The panel to the right of Gaṇeśa depicts a group of female musicians, all seated on the ground. Two are playing long Indian drums, while another plays a flute. Two smaller figures are placed in the upper corners, to the left a female figure holding an offering, and to the right another figure playing a drum. To the left of the Kārttikeya relief is a meditation scene similar to the one just mentioned. Again flanked by female attendants, here the central female figure holds her hands together with palms facing outward. The hands are badly damaged, as are the face and the faces of the attendant figures to the left.

The panel to the right of Kārttikeya depicts a female dancer in the center, surrounded by four musicians. In her foot positions and gestures the central dancer seems to be imitating, like Gaṇeśa, the dance of Śiva. The four triangular reliefs below the trapezoidal ones show essentially the same scene; a woman seated in meditative posture upon a lotus pedestal, flanked by rearing leogryphs. There is slight variation in the poses, two of the figures sit in the *siddhāsana* (adept's pose), while the two others sit in a more relaxed posture, similar to the posture referred to as *mahārājalīlā*.[18] The supporting leogryph below the southwest panel is missing, and below the lotus pedestal the indentation within which the leogryph was originally attached is visible (see fig. 5).

ENTRANCE TO THE GARBHAGṚHA

The entrance to the *garbhagṛha* (figs. 89-91) is as elaborately decorated as that of the *maṇḍapa*. Entry to the sanctum is gained by a low, undecorated semi-circular stepping stone, which is flanked by two high relief figures of crouching lions. The recessed doorway is bordered by three decorative bands, very similar to those on the outside. The outer band consists of the "acanthus leaf", with the lintel band displaying a variation, with deeply incised swirling lines around two node-like bumps. The middle band contains a pattern of delicately carved scroll work.

The bases of the doorframe are flanked by two *dvārapālas* with female attendants. The male figures are four-armed and hold the trident and other indistinct objects. They are enclosed within a rectangle bordered with bead work. The *cauri*-bearing female figures are on the outer edges of the doorframe. They are smaller than the males, and are contained within beaded framed of their own.

The lintel (fig. 91) bears a large plaque representing Gaja-Lakṣmī. The goddess sits on an elaborate lotus pedestal. She is flanked by two small female *chauri*-bearers, and above them are two elephants on lotus bases, offering their lustrations to the goddess. The space above this recessed lintel contains a relief frieze of the *Navagrahas* (the "nine graspers", the planets). The figures are housed within shallow niches flanked by pilasters growing out of pots, and surmounted by niches flanked by very simple two-leveled miniature *śikharas*, capped with *āmalakas*. The figures are all seated cross-legged upon lotus seats. They are undistinguished iconographically, but for Sūrya, the Sun (far left), who typically holds two lotuses, and Rāhu and Ketu, the ascending and descending nodes of the moon (far right), the former represented by a grotesque head, the latter only from the upper torso, and who holds his hands in a respectful *añjali* pose.

PRĀSĀDA

The *prāsāda*, the shrine proper of the temple (fig. 92), is square is plan, and surmounted by tall curvilinear *śikhara*. Each will except the mainly hidden west wall, (connected to the *maṇḍapa* by a buffer wall), is articulated in exactly the same manner, while the imagery placed around the temple on the lower *rathas*, the *kaṇṭha* (the recessed horizontal band between the upper portion of the wall and the *śikhara*), and the heraldic *candraśālā* panels, varies from side to side. For this reason, the basic architectural elements of the *prāsāda* will be discussed first, with the individual figures and reliefs being described under separate sections.

LOWER WALLS (NORTH, SOUTH AND EAST)

In describing the wall surfaces of the Mukteśvara's *prāsāda* the south side can be taken as representative (see figs. 5 and 8). The height of the lower walls is ten feet, one and one-quarter inches. The entire wall surface, as well as the entire surface of the *śikhara* is divided into three basic parts, a central outward projecting "buttress" (*bhadra*), flanked by symmetrically formed and articulated side walls. These side walls, divided into three "pilasters", or *rathas*, recede back from the central *bhadra*, creating in plan a kind of truncated Greek cross.

BHADRA

The *bhadra* (fig. 93) consists of a central niche with two pilasters on either side, and above and below, elaborate canopy and base elements, multi-course mouldings taking the shape of miniature shrines. The base is made up of seven courses. At the lowest level is placed a "triptych" depicting a female figure flanked by *vyālas*. Above this are the remaining centrally projecting courses which form a miniature *śikhara* (compare with the shrine motifs on the bases of the *toraṇa*, fig. 42). The canopy consists of six similarly formed mouldings, and is capped with a small *āmalaka* stone. The canopy serves, then, as a miniature *śikhara*, signifying the niche as a miniature shrine, housing the now missing image.

The outermost niche pilasters are of the same basic format as the *karṇas* of the *maṇḍapa*. The *prāsāda's* pilasters, however, are longer and narrower. They also differ in their base mouldings, having five, rather than four stone courses. The middle portion of each flanking pilaster bears a female figure before a background of scroll work, with a *kīrtti mukha* emitting pearls above. The upper portion of the outer *ratha* consists of three *khura*-shaped mouldings with projecting centers, capped by a similarly articulated stone incised with upward pointing lotus petals. Above this is a square moulding facing the upper level of the wall. It is capped by a rounded *kalaśa* (water pot), which faces the level of the *kaṇṭha*.

The outer *ratha* serves as a *karṇa*, since the whole central *bhadra* projects considerably from the wall surface. The side portion is identical to the front. A recessed side wall extends behind it, connecting the projecting *bhadra* with the temple wall. It is plain, but like all connecting walls on the temple, is decorated with a *vyāla* figure.

The inner *rathas* have similar base mouldings and female figures on the mid-sections, these always being depictions of the river goddesses Gaṅgā on the left, and Yamunā on the right, identified respectively by the *makara* and tortoise upon which they stand. Replacing the mouldings on the upper levels are female figures of the *śālabhañjikā* type (girl bending the branches of a tree). Serving as an elaborate lintel over these figures and the top of the central niche canopy is a stone course with an outwardly projecting center, decorated with scroll work.

Symmetrically flanking the central *bhadra* is a series of three *rathas*, designated (moving from the innermost one), as *partibhadra, pratikarṇa* (*nāga*-pilaster), and *karṇa*. Their articulation is similar to the corresponding members of the *maṇḍapa,* but with certain differences. As mentioned above, the *rathas* of the *prāsāda* are longer and narrower, giving the wall surface a more attenuated appearance when compared to the relative blockiness of the forehall. They also emphasize how the wall rises slightly above that of the *maṇḍapa*, carrying reference, on this lower level, to the difference in height between the *śikhara* and the forehall's terraced roof.

PRATIBHADRA

The *pratibhadras* stand upon double five-part base mouldings supporting two small pilasters, which flank a small niche (see fig. 5). The niche's canopy element, much more elaborate than those on the *maṇḍapa*, consists of three carved mouldings flush with the flanking pilasters. These, however, are surmounted by two outwardly projecting mouldings, the top one consisting of a miniature *gavākṣa* housing benign or grotesque faces. A narrow cornice-like moulding incised with lotus petals caps this middle section of the *ratha*. Above it rises a panel resembling a *śikhara,* faced with a net-like pattern of *gavākṣa* windows (fig. 95). This *gavākṣa* pattern, while of the same general composition as those on the forehall, differs in the complexity of its carving (cf. fig. 50). Instead of the two flat ribbon-like lines defining the shape of the *gavākṣa*, each row of arched windows is carved in relief. Only the central arch, however, forms a complete *gavākṣa* shape. These central arches consist of five inwardly receding ridges, the outer two being pointed, while the inner ones are round, creating a miniature whirlpool effect. Above and below it are simple double bow-like designs. Two more arched motifs flank each side of the central one. These consist of two "half-arches", joined together at different levels and bisected with a vertical line extending the entire length of the panel. This simple variation of the basic form, repeated vertically up the length of the panel, creates a pattern much different from the rather stable, static one of the forehall's *gavākṣa* panels. Here, the off-balance half-arches create a kind of undulating knot pattern, which together with the deeper shadows created by the receding relief pattern, and the sheer-amplification of linear activity, give a greater sense of visual energy to the surface.

Above this miniature *śikhara*, reaching up to the lower edge of the *kaṇṭha* is a *khura*-shaped moulding. Its bottom ridge is decorated with small relief figures, usually of ascetics in meditation or worshipping in *liṅga*. They will be dealt with in more detail below.

PRATIKARṆA

The *pratikarṇas*, or *nāga*-pilasters are much narrower than the other *rathas*. Their articulation is almost identical to the same elements on the *maṇḍapa*, but again, with differences in line with the overall attenuated nature of the vertical elements of the *prāsāda*. The base mouldings consist of six (rather than five) parts; *khura, kuṃbha,* vertical relief of a female figure, and three narrow incised mouldings, the top one decorated with a miniature *candraśālā*. Above this are two crouching elephants surmounted by lions, which are below the *nāga* image itself, encircling a round shaft, with its tail pointing upward. This portion of the *nāga* rises slightly higher here than on the *maṇḍapa*, and its topmost portion is not decorated with a *kīrtti mukha*. Instead, there is placed here a set of carvings, which project slightly over the surface of the *ratha*. This set, consisting of three separate images, is repeated vertically above the horizontal *kaṇṭha* along the entire length of the corresponding *pratikarṇa* of the *śikhara* (fig. 96). The lowest image is that of a girl at a door. The pose is standardized among all the repeated images; the girl leans against the door with her legs crossed, her weight on one foot. A parrot is sometimes perched on top of the door. A narrow moulding with scroll work separates the girl from a figure of a meditating ascetic-*yogin*, seated cross-legged within a *gavākṣa*. These figures also have little variation; the hands are either folded on the lap, or raised in a slightly more complex *mudrā*. Above the ascetic is another *gavākṣa*, housing a small male head, frontally placed, which gazes steadily from the window space.

KARṆA

The *karṇas* are articulated identically to those on the *maṇḍapa*, but again, are longer, narrower, and have an additional capping element. They begin with a four-part base moulding, the upper two courses of which are spanned by a vertical relief of either a female figure or a standing ascetic. The middle part bears a flat panel of scroll work, at the top of which is a *kīrtti mukha* emitting pearls, and is faced with a female figure in high relief. Above this are two carved courses, connected by a vertical leaf. They are topped by a square panel housing a squat atlantid dwarf. The *ratha's* top sections consist of *khura*-mouldings similar to those on the *pratibhadra*, and also bear relief carvings of ascetics.

WEST WALL

The west wall of the *prāsāda* consists of two symmetrical sections, made up of *karṇa*, *nāga*-pilaster, and about one and three quarters of a *pratibhadra* which runs into the buffer wall. These three-part sections flank and are divided by the north and south buffer walls that connect the *prāsāda* to the *maṇḍapa*. The west wall, then, has no *bhadra* element. However, the *rathas* flanking the buffer walls are identical in form and decoration to those on the north, south and east walls.

PRĀSĀDA, LOWER WALL SCULPTURES

West wall (north side)—(fig. 97). *Karṇa* figure (*śālabhañjikā*) and *nāga*-pilaster. The music playing *śālabhañjikā* is finely detailed but badly mutilated, most of the head is smashed away and only the elaborate chignon remains. She holds a flute in side playing position and the tree flows sinuously around her head. The *nāginī* figure, barely visible to normal view and difficult to photograph, is damaged around the face and fairly eroded.

North wall (right to left)—(fig. 98). *Karṇa* figure (*śālabhañjikā*) and *nāga*-pilaster. The *śālabhañjikā* is badly damaged; the head is completely gone, as are most of the arms and the right leg. The right leg was originally bent and lifted, probably in the conventional pose of removing a foot-thorn or painting the foot with *lak*. Below the raised leg is a pot-bellied dwarf figure (the head is broken off). The *nāga's* face and right arm are broken away. He originally held an open garland.

(Fig. 99). *Bhadra,* right side, *śālabhañjikā* and *vyāla*. The head, hands, and left forearm of the female figure are missing. Her arms are not raised as high as usual, and from their outline, it is possible that she originally held a bird, a conventional pose seen on other temples. A mutilated dwarf figure sits to the right of the composition. The *vyāla* is conventional, a male warrior on a leogryph, rearing above an elephant.

(Fig. 100). *Bhadra* niche, right side, *śālabhañjikā* (right) and Yamunā (left). The *śālabhañjikā* is eroded and damaged; the lower left leg, left arm, and face are all broken. Her left hand reaches toward the tree curving round her head, her right fondles the head of a child standing to the side (this figure is badly mutilated). The river goddess stands to the side of the now empty *bhadra* niche. She stands upon a tortoise, her animal vehicle (*vāhana*). Standing in an easy *contrapposto*, her left hand rests on her thigh. Her right hand, face and parasol above her head have all been smashed.

(Fig. 101). *Bhadra* niche, left side, Gaṅgā (left) and *śālabhañjikā* (right). The river goddess Gaṅgā flanks this side of the empty niche. She stands upon a *makara,* a stylized composite (porpoise-crocodile) animal. A parasol is placed above her head and a dwarf stands to her right. The face and left arm are badly damaged, and the whole composition is eroded. The *śālabhañjikā* stands in an unusual pose, frontally, with both arms reaching towards the branches above. The lower half of the face is broken away.

(Fig. 102). *Bhadra,* female musicians flanking niche canopy. The figure to the left stands with the right knee bent and plays a long *vīṇā*. Behind her to the left the branches of a tree spread out, though the tree trunk visible on the right is worn away. Detail of carving here is fairly eroded. The figure to the right stands in a similar pose, with the left knee bent, thus creating a symmetrical composition with het counterpart. The bottom half of her *vīṇā* is broken off. She is flanked by dwarf figures, the one the left has been broken away. Again, the details have suffered erosion.

(Fig. 103). *Bhadra,* left side, female figure and *vyāla.* Although the top of the head and the face of the female figure are broken away, the figure as a whole retains much robustness of form and clarity of detail. The torso is shown frontally while the legs are in profile, with the right one corssed over in front. She is framed by a tree; the trunk stands to the right of the composition, reaching over her head. A fantastic lotus grows from the tree trunk and curves across the composition, ending near the upper left, where it is held in the girl's right hand. As one of the Mukteśvara's better preserved examples, this figure shows a complex rhythmical composition in the interplay of crossed leg, curving hips, bending tree, and undulating flower stalks. These decorative linear plays complement perfectly the solid earthy presence of the figure. The *vyāla,* with male warrior, is of the standard type.

(Fig. 104). *Nāginī*-pilaster and *karṇa* figure (*śālabhañjikā*). The *nāginī* is well-preserved, but for damage to the face and the objects held in the hands. The female figure is badly damaged; the face, hands, and dwarf attendants at the sides have been smashed.

East wall (right to left)—(fig. 105). *Karṇa* figure (*śālabhañjikā*) and *nāga*-pilaster. The female figure is seen in multiple perspective; the crossed legs are in right profile, the torso is frontal and the head is in left three-quarter profile. The face and lower limbs are broken off. A small *gaṇa* stands to the left of the composition. The slightly curving tree trunk, creating an arch over the girl's head, echoes the linear rhythms of her body. The *nāga* figure is playing a long-necked musical instrument. The face has been completely broken away.

(Fig. 106). *Bhadra,* right side, *vyāla* and male figure. The *vyāla* is of the standard type. The male figure holds a sword and is flanked by two *gaṇas.* The face is broken off, as is the left hand.

(Fig. 107). *Bhadra, śālabhañjikās* flanking niche canopy. The two female figures again create a symmetrical composition. The trees form a kind of frame, with the branches curving over the heads of the figures. Damage is slight, confined mainly to the faces and hands.

(Fig. 108). *Bhadra* niche, right side, *śālabhañjikā* (right) and Yamunā (left). The head is broken away and the right arm and the child figure are broken and eroded. To the left, adjacent to the empty niche is Yamunā, standing on a highly eroded tortoise. The face and right arm badly damaged. The left hand rests at a slight curve on the left thigh.

(Fig. 109). *Bhadra* niche, left side, Gaṅgā (right) and *śālabhañjikā* (left). Gaṅgā is accompanied by a dwarf, who holds the stem of the parasol (mostly broken off) above her head. The upper torso is well-preserved, while the head and left arm are almost completely broken away. The right thigh is also smashed. The *śālabhañjikā* embraces a tree with her left arm, the branches of which move in a rounded curve over her head. She stands in a "scissor-step" pose, which creates a flowing "S" curve along her entire figure. The face and right arm are mostly broken away.

(Fig. 110). *Bhadra,* left side, *śālabhañjikā* and *vyāla.* This *śālabhañjikā* is well-preserved, except for the face, which is entirely smashed away, as is most of the dwarf figure to the left. Compositionally it exhibits again a pleasing interplay of linear rhythms. The tree, framing the right side of the composition, grows from a pot at its base. Its curve echoes that of the breasts, waist and hips of the figure. Particularly pleasing is the way in which the uplifted left arm winds under and around the upper part of the bending tree. The *vyāla* is of the standard type; male figure, leogryph and elephant.

(Fig. 111). *Nāginī*-pilaster and *karṇa* figure (*śālabhañjikā*). The *nāginī* holds a long stemmed lotus. The details of her jewellery are well-preserved, but the right side of her face is smashed. The whole upper portion of the *śālabhañjikā* is badly damaged. The tree is elaborately rendered, large leaves growing from the outer side of the trunk. Her body is positioned with various twists and turns, giving simultaneous front and back views.

South wall (*right to left*)—(Fig. 112). *Karṇa* figure (*śālabhañjikā*) and *nāga*-pilaster. The female figure stands legs crossed, the forward (left) leg is turned to the side, while the right with leg behind is rendered frontally, creating a dance-like pose. The upper torso is shown frontally. The bending tree and scarves complement the linear outlines of the figure. The breasts and face are broken off. The *nāga* figure holds an open garland. Here too, the face is broken off.

(Fig. 113). *Bhadra,* right side, *vyāla* and male figure. The *vyāla* is of the standard type. The male figure, clad in a simple girdle and armlets, is ample and fleshy in its rendering. The face has been broken away.

(Fig. 114). *Bhadra* niche, right side, *śālabhañjikā* (right) and Yamunā (left). The *śālabhañjikā's* tree has been entirely broken away, along with the face and the left hand. The Yamunā figure too is badly damaged; the parasol and face are smashed away. The goddess stands on a tortoise and is flanked by two diminutive figures, a female to the left, male to the right.

(Fig. 115). *Bhadra* niche, left side, Gaṅgā (right) and *śālabhañjikā* (left). The Gaṅgā figure, standing upon a *makara* and flanked by two diminutive figures is broken at the face and the left forearm. The parasol is also broken. The *śālabhañjikā* stands to the left of a tree almost creeper-like in its undulating trunk. She stands in slight *contrapposto* with the weight on her left foot. The face and right forearm are broken away.

(Fig. 116). *Bhadra, śālabhañjikās* flanking niche canopy. As on the other central niches of the *prāsāda*, these figures are symmetrically balanced. In their cross-legged *tribhaṅga* pose, one hand on the hip, the other reaching above toward the tree branches, a composition of curving and undulating lines is created. The figures are well-preserved, though the face of the figure on the right is somewhat worn.

(Fig. 117). *Bhadra,* left side, *śālabhañjikā* and *vyāla.* The *śālabhañjikā*, with legs in profile and frontal torso, lifts her right (front) leg slightly, reacting to the dwarf figure on the left, who tugs on her jewelled girdle strings. As is standard, she reaches toward the tree branches with one hand. The face has been smashed and the dwarf figure is damaged from the chest up. The *vyāla* is of the standard type.

(Fig. 118). *Nāginī*-pilaster and *karṇa* figure. The *nāginī* holds a lotus in the right hand and a jar (now broken) in the left. The face has been broken off. The female figure stands in a three-quarter profile, she is richly ornamented and well-preserved but for the broken face. She holds an unusual object in her right hand. It resembles a paddle or a pan, and a round ball rests upon it. What it represents is not known.

(*West wall*) (*south side*)—(fig. 119). *Karṇa* figure (*śālabhañjikā*) and *nāga*-pilaster. This female figure, placed in a position on the temple very difficult to photograph, lifts her right foot to her hand. She represents the standard poetic female type (*nāyikā*) of the girl removing a thorn from her foot. The *nāga* figure is one of the most beautiful and best preserved on the temple. He holds a fly whisk or lotus (broken) in his left hand and in his right the thick stalk of a creeper. The figure is full and robust, and his jewel ornaments (necklace, sacred thread), as they flow along the form, emphasize its volume.

KAṆṬHA

The *kaṇṭha*, the recessed band dividing the lower wall from the *śikhara* consists of a series of small relief panels encircling the mid-section of the *prāsāda* (see fig. 92). The reliefs above the central *bhadra* are placed to the side of the vertical axes formed by the plasters below. At the very center, directly above the niche canopy, but only about half as wide, is a *śālabhañjikā* figure. She is immediately flanked by *gaṇa* atlantids contained within small square panels placed upon small double *kapotāli* bases. Flanking these figures are very plain vertical recesses, which may have served as niches for now missing figures. Two more atlantid dwarf panels follow, their edges coming just to the mid-points of the *bhadra's* corner pilasters. Surmounting the top mouldings of these pilasters, and framing the reliefs of this central portion of the *kaṇṭha* are two *amṛta kalaśas.* The *kaṇṭhas* along both side portions of the *bhadra* bear an image of a crouching leogryph.

The reliefs above the walls flanking the *bhadra* are all vertically aligned to, and form compositional units with the figures carved upon the *khura* mouldings which cap the *rathas* below. Above the *karṇas* and *pratibhadras* are various scenes depicting ascetics in worship, ritual dance, and other scenes. Above the *nāga-*

pilasters are figures of two elephants facing each other with trunks intertwined. The *kaṇṭha* reliefs above the *karṇas* and *pratibhadras* along with the reliefs on the *khura* mouldings directly below them, will be described as follows, moving around the temple clockwise from the north:

North wall, right of center (fig. 121)—Karṇa, kaṇṭha. Liṅga worship. A male figure in a combined squatting and kneeling position holds an offering (flowers or food) above a *liṅga-pīṭha*. In the upper left corner is a flying *vidyādhara* figure. In the upper right corner is a kind of a lotus disk, in its corner placement only one quarter of it being visible.

Karṇa, khura. Here is a corpulent male figure, seated in a kneeling position, looking at himself in a mirror.

Pratibhadra, kaṇṭha. Guru with disciples. The teacher, his legs secured with a *yogabandha*, is flanked by two disciples. The left figure is reading from a book. The figure on the right is slightly damaged and his gestures are not clear.

Pratibhadra, khura. A guru (left) sits facing a single disciple. The teacher seems to read from a manuscript. Both figures are emaciated, with piled up matted hair, the guru figure is bearded. A small cross-legged table is placed between the figures.

North wall, left of center (fig. 122)—Pratibhadra, kaṇṭha. Guru and disciple. A large cross-legged tale is placed between the two figures. The guru (right) reads from a book and is seated with *yogabandha*. The attitude of the disciple suggests attentive listening. *Pratibhadra, khura.* The image here is broken off.

Karṇa, Kaṇṭha. Liṅga worship. Two figures flank a *liṅga-pīṭha,* the figure on the left is partly broken away.

Karṇa, khura. Female dancer. The dancer holds a pose similar to that of the Naṭeśa figures on the *śikhara* above; the right leg is lifted and bent, the right arm crosses in front of the body (*hasta-mudrā*).

East wall, right of center (fig. 123)—Karṇa, kaṇṭha. Liṅga worship. A single figure stands to the left of a *liṅga* in a high *pīṭha.* He holds a lotus, which he is perhaps placing as an offering. A lotus disk is placed in the upper right side of the panel, half visible because of its corner placement.

Karṇa, khura. Family scene. A man lifting a farming implement(?) onto his shoulder faces a woman holding a baby. Another child stands to the left, and a small, pot-bellied dwarf-like figure sits to the right.

Pratibhadra, kaṇṭha. Three figures, two standing, one squatting, worship, not at a *liṅga,* but at an altar consisting of a low table piled with three-tiered layers resembling folds of cloth. On top of this is placed a long vertical oval shape. It perhaps represents fire, but bears no surface detail to suggest this further. The whole form is rather indistinct.

Pratibhadra, khura. Woman with ascetic. A woman stands, back to front, with an emaciated ascetic. The carving is worn. She appears to be leading him along, pulling either at his loincloth, or his phallus.

East wall, left of center (fig. 124)—Pratibhadra, kaṇṭha. Caravan scene (?). A procession of four men carrying bundles attached to poles.

Pratibhadra, khura. Woman with ascetic. The two figures sit on a low table with a small cross-legged table between them.

Karṇa, kaṇṭha. Liṅga worship. Two standing male figures flank a *liṅga* in a low *pīṭha.* One figure holds two small brass pots, the other is about to place a flower on top of the *liṅga.*

Karṇa, khura. Yogin. The slightly emaciated figure sits on a low table, one leg bent and placed in a vertical position. He appears to be reading a book.

South wall, right of center (fig. 125)—Karṇa, kaṇṭha. Linga worship. Two figures (ascetics?) flank a large *liṅga pīṭha.* The figure on the right is holding a bell, the other figure is perhaps waving a container of incense.

Karṇa, khura. Guru with disciple. The emaciated teacher sits on a low table. He holds an indistinct object in his right hand. The disciple sits before him with hands reverently folded.

Pratibhadra, kaṇṭha. Caravan scene (?). Four male figures in a procession similar to the one in figure 124. The figures, wearing short loincloths, carry poles with bundles across backs.

Pratibhadra, khura. Guru with disciple. The figures flank a low, cross-legged table. The emaciated guru, legs wrapped with a *yogabandha,* holds a rosary, the students lean forward attentively.

South wall, left of center (fig. 126)—Pratibhadra, kaṇṭha. Dance scene. An emaciated ascetic with wild, matted hair dances. In his right hand he perhaps holds a rattle. He is flanked by musicians. To the left a bearded drummer stands also in a dance position. Between them sits a small squatting figure. Another dancing drummer stands to the right.

Pratibhadra, khura. Guru with disciple. The figures flank a low, cross-legged table. The emaciated guru, legs wrapped with a *yogabandha,* holds a rosary or garland. The disciple sits before him, his eyes cast downward.

Karṇa, kaṇṭha. Liṅga. A large *Liṅga pīṭha* is flanked by two ascetics. They seem to be waving streamers or fly whisks above the *liṅga.*

Karṇa, khura. Guru with disciple. This relief is moderately worn down. The two figures face each other, the guru sits on a low table.

ŚIKHARA

Except for the *śukanāsā* of the western *bhadra,* which has been left unfinished, the decoration and articulation of the Mukteśvara's *śikhara* is identical on all four sides. Its seven vertical divisions are aligned with and match in their degree of outward projection those of the walls below. A broad central *bhadra* is flanked by *pratibhadras.* The next horizontal element is the narrow *pratikarṇa,* and finally the *karṇas* themselves. The outline of the tower has a gradual inward curve, which becomes most pronounced at the summit. Here the *śikhara* is terminated by a continuous stone course of a modified cruciform shape, having slight outward projections over the *bhadra* and *pratibhadras.* Above this is a round stone course smaller in circumference than the cruciform course. Capping the entire superstructure is the great *āmalaka,* a flat, circular cushion or myrobalan-shaped stone extending over the course below it and articulated with a continuous pattern of vertical ribs. Its topmost portion is a low dome-like stone layer. At the summit is an *amṛta kalaśa* (jar of the nectar of immortality), which is, however, a modern replacement.[19] Capping this is a *triśūla* (trident, emblem of Śiva), also modern.

Bhadra (figs. 5, 92)—Above the *candraśālā* (the central image of the *śikhara*), the *bhadra* consists of a wide panel carved with a continuous *gavākṣa* net. A row of five individual *gavākṣa* windows, carved in the same relief technique as those on both the lower and upper *pratibhadras* is repeated without variation upon a series of narrow horizontal courses. The effect of the *gavākṣa* pattern on the *bhadra* is somewhat different than that on the flanking *rathas,* in that each windows motif is on the same horizontal level, i.e. the middle ones do not rise above. Also, each motif is whole, in contrast to the "split" motifs of the *pratibhadras* (see fig. 131). Instead of an upward moving, winding pattern, then, we have here more of an overall continuous design of horizontal rows.

The heraldic *candraśālā* dominates the surface of the *bhadra.* It rests upon a series of horizontal courses, the central portions of which project outward. The two lowest courses are of a continuous *khura* shape, with the lower ridges decorated with scroll work. The upper ridges, on the front and sides, bear relief figures of animals or squatting ascetics, similar to the figures on the upper elements of the lower *rathas.* The upper two courses are narrower, one consisting of a band of scroll work, the other having the shape of a lotus pedestal, and decorated with incised upward pointing lotus petals. Three vertical leaves connect this upper course to the lowest portions of the heraldic emblem proper.

The lowest part of the *candraśālā* consists of a narrow relief frieze. The side portions contain animal scenes, while the central projecting portions depict seated male figures surrounded by attendants. These scenes seem to represent not scenes of gurus giving discourse, as is usually thought,[20] but rather royal figures. As they vary in details, the friezes will be discussed separately below.

Directly above the central scene, and also projecting outward is a small *gavākṣa* window, which houses an outward gazing male head (except on the north, which contains a miniature Naṭeśa figure). The upper portion of each *candraśālā* is completely contained within the *bhadra.* Its main compositional element is a very elaborate *gavākṣa* window. At its very center is a roundel containing a cushion-like lotus medallion, superimposed, however, by the projecting *gavākṣa* window containing the face. A round border of bead work surrounds the lotus. Surrounding this are four figures of flying celestials holding thick vine stalks. These figures are surrounded by a more elaborate border consisting of three bands, which come to a point at the top center. This center part, however, remains slightly open, allowing the entrance of a chain, the bell at its end being situated between the upper two flying figures. The chain appears to emerge from the mouth of a high relief *kīrtti mukha*, at the top center point of the entire composition.

Along the outer edges of the window shape, flanking and above, are vegetal scroll motifs. The top two motifs are round. They flank the pointed area of the window arch, but are architecturally unconnected to it. The lower motifs form the ends of a kind of a scroll arabesque, and are highly elaborate versions of the decorative flanking elements of all the other *gavākṣa* windows on the temple.

Flanking the whole central motif are two dwarf figures. Short and stocky in proportions, they stand with one foot upon each of the arabesques just mentioned. They hold the end of a chain, which is draped across the upper portion of the central window. The dwarfs wear arm bands, bracelets, torques, and large round ear-rings. Their faces, framed by tightly curled beards, hold intense grimaces, with teeth bared and eyes bulging. Their hair is arranged in two rows of tight curls. At the center of their foreheads they wear a single cobra hood.

The projecting side portions of the *bhadra* adjacent to the *candraśālā* bear a half-*gavākṣa* arch, of the same elaborate style as that on the front (see figs. 7 and 12). The flanking dwarfs and the small central *gavākṣas* with male heads are missing, but the closed lotus medallion (cut in half) is included.

On the western side of the *śikhara*, above the juncture between the *prāsāda* and *maṇḍapa*, the *śukanāsā* (as the *candraśālā* is called when placed above the entrance) has been left unfinished (fig. 133). The central medallion itself is roughly blocked out, however, and the decorative elements have been slightly indicated by incised lines. No relief frieze appears at its base. The *makara* head, and the two flanking dwarfs have been fully carved.

RELIEF FRIEZES OF THE CANDRAŚĀLĀS

North (figs. 127 and 128)—The central relief panel, just below the *gavākṣa* window housing a Naṭeśa image depicts a male figure flanked by two ladies. The figures are in hieratic scale, the male being about twice as large. He sits on a low, short-legged dais. His pose is relaxed and easy; his left foot is crossed over the right thigh, his right hands rests on the surface of the dais and his left hand, resting on the left knee, holds an indistinct object. His figure is ample and his stomach protrudes. His hair is pulled back into an elaborate chignon. The two ladies, each bearing fly whisks, are standing, one facing the male, the other behind him.

The two rectangular friezes flanking this central panel depict an elephant caravan. On the right, three elephants, separated by trees, are pulled along toward the right by two male figures riding the first and third animal. On the left side, an elephant is mounted by the figures and followed by three others, the last one carrying a pole with two bundles across his back. This last figure is followed by another elephant. The scale here is totally disproportionate, the people being taller than the elephants. The frieze continues around the sides with additional elephant figures.

East (figs. 129-130)—The eastern relief frieze is much more weather-worn than those on either the north or south sides. The male head within the *gavākṣa* window is particularly worn. The scene below it is similar to the one on the north side. A seated male figure is flanked by two smaller attendants. The middle figure sits on ground level rather than on a dais, but in pose, proportion and hair style is similar to the corresponding figure to the north. He seems to have a knife strapped to his belt. Before him stands a male spear bearer, behind him, a female *cauri* bearer.

The flanking reliefs again show elephants. There on each side, they move away from the center in opposite directions. There are trees between each elephant. The frieze continues with additional elephant figures around the sides.

South (figs. 131-132)—The head within the *gavākṣa* motifs above the central relief panel bears a half smiling, almost quizzical expression, and is similar to the Buddha heads housed in similar arches at Ratnagiri.[21] The scene below shows a seated male figure with three attendants. The main figure sits on the ground in a pose similar to those already described, and holds an object, possibly a sword, in his right hand. Again, he is amply proportioned and wears his hair in a chignon. Though not carved with great detail, various pieces of jewellery are evident, necklace, arm bands and bracelets. One figure squats before him while behind stand two males, one holding a spear with a banner attached to it. The figures in this, and the other reliefs do not resemble in type or physiognomy the various images of ascetics found elsewhere on the temple. Rather, they seem to be royal figures with courtly attendants.

The flanking reliefs carry a touching and vividly depicted hunting scene. On the right side a hunter bending on one knee wounds an antelope with an arrow. Another antelope turns back its head in alarm while two other animals, a boar (with disproportionately long legs) and another antelope attempt to flee. On the left side, more human figures populate the scene. At the right, the figures (one of them placed on the side of the central projection) carry a dead animal hanging upside-down from a horizontal pole. To the left of these figures an archer shoots arrows at the boar he has wounded. A female figure appears to be comforting the animal, as does a small weasel-like creature placed behind him. At the far left, we again see three fleeing antelopes, the middle one turning its head to look behind.

NAṬEŚA IMAGES OF THE BHADRA

Just above the *makara* heads, at the lowest portion of the *bhadra's gavākṣa* pattern is placed on all four sides a high relief image of Śiva as Naṭeśa, Lord of Dance. All four images are iconographically similar and follow the traditional type of Naṭeśa seen in the earliest temples of Orissa.

North (fig. 134)—The figure has a tall crown of matted hair, wears many ornaments and is ithyphallic. He has six arms. His upper right and left hands hold a snake above his head. Two lower hands carry a *ḍamarū* (right) and a *triśūla* (left). The two remaining right arms are in *hastamudrā* (holding the arm across the torso in a manner suggesting an elephant trunk), and *varadamudrā* (gesture of bestowing gifts). The two remaining left hands are in *abhayamudrā* (gesture of reassurance), and *varadamudrā*.

East (fig. 135)—This eight-armed figure also holds up a serpent with his upper hands. The remaining right hands hold a *triśūla*, and one is in *hastamudrā*. The lowest right hand is broken. The left hand are in *abhayamudrā* and *varadamudrā*, and one of them holds a staff.

South (fig. 136)—This figure has eight arms. He holds the snake overhead and carries a *ḍamarū* in a right, a trident in a left hand. A lower right arm is in *hastamudrā*. The lowermost left hand cups the chin of a diminutive female figure.

West (fig. 137)—This figure has two of the lower arms broken. Originally six-armed, the two upper ones hold a serpent, a lower right was in *hastamudrā*, and another right hand holds a *ḍamarū*. The remains of a left arm carries a *triśūla*. The figure is ithyphallic. A small Nandin lifts his head between Śiva's legs.

PRATIBHADRAS

The *pratibhadras* (fig. 138) bear a continuous *gavākṣa*-net pattern, similar to that on the *pratibhadra* of the lower wall. Each horizontal course, however, carries only three, rather than five motifs, a central *gavākṣa* flanked by off-center, "split" ones on a slightly lower level. The same relief technique seen on the lower *pratibhadras*, which creates recessed concentric ridges, has been used here.

PRATIKARṆAS

The *pratikarṇas* (fig. 139) carry units of repeated imagery, which begin on the upper levels of the *nāga*-pilasters below. Upon a simple double *kapotāli* moulding is placed a relief depicting a girl at a door. She stands in a *tribhaṅga* pose, with legs crossed, and has a parrot perched on top of her door. Above this is a simple *khura* moulding decorated with a low relief animal carving. Next is a *gavākṣa* window, containing either a male head or a lotus medallion. This sequence of images is repeated along the entire *ratha,* though toward the summit, consistency as to the exact sequence of the pattern has been sometimes neglected (this is true also of the *karṇa* imagery). Many individual reliefs have also been left unfinished.

KARṆAS

The *karṇas* are made up of five sets of vertically placed stone courses, each of these also consisting of five parts (see fig. 5 and detail, fig. 138). In each set, the lowest four are identical in shape, resembling squat *khura* mouldings, with their lower ridges decorated with scroll work. Their upper portions carry imagery which is repeated continuously up the entire length of the *śikhara.* The lowest course has a simple *gavākṣa* window, bearing no image. The second course has a larger window, within which is placed a seated ascetic, each individual figure displaying one of various hand gestures. The third course also bears a *gavākṣa* window. These usually bear either an outward gazing male face or a closed lotus medallion. Occasionally, different deities, for example Gaṇeśa, are shown. The fourth course bears a simply carved leaf, many of which were left unfinished. The fifth, final course is a miniature *āmalaka* stone, which serves as a capping and dividing element to the sets of courses above and below it.

NOTES

1. See R. L. Mitra, *Antiquities of Orissa.* See also ARB, pp. 21-22, 214-15. The *Ekāmra Purāṇa, Ekāmra Candrikā, Kapila Saṃhitā,* and *Svarnadri Mahodaya,* all written in praise of Ekāmra, date from at least the 14th century or later. They basically are pilgrim guides to the temples, which are attributed mainly to the various Hindu gods (Brahmā for the Brahmeśvara, Yama for the Yameśvara, etc.). These texts have not been translated into English.

2. Kanwar Lal, *Temples and Sculptures of Bhubaneswar* (Delhi, 1970), p. 53; M. M. Ganguly, *Orissa and Her Remains: Ancient and Medieval* (Calcutta, 1912), p. 274.

3. Ganguly, *Orissa,* p. 275.

4. Debala Mitra, *Bhubaneswar,* 7th ed. (New Delhi, 1977), p. 47. Mitra states that the water is thought specifically to cure the barrenness of women. Today, one can see visitors continually throw coins into the water.

5. ARB, p. 93.

6. *Ibid.,* p. 93.

7. *Ibid.,* p. 93.

8. For example at Nalanda [Debala Mitra, *Buddhist Monuments* (Calcutta, 1971), p. 73; Roy Craven, *Concise History of Indian Art* (New York and Toronto, 1976), fig. 124]; Ratnagiri [R. L. Brown, "The Four Stone Facades of Monastery I at Ratnagiri", AA, 40.1 (1978), figs. 17 and 25]; and Ellora [Michael W. Meister, "Phāṃsanā in Western India", AA 38.2/3 (1976), fig. 7].

9. This is ascertained by the pre-restoration photographs in M. H. Arnot, *Report with Photographs of the Repairs Executed to Some of the Principle Temples at Bhubaneswar and Caves in the Khandagiri and Udayagiri Hills, Orissa, India, Between 1898 and 1903* (London, 1903).

10. Ganguly, *Orissa,* p. 280.

11. *Ibid.,* p. 279.

12. O. C. Ganguly, *Orissan Sculpture and Architecture* (Calcutta, 1956), p. 7.

13. ARB, pp. 86 and 91.

14. See Chapter 5, p. 116 and notes 19 and 20.

15. See Odette Viennot, *Temples de l'Inde Centrale et Occidentale* (Paris, 1976), fig. 108.

16. For additional illustrations see Walter Smith, "The Ceiling of the Mukteśvara in Bhubaneswar", AA, 45.1 (1984), pp. 77-84.

17. For a discussion of the Kārttikeya relief as a depiction of the *Skanda-parivāra* (family of Skanda) see P. K. Agrawala, Tetrad of Skanda Deities in a Relief at Bhubaneswar", *East and West,* 29.1-4. (1979), pp. 156-61.

18. C. Sivaramamurti, *Rishis in Indian Art and Literature* (Delhi, 1981), p. 221 and fig. 6.

19. Ganguly, *Orissa,* p. 287. For photographs showing the *śikhara's* pre-restoration state *see Ibid.,* pl. 8; and James Fergusson, *History of Indian and Eatern Architecture,* vol. 2, 2nd ed., rev. and ed. by James Burgess (London, 1910), fig. 313.

20. Alice Boner and S. R. Śarmā, trans., *The Śilpa Prakāśa* (Leiden, 1966), pp. 44-45; Thomas Donaldson, "Development of the *Vajra-Mastaka* on Orissan Temples", *East and West,* 26.3-4 (1976), pp. 427-28. More recently, in HTAO, Donaldson identifies the Mukteśvara reliefs and similar examples as depictions of kings, but does not give a detailed explanation for his identification. See pp. 1170-74, and figs. 4188, 4189, 4197, 4212, and *passim.*

21. See note 8.

CHAPTER 4

AN INTERPRETATION OF THE MUKTEŚVARA TEMPLE

The Symbolic Meaning of the Hindu temple is usually discussed in very general terms, following the interpretation put forth by Stella Kramrisch in her monumental study, The *Hindu Temple.*[1] Kramrisch views the temple as a representation of the Cosmic Puruṣa, an image of the body of God and the universe. To the extent that this metaphysical interpretation is supported by literary evidence, it is valid and meaningful, and brings into focus how various ideas and concepts of medieval Hinduism were incorporated in the temple's form and functions. The concept of the temple as an image of the Universal Being (Puruṣa) has its basis in the abstract diagram called the *vāstupuruṣamaṇḍala.*[2]

In the center of this grid diagram of sixty-four or eighty-one squares is Brahmā, the creator god, identified here with Brahman, the neuter, unmanifest absolute. Surrounding Brahmā are various gods from the Vedic pantheon, including at the outer borders the eight guardians of the directions. In Utpala's commentary on the *Bṛhat Saṃhitā*, the gods of the *vāstupuruṣamaṇḍala* are identified with various celestial bodies (the planets and constellations), and the diagram as a whole constitutes a cosmic map, embodying all aspects of celestial manifestation as emanations of the absolute.[3] This abstract ''plan'' holds the essential meaning of the Hindu temple, individual monuments exhibiting their own particular variations on the theme of the temple as the body of God, or Cosmic Puruṣa.

Hindu temples tend to be broadly interpreted, partly because many architectural and sculptural features are very similar from monument to monument, even from region to region in northern India. Such features as the curvilinear *śikhara* (the world mountain encompassing the axis of the universe), the *vyāla* motif and female figures (both manifestations of Śakti, the former also being a royal symbol), the *kīrtti mukha* (an "essential symbol of supreme Reality"), and the *āmalaka* (a celestial/solar symbol), have been lucidly but generally discussed by Kramrisch. The present task is to build upon these generalities in order to come closer to the particularized meanings of individual monuments.

While the symbolism of the Mukteśvara temple can be discussed in broad and general terms, much of its distinctive and even unique imagery suggests more specific statements of symbolism and meaning. In this chapter, while adhering broadly to the concepts outlined above, these unique features will be emphasized. The chapter is divided into two main parts. Each discusses one of the major areas of the temple that can be said to display a particular sculptural program, the *prāsāda* and the ceiling of the *maṇḍapa*.

Two major elements of the temple, the enclosure wall and the *toraṇa* do not display iconographical programs as such. The images on the corners of the enclosure wall, depictions of various deities and human figures (see figs. 3, 16-40), are arranged more or less at random, and are not connected thematically, even though some figural types (meditating yogins, royal figures) are prominent on the temple itself. The *toraṇa*, with its abundance of floral, abstract and figural motifs, is a decorative *tour de force*, but it can also be seen as a kind of essentialized prelude for certain aspects of the temple's sculptural program, such as the small yogin figures, but perhaps more importantly, the female figures, who here recline along the gateway's arched lintel (figs. 44, 45). They perhaps serve a symbolic function similar to the female figures on the temple, as *ākarṣiṇīs* (attractions), who draw the devotee into proximity with the divinity within the temple. This concept will be discussed in greater detail below.

THE PRĀSĀDA

The *prāsāda*, the "temple proper", which houses the emblem of Śiva (the *liṅga*) within the small space of the *garbhagṛha*, is a square structure surmounted by a curvilinear superstructure (*śikhara*). This tall, mountain-like architectural image can be divided horizontally into two broad parts, the lower walls and the *śikhara*, these being divided by a slightly recessed horizontal band (*kaṇṭha*) containing relief carvings. The following sections will discuss the *prāsāda's* iconography, beginning with the imagery on the lowest portion of the temple, discussing finally that of the superstructure. The three main ideas will be put forth: that as an image of the cosmos, the temple represents the terrestrial, celestial and supercelestial realms of existence; that as a temple dedicated to Śiva, the Mukteśvara can be read as an architectural *pañcamukhaliṅga* (*liṅga* with five faces), a universal form of Śiva having great symbolic and metaphysical importance; and that certain aspects of the temple's sculptural imagery relate to Hindu concepts of divine kingship.

THE LOWER WALLS

All around, the *prāsāda* bears niches in the *bhadras* and *pratibhadras*, as do the other *rathas* (vertical "pilaster" elements) of the *maṇḍapa*.[4] These niches are now all empty; originally, they must have held free-standing statues, perhaps made expressly for them. The probable kinds of images originally contained in these niches is not problematic, and can be ascertained through comparisons with earlier temples. The imagery of these prominent positions (the center and corners of the *prāsāda's* walls) was more or less standardized from the earliest surviving monuments. The *prāsāda* of the Mārkaṇḍayeśvara temple in Bhubaneswar, for example, bears images of Gaṇeśa, Kārttikeya and Pārvatī, respectively in the south, west and north *bhadra* niches.[5] The same arrangement is found on the Śiśireśvara temple. Both temples are entered from the east. The Paraśurāmeśvara temple, which like the Mukteśvara is entered at the west, has images of Kārttikeya and Gaṇeśa at the east and south. The northern niche is empty, but must have contained a Pārvatī image, since this goddess is also depicted on the lintel above the niche. We can reasonably assume that these same deities were housed in the Mukteśvara's *bhadra* niches.

These centrally placed figures, the *pārśvadevatās*, or "accompanying deities",[6] are directionally aligned with the Śiva-*liṅga* within the temple. They can be thought of as primary emanations, or aspects of Śiva, radiating out from this core image. Taken together with the *liṅga*, these figures also constitute an architectural tableau of Śiva and his family.

The niches of the *pratibhadras*, the pilasters flanking the central vertical salient, originally held the *āvaraṇadevatās*, or "surrounding deities".[7] These niches usually bear one of the various *mūrtti* of Śiva, such as Ardhanārī, Aja-Ekapāda, Bhikṣāṭana, and so forth.[8] The *ratha* niches of the *maṇḍapa* may also have held images of these dieties, or, they perhaps housed images of the *dikpālas*, the guardians of the directions.[9]

Much figural sculpture, however, does survive on the walls of the *prāsāda* and *maṇḍapa*. The *karṇas* and *pratibhadras* each bear a female, occasionally a male figure, these alternating with *nāga*-pilasters (*pratikarṇas*). The *bhadra* niches of the *prāsāda* are each flanking with two female figures, those closest to the niche being the river goddesses Gaṅgā and Yamunā. These dieties are usually placed on door frames leading into temples,[10] and we can see here how the niches themselves are conceived as a type of door, conceptual penetrations in the walls, where the god's being manifests itself in the images of his consort and offspring. (Curiously, the entry to neither the *maṇḍapa* nor the *garbhagṛha* bears images of the river goddesses; instead they hold the usual Śaivite door guardians, Caṇḍa and Pracaṇḍa.

The remaining female images are uniformly of the same type, the *śālabhañjikā*. The "girl embracing a tree" is one of the most long standing and conventional images in Indian art, its basic iconography being standardized as early as the Mathurā stūpa railings of the second century A.D., or even Bharhut.[11] Most of the figures represent a particular sub-type of *śālabhañjikā*, designated *dohadā* (literally, "two-hearted", i.e. pregnant). This particular type is to be shown kicking the tree she embraces. This practice, when performed by ordinary women at trees held to be magical or sacred, such as the *aśoka* or *kurabaka*, is meant as a fertility rite.[12] The promise of fertility is seen, not only in the flowering trees themselves and the voluptuous forms of the women, but also in the child occasionally accompanying the figure, either in her arms or standing to the side.[13]

From the earliest period, however, these figures have represented not ordinary mortal women, but *yakṣiṇīs*, "forest dryads", fertility deities who have the power to bring trees to flower by a mere touch of the foot.[14] This life-giving kick reveals the tree goddesses as manifestations of Śakti, the feminine aspect of the divine, which consists of "energy", or "power". The *Purāṇas* recount how the various aspects of Śakti came into being at the beginning of creation. After the supreme Śiva divided himself into a male and female part, the male further split into the "Eleven Rudras", while the female was divided into a multitude of Śaktis. Through these Śaktis, "the Supreme Goddess pervades the universe''.[15] The minor female divinities represent the various "conditions" (*upādhi*) of the Supreme Goddess, who "with superior and inferior forms, plays in his (Śiva's) presence".[16]

The *yakṣiṇīs* surrounding the temple can be identified as so many of these minor manifestations of Śakti. Kramrisch identifies such female figures in general, however, with the *ākarṣiṇīs*, the "attractions", the peripheral goddesses of the *śrī yantra.*[17] A *yantra* is a geometrical diagram used as a kind of aniconic emblem of a divinity. In the *śrī yantra*, sacred to the Supreme Goddess in conjunction with Śiva, the Absolute is represented as a dot in the center, with the intersections of the various interlaced triangles indicating the places of various emanatory principles.[18] Through their attractiveness and power (*śakti*), these goddesses pull the devotee inward to the presence of the central divinity (of the *yantra* or of the temple, which in itself can now be seen as an architectural *yantra*. The ground plan of the temple is quite suggestive of a *yantra*, as are the contours of the low wall enclosing the temple).[19]

The *yakṣiṇīs* also retain here much of their original meaning, which is complementary to their role as manifestations of Śakti. As forest (earth) deities, they represent the terrestrial realm of existence. This is in contrast to the figures that alternate with them on the *pratikarṇas*, the *nāgas* and *nāginīs*. These serpent divinities are associated with the subterranean realm and are guardians of the earth's treasures. They reside in a fantastic city, Pātāla, which is said to be even more splendid than Indra's heaven.[20] The *nāgas* and *nāginīs* display their wealth here on the temple by their jewellery—heavy necklaces, arm bands, even crowns—and by the jewel-offerings they hold in their hands. On the walls of the temple, the *nāgas* take on a worshipful role, offering garlands as well as jewels. Some hold fly whisks, an ancient accouterment of a royal or divine attendant.

The lower walls of the temple, with the subterranean *nāgas* and the terrestrial *yakṣiṇīs*, represent two levels of the material plane of existence. The *nāgas*, on their recessed pilasters, are most often in the shadows created by the flanking projections, an effect which calls to mind their dark underground kingdom. The *yakṣiṇīs*, however, are in full sunlight, at play on the surface of the temple as they are on that of the earth. In their placement on the lower walls, these terrestrial deities play a role in the temple's symbolism as an image of the universe. They signify the realm of physical manifestation, with the celestial and supercelestial regions looming above them, all being part, however, of the same cosmic body.

SCULPTURES ON THE KAṆṬHA (HORIZONTAL RECESS)

The images of the *kaṇṭha* and those on the mouldings below them show primarily two types of scenes, *liṅga* worship and ascetic gurus with their disciples. The figures here are anonymous—the scenes do not depict mythological episodes (except perhaps one), but represent conventional, contemporary views of devotional life. The practices here are completely orthodox, a very standard kind of *liṅga-pūjā*, where the icon is revered with offerings, oblations, etc. There is, however, a strong emphasis on the practice of yoga and meditation, and on the relationship of the guru and disciple. The guru is essential to salvation, and as a manifestation of the deity, is the most direct means toward spiritual liberation. The role of the guru held this exalted status from as early as the *Upaniṣads*; the guru is deified throughout the literature of the *Tantras*, and has divine status even today.[21]

We can speculate that the prominence of yogic imagery owes something to the Śiva sect, with its strong tradition of yoga and asceticism, as practised by the Mattamayūra order of Śaivācāryas.[22] This may also account in part for the yogic imagery on the *śikhara*, to be discussed shortly.

Of the remaining reliefs, certain of the images; the caravan scenes, female dancers, the woman with the ascetic (figs. 121-125); seem purely anecdotal, even playful. One relief, however, is rather enigmatic, that of the dancing ascetic (fig. 126). One scholar has interpreted this figure as a dancing Bhikṣāṭana (Śiva as mendicant).[23] This may, however, simply be a devotional dance, practised by an anonymous ascetic. Possibly, the relief represents the myth of Maṅkaṇaka. This ascetic devotee of Śiva danced ecstatically at the realization of his own great ascetic power when an accidental wound produced not blood but plant sap. Bewitched by his energy, the whole universe began to dance, until Śiva appeared and shamed the proud ascetic by producing ashes from a similar wound. This meeting's final result was that the sage's ascetic power was increased a thousand-fold.[24] Possibly, the relief was meant to bring to mind both human limitation and the limitless possibilities inherent in asceticism.

THE ŚIKHARA

The *śikhara* can be taken as a symbol of the celestial realm of existence primarily in that many of its decorative elements are solar-celestial symbols. Kramrisch's discussion of both the *gavākṣa*-net and the *āmalaka* bear this out.[25] The *śikhara's bhadras* and *pratibhadras* are covered with this continuous *gavākṣa* pattern. A basic meaning of *gavākṣa* is "sun-arch". Through those innumerable sun-arches of the *śikhara* shines a celestial light from within, which is nothing other than the transformed "superluminous darkness" of the divinity within the temple.

The *karṇas* are divided into five "stories" by a series of *bhūmi-āmalakas*. These are miniature repetitions of the large *āmalaka* crowning the temple's superstructure. The *āmalaka* is also a solar symbol, its ribbed surface being likened to the rays of the sun.[26] At the summit of the temple, the *āmalaka* "symbolizes the celestial region where the rays of the sun spread like the filaments of the lotus of the zenith".[27] The *prāsāda* as a whole, then, is an image of the universe, from the subterrestrial to the supercelestial regions (the latter being symbolized also by the *amṛta kalaśa*, the "jar of the nectar of immortality". This meaning is summed up in many architectural texts and *Purāṇas.* The door is the mouth, the *āmalaka* the head, the *bhadrās* the arms, the *kaṇṭha* the throat, and so on.[28] This basic interpretation is valid for all Hindu temples, whether dedicated to Śiva, the Goddess, or Viṣṇu. The Mukteśvara temple, however, is a particularly Śaivite representation of the universe/cosmic Puruṣa in that the *śikhara* can be read as an architectural *pañcamukhaliṅga* (*liṅga* with five faces). This *liṅga* symbolism can be seen as being inextricably linked, moreover, with images representing earthly kings. They are portrayed, through their position on the temple, as divine figures themselves, and also as worshippers of Śiva. The images refer not to a cult where the king himself was worshipped as a high god, but to a conception of the king as a "deputy" of the major divinity, namely Śiva, the kings's reign being legitimized through his close relationship to the deity. Additional layers of symbolism relate again to the concept of the *śikhara* as a representation of the celestial realm, the imagery on the Mukteśvara presenting a unique and engaging variation on this theme.

THE ROYAL IMAGES

The depictions of kings are placed at the lowest level of the elaborate and heraldic *candraśālās* on the north, east, and south sides of the *śikhara* (figs. 127-132). As stated earlier, these reliefs have sometimes been identified as depictions, not of kings, but ascetic gurus giving instruction to their disciples. Interestingly, images of yogins or ascetics are found all over the Mukteśvara, and on several other Orissan temples as well. In examples (figs. 121-126), from the *kaṇṭhas* of the Mukteśvara, the gurus, and their disciples as well, are depicted as extremely thin and emaciated, the result of their ascetic practices, this being in complete contrast to the robust figures of the *candraśālā* reliefs.

An early iconographical treatise, the *Viṣṇudharmottara* (ca. seventh century), describes the way ascetic figures are to be depicted: "The sages are to be adorned with bundled up locks of hair, . . . and though physically weak, are full of spiritual lustre (*tejas*)."[29] The benign expressions of the *kaṇṭha* figures convey well this idea of inner spiritual radiance, but it is the textual emphasis on the "physical weakness" of the ascetics, portrayed visually by thin, almost skeletal figures, that is important here, for it is a physical description in complete contrast to the *candraśālā* reliefs. Those robust figures are much more analogous to textual descriptions of the ideal king, who is most strongly characterized by his strength and sense of physical well-being. He is also often likened to the great heroes of epic and legend, as well as to warrior-deities like Indra, king of the gods.[30] The overall compositional layout of the teaching ascetic panels, however, (as well as the emphasis on hieratic scale that is seen in such images on the Rājarāni and Liṅgarāja temples) is quite similar to that of the royal reliefs, and helps to explain how the latter could be taken as depictions of ascetic sages.[31]

That the *candraśālā* panels indeed depict kings can be ascertained through comparison with sculptures that we know with certainty are depictions of royal figures. Of the many images of king Narasiṁhadeva I, the thirteenth-century monarch who built the Sun temple at Koṇārka, one is carved on the base of the large image-pedestal placed within the Sun temple's sanctum (fig. 140).[32] Larger than all surrounding figures, he greets the man seated before him while the other figures offer obeisance. The physical build of the king, his hair style, ornaments and weapons, are all strikingly similar to those of the main figures of the Mukteśvara reliefs.

Additional imagery, on the horizontal strips flanking each of the reliefs, also relates to royalty. In figures 127 and 129 are a representation of an elephant caravan. Another relief from Koṇārka again shows Narasiṁhadeva, this time mounted on an elephant, with a caravan led by soldiers depicted below.[33] Another activity closely associated with royalty is that of the hunt, as seen throughout Epic and Purāṇic literature, and in all periods of Indian art.[34] This is the subject-matter of the relief bands flanking the southern reliefs (fig. 131).

To briefly summarize, then, here we have the iconography of kings in Indian art. They are shown as robust, full-bodied figures, adorned with jewellery, bearing weapons, and attended by courtiers, and are surrounded by references to the hunt and the battle. This iconographical scheme, depicting kings at court, is strongly differentiated from representations of gurus with their disciples.

As stated previously, the depictions of kings on the Mukteśvara temple show the royal figures not simply as earthly rulers, but through their placement and other iconographical associations, are presented in a way that affirms their own divinity and their close relationship with Śiva, the god worshipped within the temple. Before going into this, however, it is necessary to more fully set the stage for an interpretation of the Mukteśvara reliefs as images of divine kings, discussing first the idea of divine kingship in ancient India in general and in Orissa in particular, showing the conceptual context out of which the images arise, and second the conception of the temple itself as a divine image, specifically, as an architectural parallel of an image presenting Śiva as an absolute, supreme, all-encompassing totality, the *pañcamukhaliṅga*.

DIVINE KINGSHIP IN THE BRAHMANICAL AND ORISSAN TRADITIONS

On many levels, the symbolic, the metaphorical, and at times even the literal, the Indian king is considered to be divine.[35] This divinity is instilled in him during the ceremony of consecration, the *mahābhiṣeka*, a ritual bath which constitutes a re-enactment of the consecration of Indra, a ritual that endows the king with divine power and prosperity (*śrī*).[36] A painting from Ajanta illustrating the *abhiṣeka* of Prince Mahājanaka (fig. 141) shows the royal figure flanked on either side by attendants who literally shower him with water poured from huge pots. The overall composition, with the symmetrical arrangement and the hieratic scale of the prince, closely resembles the standard image of Gajalakṣmī, the goddess of fortune, also called Śrī, being lustrated by elephants, who in Orissa particularly is often depicted on the lintels of temple entrances (fig. 91, see also fig. 52).[37] This visual analogy suggests that the king is not only being consecrated, but worshipped or venerated through lustration, as is the goddess. The parallel also suggests that the king, like Gajalakṣmī, was seen as a god of prosperity, whose very presence endows the kingdom with good fortune, peace, security, abundance, and so forth.[38]

In India, the king was not identified with the highest, absolute form of divinity, as he may have been in the *devarāja* cult of southeast Asia.[39] Instead, he was seen more on the level of the Vedic gods, who during the post-Vedic period are minor figures, but who embody traits and virtues to be valued in a king, particularly physical strength and prowess. Numerous passages in the *Mahābhārata* refer to the strength of the king, to the might of his arms, and such an ideal king is often called *rājendra*, "Indra among kings" (Indra of course being the king, of the gods).[40] Kings are said to embody the essences of the *lokapālas*, the guardians of the directions, Vedic deities who oversee the limits of creation.[41] Having the essence of these gods who oversee and protect the entire world, the king is first and foremost a protector, a preserver of order, or *dharma*. His very presence or existence is thought to preserve order, and a land without a king is a land in complete chaos.[42]

The role of the king as protector *par excellence* apparently gave rise to an identification of the Indian king with Viṣṇu, the supreme protector, the preserver of the universe, by the early Purāṇic period. Texts like the *Vāyu Purāṇa* (52.72), show the nature of this identification: "Every emperor. . .is born with a portion of Viṣṇu within him."[43] This identification was made not only within theoretical religious texts, but also with historical kings. At the end of Viśākhadatta's *Mudrārākṣasa*, the author refers to his royal patron (possibly Candragupta), as Viṣṇu.[44] More relevant to the present discussion is an inscription of the ninth-century Orissan king Śivagupta Bālārjuna, who is described as an aspect of Viṣṇu. Śivagupta, like most kings of both the early and later Somavaṃśī dynasties was a devotee of Śiva [the usual epithet describing them is *paramamaheśvara*, "having Śiva (Maheśvara) as one's chief aim"], and it is interesting in this light that the inscription also gives expression to the idea of Viṣṇu's subservience to Śiva.[45] A mythological parallel is seen in the myth of Liṅgodbhava, where Śiva reveals himself as the essence of a fiery shaft, or *liṅga*, of which neither Viṣṇu nor Brahmā could find the source, and thus were compelled to worship Śiva as the supreme lord.

Here then are two apparently contradictory aspects of divine kingship in India, for while the king is a *deva*, or an aspect of Viṣṇu, he is still a worshipper (albeit the chief one) of the supreme deity. This leads to the important point that the role of the king as a divine worshipper, while superficially contradictory, is really essential to his function. This has been pointed out by Jan Gonda. A consideration of the Vedic gods shows that they themselves perform sacrifices in order to gain victory, possessions, and to insure universal order.[46] The gods, then, perform rituals and acts of worship for many of the reasons that mortals do. In the Orissan tradition (particularly before the twelfth century) the king is consistently referred to as *paramamaheśvara*. The role of king as chief worshipper is also seen in the cult of Jagannātha, which began to achieve great prominence in the twelfth century, with the building of the great Jagannātha temple at Puri. By the thirteenth century a true royal cult is fully observable, with the king as the chief worshipper and a kind of deputy, or even earthly reflection, of the great god.[47]

Two more images of the thirteenth-century king Narasiṁhadeva clearly show the king's role as both god and worshipper. One stele shows the king worshipping a triad consisting of the goddess Durgā, Puruṣottama (later known as Jagannātha), and a Śiva-*liṅga*.[48] The king is of regal bearing and heroic proportions, but he is nevertheless shown in the subservient role. An altogether different conception is seen in another stele showing Narasiṁha enthroned on a swing (fig. 142). The format is frankly iconic, with the king in a frontal pose, and flanked symmetrically by worshipful attendants. The arch of the swing that frames the king is very similar to the arches surrounding Durgā and Puruṣottama in the stele showing King Narasiṁha worshipping these gods. In both cases, it acts as an enclosing shrine.[49] A devotional attitude is seen particularly in the figures below, who worship the foot of the king as it extends down toward them. As Hermann Kulke points out, this motif of worshipping feet is a standard feature of many icons, as several examples clearly show (fig. 143).[50]

Narasiṁha's conception of himself as a deity corresponds with the status of the king of Puri today, Puri being the center of the Jagannātha cult. The king of Puri is known as *calantī Viṣṇu*, "mobile Viṣṇu", in other words, a living incarnation.[51] In line with this, the audience he gives to pilgrims is called *darśana*, "vision", a term which usually refers to the viewing of a god. Also, many rituals usually thought of as belonging to gods (or images of gods), are performed for the king (ritual waking up, bathing, offering of food, and so forth).[52] As pointed out above, this had occurred in earlier periods, and in ancient India the king also gave *darśana* to his subjects,[53] hence the practices at Puri are nothing new. However, they do show a firmly documented occurrence of worshipful veneration of kings in Orissa. It should be pointed out too, that the king of Puri also acts as the chief ritual functionary of Lord Jagannātha, a role that seems inextricable from his own divine status.

There are no historical records to indicate whether the earlier temples at

Bhubaneswar were expressions of a royal cult of the same magnitude that appears at Puri. But we can see with particular clarity in the Mukteśvara temple an expression of the king as both a divine being and the chief worshipper of the supreme lord.

As stated earlier, the *candraśālā* designs which bear the relief depictions of kings are placed on all four sides of the superstructure of the Mukteśvara temple. There are only three reliefs depicting kings, however, because the *candraśālā* above the entrance way (in this position called the *śukanāsā*), hidden as it is by the pyramidal roof of the forehall, is unfinished. But conceptually, there are four *candraśālās*, and by extension, four images of kings. The fourfold *candraśālās* embody a complex iconography, whereby they can be seen as constituent parts of an abstract image of Śiva, specifically, the *pañcamukhaliṅga* (fig. 144). Relating the temple to the symbolism of the *pañcamukhaliṅga* is complementary to what has become the classic interpretation of the Hindu temple as an image of the cosmic *puruṣa*, having at its base the *vāstuprurṣamaṇḍala*.[54] The directional, celestial, and cosmic symbolism of the *vāstupuruṣamaṇḍala* strongly parallels that of the *pañsamukhaliṅga*. In its turn, the symbolism of the *liṅga* provides a specifically Śaivite perspective in interpreting temples of Śaiva dedication. The relevance of this symbolism to the Mukteśvara's royal images will, I hope, become clear in the following pages.

THE MUKTEŚVARA TEMPLE'S ŚIKHARA AS PAÑCAMUKHALIṄGA

Observations on the similarities of north Indian *śikharas* in general to the Śiva-*liṅga*, specifically the *pañcamukhaliṅga*, have been made previously by Kramrisch. Referring to the Siddheśvara temple at Bhubaneswar, she states that the central *rathas* of the *śikhara* "are akin to the form of a four-faced Śiva-liṅga", adding that the *liṅga* is, in anthropomorphic imagery, analogous to the architectural symbolism of the temple buttresses facing the four directions.[55] What Kramrisch alludes to is that just as the faces of Śiva seem to emerge from the surface of the *liṅga*, so too do the *rathas* seem to project out from the *śikhara's* core. This analogy can be taken much further, particularly when temples with richer sculptural programs than the Siddheśvara's are studied. It will be shown here how the elaborate imagery of the *śikhara* itself leads to an interpretation of the Mukteśvara, and various other temples as well as architectural analogs to the *pañcamukhaliṅga*.

The *pañcamukhaliṅga* represents Śiva as Sadāśiva, "eternal and immanent Śiva", the supreme embodiment of all existence. The five different faces or aspects each represent some facet of this totality, and each on a variety of levels.[56] Briefly, each aspect is associated with one of the five directions, one of the five elements, and with one of the five ontological principles of Sāṁkhya philosophy. Each is also assigned a *śakti*, or female power. Sadāśiva-Īśāṇa, the face of the zenith, is the aspect of Śiva beyond manifestation, and is the god in complete transcendency. In sculpture he is rarely depicted anthropomorphically, but is understood to exist at the curved summit of the *liṅga*. In accordance with his rarified nature, he is associated with the element *ākāśa,* "ether" or "space". His *śakti* is Parāśakti, transcendental consciousness. The progressively tangible aspects of existence are embodied in the four directional faces below; Mahādeva-Tatpuruṣa, Bhairava-Aghora, Umā-Vāmadeva, and Nandin-Sadyojāta. This whole complex scheme is known as the *pañcabrahmans,* or the "five *mantras*" of Śiva. Its overall meaning is summed up in a passage from the *Pañcabrahman Upaniṣad*:

> With the knowing of the fivefold Brahmans, . . . one should know that all this phenomenal world is Parābrahman, Śiva, . . . whatever is seen or heard or falls within or lives beyond the range of his inner or outer senses, (one should know) as Śiva of the character of the fivefold Brahmans alone.[57]

The *pañcamukhaliṅga* then, is a symbolic representation of God as totality, and the phenomenal universe is but a part of his body.

Now to return to the suggestion that the Mukteśvara temple has a conceptual basis similar to that of the *pañcamukhaliṅga*. First, the formal similarities pointed out by Kramrisch are strongly evident, with the central offsets of the *śikhara* projecting into space just as the faces of the *liṅga* do (cf. figs. 144 and 7). In addition, the lower levels of the *śikhara* on the north, south, and east sides, contain elaborate networks of imagery in the large *candraśālā* devices described earlier, superimposed upon the central offsets, with the west one, obscured by the roof of the forehall, left unfinished. At the center of the large window is another, much smaller *candraśālā*. It projects out from the surface of the larger design and has within it a small face resembling that of a Buddha image, which I would argue, is a representation of Śiva. Behind this *candraśālā,* and largely hidden by it, is an image of a closed lotus, well-known as a symbol of the Goddess (figs. 129 and 131).

Each element of these compositions bears some sort of Śaivite reference, which in their fourfold repetition are analogous to the faces of Śiva on the *pañcamukhaliṅga*. The *kīrtti mukha* above each large window is the first of these references. While seen in conjunction with many gods of the Hindu pantheon besides Śiva, its origins are discussed in Purāṇic myths specifically within a Śaivite context.[58] The *kīrtti mukha* is born from the wrath of Śiva, in some myths being emitted from the god's third eye. In the *Padma Purāṇa,* Śiva assigns the self-devouring monster a place of honor on his temples, and requires worshippers to acknowledge its presence. The *kīrtti mukha,* originating from Śiva's wrathful side, presents to the viewer a theophany of Śiva and Śakti, and is a constituent part of it.

On the north side of the *śikhara,* the small *candraśālā* bears an image of Śiva Naṭeśa, Lord of Dance (fig. 128), and so the entire window here is unproblematic as a presentation of Śiva. The small faces within the south and east windows, however, are rather innocuous, and have no iconographical features identifying them specifically with Śiva, at least at first glance. As mentioned earlier, they resemble

Buddha-heads, and it can be noted that one particular aspect of Śiva, one seen over and over in Orissa, that of Lakulīśa, is closely related to the Buddha image and obviously is derived from it.[59] Images of Lakulīśa based on Buddha images take on the seated meditative posture (perhaps the original *raison d'être* for the adaptation, as both Buddha and Lakulīśa are yogin-ascetics), the snail-curls or smooth skull, cranial extension (though sometimes omitting it), and distended ear lobes. The Lakulīśa images are instantly distinguishable, however, because of the attribute of the club and the lack of monastic garb (figs. 15 and 20).[60]

Figures or heads of deities within *candraśālā* or *gavākṣa* windows, particularly on Buddhist monuments, can be cited from all over northern India,[61] and it seems that from the Gupta period on, many of these images depict gods or celestials, not simply anonymous, decorative portraits. The general similarity between a figure of Lakulīśa on the Mukteśvara's enclosure wall and the faces within the *candraśālās* is evident (cf. figs. 20, 130 and 132).

That the *candraśālā* images superimposed upon lotuses represent the conjunction of Śiva and Śakti can be ascertained through comparisons with other Orissan monuments. On the west side of the Paraśurāmeśvara temple's *śikhara* there are two superimposed *candraśālās* placed directly above the entrance to the shrine, each bearing an image of Śiva (fig. 150). The bottom one depicts Śiva and Pārvatī on Mount Kailāsa, with the demon Rāvaṇa below (Rāvaṇānugrahamūrti). The *candraśālā* above holds an image of Śiva Naṭeśa, and above this is a figure of Lakulīśa. On the Mukteśvara temple, the upper *candraśālā* is eliminated, and an unframed relief of Naṭeśa is attached to the surface. The lower emblem is also simplified, with Śiva represented as a face, and the Goddess as a closed lotus behind it. The emblematic function of this lotus motif is seen more clearly on the *śikhara* of a temple dedicated to the Goddess herself, the Gaurī temple at Bhubaneswar, which is contemporary with the Mukteśvara (fig. 172). Here the face of Śiva is excluded, and the dwarf figures display only the symbolic image of the Goddess. The Mukteśvara, however, shows Śiva and the Goddess in conjunction. The mythological associations of the Paraśurāmeśvara's *candraśālās* are eliminated, replaced with emblems of a more abstract nature. But aside from this, the Śiva-Śakti images, repeated on each directional face of the Mukteśvara, suggest that the Śaktis of the *pañcabrahmans* have been represented along with the faces of Śiva.

The Śaivite identification of the *candraśālā* faces of the Mukteśvara can be further strengthened by comparison with other temples. A *candraśālā* from a niche on the Paraśurāmeśvara temple bears the typical third eye and matted hair of Śiva (fig. 145). Another *candraśālā* from the same temple shows a three-headed image of Maheśamūrti (fig. 146). The three-faced Maheśamūrti has been interpreted by Kramrisch as identical with the five-faced deity of the *pañcamukhaliṅga*, with the rear face hidden from view, and the top one being invisible.[62] This image, along with the *liṅga* in figure 144, clearly shows that the concept of the *pañcabrahmans* was well-known in early medieval Orissa,[63] indicating also its all Indian importance.

Another Maheśamūrti image is found on the western side of the Paraśurāmeśvara's *śikhara,* near the summit of the central *ratha,* capping the sequence of Rāvaṇānugrahamūrti, Naṭeśa, and Lukulīśa (just visible at the top of figure 150). The placement of the image is significant in that the profile heads and the "hidden" rear one can be related conceptually to the remaining sides of the *śikhara*. In this it bears great similarity to several temples further north, specifically, in the Himalayan regions. The Maheśa shrine at Jagatsukh (Himachal Pradesh), for example, shows an image of Maheśamūrti on the *candraśālā* above its entryway.[64] The Viśveśvara Mahādeva temple in Bajaura (Kulu Valley, Himachal Pradesh), has on *each* side of the *śikhara* a *candraśālā* bearing a Maheśamūrti, with the central faces each depicting a different aspect of Śiva, precisely as would be seen in circumambulating a *pañcamukhaliṅga*. Thomas Maxwell has taken steps toward interpreting this temple as a *pañcamukhaliṅga*. Since, however, he could discern no representation of Īśāṇa-Śiva, the face of the zenith, he did not adapt this view, stating instead that the temple, or the *śikhara* itself represents Īśāṇa, surrounded by the manifest aspects of Śiva.[65] This most rarified aspect of Śiva, however, is non-manifest and beyond form, while the temple, interpreted as Puruṣa, the body of god, as well as the four visible faces of Śiva, relates to God's manifestation on the phenomenal plane. Further, the relevant texts never state, to my knowledge, that the *liṅga* itself is Īśāṇa—rather, the *liṅga* is the totality, and bears the images that emanate from it. Īśāṇa, associated with the element *ākāśa,* would be more appropriately represented by the temple's capping elements, the *āmalaka* stone, the *karpara* ("skull", the curved surface above the *āmalaka*), and the finial.

Again the standard interpretation of the temple's capping elements lends credence to their identification in a Śaivite context, with the uppermost face of the *pañcamukhaliṅga*. It is easy to make analogies between this most subtle aspect of Śiva, associated with the element *ākāśa*—ether or space—and the uppermost parts of the temple. By their very position, the capping elements symbolize the celestial world. Kramrisch discusses the *āmalaka* in particular as a symbol of passage, of exit from the world and of entry into heaven.[66] And remembering how texts like the *Agni Purāṇa* (ca. ninth century) and the *Samarāṅgaṇasūtradhāra* (mid-eleventh century) describe the parts of the temple as parts of the human body, with the area above the *śikhara* being likened to the head, the name for the curved area above the *āmalaka*, the *karpara,* or skull, is most suggestive.[67]

But the capping element with which the most intriguing analogies with the Īśāṇa-face of Śiva can be formed is the finial, the *amṛta kalaśa,* the vase of the nectar of immortality. These analogies are made in light of the existence of another type of finial, discovered by M. A. Dhaky, called the *ākāśaliṅga*.[68] The *ākāśaliṅga* finial is described in various texts, such as the *Samarāṅgaṇasūtradhāra,* and the *Lakṣaṇa-samuccaya* (ca. thirteenth century). Temples with *ākāśaliṅga* finials are found on several Orissan temples dating from the seventh to tenth centuries, for example the Paraśurāmeśvara at Bhubaneswar, the Kutai Tundi at Khiching, and the Siddheśvara at Gandharadi. Other similarly dated examples are found in Andhra Pradesh and in the Himalayan regions.[69]

The term *ākāśaliṅga* can be translated variously as "the *liṅga* open to space", "*liṅga* consisting of space", or as the "*liṅga* consisting of ether, *ākāśa*". This latter reading indicates that the *liṅga* represents Sadāśiva-Īśāṇa, associated with the subtle element *ākāśa*.

The term *ākāśaliṅga* alone suggests the finial's identification with the fifth, invisible head at the summit of the *pañcamukhaliṅga*. This is further suggested by the *Agni Purāṇa,* which refers to another finial, the *Īśascūḍa,* the finial of Īśa, or Īśāṇa, which is defined as "having its upper part in *liṅga* form". Dhaky suggests the possibility that many, if not all early medieval Śiva temples from Orissa and Andhra were originally crowned with *liṅga*-finials, since most of these temples have lost their original crowning elements.[70] If so, then the four *candraśālā* reliefs, along with the *ākāśaliṅga* finial, would have presented a powerful architectural expression of the conception of the five faces of Śiva.

The *amṛta kalaśa,* the more usual temple finial, seems however itself to have a conceptual affinity with the *ākāśaliṅga*. Keeping in mind the idea of the temple as the body of God, Śaivite myths often describe *amṛta*, the nectar of immortality, as flowing from the crescent-moon embedded in Śiva's hair.[71] Similarly, *ākāśa* is associated with the topmost head of Śiva, and is itself space, the uppermost reaches of the universe where *amṛta* dwells. In the context of yoga, the meaning of *amṛta* taken on a much broader scope. It becomes a subtle element, flowing from the *sahasrāra cakra* (located at the top of the skull), during the highest state of meditation.[72] At this it becomes all-pervasive, permeating the being of the enlightened devotee. Here *amṛta* takes on a subtle, expansive character, similar to that of *ākāśa*—ether.

The similarity of *ākāśa* and *amṛta* is further indicated in the *Yogatattva Upaniṣad,* which describes yogic physiognomy.[73] In the subtle, or spiritual body, *ākāśa* is located at the region from the middle of the eyebrows to the top of the head, that is, at the *sahasrāra cakra,* which another text, the *Śiva Saṃhitā* (ca. tenth century), calls the *ākāśa paṅkaja,* the *ākāśa*-lotus, or *cakra*. Reference to the *sahasrāra cakra* is relevant in terms of the temple's symbolism both as the body of Puruṣa and as *pañcamukhaliṅga,* since *amṛta,* symbolised by the *amṛta kalaśa,* is housed within the same portion of the spiritual body as is *ākāśa*.[74]

A parallel meaning for the two elements *ākāśa* and *amṛta* is suggested architecturally by the finial of the Svargabrahmā temple at Alampur (Andhra

Pradesh),[75] where an *amṛta kalaśa* is placed above an *ākāśaliṅga*. That the summit of the temple can be taken specifically as the crown of Śiva's head is again suggested textually in the *Viṣṇudhramottara,* where another finial, the *āmalasāraka* is described. Here a cylindrical shaft *(ākāśaliṅga)* is crowned with the Śaivite crescent moon, the vessel of *amṛta*. This suggests as strongly as the Alampur temple, parallel meanings for *amṛta* and *ākāśa*.

KINGS AS GODS ON THE MUKTEŚVARA TEMPLE

A detailed discussion of the *liṅga* symbolism of the Mukteśvara's *śikhara* is of great relevance to the meaning of the royal images placed on the superstructure's *candraśālās*. As a support for the royal images, the *śikhara* serves several functions. First, as an image of Puruṣa, who embodies the entire cosmos,[76] the *śikhara* lends a kind of cosmic, celestial setting for the images, placing them in the "heavenly sphere", which strongly suggests the Kings' divinized status.[77] Also, regarding the directional symbolism of the temple—set forth in the iconography of the *vāstupuruṣamaṇḍala* as well as in the directionally oriented *pañcamukhaliṅga*—the kings can be seen as embodiments of the *lokapālas,* the guardians of the four cardinal directions.

The formal layout of the *candraśālās* suggests further a close proximity between the king and Śiva, with the royal images placed directly below the faces of Śiva, the whole *candraśālā* device itself being a manifestation of an aspect of Śiva's being. The king can also be perceived as being in a worshipful attitude, looking upward at the image within the *candraśālā*. Various comparisons can again be made. Of similar conception is the image of the Cola king Rajendra I, from the eleventh-century Bṛhadīśvara temple at Gangaikondacolapuram, where the ruler, in worshipful obeisance, receives a garland of victory from Śiva and Pārvatī, a more pictorial version of the abstract representation on the Mukteśvara.[78] In Orissan art, the image-pedestal from the Sūrya temple (fig. 140) perhaps served a similar function, with the king, while receiving obeisance from his retinue, is seated at the feet (the worshipful attitude *par excellence)* of the sun god.

If we accept the interpretation of the Mukteśvara reliefs as images of divine kings, the question which remains is, "why are such images placed so prominently on this particular temple?" Nothing has been mentioned so far as to who exactly the kings depicted on the Mukteśvara temple might be. With a date of ca. 950-75, the Mukteśvara was built during the first century of the "later" Somavaṃśī dynasty, which most likely reigned either from ca. 882-1110[79] or from ca. 929-1118.[80]

By around the middle of the tenth century, the Somavaṃśīs (literally, "whose lineage is from Soma", the moon, but also one of the *lokapālas)* appear to have become firmly established on coastal Orissa.[81] According to Orissan tradition,[82] the Mukteśvara temple was built by Yayāti I Mahāśivagupta, the second Somavaṃśī king, who probably ruled either from ca. 922-55, or as late as ca. 963-91.[83] The tradition seems authentic, since Yayāti's dates correspond closely to the date of the temple, arrived at through stylistic analysis. The site of Bhubaneswar, near the eastern coast, had been a pilgrimage site sacred to Śiva from at least the early seventh century.[84] It is possible that Yayāti built the small but elaborate Mukteśvara temple as a symbol, not only of the dynasty's growing supremacy, but of the divine legitimacy of its royal power as well. Kulke discusses how royal patronage at pilgrimage sites:

> Had great significance for the legitimation of royal power . . . The *tirthas* (places of pilgrimage) became centres of a multicentered royal network which united the different nuclear areas religiously and even economically.[85]

And so, even though Bhubaneswar was not their political capital, the Somavaṃśī declaration of affiliation with Śiva at this important pilgrimage site and religious center, was crucial to their establishment of divine legitimacy. As examples of this "royal temple policy", Kulke cites, among others, the Bṛhadīśvara temple at Tanjore (eleventh century), the Kandarya Mahādeva at Khajuraho (eleventh century), the Liṅgarāja at Bhubaneswar (eleventh century), and the Jagannātha temple at Puri (thirteenth century).[86] As "royal temples", these works are most notable for their extreme monumentality, in contrast to the tenth-century Mukteśvara temple, which is of the same modest proportions as most of its predecessors, being built at a time before the trend toward grandiose size become established. In spite of this, the Mukteśvara fits well into Kulke's scheme in that it was built after a long hiatus of architectural activity in Bhubaneswar, the Mukteśvara's immediate predecessors being the Vaital Deul and Śiśireśvara temples, both dating to ca. 800, and possibly sponsored by the Somavaṃśīs' predecessors, the early kings of the Bhauma-kara dynasty (ca. 736-923). Most politically powerful during their first century, the quarter of the ninth century.[87] The Mukteśvara temple, then, was possibly built as a declaration of Somavaṃśī legitimacy as the Bhauma-karas' successors, showing the dynasty's kings (Yayāti himself, and/or his predecessors?) literally at the center of a newly formed royal cult dedicated to Śiva.

The reliefs on the *candraśālās* of the Mukteśvara temple, placed in close proximity to a symbolic and visually powerful representation of Śiva, give form to the idea of the king as a deputy of the supreme lord, who himself contains a portion of the divine essence. The reliefs can also be seen as indicators of a royal cult centered around Śiva. If such a cult existed, it strongly parallels the cult of Jagannātha (which is much more clearly documented and observable, due mainly to the fact that it is a living tradition), and was an important precedent for it.

THE ŚIKHARA'S PRATIKARṆAS

The narrow recessed vertical areas between the *pratibhadras* and *karṇas* bear repeated units of imagery unique to the Mukteśvara temple (see details, figs. 138, 139). This unit, which begins on the upper portion of the *pratikarṇa* of the lower wall (fig. 96), and sweeps upward to the temple's summit, consists of three parts. The lowest section bears a female figure standing at door. She can be identified with the *vāsa kasajjikā nāyikā* the lady waiting for her beloved.[88] Above her sits a meditating yogin, housed within a *gavākṣa* and seated in the lotus posture. The final image of the unit is another *gavākṣa*, which houses a human head.

In the context of mysticism, the *nāyikā* can be seen as longing, not for a human lover, but for the divine, as she does in this seventeenth-century poem dedicated to Kṛṣṇa:

Today is an auspicious day.
Let my Lord come like a king.
Why does he play hide and seek with me,
He, who is Gopala of Muvva?
O friend! My entire being belongs to him.
Emaciated I may become,
Strength may leave me,
Let him come soon.
I cannot stay alone,
Where is the Kind-hearted One?
Why does he not come?
Wherefore does he hesitate?
This is the house of the moon-faced one.
I adorned myself
With beauty only for him.
Has another prevented him?
But alas, even so,
Why does he not come?[89]

This longing for the divine beloved mirrors the struggle of the yogin for union with God. As a group, these *nāyikās* may also be interpreted, like the *yakṣiṇīs* of the lower walls, as *ākarṣiṇīs* "attractions", who lead the yogin into the state of *yoga,* the mystical union with God, symbolized in the *gavākṣa* head above. The attitude of Vāsakasajjikā Nāyikā strongly suggests an identification with *ākarṣiṇī*; she decorates both herself and her stands at the threshold waiting for her beloved.[90]

That the uppermost image of the three-part ensemble, the head within the *gavākṣa,* symbolizes Śiva, is in keeping with the interpretation of the *gavākṣa* as a sun/celestial window, within which the superluminous darkness of the deity inside the temple is made manifest. Comparisons with similar motifs at sites like Ellora and Ratnagiri,[91] and the images within the *candraśālās* of the *śikharas* discussed above,[92] also suggest that a divine personage is being depicted here.

This tripartite unit moves consistently up the *śikhara* except for minor details—some *gavākṣas* omit the yogin or the head above him, substituting a closed lotus, or occasionally an image of Gaṇeśa. But the vertical composition of *nāyikā*, yogin, and god-image is consistent as an overall pattern, and as the figures move higher on the temple the precision of details becomes less important. Eight of these vertical image sequences are placed around the temple. Adjacent to them, on the *karṇas*, is a similar composition made of two elements—yogin and *gavākṣa* (enclosing a head or a closed lotus) placed between each *bhūmi āmakala* (see figs. 138, 139). The *śikhara* is thus pervaded with an images of yoga, which is repeated with a constant unflaging rhythm, like the repetition of a *mantra,* all over the upper surface of the temple.

The *pratikarṇa* reliefs can be interpreted on another level, in tune, once more, with the idea of the temple as Puruṣa. In taking the *śikhara* as an image of the celestial realm, once can draw a parallel between the *nāyikā*-yogin composition and the description of Indra's heaven found in Kalidāsa's *Abhijñānaśākuntalam.* King Duṣyanta, upon arrival in Indra's heaven, marvels at the wonders seen at the hermitage of Mārīca:

> . . . Here in the forest of Kalpa trees, they draw from air life's necessary substance, in waters yellow with the golden dust (pollen) of the lotus, they perform ablutions for religious ends, on jeweled slabs they meditate, and restrain their passion in the midst of celestial nymphs. They practice penance in a place which other sages by their austerities seek to win.[93]

The image of yogins meditating in a realm of heavenly pleasures serves as a supreme metaphor for *vairāgya,* "indifference" (literally, "disgust"). The Mukteśvara temple depicts repeated images of the ideal yogin who has risen above the common man of the world:

> When he dwells in ignorance and is deluded by Kāma's magic, man sees the world filled with the glances of women, but when he achieves the state of dispassionate calm, his senses are disengaged, and he rests in the pure vision of absolute reality.[94]

This imagery may have been inspired by the ideals held by such groups as the Mattamayūra "clan" (order) of Śaiva *ācāryas,* with their strong tradition of austerity and yoga.[95]

NAṬEŚA IMAGES

Presiding over all this, isolated on the *bhadra* directly above the *candraśālā* is Śiva Naṭeśa, performing his cosmic dance of creation (figs. 134-137). That Śiva is creatively (not destructively) dancing here is indicated by his peaceful countenance. Also, Śiva's drum attribute is a well-known symbol of the god's creative nature, and certain texts relate how he plays it during his dance of creation.[96] From his place on the temple, Naṭeśa oversees the vast play of the three realms of existence, which through his creative dance he is responsible for bringing about.

The image of Śiva Naṭeśa, like the *candraśālā* below is a kind of theophany, where the god reveals himself to his devotees in his divine glory. A textual parallel with this architectural theophany from the *Kūrma Purāṇa* (part two, the *Īśvara Gītā)* is relevant here. In the text, Śiva delivers a lengthy exposition to the assembled *ṛṣis* (sages) on the nature of the universe. The essence of his message is seen in one verse: "Being the master of and one with Māyā (cosmic illusion, *prakṛti*), I become united with Kāla (Time) and create the universe and also draw it together (i.e., destroy it)''.[97] Following this, while being praised by the *ṛṣis* as Yogeśvara (Lord of Yoga), Śiva ascends to the sky and in a transfigured, multi-limbed effulgent form, dances.[98] The Mukteśvara temple approximates this visionary description; the figure of Śiva is seen against the swirling light and dark patterns of the *śikhara's gavākṣa* patterns and the sages/yogins are assembled as ecstatic witnesses in the vertical modules of the *pratikarṇas.*

THE CEILING OF THE MAṆḌAPA

The ceiling of the *maṇḍapa* exhibits a distinctive sculptural program that can be interpreted on various levels (figs. 6, 87).[99] It can be read initially as a narrative tableau depicting key events in the mythology of Śiva and Pārvatī, specifically, the Austerities of Pārvatī, while also bearing reference to the births of Gaṇeśa and Kārttikeya, with particular emphasis upon the latter's relationship to the Kṛttikās, the Wives of the Seven Sages. It can also be interpreted as a *maṇḍala*, a circular diagram wherein is expressed a whole complex of metaphysical meaning.

The *maṇḍala* imagery of the Mukteśvara ceiling can be read in several ways. It represents on one level deities emanating from the center, who can be identified with various aspects of the celestial realm of existence.[100] On yet another level it represents a concept of greater abstraction, where the *maṇḍala* can be seen as an exposition on the theory of the *mantras,* the basic constituents of a complex system of sound symbolism, which had become highly developed during the early medieval period. This esoteric meaning becomes clear as we compare the ceiling's imagery with ideas expressed in various religious texts, generally accepted as dating to the early medieval period.[101] These texts, which can be typified as Tantric in nature, contain striking parallels with the ceiling's imagery, as we shall see when various correspondences are made.

NARRATIVE ASPECTS OF THE CEILING

On a basic narrative level, the ceiling reliefs represent key events in the legend of Śiva's family. The two trapezoidal meditation scenes represent the Austerities of Pārvatī, Śiva's consort.[102] This can be ascertained by comparing the reliefs to mythic accounts of this story, found in various Purāṇic texts, which recount how Pārvatī resorted to asceticism on various occasions. Two particular episodes record major events in Śiva's and Pārvatī's mythology. The goddess first took up austerities in order to win Śiva, himself the implacable yogin as her husband.[103] Pārvatī's second retreat to the ascetic grove was the result of an insult from her husband. Highly offended when, referring to her dark skin Śiva teasingly called her Kālī, or "Black", she vowed not to return to him until she attained through ascetic power a light complexion. In reaching this goal she won the appelation Gaurī, or "Golden One".[104]

The developmental sequence in both penance episodes is quite similar—beginning with the goddess's departure to the Himalayan forests, progressing to the penance itself, the attainment of the fruits of asceticism in the form of boons from gods or sages, and finally union or reunion with Śiva. The goddess arrives at her remote mountain retreat, both times accompanied by hand maidens. One account of her second bout with asceticism specifically states, however, that four goddesses; Jayā, Vijayā, Jayantī, and Aparājitā; were called to mind by the goddess and then "began to render necessary services".[105] At the end of countless years, Pārvatī's goals were attained on both counts. In various versions of the earlier episode, it is announced to Pārvatī either by the Seven Seers (great legendary figures very prominent in the Epics and Purāṇas), by the god Brahmā, or by Śiva himself, that the god would marry her.[106] The second time, the goddess's asceticism won the particular favor of Brahmā, who caused her to shed her dark skin, and attain a golden complexion.[107] When Śiva and Pārvatī were reunited, a series of complex events following their intense love-making resulted in the birth of Kārttikeya.[108]

Because these reliefs lack specific narrative details, it cannot be precisely determined which panel represents which event. In the scene to the west, the goddess sits in quiet meditation, at the beginning, or in the midst of her long austerities. In the eastern panel, her hands are raised in a specific gesture. Although damaged, her hands seem to be joined at the thumbs and open outward, in a kind of expanded *añjali*, the gesture of greeting. Her hand pose is very similar to one described in the medieval text on dramatic dance gesture, the *Abhinayadarpaṇa*. According to this text, the gesture, called *kapota* (dove) is made by joining the hands at the sides, base and top. The gesture can variously indicate the taking of an oath, salutation, addressing a preceptor, or humble acquiescence or agreement.[109] As a gesture of oath taking, it is appropriate to the goddess's vow that she should remain an ascetic until her goals were accomplished. On the other hand, the gesture would serve also as an appropriate reply to the Seven Seers, or especially to Brahmā, with Pārvatī humbly acknowledging the god's favor to her.

The four triangular meditation scenes are even more iconographically spare than the two just discussed. Although the figures of the meditating women are centrally placed and symmetrically flanked, the relaxed poses of the figures negate any strong iconic impression. The figures seem to be general representations of Pārvatī's Penance, showing no particular episode, but in their repetition, make this the pervading narrative theme of the ceiling's program.

Gaṇeśa and Skanda, the two sons of Śiva and Pārvatī, are depicted on the two largest relief panels, at the west and east end of the ceiling respectively. That the Gaṇeśa relief may represent the birth of this god is indicated by a passage from the *Liṅga Purāṇa,* stating that as soon as he was born, "the embodied form of gentleness, and terrific in appearance, the abode of all auspiciousness, Gaṇeśa danced."[110] The particular pose of the figure, holding a cobra above his head, indicates that his dance is imitative of that of his father. That the dancing form of Gaṇeśa was popular in eastern India can be seen in several examples from Bengal and Orissa.[111]

The image of Skanda represents the god in a basically iconic form, devoid of any narrative references. The central image of the ceiling, the circle of the Seven Mother Goddesses, however, can be seen as referring specifically to Skanda's birth, in that the Sapta Mātṛkās can here be identified with the Kṛttikās, the nursemaids of Skanda. The cult of the Seven Mothers, which had been gaining popularity in northern India from the sixth or seventh century, found particular favor in medieval Orissa, as can be seen in the many surviving sculptural depictions of them.[112] The most complete mythological account of the Seven Mothers is in the *Devī Māhātmya,* a text glorifying the exploits of the great goddess Durgā, the slayer of Mahīṣāsura, the Buffalo Demon.[113] Here the Mothers, created out of the energy of their male counterparts for the purpose of battle, are depicted as ferocious demon slayers. The first six goddesses; Brahmāṇī, Maheśvarī, Kaumārī, Vaiṣṇavī, Vārāhī, and Indrāṇī are female versions of the male deities Brahmā, Śiva, Skanda, Viṣṇu, Varāha and Indra. Cāmuṇḍā is an independent figure, although she too was created for battle against Mahīṣāsura and other demons. The Mothers on the Mukteśvara ceiling have been identified in Chapter 3 by their various attributes, headdresses, and animal vehicles. At the northwest section of the circle is Vīrabhadra, an aspect of Śiva, who here, and in almost all representations of the Seven Mothers, holds a *vīṇā* (a long-necked instrument resembling a lute).

By the time their cult was codified, the Mothers had acquired—but for the emaciated devourer Cāmuṇḍā—nurturing, maternal personalities, and by the tenth century in Orissa they are almost always represented with babies in their arms. This emphasis upon the goddesses' maternal natures is important, for it points to their connection with the Kṛttikās. The Kṛttikās are one of the many feminine heptads mentioned throughout Sanskrit literature and are identified with the constellation Pleiades.[114] In every version of the Birth of Kārttikeya, the Kṛttikās (from whom his name derives) play a greater or lesser role, sometimes actually becoming collectively pregnant with the divine embryo, other times acting only as his nursemaids.[115] A relief frieze from the Kushan period (second to third century A.D.) depicting Kārttikeya and seven undifferentiated female figures is clearly a prototype for later Sapta Mātṛkā representations.[116] In later renditions, including that of the Mukteśvara ceiling, Skanda's place is taken over by Vīrabhadra, who as a youthful, comely, but at times ferocious god, and as an offspring of Śiva, bears a certain resemblance to the more mythologically appropriate Skanda.[117] In the Mukteśvara ceiling, however, with the close proximity of the image of Skanda on the eastern trapezoidal relief to those of the Seven Mothers at the center, the latter's identity with the Kṛttikās is strongly established.

The entire ceiling, then, constitutes both an iconic and a narrative representation of Śiva and his family. Śiva himself is represented abstractly as a crescent moon at the center of the lotus medallion. His wife Pārvatī is shown twice (perhaps even six times), engaged in ascetic practices having highly important consequences. The two most iconic images on the ceiling, those of Skanda and Gaṇeśa, are shown in ways that make allusions to their births; Gaṇeśa, who danced at his birth, and Skanda, whose birth is referred to by the presence of the Kṛttikās, his nurses.

THE CEILING'S MAṆḌALA SYMBOLISM

A more esoteric level of meaning also exists in the imagery of the Mukteśvara ceiling, which when considered as a whole, becomes a three-dimensional *maṇḍala*. On a primary level, a *maṇḍala* can constitute an image of the universe, which emanates from a supreme absolute principle, itself unmanifest yet responsible for all creation. One of the clearest expressions of this idea is found in the *maṇḍala* conceived specifically within the symbolic context of the Hindu temple, the *vāstupuruṣamaṇḍala*. This grid diagram symbolically houses the entire universe and the extent of the directions, symbolized by its *dikpālas* (guardians of the directions).[118] It seems possible that in the Mukteśvara ceiling the Seven Mothers with Vīrabhadra have a symbolism comparable to that of the eight *dikpālas* of the *vāstupuruṣamaṇḍala*, i.e. as representations of the directions and the planets. First of all, the very number of image in the central circle (eight) suggests a directional symbolism, and we should keep in mind that from its earliest conception, the *maṇḍala* had strong directional orientation.[119] The presence of celestial symbolism becomes even more clear in that in their identification with the Kṛttikās, the Mothers represent the Pleiades, one of the constellations, or lunar mansions. The *Mahābhārata* states that "after having fed Skanda, the Kṛttikās entered into the sphere of the stars".[120] This identification with the Kṛttikās perhaps influenced the strong connection made between the Seven Mothers in certain other contexts, specifically with the planets. There are a number of northern Indian temples which superimpose friezes of the Seven Mothers with Vīrabhadra and Gaṇeśa over door lintels bearing images of the Navagrahas (the "Nine Graspers"), the seven planets plus the ascending and descending nodes of the moon.[121] The Mothers themselves are, in fact, also describes in the *Mahābhārata* as *grahas,* and the use of this term is clearly denotative of their role as planetary powers. In this role, we see a dark side to the nature of the Mothers, to whom Skanda gives power over the fates of children to the age of sixteen.[122] Inscriptional remains refer to the goddesses as "mothers of the seven worlds",[123] and the *Mahābhārata* calls them "great mothers of the universe".[124] While these last references are not specifically planetary, they do bestow a cosmic dimension upon the Mothers, making them all-expansive and omnipresent.

There is reason to suggest, therefore, that the Seven Mothers with Vīrabhadra represent on the Mukteśvara ceiling both the eight directions and the planets, and are thus conceived as the constituents of the celestial sphere of existence, emanating from the Absolute.[125] The remaining imagery of the ceiling is consistent with a cosmological interpretation. The four narrative reliefs flanking Kārttikeya and Gaṇeśa represent particular events occurring on the terrestrial plane, while attached to the lower parts of the ceiling, below these reliefs, are high relief figures of *nāgas,* deities of the subterranean world, who serve here as the earthly supports of a celestial canopy.

A further level of symbolism can be discerned through a correspondence that stands between much of the ceiling's imagery and various aspects of Tantric metaphysics. An interesting connection can be seen, first of all, between the *nāga* couples occupying the corners of the square enclosing the lotus medallion and the abstract representation of the Absolute at the center. According to the *kiraṇāgama,* a Śaivite text which dates before the tenth century, the phenomenal world was created through the interaction of Śiva's *śakti,* or female energy, and Ananta, the great serpent who supports the earth.[126] Ananta is more usually seen in a Vaiṣṇava context. The *Kiraṇāgama,* however, describes him as an aspect of Śiva, specifically a creative aspect, who through interaction with Śakti, "gives birth to a series of derivatives which constitute the world."[127] Their union is depicted on the Mukteśvara ceiling through the image of the serpent couples, who on the periphery of the *maṇḍala* preside over the earthly levels of creation.

The disk at the very center of the lotus medallion, if interpreted as the center of a *maṇḍala,* represents the Absolute. It can be stated even more specifically, however, that we have here symbolised the transcendental union of Śiva and Śakti. The incised crescent moon at the center of the lotus certainly must be taken as symbol for Śiva. The full-blown lotus within which it is placed is emblematic of the Supreme Goddess. As is well-known, the lotus as a symbol of the Goddess appears as early as the first century B.C.[128] The symbol's continuity into the medieval period can be seen in several images of lotus-headed goddesses,[129] and more relevant to this study, in the *candraśālā* reliefs identically placed on three sides of the *śikhara* of a temple dedicated specifically to the Goddess, the Gaurī temple at Bhubaneswar (fig. 172). Here a closed lotus is displayed on the *candraśālā* held by two dwarfish attendants. This is similar to the corresponding element of the Mukteśvara temple, where the lotus, rather than being represented alone, has placed before it an arched window motif beating a face, probably meant to indicate that of Śiva (figs. 129, 131).[130] It is this same motif of the Goddess as lotus, together with Śiva, that appears more abstractly in the interior ceiling, where at the apex of the *maṇḍala,* Śiva and Śakti are the absolute center from which all existence emanates.

With the images of the Mātṛkās on the eight surrounding lotus petal cusps, and the abstracted symbol of the Absolute at the center, the Mukteśvara ceiling resembles, both formally and conceptually, Hindu and Buddhist *maṇḍalas* of the later medieval period, which represent deities surrounding a central figure symbolic of the absolute principle from which they emanate.[131]

A great number of *maṇḍalas* of the later medieval period, however, often have placed on their major divisions not images, but rather *mantras,* the sacred and magically potent sound elements which assume such great importance in Tantric ideology.[132] It is suggested here that *mantra* symbolism has a prominent role in the total symbolism of the Mukteśvara ceiling.

As stated by Dirk Jan Hoens in the book *Hindu Tantrism,* "one of the most essential traits of Tantrism is its conception of a phonic plane of existence, parallel to, and even basic to, the objective world. It is a leading factor in cosmic evolution."[133] The universe as a system of variously subtle sound elements emanating from the primordial, transcendent sound (*nāga*) is conceived either as a manifestation of Śiva alone, or as the result of his union with Śakti.[134] Relevant to the present discussion is that *nāda* can be symbolized by a crescent.[135] This motif on the Mukteśvara ceiling may, then, have a double meaning, signifying Śiva himself, as well as the primordial sound which he produces, either alone or through union with the Goddess.

According to the *Kiraṇāgama,* it is not the *mantras* proper that initially emanate from primordial sound, but rather, more subtle elements, the phonemes. They are represented by the letters of the alphabet, the basic constituents from which first the *mantras,* and then the words of language, ariṣe.[136] These phonemes are given the apellation *mātṛkās* (mothers), and in other contexts are *mantra-mātṛkās* (mothers of the *mantras*), for it is this limited number of phonemes, analogous to the creative power of Śiva, from which all *mantras,* and finally words, corresponding to the various aspects of phenomenal existence, are created.

It is through the evolving forms of the basic sound elements, the *mātṛkās,* that passage is made from the Absolute to the many, from inexpressible to expressible knowledge. For just as the world is seen to evolve from the pure absolute to the realm of phenomenal existence, so from transcendent sound evolve first the phonemes, then sacred *mantras,* and finally, words, the human means of expressing knowledge. Thus knowledge, like existence, has a supreme, transcendent source.

Two other Tantric works, the *Svacchanda Tantra* and the *Kubjikāmata Tantra* describe the phonemes, or *mantra-mātṛkās,* in a way that seems highly analogous to the Mukteśvara ceiling's imagery. In these texts, a group of eight goddesses (the Seven Mothers plus Mahālakṣmī), reside over eight sections of the alphabet, and are thus identified with the *mantras mātṛkās.*[138] The image of Vīrabhadra is most likely retained in the Mukteśvara ceiling because of the long standing convention of representing him with the Mothers. The *Kiraṇāgama* also describes how the letters of the alphabet (the *mātṛkās*) are to be disposed upon a circular *maṇḍala.* In their ensemble they constitute the "Śakti of the Word" (Vagīśvarī-Śakti), who appears personified to the devotee in the course of meditation.[139]

If the Absolute is represented by the central lotus and crescent and its immediate emanations by the Mothers, a third level of existence, the realm of manifestation, is represented by the reliefs surrounding the central *maṇḍala*—the depictions of Gaṇeśa and Skanda, Pārvatī's Penance, and the two reliefs showing music and dance. In a general way, all these scenes represent events occurring on the phenomenal plane, and in their placement, they may be read as evolving immediately from the differentiated Mātṛkās, and ultimately from the Absolute. In terms of sound symbolism, however, the Gaṇeśa image and the music and dance scenes can be read as phenomenal manifestations of the primordial *nāda.* In their representations of musicians clanging cymbals and beating drums, the reliefs depict in a most appropriate way the pheonomenal evolution of primordial unheard sound. The drum is of particular symbolic importance here. It is well-known that the drum is a symbol of the creative power of Śiva, and that he plays it during his dance of creation.[140] Śiva dancing in his creative, peaceful aspect is prominently depicted on the *śikhara* of the Mukteśvara temple. This creative dance is imitated in the interior by Gaṇeśa and the female dancer, while its accompanying music, particularly the beating of the drum, is played by the attending musicians. The associations here are subtle and rather ingenious. Not only is manifested sound depicted on the plane of creation; also given visual form is the idea of creation *through* sound, through both the evolution of *nāda* and the beating of Śiva's drum.

The final textual sources to be considered here not only support an interpretation of the ceiling of the Mukteśvara temple as a *maṇḍala,* but also suggest that the forehall in which it stands was conceived specifically as a meditation hall. A meditation is described in the Kashmiri *Mālinīvijaya Tantra* (ca. tenth century), where after offering *pūjā* to Gaṇeśa, the devotee contemplates an image of Śiva surrounded by eight goddesses, who can be identified with the Sapta Mātṛkās.[141] Also from the tradition of Kashmir Śaivism comes a similar meditation where the object of contemplation, the Absolute and its emanations, is internalized, identified with the very being of the yogin. Here, various gods are to be identified with constituent parts of the individual's psyche. Intellect, ego, mind, and the five senses are connected with a group of eight Mothers, here called *indriya devīs,* or goddesses of the senses. They are located in a circular formation in the heart lotus, around the supreme pair, Śiva-Śakti.[142]

SUMMARY

The textual analogies made with the ceiling of the Mukteśvara temple show that a cohesive group of ideas, prevalent at the time of its production, certainly played a role in the formation of its iconography, and help us to understand its deeper meanings. On one level the Mukteśvara ceiling has a simple iconic-narrative function, depicting a group of interrelated deities. On another level, it shows a complex conception of the Absolute and its emanations, which can be interpreted as both tangible and objective (celestial phenomenon), and subtle and mystical (the *mantra-mātṛkās*), the essential substance of all that has potential for existence. Finally, the ceiling perhaps served very specifically as a *maṇḍala* or *yantra* (instrument), as an aid to spiritual practice, helping the devotee to visualize some of the abstract ideas which bore specifically upon his meditation.

If the ceiling seems to be Tantric in its overall program, the *prāsāda* is decidedly orthodox, representing the temple as the body of Puruṣa. We have been able to perceive, however, that there is perhaps an additional, particularly Śaivite level of meaning to this primary interpretation, the temple as *pañcamukhaliṅga*. This meaning possibly exists in all Śiva temples, not only the Mukteśvara. It comes particularly clear in those examples bearing *ākāśaliṅga* finials, which are representations of Īśāna-Sadāśiva, the head of the zenith on the *pañcamukhaliṅga*, symbolic of Śiva's subtle and unmanifest aspect. It can be further suggested that this *liṅga* symbolism provides a support for an iconography of kings as gods, minor *devas* who serve as the chief worshippers of Śiva. Placed prominently on a temple built in the chief pilgrimage center of coastal Orissa, these images, probably of the Somavaṃśī ruler who built this temple, proclaim him as the supreme ruler of the Somavaṃśī empire that came to be consolidated in the mid-tenth century.

NOTES

1. Stella Kramrisch, *The Hindu Temple*, 2 vols. (Calcutta, 1946).

2. For a complete discussion of the *vāstupuruṣamaṇḍala* see *ibid.*, vol.1, pp. 19-55, and illustration.

3. *Ibid.*, p. 34, citing Utpala's commentary on the *Bṛhat Saṃhitā,* 5.2.73.

4. The *maṇḍapa* has the same essential divisions as the *prāsāda*, but has no *kaṇṭha*, not the elaborate imagery of the *candraśālās.*

5. Thomas Donaldson, HTAO, vol. 3, p. 1051.

6. Kramrisch, *Hindu Temple*, vol. 2, pp. 300-301.

7. *Ibid.*, p. 301.

8. Mārkaṇḍayeśvara temple bears *karṇa* figures of Ardhanārīśvara, Aja-Ekapāda, Bhikṣāṭana (?), Hari-Hara, and a four-armed aspect of Śiva. The Someśvara temple, Mukhaliṅgam, has a niche layout similar to the Mukteśvara's. The *āvaraṇadevatās* here are Aja-Ekapāda, Bhikṣāṭana, Ardhanārī, Hari-Hara, Gaṅgādhara, and Lakulīśa.

9. The Bhrameśvara temple has figures of the *dikpālas* on both the *prāsāda* and *maṇḍapa*. P.P. Acharya feels, however, "that no temple before 1000 was adorned with *dikpālas*." ("Dikpālas and their Śaktis", *Studies in Orissan History, Archeology, and Archives* (Cuttack, 1969), pp. 312-15.

10. See Odette Viennot, *Les divinités fluviales Gaṅgā et Yamunā aux portes des sansctuaires de l'Inde* (Paris, 1964).

11. See J. P. Vogel, "The Woman and Tree, or Śālabhañjikā in Indian Art and Literature", *Acta Orientalia*, 7.2.3, (1928), pp. 201-31. Vogel ascertains that *śālabhañjikā* was from an early date a general technical term denoting practically any standing female figure, and not exclusively "she who bends the *śāla* tree" this meaning having its origin in a fertility rite recounted in the Buddhist Jātaka tales.

12. See C. Sivaramamurti, *Sanskrit Literature and Art*: Mirrors of Indian Culture (New Delhi, 1970), p. 40. See also A. K. Coomaraswamy, *Yakṣas* (New Delhi, reprint 1971) p. 36.

13. Cf. Coomaraswamy, *Yakṣas*, p. 32.

14. See *ibid.*, pp. 32-36.

15. A. S. Gupta, ed., *Kūrma Purāṇa* (Varanasi, 1971), 1.11.7 (p. 75).

16. *Ibid.*, 1.11.24 (p. 76). For another discussion of Śiva and Pārvatī in terms of a theistic interpretation of Sāṃkhya philosophy see J. L. Shastri, ed., and trans. "A Board of Scholars", *Liṅga Purāṇa*, Ancient Indian Tradition and Mythology (Delhi, 1973) 2.11 (pp. 640-44).

17. Kramrisch, *Hindu Temple*, vol. 2, pp. 338-39.

18. For an illustration of the *śrī yantra* see H. Zimmer, *Myths and Symbols in Indian Art and Civilization* (Princeton, 1946), fig. 36.

19. For an illustration and further discussion see Guiseppe Tucci, *The Theory and Practice of the Maṇḍala* (London, 1961).

20. Y. Krishnan, "the Nāga Cult in Indian Art and Literature", *Oriental Art*, 13.3 (Autumn, 1967), pp. 180-92, citing the *Viṣṇu Purāṇa* (Wilson trans., p. 168).

21. See J. Gonda, "The Guru", *Change and Continuity in Indian Religion* (The Hague and London, 1966) pp. 229-83; and Sanjukta Gupta, *et al.*, *Hindu Tantrism* (Leiden, E.J. Brill, 1879), pp. 75, 76, 78, and *passim*.

22. See above, Chapter 2, pp. 67, 68.

23. Anne Marie Gaston, *Śiva in Dance, Myth and Iconography* (Delhi, 1982), pp. 162-63. Gaston's evidence for this identification is at best, contrived. She states that her only reason for identifying the figure as Bhikṣāṭana is that he is an ascetic who dances, admitting both that no other images of Bhikṣāṭana dancing exist, and that he is depicted both in myths and in South Indian medieval sculpture as a comely youth, not old and emaciated.

24. See Wendy K. O'Flaherty, *Hindu Myths* (Baltimore, 1975), pp. 173-74.

25. Kramrisch, *Hindu Temple*, vol. 2, pp. 318-21, 348-56.

26. *Ibid.*, 351, note 175.

27. *Ibid.*, citing the *Bṛhadāraṇyaka Upaniṣad* 6.3.6.

28. *Ibid.*, citing *Agni Purāṇa* 61.23.24; and *Śilparatna* 16.115.

29. C.Sivaramamurti, *Chitrasutra of the Vishnudharmottara* (New Delhi, 1978), p. 185.

30. See Jan Gonda, *Ancient Indian Kingship from the Religious Point of View* (Leiden, 1966), p. 35, where abundant references from epic literature are cited, such as *Rāmāyaṇa* 1.1.8ff., where Rāma is described as broad-shouldered and long-armed, a description given to various other rulers,

such as Nala (*Mahābhārata* 3.53.11, also *Mārkaṇḍeya Purāṇa* 74.51. It should be noted also that the epithet *mahābāhu*, "having great arms", is also given to Viṣṇu, the prototype for the protective role of the king (*Mahābhārata* 5.70.9). The ideal of the *cakravartin* of course immediately comes to mind.

31. For images of teaching ascetics from the Liṅgarāja temple see Donaldson, HTAO, fig. 4215. The controversial architectural treatise, *Śilpa Prakāśa*, p. 44, refers to such scenes as *śikṣadāna*, "imparting instruction".

32. For additional images of Narasiṁhadeva I see HTAO, figs. 1359, 4225.

33. *Ibid.*, fig. 4241.

34. To give a brief overview here, we may cite the various *jātaka* stories in which the Bodhisattva, in an animal incarnation, is the subject of a king's hunt [*Rurujātaka* (E. B. Cowell, ed., *The Jātakas or Stories of the Buddha's Former Births* (London, 1957), vol. 4, p. 163; and *Sāmajātaka* (*ibid.*, vol. 6, p. 43)]. At the beginning of the tale of Śakuntalā in the *Mahābhārata* [J.A.B. van Buitenen, trans., *The Mahābhārata*, vol. I; *The Book of the Beginning* (Chicago, 1973), pp. 156-60], and in the opening scenes of Kalīdāsa's play [A. W. Ryder, *Shakuntala and Other Writings by Kalidasa* (New York, 1959), pp. 5-6] the story begins with a description of King Duṣyanta pursuing deer into the sacred hermitage of Kaṇva. Depictions of royal hunts (illustrating the jātakas mentioned above) are found at Ajanta, Caves 10 (*Sāmajātaka*), and (*Rurujātaka*). See M. Singh, *Ajanta* (New York, 1965), fig. 3, pls. 17-19. For the *Rurujātaka* at Bharhut see H. Zimmer, *The Art of Indian Asia* (New York, 1960), fig. 31a. Other published examples of royal hunting scenes are from the Rani Gumpa, Udayagiri, Orissa (Zimmer, *ibid.*, pl. 57), and the Lakṣmaṇa temple, Khajuraho [E. Zannas and J. Auboyer, *Khajuraho* ('S-Gravehage, 1960), p. 64].

35. Fundamental studies of Indian kingship are E. W. Hopkins, "The Divinity of Kings", JAOS (1931), pp. 309-16; and John W. Spellman, *Political Theory of Ancient India* (Oxford, 1964) Enlightening recent studies are Jan Gonda, *Ancient Indian Kingship*; and Sheldon Pollock, "The Divine King in the Indian Epic", JAOS 104.3 (1984), pp. 505-28. That the question of the Indian King's literal divinity is controversial can be seen in two papers published in *The Sacral Kingship: Contributions to the Central Theme of the VIIIth International Congress for the History of Religions* (Leiden, 1959). A. Basu in "Hindu Doctrine of Divine Kingship", pp. 167-71 considers that is Indian *kingship* and not the person of the king himself that bore divine status. J. Gonda in "The Sacred Character of Ancient Indian Kingship", pp. 172-80 states emphatically that the Indian king is indeed a god, specifically a *deva*, having within his being the essence of the *lokapālas*, the guardians of the universe. In "Divine King", Pollock provides numerous references to the king's divinity, particularly from the epics (pp. 552ff.). Considering the negativity toward the notion of the king's divinity, particularly from *dharmaśāstras*, Pollock rightly states that "even if these denials are contemporary with (the epics) the fact that they at the same time imply a widespread belief is something we should not ignore" (p. 523).

36. See J. Gonda, *Ancient Indian Kingship*, pp. 80-81. The main text Gonda cites in his discussion is the *Aitareya Brāhmaṇa*, specifically 7.20.5ff. and 8.14.4.

37. For an illustration and discussion of a god's *abhiṣeka* see J. Williams, *The Art of Gupta India* (Princeton, 1983), p. 76 and p. 72, a fifth-century image from Mathurā, where Kumāra is "anointed" as the general of the gods by Śiva aad Brahmā, both holding jars.

38. Various references suggest a subtle conceptual interrelation between Lakṣmī/Śrī and the prosperity (*śrī*) of the king. Gonda has shown how parts of the king's throne are to be identified with *śrī* [*Aspects of Early Viṣṇuism* (Delhi, 1954), pp. 188 ff.]. The Viṣṇu Smṛti states that Lakṣmī

Śrī resides in the white sunshade of State (99.12), as well as in the royal consecration [(*abhiṣeka*) itself (99.16)]. See Gonda, *Ancient Indian Kingship*, p. 37.

39. This is the classic interpretation given by G. Codès in such work as "Le culte de la royauté divinisée, source d'inspiration de grands monuments du Cambodge ancien", *Serie Orientale Roma*, vol. 1 (1952), pp. 1-23. An extensive challenge to Codès' ideas is H. Kulke, "Der Devarāja-Kult. Legitimation und Herrscherapotheose in Angkor Reich", *Saeculam* 25 (1974). Trans and reprint 95, Southeast Asia Data Program Paper, no. 118, Ithaca, 1978). A full list of Codès's writings on the subject can be found in Kulke's bibliography.

40. See note 30.

41. Gonda, *Ancient Indian Kingship*, pp. 9 and 16 (citing *Mānava Dharmaśāstra* 7.3 and 5.97), and 36 (citing *Bhāgavata Purāṇa* 4.13.23). For a definition of *lokapāla* as a guardian of one of the four cardinal directions (as opposed to all eight, as Gonda takes the term), see Kramrisch, *Hindu Temple*, p. 91.

42. Pollock, "Divine King", p. 526, citing the *Ahirbudhnya Saṃhitā* 16.14-19.

43. *Ibid.*, p. 526.

44. *Ibid.*, citing *Mudrārākṣasa* 7.19.

45. S. N. Rajaguru, *Inscriptions of Orissa* (Bhubaneswar, 1966) vol. 4, pp. 48-51. Several other inscriptions from the Somavaṁśī period make allusions to royal godhood. See *ibid.*, pp. 63, 76, 223 (referring to minor kings who worship the king's feet); 227, where Yayāti II is referred to as the son (*jāta*) of Madhusūdana. Yayāti II is also referred to as *pratinidhir madhusūdana* "the representative (or likeness) of Madhusūdana". *Inscriptions of Orissa*, vol. 4, no. 36, cited by H. von Stietencron, "The Advent of Viṣṇuism in Orissa", CJRTO, p. 21. A predecessor of the Pāṇḍava king Bharatabala is called "a deity and a supreme divinity (*abhidaivatā*)", *ibid.*, pp. 10, 15, while his consort is called "of divine origin", *ibid.*, pp. 9, 16.

46. Gonda, *Ancient Indian Kingship*, p. 15, citing *Rāmāyaṇa* 2.113.23; and *Mahābhārata* 1.74.129, 3.293.2.

47. H. Kulke, "Early Royal Patronage of the Jagannātha Cult", CJRTO, pp. 151-53; H. Kulke, "Jagannātha as the State Deity under the Gajapatis or Orissa", *ibid.*, pp. 200, 201. The usurper kings of the early Sūryavaṁśī dynasty tried to set themselves up as Jagannātha's deputies in the mid-15th century, necessary in a kingdom that had been dedicated to the god two centuries earlier. See Kulke, "Jagannātha as State Deity", pp. 204-05.

48. HTAO, fig. 3843.

49. In Indian imagery the arches behind image-pedestals and thrones generally bear similar symbols, a *makara* at the top, *vyālas* (leogryphs) at the sides, and elephants at the base, these referring to the celestial, intermediate, and terrestrial realms respectively. In the context of the throne, these symbols caractère royal et divin du trône dans l'Inde ancienne, Paris, pp. 105-85.

50. Kulke, "Jagannātha as State Deity", p. 203. See also HTAO, figs. 3667, 3677 and *passim*.

51. L. K. Mahapatra, "Gods, Kings, and the Caste System in India", A. Bharati, ed., *Ninth International Congress in Anthropological and Ethnological Sciences* (Chicago, 1973), pp. 53-54.

52. *Ibid.*, p. 54.

53. Gonda, *Indian Kingship*, p. 73, citing *Raghuvaṁśa* 19.7, *Mahābhārata* 7.5.86; *Rāmāyaṇa* 2.100.51 and 3.33.5.

54. S. Kramrisch, *Hindu Temple*, pp. 21-57, 67-97, 357-361.

55. Kramrisch, "Wall and Image in Indian Art", B. S. Miller, ed., *Exploring India's Sacred Art:*

Slected Writtings of Stella Kramrisch (Philadelphia, 1983), p. 258 and figs. 14-6, 14-7. Donaldson suggests that four images of Śiva at the summit of the liṅgarāja temple may allude to *liṅga* symbolism (HTAO, pp. 1089-90 and figs. 3452-55).

56. See Stella Kramrisch, *Presence of Śiva* (Princeton, 1981), pp. 178-89.

57. *Pañcabrahman Upaniṣad* 26, cited in Kramrisch, *Presence*, p. 187.

58. See Kramrisch, *Hindu Temple*, vol. 2, pp. 322-31; and V. S. Agrawala, *Studies in Indian Art* (Varanasi, 1965), pp. 234, 237-40.

59. For example see Donaldson, HTAO, figs. 3471-68 and *passim*.

60. Buddha images from various Orissan sites, notably Ratnagiri, must have served as the prototypes of the Lakuliśa images. See D. Mitra, "Ratnagiri, 1958-61", MASI 80 (1981-83), pp. 216-24 and *passim*.

61. Figures or heads of deities within *candraśālās*, particularly on Buddhist monuments, occur with great frequency, and its seems that from the Gupta period on, many of these images depict gods or celestials, not simply anonymous, decorative portraits. See for example Ellora, Cave 9 [O. Viennot, *Temples de l'Inde centrale et occidentale* (Paris, 1976), p. 10]; votive stūpas at Nalanda [R. Craven, *A Concise History of Indian Art* (New York, 1976), fig. 124]; and most importantly, Ratnagiri, Monastery I, third shrine façade, showing details of large *candraśālā* devices with smaller *candraśālās* bearing seated Buddhas. See R. Brown, "The Four Stone Façades of Monastery I at Ratnagiri", AA 40.1 (1978), figs. 17, 25. These can be compared iconographically (as Brown does stylistically), with the large *candraśālās* of the Mukteśvara, the Buddha figures corresponding to what I identify as the heads of Śiva (see *ibid.*, fig. 24). Hindu examples from Orissa are cited in the text below, and in figs. 143, 144.

62. See S. Kramrisch, "The Image of Mahādeva in the Cave Temple on Elephanta Island", *Ancient India*, 2 (1946), pp. 4-8; and *Presence of Śiva*, pp. 443-47.

63. For illustrations of other Orissan *pañcamukhaliṅgas* see HTAO, figs. 3435, 3436, 3438.

64. Illustrated in A. de Lippe, *Indian Medieval Sculpture* (New York and Amsterdam, 1978), fig. 41, 44.

65. T. S. Maxwell, "The Five Aspects of Śiva in Theory, Iconography and Architecture", *Art International*, 25.3-4 (March, April 1982) pp. 41-47 and pls. 19-23.

66. Kramrisch, *Hindu Temple*, p. 356.

67. See M. A. Dhaky, "The Ākāśaliṅga Finial", AA 36.4 (1974), p. 307; and Kramrisch, *ibid.*, p. 367.

68. Dhaky, "Ākāśaliṅga Finial", pp. 307-15.

69. In Andhra Pradesh the Svargabrahmā temple, Alampur (ca. 725-50); Mahānandīśvara temple, Mahanandi (ca. 800); Bhṁaliṅgeśvara and Rāmaliṅgeśvara temples, Stayavolu (ca. 9th century). In Himachal Pradesh the Kedāra and Bāleśvara temples, Jaheshvar (10th century); Baijanātha, Bānanidevāl and Rakasidevāl temples, Kumaon area (ca. 10th century). See Dhaky, *ibid.*, p. 308.

70. *Ibid.*, p. 308.

71. Bhāravi, *Kirātārjunīya* 5.44; and Somadeva, *Kathāsaritsāgara* 74.111: "The tasteful water of the Ganges, which seemed to be impregnated with the nectar of the moon, from dwelling on Śiva's head." Cited in J. Gonda, *Viṣṇuism and Śivaism: A Comparison* (London, 1970), p. 121.

72. S. Gupta, K. J. Hoens, and T. Goudriaan, *Hindu Tantrism* (Leiden, 1979), p. 62. citing *Vijñānabhairava Tantra*, 65 and *Netratantra*, 7.49.

73. M. Eliade, *Yoga: Immortality and Freedom* (Princeton, 1969) p. 131, citing the *Yogatattva Upaniṣad.*

74. *Śiva Saṃhitā* 5.109-10, cited in S. Ghose, *The Original Yoga as Expounded in the Śiva Saṃhitā, Gheraṇḍa Saṃhitā and Patañjali Yogasūtras* (Delhi, 1980), p. 91.

75. Dhaky, "Ākāśaliṅga", fig. 3.

76. See note 53.

77. In this, the Mukteśvara's *candraśālās* bear a great conceptual affinity, and are striking visual analogies as well, to images of apotheosis from the Greco-Roman and Byzantine traditions (which themselves have roots in Ancient Near Eastern and Egyptian art). See H. P. L'Orange, *Studies on the Iconography of Cosmic Kingship in the Ancient World* (New Rochelle, New York, 1982), especially p. 97 and figs. 69, 72, 73, 89.

78. G. Michell, *The Hindu Temple: An Introduction to its Meaning and Forms* (New York, 1977), fig. 17. J. M. Somasundaram Pillai, *The Great Temple at Tanjore* (Tanjore, 1958), p. 107, however, identifies this images as "Chandeśanugrahamūrti . . . a form assumed by Śiva to confer blessings on His fervent devotee Chandeśa."

79. K. C. Panigrahi, *Chronology of the Bhauma-karas and the Somavaṃśī of Orissa* (Madras, n.d., 1961?), p. 17.

80. B. K. Śarmā, *The History of Somavaṃśī Rule in Orissa* (Calcutta, 1983), pp. 9-16. Śarmā's chronology, while bases on a more critical assessment of various records than Panigarhi's—particularly those of dynasties like the Kalacuris and Colas, with whom the Somavaṃśīs were in conflict—fails to relate the probable beginning of the previous Bhauma-kara dynasty (736 A.D.) to her chronological sequence (Śarmā, *ibid.*, p. 15), which would give the Somavaṃśī dynasty an earlier beginning than she allows.

81. N. K. Sahu, "History of Kosala and the Somavaṃśīs of Utkala", OHRJ 3.8 (1954), pp. 127-32; HCIP, Vol. 3, pp. 220-22; Panigrahi, *Chronology*, p. 9; K. C. Panigrahi, *History of Orissa* (Cuttack, 1981), pp. 96-97; Śarmā, *Somavaṃśī Rule*, p. 70.

82. ARB, pp. 159-61.

83. Panigrahi, *Chronology*, p. 17; Śarmā *Somavaṃśī Rule*, p. 16.

84. The earliest period of temple-building activity.

85. Kulke, "Royal Temple Policy", p. 133.

86. *Ibid.*, p. 135.

87. See Panigrahi, *Chronological*, pp. 7, 9, 22, 27, 30; and B. Das, *The Bhauma-karas: Buddhist Kings of Orissa and Their Times* (Bhubaneswar, 1978), pp. 81-82, 192-93.

88. See M. Sarabhai, *Longing for the Beloved: Songs to Shiva Nataraja in Bharata Natyam* (Ahmedabad, 1976), p. 30.

89. Poem by Khestragna, quoted in M. Sarabhai, *The Eight Nayikas* (New York, 1965), p. 30.

90. G.C.O. Hass, trans., *The Daśarūpa: A Treatise on Hindu Dramaturgy* (New York, 1965), p. 54 (2.38).

91. See above, Chapter 3, note 8.

92. See pp. 165ff.

93. C. R. Devadhar and N. G. Suria, ed. and trans., *The Abhijñānaśākuntalam of Kālidāsa* (Delhi, 1934), 7.12.

94. B. S. Miller, *Bhartrihari: Poems* (New York, 1967), p. xviii.

95. See above, Chapter 2, p. 27.

96. See Zimmer, *Myths and Symbols*, p. 152; and Kramrisch, *Presence of Śiva*, p. 440. See also A. K. Anandakumaraswamy (sic), "The Dance of Śiva", reprinted in T.A.G. Rao, *The Development of Hindu Iconography* (1914. Reprint New Delhi, 1968), vol. 2, part 1 p. 239, quoting the *Unmai Vilakkam* (v. 36), "creation arises from the drum (of Śiva)...", and the *Chidambara Mummani Kovai* (no verse no. given), "O my Lord, they hand holding the sacred drum has made and ordered the heavens and earth and other worlds and innumerable souls..."

97. Anand Swarup Gupta, ed., various trans. *Kūrma Purāṇa* (Varanasi, 1972), 2.4.22 (p. 306).

98. *Ibid.*, 2.5 (pp. 309-10).

99. W. Smith, The Ceiling of the Mukteśvara Temple in Bhubaneswar", AA 15.1 (1984), pp. 73-95.

100. For discussions of celestial symbolism in ceiling imagery see the seminal studies of K. Lehman, "The Dome of Heaven", *Art Bulletin*, 27.4 (1945), pp. 1-27; and A. Soper, "The Dome of Heaven in Asia", *Art Bulletin*, 29.4 (1947), pp. 225-48.

101. For the dating of the texts under discussion I rely on the opinions expressed in Gupta, *et al.*, *Hindu Tantrism*, and J. Gonda, *Medieval Religious Literature in Sanskrit* (Wiesbaden, 1977).

102. This identification was first made by K. C. Panigrahi, ARB, p. 92. He does not discuss, however, how the identification was arrived at.

103. *Śiva Purāṇa*, ed., J. L. Shastri, trans., "A Board of Scholars", Ancient Indian Tradition and Mythology (Delhi, 1970), 2.3.22-28 (pp. 554-89); *Skanda Purāṇa*, 5.2.55.1-5, 1.1.22.38-40, cited in W. D. O'Flaherty, *Śiva, The Erotic Ascetic* (London 1981), p. 153; *Matsya Purāṇa*, trans., a Taluqdar of Oudh (1916-17, 2nd ed., reprint New Delhi, 1980), 154-57 (pp. 94-111).

104. See *Skanda Purāṇa*, 1.2.27.58-73a, 74-84; 1.2.28.1-4; 1.2.29.1-69a, 726-81; trans. in O'Flaherty, *Hindu Myths*, pp. 252-61. See also *Śiva Purāṇa*, 7.1.24.26 (pp. 1857-65), *Vāmana Purāṇa*, trans., S. M. Mukhopadhyaya (Varanasi, 1968), 28 (pp. 321ff.).

105. *Vāmana Purāṇa*. 28.12-13 (p. 321ff.).

106. See note 104 for references. In the *Matsya Purāṇa*, Pārvatī is told of her success by the Seven Sages. According to O'Flaherty (*Erotic Ascetic*, p. 153), Brahmā is forced to grant Śiva hand to Pārvatī in marriage. In the *Śiva Purāṇa* (2.3.28, p. 584), Śiva appears to the Goddess and tells her with great devotion that they will marry.

107. See note 105, especially the *Skanda Purāṇa* sections translated by O'Flaherty, *Hindu Myths*, pp. 252-61.

108. See *Śiva Purāṇa*, 2.4.1.44-63; 2.4.2.1-73 (O'Flaherty, *Hindu Myths*, pp. 161-68; Shastri ed., pp. 714-22).

109. A. K. Coomaraswamy and G. K. Dugsirals, *The Mirror of Gesture, Being the Abhinaya Darpaṇa of Nandikeśvara* (Cambridge, Mass., 1917), p. 39; M. Ghosh, trans., *Abhinaya Darpaṇa* (Calcutta, 1957), p. 178.

110. *Liṅga Purāṇa*, 1.105.11, trans. in S. Kramrisch, *Manifestations of Shiva* (Philadelphia, 1981), p. 74. See also *Liṅga Purāṇa* (Shastri ed.), p. 577.

111. P. Pal, *The Sensuous Immortals* (Los Angeles, 1977), fig. 56; D. N. Patnaik, *Odissi Dance* (Bhubaneswar, 1971), p. 15, fig. 1-4.

112. For depictions of the Seven Mothers with Gaṇeśa and Vīrabhadra see Rao, *Hindu Iconography*, vol. 1, part 2, pl. 119; Pal, *Sensuous Immoratals*, p. 65, Kramrisch, *Manifestations of Shiva*, fig. 56. For Orissan images of the individual Mothers see J. N. Banerjea, *The Development of Hindu*

Iconography, 2nd ed. (Calcutta, 1956), pl. 43, figs. 1, 3, 5; pl. 44, figs.1-5.

113. See V. S. Agrawala, trans., *Devī Māhātmya* (Varanasi,1963), 8.11-20 (pp. 105-06). The Mothers are described in various other texts where although the particular story line is different from that in the *Devī Māhātmya*, they are still portrayed as blood-thirsty demon slayers. For a survey of texts in which these stories occur see K. A. Harper, "An Iconological Study on the Origins and Development of the Saptamātṛkās" Ph.D. thesis, University of California, Los Angeles, pp. 270-73.

114. For discussions of female heptads see Harper, "Saptamātṛkās"; and S. Kramrisch, "The Indian Great Goddess", *History of Religions*, 14.4 (May, 1975),pp. 235-65 (especially pp. 262-63); and J. N. Banerjea, *Purāṇic and Tāntric Religion* (Calcutta, 1966), pp. 116-17, 125.

115. For various accounts of the role of the Kṛttikās in the birth of Skanda see P. C. Roy, trans., *The Mahābhārata* (Calcutta, 1927-32), 9.44-46 (vol.7, pp.130-43), *Śiva Purāṇa*, 2.4.1.49-63, 2.4.2.1-73 (O'Flaherty, *Hindu Myths*, pp. 161-69, Shastri ed., pp. 714-21).

116. See line drawing in V. S. Agrawala, *Indian Art* (Varanasi, 1965), fig. 184.

117. In the *Kūrma Purāṇa*, Vīrabhadra is generated by Śiva at the time of the destruction of Dakṣa's sacrifice. In this text he is described as horrific in appearance (Rao, *Hindu Iconography*, vol. 2, part 1, pp. 182-83). In the *Devī Bhāgavata Purāṇa* (7.30), Vīrabhadra is engendered by Śiva, along with the army of Bhadrakālī (O'Flaherty, *Hindu Myths*, p. 251). In the *Matsya Purāṇa*, Vīrabhadra, described as "covered with buckskin, clean in person . . . wearing the wreath of stone heads, with handsome form", becomes the adopted son of Pārvatī (Taluqdar of Oudh trans., 154.550ff. (pp. 105-06). For an iconographical description of Vīrabhadra as an attendant of the Seven Mothers conforming to the standard representations see Banerjea, *Hindu Iconography*, p. 505 (citing the *Rupamaṇḍana*).

118. See above, notes 2 and 3.

119. See D. Snellgrove, *The Hevajra Tantra: A Critical Study* (London, 1959), p. 39. The *Hevajra Tantra* probably dates "in its present form", to the late 8th century (*ibid.*, p. 14).

120. V. Mani, *Purāṇic Encyclopaedia* (New Delhi, 1975), p. 432, citing *Mahābhārata*, 3.236.11, I have, however, been unable to locate this citation, either in V. S. Sukthankar, ed., *The Mahābhārata* (Poona, 1942), or in Roy's translation.

121. See M. A. Dhaky, "The Genesis and Development of Maru-Gurjara Temple Architecture", in P. Chandra, ed., *Studies in Indian Temple Architecture* (Varanasi, 1975), p. 138. See also HCIP (Bombay, 1955), vol. 4, pp. 339, 343.

122. Kramrisch, "Great Goddess", p. 262 (citing *Mahābhārata* 3.219.25-40), See also Van Buitenen, *Mahābhārata*, vol. 3, p. 658.

123. HCIP, p. 343.

124. Kramrisch, "Great Goddess", p. 262.

125. That the planets usually were conceived as male does not necessarily repudiate these views. Other transformations of the identities of celestial bodies can be seen in Indian literature, for example in *Mahābhārata*, 1.60.13-16 (Van Buitenen trans., vol. 1, p.148), where the twenty-seven constellations, or lunar mansions (the groups of stars through which the moon passes in its route across the heavens) are conceived as all female; "twenty-seven wives are known in the world to be the moon's these faithful wives of the moon are appointed to the precession of time. They are the fairies of the lunar mansions, which regulate the life of the world."

126. H. Brunner, "Analyse du Kiraṇāgama", *Journal Asiatique*, 253 (1965), pp. 315-16 (citing *paṭala* 4).

127. Brunner, "Kiraṇāgama", p. 316.

128. See P. K. Agrawala, "The Early Indian Mother-Goddess Votive Discs", *East and West*, 29.1-4 (Dec. 1979), figs. 24 25, 32-36.

129. For images of the Goddess as lotus see D. Desai, *Erotic Sculpture of India* (New Delhi, 1975) fig. 114; C. Radcliffe, "Early Chalukya Sculpture", Ph.D. thesis, New York University, 1981, figs. 152, 606.

130. Faces within *gavākṣa* motifs, while often anonymous, frequently bear identifiable iconographical traits. See Thomas Donaldson, "Development of the *Vajra-Mastaka* on Orissan Temples", *East and West*, 26.3-4 (Sept.-Dec. 1976) figs. 3, 5, 15, 20. On the *candraśālā* (*Vajra-mastaka*) on the north side of the Mukteśvara's *śikhara*, the lotus has placed before it an image of Śiva dancing.

131. For example see Phillip Rawson, *The Art of Tantra*, revised ed. (London, 1978), figs. 65, 78, 153, 154, 156.

132. For illustrations of *maṇḍalas* composed of *mantras* see Rawson, *ibid.*, fig. 50; and Alain Danielou, *Hindu Polytheism* (London, 1964), p. 387.

133. Gupta, *et al., Hindu Tantrism*, p. 93.

134. *Ibid.*, p. 93.

135. *Ibid.*, p. 94, citing the *Mahānirvāṇa Tantra*. While this text is usually considered to be quite late (17th century), Agehananda Bharati *The Tantric Tradition* (London, 1965), considers it one of the oldest Tantras, dating to the 11th century at the latest (pp. 66, 171).

136. Brunner, "Kiraṇāgama", p. 318, citing *paṭala* 11. See also Gonda, *Medieval Religious Literature*, pp. 186-87.

137. Gupta, *et al., Hindu Tantrism*, p. 127, citing the *Kubjikāmata Tantra*.

138. *Ibid.*, p. 65, citing *Svaccanda Tantra*, 1.33ff., and *Kubjikāmata Tantra*, 24. Also, J. Singh, trans., *Śiva Sūtras: The Yoga of Supreme Identity* (Delhi, 1979), p. 25-27 (*śūtra* 4). In his note (p. 27), the translator describes the presiding deities over the various classes of letters as Yogīśvarī (or Māhālakṣmī), Brāhmī, Maheśvarī, Kaumārī, Vaiṣṇavī, Vārāhī, Indrāṇī and Cāmuṇḍā.

139. Brunner, "Kiraṇāgama", p. 326, citing *paṭala* 7.4.

140. See above note 96.

141. Pt. M. K. Shastri, ed., *Mālinīvijayottara Tantram* (Srinagar, 1922), 8.96. The names of the goddess here are Indrāṇī, Agneyī, Nairitī, Kauverī, Yamī, Iśānī, Vāruṇāṇi. It is interesting that the Vaiṣṇā goddesses in the more standard list of Sapta Mātṛkās (Vārāhī, Vaiṣṇavī) are omitted in this Tantric Śaivite text. That many of the texts cited here originate in Kashmir does not preclude their relevance to the Mukteśvara's sculptures. According to G. C. Tripathi, the *Śāradātilaka* of Lakṣmaṇa Deśika, written in Kashmir in the 11th century was immensely influential in Bengal and Orissa, as evidenced by the numerous manuscripts of the text found in Orissa, as well as by its frequent quotation in Orissan texts. See G. C. Tripathi, "On the Concept of Puruṣottama in the Agamas", CJRTO, p. 42.

142. Gupta, *et al.*, Hindu Tantrism, p. 59, citing Abhinavagupta's *Dehasthadevatā Cakra Stotra* (3ff.), "The *indriya devīs* (eight Mothers) are located in a circular formation in the heart lotus (*anandakonda*), around the supreme pair of Ānandabhairava and his spouse (Ānandabhairavī). The Mothers worship the couple with the objects of the sense as their offerings." A description of the Mothers being worshipped in a *maṇḍala* or circle is seen also in the *Bṛhat Saṁhitā* (cited by D. C. Sircar, *Studies in the Religious Life of Ancient and Medieval India* (New Delhi, 1971), p. 99. The text refers to *matṛ-maṇḍala vidaḥ*", or *maṇḍala-krama-vidaḥ*, "those who know fully the circle of Mothers". The other reading, accepted by Utpala, explains *maṇḍala-karma as pūjā-krama*, i.e.

maṇḍala-pūjā-karma (traditional rules regarding the worship of the *maṇḍala*). There is a Jain text that is also of interest for its descriptions of a *mātṛkā-maṇḍala*, although its meaning and use are quite different from what we have discussed above. The *Jvalini Kalpa 4 describes a maṇḍala* of eight petals, containing images of Brahmāṇī, Maheśvarī, *et al.*, with an image of goblin in the center. This diagram is used in "ritual meant to bring about harm to an enemy." See R. N. Nandi, *Religious* Institutions and Cults in the Deccan (New Delhi, 1973), p. 131. The same text again invokes the Mothers in a rite "by which a person is hypnotized and brought under control" (*ibid.*, p. 131).

CHAPTER 5

THE PLACE OF THE MUKTEŚVARA IN THE DEVELOPMENT OF THE ORISSAN TEMPLE

Regarding its visual form, the Mutkeśvara temple is often described as being innovative: while having its basis in earlier stages of formal development (exemplified by the Paraśurāmeśvara temple, ca. 650), it makes many departures from earlier forms. Further, these innovative aspects provide the foundation for formal changes in later temples. Of primary importance in the Mukteśvara's approach to form is a new emphasis on verticality. This changing emphasis can be seen in comparing the Mukteśvara with the Paraśurāmeśvara temple, datable through inscription to about the mid-seventh century (figs. 148-150). The wall surface of the earlier temple consists of two differentiated sections, the lower walls and the *śikhara*. On the lower walls, two flanking niches rest upon mouldings which provide them with a horizontal base, a firmly grounded foundation. The mouldings are interrupted by an opening at the base of the central vertical projection, which makes room for an image within a niche. The two smaller niches are framed by architectural forms—pilasters and *gavākṣa*-capping elements, which transform them into miniature shrines, these being superimposed against a flat wall. The horizontal *kaṇṭha* division marks a clear boundary between the lower walls and *śikhara*, the latter being treated in a totally different way. It is divided into a series of vertically arranged courses, three on either side of the rather boldly projecting *bhadra*. While vertically organized, these mouldings have the form of horizontally placed rectangles, creating a pattern of shadows across the *śikhara*.[1] Hence, in spite of the vertical arrangement and curved outlines of the *śikhara*, a sense of horizontality pervades, and checks or modifies the vertical arrangement and the velocity of the tower's ascent. The first note of horizontality however, is struck by strong differentiation between the treatment of lower and upper walls, with the central *bhadra* being the only continuously vertical element (and it too consists of horizontally piled mouldings).

The *prāsāda* of the Mukteśvara likewise has strong, outwardly projecting *bhadras*, but to a much greater degree than the Paraśurāmeśvara. Indeed, all of its vertical wall elements (except for the *pratikarṇas*), project strongly from the wall. These vertical elements are continuous, from the foot of the temple, all the way to the summit. Each *ratha* is an alignment of several vertical elements. At ground level are a series of base mouldings, each conforming in width to its corresponding *ratha*. The side niches—like those of the Paraśurāmeśvara, taking the form of a miniature shrine, each have two base mouldings—which serve as the bases of pedestals for the pilasters of the shrine element. The central *bhadra*—the most complex of all the vertical elements—has five base mouldings, again, each corresponding to the element that rises above it. Unlike the Paraśurāmeśvara, with its strong differentiation between lower walls and *śikhara*, the *rathas* of the Mukteśvara rise in strict vertical unity. The horizontal *kaṇṭha* only briefly interrupts the vertical ascent. Just below the *kaṇṭha*, a hoof-shaped *khura*-moulding caps each *karṇa* and *pratikarṇa*, providing the first note for the series of *kumbha* mouldings that rise in a rhythmical sequence alternating with other elements—*gavākṣas* and *bhūmi-āmalakas*—cohesive consistency is put forth in that the motifs repeated on the *karṇas* of the *śikhara* begin on the upper levels of the lower walls. This is also true of the *pratikarṇas*—rising above the *nāga*-pilasters are the sculpted modules (girl at her door surmounted by *gavākṣas*, fig. 96), that are continuously repeated on this portion of the *śikhara*. Vertical continuity is most adamantly expressed, however, by the long net of *gavākṣa* interlace, beginning as a decorative overlay on the capping element of the *pratibhadra's* niches, continuing to the top of the *śikhara*. The *gavākṣa*-nets eliminate any sense of the horizontal patterning so strong on the Paraśurāmeśvara. This emphasis on upward rising, vertically oriented decorative elements, along with a certain elongation of from, gives the Mukteśvara a greater sense of soaring, upward movement, less encumbered by sheer mass.[2]

Another way in which the Mukteśvara differs from the Paraśurāmeśvara is in the more rounded treatment of the wall surface. A contributing factor to this is the high relief treatment of the *rathas*, but also, the corner elements are given a stepped articulation that rounds the corners and breaks down the sense of four separate "walls"—those of the more cubic Paraśurāmeśvara meet at sharp angles.[3]

Regarding figurative sculpture, the images on the Paraśurāmeśvara adhere to the wall surface, and are composed so that poses and arrangements of limbs conform to the outlines of the frame—the figure is part of a whole network of patternization (fig. 149). On the Mukteśvara, figurative sculpture projects strongly from the wall surface. The *śālabhañjikās* of the lower walls are very lightly attached to the panels of scroll work behind them, which serve as backdrops, rather than as frames. Even on the Mukteśvara's *kaṇṭhas* and surrounding areas (figs. 121-126), the figures seem to be moving on a stage, rather than being compartmentalized within a cubic module.

In the following pages, I will attempt to analyse the development of architectural and sculptural form as seen in the Mukteśvara. This will be done primarily through visual analysis, since only two of the temples to be discussed bear datable inscriptions, the Paraśurāmeśvara, and the Brahmeśvara.[4] I hope to clearly show that it does indeed present a developmental mid-point within the Orissan tradition, and further, that integral to its form is the inspiration of various elements from outside the Orissan tradition, specifically, from western and central India. This incorporation may have come about through direct contact with artisans trained in these traditions. Their appearance may be partly accounted for too in terms of a gradual intrusion of these elements via such disparate places as western Orissa (temples at Baidyanath and Charda) and Mukhaliṅgam, in the ancient region of Kaliṅga.[5] I will also discuss ways in which the Mukteśvara provides a basis for later developments and formal experiments, thus showing its role in the development of the fully mature Orissan temple form as exemplified in the Liṅgarāja temple.

ANTECEDENTS

VAITĀL DEUL, BHUBANESWAR, C.A. 800-25

The Vaitāl Deul constitutes a transitional point between the Paraśurāmeśvara and Mukteśvara temples.[6] The south and north, or narrow sides of the rectangular *prāsāda* are each divided into three major *rathas*. The tripartite *bhadra* houses an image of a goddess, flanked by *mithunas*. This ensemble is in turn surmounted by an elaborate *candraśālā* (fig. 152). The base mouldings are simply but forcefully articulated. The area below the central figure is recessed inward and the wall marked only by a few narrow horizontal profiles. Below the couples, however, the elaborate mouldings which begin to suggest those typically found on later temples. The bottom-most element, the *khura*, is low and squat, as are all the elements of the moulding. The corner mouldings meet with those on the walls perpendicular to them, and because of this are given a central part which advances slightly from the surface. This gives the corner mouldings a greater sculptural complexity than those on the recessed parts of the wall, and again foreshadows the rhythmic outlines of later temple mouldings.

The *karṇas* of the *śikhara* are make up of several layers of horizontal courses, which are divided by two *bhūmi-āmalakas* (flat myrobalan-form stones, repetitions of those at the summit of the temple). These courses are articulated in a way similar to the bottom-most portions of the corner base mouldings, advancing at the centre, and in plan would resemble a square, truncated cross. The underside of the course is carved in a three-leveled step pattern, each successive level being more deeply carved, until the last one is nearly level with the flat wall surface. These horizontal incisions into these piled up courses form an ascending linear pattern, while creating deep shadows which make the *karṇas* seem to advance greatly from the wall surface.

The three vertical wall divisions—defined by groups of sculptures on the lower wall, and by the *candraśālās* and piled up stone courses at the *karṇas*—mark an early phase in the development of the Orissan temple where each of these divisions will soar uninterruptedly to the summit of the temple, creating an effect of towering verticality. Such a smooth, uninterrupted outline is not attained in the Vaitāl Deul, in that the entire *jaṅghā* (lower wall) is actully recessed. Further, the niche figures are not on the same vertical plane as the base mouldings and *śikhara*, but are set back into the wall, breaking the vertical rhythm of base moulding, wall and superstructure. Furthermore, the superstructure does not have a smooth, vertical contour. The Spaces between its courses a *staccato* play, precluding any sense of a smooth contour making a vertical ascent.

It is evident, though, from the horizontal courses of the *śikhara*, the conception of the base mouldings and their vertical alignment with the wall images and the salients of the *śikhara,* that some of the elements of the style typified by the Mukteśvara have already been formulated in the Vaitāl Deul.

The sculpture of the Vaitāl Deul can also be seee as an intermediary between the geometric angularity of the Paraśurāmeśvara's sculpture, and the greater three-dimensionality aad heightened naturalism of that of the Mukteśvara. On the Vaitāl Deul (as on the Paraśurāmeśvara), figures are invariably placed within frames, with their poses adapted to the latter's rectangular outlines. The figure of a woman adorning herself while holding a mirror (fig. 153), for example, stands in a slight *tribhanga* pose. Her right leg is a stiff diagonal, with the foot pushed flush against the corner of the frame. The left leg, while also at a diagonal, is bent at the knee in a ninety degree angle, thus echoing the edge of the frame. The left arm, raised above the head also forms a sharp angle, enclosing the head almost like a second, inner frame. This overall compositional conception is very much akin to what is seen on the Paraśurāmeśvara (fig. 149), where the limbs of the seated Śiva and Pārvatī are compactly arranged as an angular geometric pattern. Yet the sculpture of the Vaitāl Deul, while adhering to the patternization of the archaic mode, advances toward naturalism as well. The proportions of the figures are more normative, less heavy and squat than those of the Paraśurāmeśvara (the niches themselves have become taller and narrower, compare figs. 148, 152). Also, the figures seem more three-dimensional, appearing to relate to the niche as an actual space, rather than a plane against which it is superimposed. A greater fleshiness comes through in the softer modeling of the torso, this being conveyed further by the pressure of the belt against the waist. The reaction of flesh to clothing and ornament, then, is being treated more realistically, in contrast to the Paraśurāmeśvara, where belts and other ornaments appear layered against the surface of the body, rather than reacting with them. The faces of the Vaitāl figures have the long, squarish proportions of those on the Paraśurāmeśvara. However, the hard, planar carving and somewhat frozen, mask-like visages of the earlier temple (fig. 145) give way to a somewhat softer, more fleshy treatment.

The abstracted means of presenting figurative sculpture on the Paraśurāmeśvara is logically consistent with the cubic planarity of the temple itself. And likewise, the more fluid, open arrangement of the Vaitāl Deul is reflected in the geometrically tempered realism of its sculpture.

An additional degree of formal complexity is seen in another female figure from the Vaitāl Deul (fig. 154). The twisted pose of this figure presents multiple viewpoints, with a combination of rear and frontal views of the torso, which conveys an impression of the figure twisting and moving within space. This type of pose can be seen in central Indian sculpture, for example at Khajuraho, and one is tempted to speculate that the Orissan artist had some knowledge of or contact with the art of regions further west. (We will see further evidence of central Indian influence in the temples of Baidyanath and Charda, in western Orissa.)

KUTAI TUṆḌI TEMPLE, KHICHING, ca. 825-50

The Kutai Tuṇḍi temple (fig. 155) bears a general resemblance to the Paraśurāmeśvara.[7] The side niches are similarly placed upon slightly outward projecting horizontal base mouldings, and are pressed almost flush against the flat, undecorated wall. Also, what remains of the side niches' crowning elements resembles those of the Paraśurāmeśvara, consisting of two superimposed *gavākṣa* motifs. The little sculpture that survives here is conservative in style, relating more to the compartmentalizing of the Paraśurāmeśvara than to the more spatially conceived imagery on the Vaitāl Deul.

Critical in dating this temple later than the Paraśurāmeśvara is the occurrence of four-part base mouldings below the *bhadra* niche, predecessors of those on the Mukteśvara temple. Their shapes lack the mature elegance and refinement of those on the Mukteśvara; the *kumbha* particularly is rather squat in its proportions.

The base mouldings of the *pratibhadras* of the both the Paraśurāmeśvara and the Kutai Tuṇḍi, even though they support a niche framed with pilasters, are not conceived as pillar bases, but as long running horizontals. The Kutai Tuṇḍi demonstrates a new conception in its *bhadra* however, where base mouldings relate in a more architecturally logical way to the vertical elements above them, and seems to be a further development of the idea presented in the *bhadra* niches on the Vaitāl Deul. This contrasts with the Paraśurāmeśvara's *bhadra* niche, where the base mouldings form a support structure, not by being rounded into *kumbha* and *khura* shapes, but simply by being cut abruptly on a vertical line to allow for the space of the niche.

Another advanced aspect of the base mouldings of the Kutai Tuṇḍi's *bhadra* is the way in which the four-part constructions have two repeated profiles emerging from the inner sides of the basic form. This creates an inward moving linear rhythm that also gives a sense of depth to the niche space. This penetration of mass through linear repetition foretells one of the most dynamic features of Orissan temples from the tenth century.[8]

SIṀHANĀTHA TEMPLE, BARAMBA, ca. 850-75

In its broad outlines, the *prāsāda* of the Siṁhanātha (figs. 156, 157) resembles the Paraśurāmeśvara and Kutai Tuṇḍi temples. An initial glance at the *śikhara*—with its horizontal *bhūmi* divisions and vertical arrangement into five broad *rathas*, suggests a date close to the Paraśurāmeśvara's. The *jaṅghā* (lower wall), however, betrays a sense of experimentation departing quite radically from the archaic prototype. The *jaṅghā* has seven vertical divisions, the central, projecting *bhadra* is flanked symmetrically by *pratibhadras*, which in turn are flanked by thin pilasters.

The conception of wall projections as pilasters, composed of base, shaft, and capital, as seen on the Vaitāl Deul and implied at Khiching, are further developed here. Each pilaster element surmounts base mouldings of the four-part variety seen on the Kutai Tuṇḍi. The pilaster shafts are flat and ribbon-like. True pilasters are also seen on the central *bhadra*, flanking its niche, although the base mouldings are not of the *kumbha-khura* type, instead consisting of a series of five squarish mouldings.

The *pratibhadra* pilasters mark a major change in the treatment of the lower walls of Orissan temples. In earlier monuments, the vertical elements flanking the central *bhadra* are superimposed upon a flat background, like elaborately framed pictures against a wall. At the Siṁhanātha the wall space is "filled in", resulting in the decorative elements of the wall surface being more closely knit. The *jaṅghā* can now begin to be likened to a tightly woven fabric, the vertically placed decorative textures moving continuously across the wall, anticipating the wall treatment of the Mukteśvara temple.

Two completely new architectural elements also anticipate forms to be seen on the Mukteśvara. Above each *partibhadra* niche are not the double *gavākṣas* of the Paraśurāmeśvara and Kutai Tuṇḍi, but a series of highly articulated horizontal mouldings, which though relatively flat, are conceived as miniature *śikharas*. Below the central *bhadra* niche is an outward projecting base. On earlier emples this area was empty, the niche image resting upon a narrow sill. The base element here takes the role of a pedestal, calling attention not only to the image,[9] but to the entire *bhadra*, which now acquires sharper focus as the wall's literal and compositional center.

SOMEŚVARA TEMPLE, MUKHALIṄGAM, C.A. 900

The Someśvara temple at Mukhaliṅgam, Andhra Pradesh, like the two temples previously discussed, utilizes various elements that will be fully developed on the Mukteśvara temple (figs, 158, 159).[10] It is evident from earlier periods that a kind of dialogue has been long standing between Orissa and the Andhra area, and this is clearer still when the Someśvara temple is examined in relation to the Mukteśvara.

The base mouldings of the side niches are made up of four parts. The *khura* and *kumbha* are connected by a stylized vertical leaf to the double *kapotāli*, consisting of two squat, oblong mouldings. It is this type of base moulding that becomes standardized on later Orissan temples. Their formative character is evident, however, when compared to the same elements on the Tīrtheśvara and Mukteśvara temples at Bhubaneswar (figs. 94 and 166). At Bhubaneswar, the *kumbha* has become narrower at the bottom, swelling upward and increasing in volume much more gradually than that of the Someśvara. Moreover, the treatment of all the base mouldings of the Someśvara is not alike. The *bhadra* niches exhibit an archaic form of moulding, showing that the four and five-part mouldings typical of later temples had still not yet been standardized or even fully developed. The more advanced base mouldings at the corners (fig. 159) create a rhythmic sequence of line and mass only partly realized on the Vaitāl Deul and Siṁhanātha temple. This is created by the convergence of the mouldings on the perpendicular sides of the wall. The mouldings on the walls' inner parts have profiles emerging from behind on either side, creating a sense of expanding form. On the corner mouldings, these emerging profiles are repeated twice, and when they converge with those of the moulding around the corner, a total of five expanding contours result. A linear pattern is generated by this repetition of contoured forms, which in conjunction with the spaces between them, tremendously animates the corner profile of the wall, blurring the very sense of a corner at all—the walls blend into each other, rather than meeting at an angle. This recession and converging of planes is repeated upon the walls above the mouldings and upon the *śikhara*, here contributing to a more rounded appearance. Again the Vaitāl Deul must be referred to, where the corners meet at angles and each wall retains its integrity as a "façade".

The three niches on each face of the Someśvara resemble those on the earlier temples in that the three framed niches are recessed. Standing upon the topmost part of the base mouldings, the flanking scroll panels do not fit squarely onto them—they do not "grow" directly from the mouldings in the way that pilasters would, but are pushed back into the wall.

A date earlier than the Mukteśvara for the Someśvara seems likely in that the latter, while using several elements in an "advanced" way, has other features that hearken back to the earlier tradition. It was built at a time when these advanced elements had not yet been standardized. This standardization occurs, however, around the middle of the tenth century. The next group of temples to be discussed shows how these elements become crystalized, while still being adapted to individual temple designs.

THE "SOMAVAṂŚĪ STYLE"

KOŚALEŚVARA TEMPLE, BAIDYANATH; KAPILEŚVARA TEMPLE, CHARDA, CA. EARLY TENTH CENTURY

Two very imperfectly preserved temples in Bolangir district, western Orissa, show strong indications of the incorporation of central Indian architectural elements. The Kośaleśvara temple at Baidyanath (figs. 160 and 161) has a *maṇḍapa* with outwardly projecting porches and inside, four columns and a raised central floor area. The closest parallels, as D. R. Das suggests, come from Khajuraho. Also distinctly central Indian is the high relief carving of human figures on the columns. Again, many central and westen Indian analogies can be made (for example, the *apsarasa* on the Ghateśvara temple, Badoli, Rajasthan).[11] Compared even with the figures on the Vaitāl Deul, those at Baidyanath seem to step out from the supporting ground, while the Vaitāl Deul figures, however plastically modeled and three-dimensionally conceived, still are bound within, and their contours and poses defined by their frames. The figures have a sense of quiet, contained energy. They are poised, alert, but not tense. Their facial treatment departs (or is of a different tradition than) the mask-like visages of the Paraśurāmeśvara and Vaitāl Deul, with their sharply contoured features. One is tempted to see vestiges of the Gupta style here and indeed echos of Gupta sculpture are seen in some of the facial expressions of figures on the Mukteśvara temple.

The Kośaleśvara's porch element does not carry over to eastern Orissa. It is, however, strong testimony to the fact that central and western Indian elements were making their way into Orissa. Another temple in Bolangir district showing this is the heavily restored and remodeled Kapileśvara temple at Charda (fig. 162). One of the most striking central Indian elements, particularly in relation to what we will see on the Mukteśvara, is the interlace of *gavākṣa* motifs on the *pratibhadras* and *bhadras* of the *śikhara*. Interesting too, in relation to the Mukteśvara is the treatment of base mouldings and the niche elements they support. These do not relate to central India and can be seen in terms of the development in Orissa of four-part base mouldings consisting of *khura*, *kumbha*, and double-*kapotāli*. At Charda these approach the forms seen on the Mukteśvara. The *kumbha* form now has the graceful, upward swelling curve that was lacking at Khiching, Mukhaliṅgam and Baramba. Yet it can reasonably be stated that the Charda temple pre-dates the Mukteśvara in that various aspect of its wall treatment, for example the proliferation of pilasters and the treatment of the large *candraśālā*,[12] lack the formal elaboration of the Mukteśvara. It could be suggested from this that artisans in western Orissa, working within the developing Orissan style and also familiar with architectural forms from further west, made their way to coastal Orissa by the mid-tenth century. Intriguing also is that the Somavaṃśī dynasty has its origins in western Orissa, and during the early tenth century was still based there, not making significant political gains on the coast until the mid-tenth century. Possibly then, we have at Baidyanath and Charda the beginning of what could actually be called a "Somavaṃśī'' style, characterized by an adaptation of elements from the Nāgara tradition outside of Orissa, that has its finest achievement in the Mukteśvara temple.

''TWIN" TEMPLES, GANDHARADI, ca. 950

The idea of a "Somavaṃśī style" is further suggested by the temples of Nīlakaṇṭha and Siddheśvara at Gandharadi, which, as suggested earlier, were possibly erected by the Somavaṃśīs as a proclamation of their power over regions previously ruled by the Bhañja dynasty. The formal treatment here seems indeed to carry on developments begun at Charda, and as these temples stand unaltered and relatively well preserved, they give us a clear picture of the stage in the formal development of the Orissan temple just preceding the Mukteśvara.

Though unfinished, the Siddheśvara temple (figs. 163-64) shows an advanced stage of development that can be seen in comparing it with the Siṁhanātha temple in Baramba (figs. 156, 157). There is general similarity in that the lower walls of the *prāsāda* are divided into a series of vertical sub-divisions, with a conceptual similarity seen in the treatment of *pratibhadras* with niches framed by pilasters and surmounted with a "superstructure". The proportions of the Gandharadi temple, however, have changed dramatically. The *rathas* of the lower wall have become more elongated, and this sense of attenuation continues up through the *śikhara*. Indeed, a correspondence between the *rathas* of the *jaṅghā* and *śikhara* is now strictly adhered to, making the sense of vertical, rather than horizontal piling, the dominant effect.

Also at Gandharadi, there is an emphasis on the independent nature of each *ratha*, which creates strong solid-void, light-dark rhythms. The recession of the *karṇa* rounds the edges of the walls, softening their perpendicular conjunction. This treatment continues on the superstructure, the corners of which are also rounded stone courses.

The *bhadras* of the lower wall are treated with a complexity heretofore unseen. The *bhadra* niches have two pilasters on either side. The outer ones, which extend above the projecting roof of the niche, have elaborate capping structures resembling miniatures *śikharas.* Between the pilasters and above the projecting roof of the niche is an unfinished *candraśālā*. Above this is a relief carving of a miniature shrine, the *śikhara* of which extends on to the lower levels of the actual *śikhara*. Similar miniature shrines are repeated on other parts of the temple; above the side niches of the *prāsāda* and those of the *maṇḍapa*.

The character of these motifs is highly three-dimensional, and those capping the pilasters especially extend more organically from them. The use of miniature *śikharas*, seen very conceptually as early as the Paraśurāmeśvara, is here taking a more literal form, and will culminate with the Rājarāni temple in Bhubaneswar.

Continuing at Gandharadi is the use of decorative motifs which before this time were prevalent in central and western India. On the *śikhara*, the *bhadras* and *pratibhadras* are faced with a continuous vertical pattern of interlaced *gavākṣa* motifs, as seen also at Charda. This type of *śikhara* decoration has been present in temples of the Nāgara style from all over India, not only central and western India, but also in the Deccan.[13] By the ninth and tenth centuries, these *gavākṣa* patterns become extremely delicate and refined, resembling almost a net of lace cast over the surface of the *śikhara*, for example the Sun temple at Mankheda (fig. 168). Only the bare outlines of the *gavākṣa* elements can be seen on the Gandharadi temples, the delicate carving was never completed. Has it been, it may have resembled the *śikhara* decoration on the Mukteśvara temple, where a unique Orissan variant of the *gavākṣa*-net pattern occurs.

The most advance aspect of the Gandharadi temples is the increased emphasis on tall proportions and vertical continuity between the lower wall and *śikhara*. Before seeing how this trend culminates with the Mukteśvara, however, we should look briefly at two other monuments, which while nearly contemporary with the Mukteśvara, show what can be seen as certain conservativism, specifically in regard to the use of non-Orissan forms.

TĪRTHEŚVARA TEMPLE, BHUBANESWAR, ca. 960

The Tīrtheśvara temple (figs. 165, 166) exhibits the essential characteristics seen in more refined form on the Mukteśvara temple. These characteristics include fully developed four-part base mouldings, the developed niche base and canopy, and *nāga*-pilasters as *pratikarṇas* (the vertical elements flanking the *karṇas*). Also, the elevation of the temple in general has become more refined. The *śikhara* appears tall and thin in its proportions, and a continuous outline is formed by the lower walls and superstructure. This sense of upward rising verticality is less hindered by sheer mass, as are for example the temples of Siṁhanātha at Baramba and Someśvara of Mukhaliṅgam. The lower walls, too, are lengthened in their proportions, and are faced with seven distinctly articulated salients (*rathas*).

A comparison of the lower walls of the Tīrtheśvara and Someśvara, Mukhaliṅgam (figs. 159, 165), indicates the development taking place. On the Tīrtheśvara, two wide *rathas* (the *karṇas* and the *pratibhadras* with very narrow *nāga*-pilasters between them), flank a wide *bhadra* niche. The bases of the *karṇa* and *pratibhadra* consist of a four-part base moulding similar to those on the Someśvara. Their forms and outlines, however, have become more refined. The *kumbha,* for example, is drawn in or constricted at its base, swelling gradually upward, and compared to those of the Someśvara, is more vertical, and less rounded and squat. A departure from rounded forms is also seen in the double-*kapotāli.* Its bottom half curves in a way similar to the *khura*, but is much shorter, and is superimposed by a mirror image of itself. Decorative facings of *gavākṣa* motifs and vertical leaves have been applied to the Tīrtheśvara's mouldings, serving as connecting elements for the three lower parts of the mouldings, unifying the whole composition.

The mouldings serve as foundations for a series of vertical pilasters (*rathas*). The panels of scroll work decorating these pilasters bear the same decorative motif, a small *kīrttimukha* relief at the top, which spews from its mouth strands of pearls which drop straight down, then curve away in opposite directions. This motif, repeated throughout the upper portions of all the scroll panels, is a standard decorative feature for temples contemporary to the Mukteśvara (and interestingly, is first seen at Charda).

The *rathas* of the Tīrtheśvara no longer recede into the wall, as do the image bearing panels of the earlier temples (except at Gandharadi and Charda). They are on the same vertical plane as the base mouldings, which here closely resemble the base elements of columns. These *rathas*, then, can be called "pilasters" with greater accuracy than those of earlier temples.

The *bhadra* of the Tīrtheśvara is flanked by pilasters bearing scroll work and figural reliefs, and supports an outward projecting roll cornice. Two new elements, standard in mid-tenth century temples, appear here—the projecting base serving as a support for the image (now lost), along with a similarly formed niche "canopy". This bears a certain resemblance to a miniature *śikhara*, and gives the entire niche the appearance of a small shrine within the temples's wall. The entire *bhadra* juts considerably outward, and the niche base and canopy lend a greater cohesiveness to this whole projecting element. It is this cohesive unity, and, it should be said, highly sculptural conception of the *bhadra*, seen also at Gandharadi, that is rendered with such sophisticated elaboration on the Mukteśvara.

PAÑCAYATANA VIṢṆU TEMPLE, GANESWARPUR, ca. 970

Only three of the corner shrines of this temple complex are still standing in various stages of preservation—all that remains of the main central shrine are the lower walls.[14] Built of a low grade sandstone, which contributes to an overall lack of refinement, the corner shrines (fig. 167), are miniature versions of the *prāsāda* of the Mukteśvara. The Ganeswarpur temple is the Mukteśvara's more conservative contemporary, or perhaps slightly post-dates it. It uses elements seen at Gandharadi, while also incorporating features seen on the Mukteśvara, though not in as integrated a way.

The forms of the *bhadra* niche and of the side niches are similar to those at Gandharadi, while the crowning elements of the niches are more advanced. They consist of horizontal courses decorated with scroll work and have highly articulated centers. They are crowned by *gavākṣa* motifs consisting of wide, ribbon-like bands of tracery. These crowning elements, as well as the flanking pilasters of the central niche, indicate a phenomenon that appears also on the Mukteśvara temple, that is, the *rathas* are beginning to assert a three-dimensionality. Those of the Mukteśvara always retain a rather angular, squared off character. At Ganeswarpur, however, they are more softly rounded, and foreshadow the highly articulated pilasters of the Gaurī temple in Bhubaneswar.

The *śikharas* of the Ganeswarpur shrines contain many elements that will be developed further in the Mukteśvara temple. They have *bhadras* and *pratibhadras* covered with decorative net-*gavākṣas*, and give an indication of what the Gandharadi shrines would have looked like had they been finished. The *śikharas*' subtly curving outlines are also almost identical to the Mukteśvara's, which is almost vertical up to the fourth *bhūmi-āmalaka,* from where it begins to curve in slightly. The curve of the Mukteśvara is perhaps subtler because of the *śikhara's* greater height.

MUKTEŚVARA TEMPLE, BHUBANESWAR, ca. 970

The Mukteśvara temple conceptually advances beyond the shrines of Ganeswarpur, incorporating additional eclectic elements—several of which occur only here—and experimenting further with the articulation of the wall surface.

Each individual *ratha* of the Mukteśvara (disregarding the figurative sculpture), is quite flat. This is emphasized by the scroll panels facing each *ratha* and the flattened decorative treatment of many of the upper and lower mouldings.

The *bhadra,* while proportionately larger than those of the Gandharadi temples, is also more complexly articulated. The central niche is flanked by pairs of pilasters, which are taller and more elaborately articulated than those at Gandharadi. Appearing again on the *bhadra* are the niche base and canopy, the multi-coursed elements seen in earlier forms on the Siṁhanātha temple, at Gandharadi (bases only), and on the Tīrtheśvara. The form of the Mukteśvara's niche base is closer to that of the Gandharadi temples, while the niche canopy is similar to that of the Tīrtheśvara—it is elongated by additions of several stone courses and is topped by a small *āmalaka* stone, adding to its function as a miniature *śikhara.*

On either side of the Mukteśvara's *bhadra* the wall is divided into three vertical divisions. The *karṇa* consists of a four-part *kumbha* base moulding (now fully developed), and a flat pilaster bearing a high relief female figure. Next to it is a very narrow, slightly recessed round pilaster with an intertwined *nāga* figure (*pratikarṇa*). Next, the *pratibhadra* is salient with two narrow *kumbha* base mouldings which are faced with a decorative, lace-like network of *gavākṣa* arches.

In their attention to fluctuating surfaces, contrasting patterns of light and dark, and concern with architectural rhythm and proportions, the lower walls of the Mukteśvara show what greater compositional possibilities lie within the basic design found at Gandharadi, Ganeswarpur, and at the Tīrtheśvara temple. Compared to the Mukteśvara, the treatment of these temples seems somewhat conservative.

Many of the formal advances found in the Mukteśvara have their sources in temples from central India, Rajasthan, and Gujarat. One of the most obvious eclectic elements of the Mukteśvara is the network of *Gavākṣa* motifs decorating the *bhadra* and *pratibhadras* of the *śikhara,* as well as the side niches of the lower walls of the *prāsāda* and *maṇḍapa.* The use of the *gavākṣa*-net, seen before at Charda, Gandharadi and Ganeswarpur, has precedents that have already been pointed out.[15] Comparison shows, however, that the artisans of the Mukteśvara created their own unique variant, consisting of a network of raised lines, in contrast to the central

Indian examples, where the *gavākṣa* shape is formed out of flat, ribbon-like bands.[16] The particular arrangement of the Mukteśvara's *gavākṣa* pattern is also unique, where the central arch motif is flanked by what can be called "split *gavākṣas*", two half-arches connected by a vertical line, with one side slightly higher than the other.[17] The Mukteśvara's *gavākṣas* also reflect central Indian influence in that they occur not only on the *śikhara*, but on the lower walls of the temple as well,[18] contributing to a sense of vertical continuity along the whole length of the temple.

Two other eclectic elements are the ribbed awning-like roofs and *gavākṣa*-pediments over the lattice-grilled windows of the *maṇḍapa* and above the entrance. This awning-pediment composition has a general similarity to such temples as the Nīlakaṇṭha Mahādeva at Kekind (ca. early tenth century)[19] and the Mahādeva temple at Bhumdana (ca. ninth century).[20] It resembles even more closely the *maṇḍapa* elements of the Lakṣmaṇa temple, Khajuraho (ca. 965, fig. 178), and particularly, in the way the pediment relates to the design of the *maṇḍapa* as a whole, the Śiva temple at Kotai, Gujarat (ca. 950, fig. 169).[21] This form of *gavākṣa*-pediment was continued only with distinctive variations in later Orissan temples (e.g. the Rājarāni, Brahmeśvara, and Liṅgarāja), never becoming a major Orissan motif.

The terraced pyramidal roof of the Mukteśvara's *maṇḍapa*, however, becomes standard for the forehalls of subsequent Orissan temples. While these roofs are sometimes traced to indigenous sources,[22] an outside source seems more likely. The strongest conceptual analogies for the Mukteśvara's *maṇḍapa* roof are in western India. An early stage of the development of the pyramidal roof is seen in the Gāyatrī temple at Pasnavada, Gujarat (early eighth century).[23] The receding tiers of the temple's roof, much thicker than those of later temples, are punctuated by single *gavākṣa* motifs, which are continued in smaller form in the Mukteśvara.

A temple much closer in spirit to the Mukteśvara and roughly contemporary with it, is the Śiva temple at Kotai.[24] While the overall articulation of the *rathas* is quite different, the elevations of their *maṇḍapas* have a general similarity; both have large central windows flanked by wide pilasters, covered by an awning-like roof crowned by a *gavākṣa* pediment. The *gavākṣa* motifs along the terraces of the Kotai temple's roof are much simpler than those of the eighth century Gāyatrī temple and are toned down even further in the Mukteśvara.

While certainly not a direct source, the Śiva temple at Kotai is of a general type, from which the builders of the Mukteśvara obtained several new ideas. For aside from contributing new motifs, the western Indian temple type seems also to have provided an example of how a greater sense of harmony could be obtained between the *prāsāda* and *maṇḍapa*, in part by giving greater emphasis to the latter's roof. This harmony between the two major parts, basically lacking in the temples of Gandharadi, is one of the most striking features of the Mukteśvara temple.[25]

The treatment of the Mukteśvara's *maṇḍapa* roof is not entirely satisfactory, however. We can surmise from the western India examples that the Mukteśvara's builders desired a roof rising at a gradual angle of forty-five degrees, with the top-most level being the platform for a *kalaśa* finial. To this aim, each terraced slab recedes lightly inward, and a forty-five degree angle is produced up to the seventh level. Beyond this, the slabs begin to recede too far; the angle is broken up and the contour of the roof becomes rounded. If the eighth through eleventh slabs had continued along the forty-five degree angle, at least three more levels would have been necessary, so that the top-most one would be small enough for the *kalaśa*. Had this been done, the roof would have been much too high—rising above the *śukanāsā* of the *śikhara*, and overly massive. A smooth geometric line apparently was sacrificed in order to attain pleasing proportions (approximately 1 : 2) between the roof and the *śikhara*. This same treatment of the *maṇḍapa* roof is seen on the Siddheśvara (Bhubaneswar) and Rājarāni temples, and a resolution between geometric outline and satisfying proportions is reached with the Brahmeśvara.

The Mukteśvara temple advances from its predecessors in the bold articulations of the *bhadra*, and in the fluctuating surfaces of the walls, resulting in an unprecedented complexity of pattern. It advances further in the vertical continuity of the *prāsāda's* lower and upper parts, attained through the continuation of the *gavākṣa*-net along the whole length of the *pratibhadra*. This usage was experimental and never continued. However, uninterrupted verticality will be an overriding concern in all subsequent temples.

Analogous to the forceful articulation of the *bhadras*, and indeed of the all *ratha* elements, is the sculpture of the lower walls (fig. 93). These high relief figures, extending from their pilaster-like *ratha*-supports (just as the *rathas* themselves extend from the wall of the temple), are a total departure, formally, from Orissan tradition, and like the sculptures of Charda, indicate exposure to central Indian idioms.

The Mukteśvara figures, generally standing on lotus pedestals, take poses of dance-like freedom of movement (figs. 58, 103, 112 and 119). Comparison with the Vaitāl Deul (fig. 153) shows both similarities and differences. While the Mukteśvara figures still have large flattish feet and at times stiff, tubular legs, overall proportions have become more slender, and modeling softer and more naturalistic. Compositional possibilities are expanded by releasing the figures from frames. In many cases, the tree held by the *śālabhañjikā* functions as a kind of frame, however, one that is not all enclosing, and made up of loosely flowing contours. This integration of tree and plant forms into the composition is especially striking in figure 103, where a long lotus stalk extends from the lower trunk, and held in the lady's hands, echoes the curving forms of her body.

Greater compositional daring is also seen in the figures standing in twisting poses showing the body from multiple viewpoints (figs. 58, 119, cf. fig. 154). They are at once more naturalistic and more complex. The Vaitāl Deul figure is twisted into a vertical, "corkscrew" arrangement, and movement within the frame is strictly upward. The figure compositions on the Mukteśvara are given greater horizontal expansion, conveying more strongly a sense of movement through space.

It has been stated above that the Vaitāl Deul's sculptures show a fleshy quality made more palpable by the way clothing and jewellery constrict the body. But compared with the Mukteśvara, the treatment of jewellery on the Vaitāl Deul still retains the archaic style's sense of planar overlay (figs. 153, 154). On the Mukteśvara, jewellery is the final step in the outward expansion of wall, *ratha*, and figural sculpture. Ornaments are deeply modeled, like a high relief on the "ground" of the figure (fig. 119), while also echoing the body's expanding volumes (fig. 120).

A final comparison, between the figures of Naṭeśa on the superstructure of the Mukteśvara, with similar figures on the Paraśurāmeśvara, clearly shows how radically the relationship between sculpture and architecture has changed. On the Paraśurāmeśvara, Naṭeśa is confined within an elaborate *candraśālā* (fig. 150). The multi-armed figure squats in his dance-pose in order to fit within his circular enclosure. The arms move in a circular rhythm that seems to spin like a pinwheel around the mask-like visage. No *candraśālā* encloses the Naṭeśa on the Mukteśvara temple (see especially detail, fig. 137). His knees are bent, but he does not squat, his dance-like movements are more flowing and relaxed—the arm positions suggest a vigorous rhythm, but not one that is confined by a geometric enclosure. While not set within a *candraśālā*, the traditional window motif still pervades on the Mukteśvara, but as a delicately interlaced field that provides a pulsating backdrop for the dancing figures.

ŚIKHARA-CLUSTER TEMPLES

GAURĪ TEMPLE, BHUBANESWAR, ca. 970-75

The rectangular-shrine Gaurī Temple (figs. 171, 172), resembles the Mukteśvara in the outline and decoration of its architectural elements. The articulation of these elements on the Gaurī, however, is very different, and signals the early development of temples exhibiting clusters of miniature *śikharas* along the bodies of their main superstructure. The use of miniature *śikharas* (*śṛṅgas*) was abandoned in Orissa soon after having reached a high degree of accomplishment in the Rājarāni temple. The rounded articulation of these elements on the Gaurī, however, is very different and becomes characteristic on all later monuments, the most famous example being the Liṅgarāja in Bhubaneswar. The Mukteśvara and Gaurī temples, then, are of great importance for the development of the mature Orissan temple, as the earliest examples with highly articulated, strongly differentiated *rathas*. The elevations of the lower walls of the Gaurī and Mukteśvara temples are very similar. The bases, canopies, and pilasters of the *bhadra* niches are virtually identical. The pilasters of the Gaurī, however, are slightly narrower and more elongated.

The formal arrangement of the Gaurī's *pratibhadras* resembles more closely the Viṣṇu temple at Ganeswarpur. The latter's two adjacent base mouldings supporting a niche are replaced by narrower base mouldings, and a base just below the empty niche itself. The Muktesvara is the only known temple which places adjacent mouldings under the *pratibhadra* niche. This format was probably abandoned as not conveying the sense of actual columns supporting a niche superstructure, a more convincing impression of which is seen at Ganeswarpur and in the Gaurī temple. The *pratibhadra* also abandons the *gavākṣa*-net of the Mukteśvara. Even though the *pratibhadras* of the Mukteśvara are quite highly articulated, the fabric-like nets of *gavākṣas* give them a flattened appearance. The *pratibhadras* on the Gaurī temple are faced with vertical scroll panels, resulting in a more rounded effect.

The real differences between the Mukteśvara and Gaurī temples lie not in their basic architectural forms, but in how these elements are articulated from the wall surface. Both temples have three angular pilasters on either side of the *bhadra*. On the Mukteśvara, they advance only slightly from the wall, while on the Gaurī temple, they are almost more precisely described as engaged columns. Also, the Gaurī eliminates *nāga*-pilasters, making the interstices between each *ratha* all and more prominent. Though individually angular, the three *rathas*—the *karṇas* and the *pratibhadras* of the adjacent sides—together form a sweeping curve around the body of the temple, producing a rounded effect only nascently present in the Mukteśvara. This curve is further emphasized by the articulation of the *bhadra*; highly independent of its flanking *rathas*, it does not de-emphasize their collective roundness by making them flow directly into its rectangular surface.

The Gaurī temple differs further from the Mukteśvara in the treatment of its superstructure. The three *rathas* between each central *bhadra* elements are now directly crowned with superstructures similar to those above the central niches. These miniature *śikharas*—for in their rounded surface and gradually upward tapering form, this is precisely what they resemble—extend upward onto the lower levels of the superstructure. This upward extension breaks down the distinction between lower walls and *śikhara*, and this will be a feature also of square-shrine *śikhara*-cluster temples.

Because of the basic similarity of their architectural features—the types of base moulding, the decorative elements of the *rathas*, the style of the *candraśālā*,[26]—the Mukteśvara and the Gaurī must be nearly contemporaneous. The Gaurī, however, experiments further with *ratha* articulation. These become almost free standing units, clustered together to give a sweeping roundness to the lower walls, and continuing upward, onto the level of the superstructure, show the beginnings of a verticality that breaks down the barriers between lower and upper levels.

THREE ŚIVA TEMPLES, BAUDH, ca. 970-75

The *ratha* articulation of the Gaurī temple is given further experimental treatment in this set of temples with curvilinear superstructures (figs. 173, 174). In plan the virtually identical Baudh temples resemble eight-point stars. In elevation each of these jutting corners resemble the three *rathas* between each *bhadra* section of the Gaurī temple, except that at Baudh, the entire extending element consists of five, rather than three *rathas*, the two inner ones based on the composition of the Mukteśvara's *bhadra* niches. The niches of these *rathas* consist of two thin pilasters and a small canopy. With the adjacent wall-face placed at a forty-five degree angle, horizontal series of four such niches result. This reduction of the formation of the Mukteśvara's *bhadra* niche to a series of repeated miniatures shows a derivation where a large prominent element takes on a less dominant role, reduced to a motif in an overall decorative pattern.

When the corners are viewed face on, they closely resemble the corresponding sections of the Gaurī temple. The upward vertical sweep of the Baudh temples, however, is not broken by terminating the *rathas* and introducing a second storey, but rather, continues with an uninterrupted contour to the summit of the temple. Taken as a single unit, these corner projections resemble "quarter-*śikharas*". In their projection, and their almost three-dimensional independence, they begin to foreshadow not only the rounded pilasters of later temples like the Rājarāni, but also their clusters of miniature *śikhara*.

VĀRĀHĪ TEMPLE, CHAURASI, ca. 985

This rectangular-shrine temple takes the innovations of the Gaurī temple further, creating through both manipulation of architectural forms and a high degree of ornamentation, a work of unprecedented baroque character (figs. 175, 176). The ninth-century date put forth by various scholars cannot be maintained.[27] It is based mainly on the flat roof of the temple's *maṇḍapa*, terraced ones first appearing on the Mukteśvara. Despite its archaic roof, the Vārāhī temple's forehall bears similarities to those of tenth-century temples. In elevation it resembles the Mukteśvara—an equal number of small niches crowned by miniature superstructures (four on the Vārāhī, two on the Mukteśvara) flank a central lattice-screen window. The whole *maṇḍapa* is much larger in proportion to the shrine, however, which is true also of the even more similar forehall of the Śiva temple at Gandharadi. The Gandharadi forehall is in much more pleasingly proportionate scale to its shrine than that of the Vārāhī temple, where like the Mukteśvara, only two niches flank the central window (fig. 163). The windows of the Gandharadi and Chaurasi temples bear a strikingly similar feature, however, both being flanked by massive engaged columns intertwined with upward ascending *nāga* figures, also found at the entrance to each *maṇḍapa*. These *nāga* columns will be seen again only at the entrance of the Rājarāni temple.[28] It can be concluded that this feature is confined to a group of monuments having relatively close dates, since it is not found earlier than Gandharadi, nor later than the Rājarāni.

The Chaurasi temple moves ever closer to a more rounded treatment of its entire surface, begun in the Gaurī temple, but not fully realized in that its square, jutting *bhadras* effectively interrupt the rounded curve of the unit of three *rathas*. The outer walls of the Vārāhī temple take on an almost oval form. The *bhadra*, while still advancing more than its adjacent *rathas*, does not dominate the wall to the same degree as the Gaurī,[29] as a comparison of the walls clearly shows.

The flanking *pratibhadras* are composed in a way similar to the Gaurī, the central portions bearing a vertical panel of scroll work. Unlike the Gaurī temple, these *rathas*, because of their step-like articulation, have a certain "splayed out" effect, further emphasized by their base mouldings. The corner and *pratibhadra* mouldings are also necessarily widened, since a single, rather than double moulding supports these widened pilasters.

The stepped articulation of the *karṇas* and *pratibhadras*, though basically flat, viewed as an ensemble, produces a rounded appearance in the walls, and the adjacent walls, each sharing half a *karṇa*, flow effortlessly into one another. Though this effect is present on the Gaurī and even Mukteśvara, it is here more fully realized by the de-emphasis of the *bhadra*, which no longer interrupts the smooth horizontal sweep.

The superstructure of the Vārāhī temple has the same basic format as that of the Gaurī (two storeys marked by miniature *śikhara* surmounted by a barrel-shaped capping structure). Though the general conception has not changed, the way in which the individual elements have been articulated has, the overall effect being much more sculptural, more concerned with the effects of solids against space, and rhythmical interplay.

The miniature *śikharas* (*śṛṅgas*) at Chaurasi have become much more rounded compared to those of the Gaurī temple. They are articulated with a step-like pattern, as are the *rathas* below them. The central, outward jutting portions are, however, narrower than those on the courses of the Gaurī's *śṛṅgas*, which extend across almost the entire surface. Also, they are not stacked so closely together; rather, a certain amount of space exists between each moulding, creating an interplay between the dark shadowy voids and the ornately carved solids. Further rhythmical play is created by the different horizontal levels of the *pratibhadra* and *karṇa śṛṅgas*.

The Vārāhī temple shows a variation on the treatment of the *śikhara*-crowned *rathas* of the Gaurī temple. At Chaurasi, the stepped articulation of each *ratha* gives it greater independence from the wall. They sweep across the temple's surface, and with the less dominating *bhadra*, the sense of four independent walls is further reduced.

RĀJARĀNI TEMPLE, BHUBANESWAR, ca. 1030

A small number of square-shrine temples dating to the eleventh century also exhibit "core" superstructures enveloped by clusters of *śṛṅgas*. With square, rather than rectangular *śikharas*, they are formally quite different from the temples just considered, but they nevertheless result from the same conception, where the miniature *śikhara* is a smooth continuation of the lower *ratha*, and with its counterpart, surrounds the embedded core structure. In addition, the rounded appearance of the *rathas* blurs the sense of four distinct walls.

The best known Orissan temple of this type is the Rājarāni in Bhubaneswar (fig. 177).[30] Since there are so few examples of *śikhara*-clusters in Orissa, many scholars have pointed to central India as a source for this isolated development. These discussions have been confined primarily to brief comments on Khajuraho as the source of this phenomenon.[31] While it is obvious that central India did have a certain role, it is equally clear that the temples of Khajuraho relate only indirectly to the Orissan *śikhara*-cluster. Comparing the Rājarāni and the Lakṣmaṇa temple in Khajuraho (ca. 954) for example (fig. 179), it is seen that the Rājarāni is marked by a strong sense of mass. Its relatively squarish and somewhat stunted "core" *śikhara* is embedded within a system of smaller versions of itself. In their rounded appearance, these *rathas* complement the massiveness of the core and seem to be almost bulging out from the central structure, creating a sense of outward expansion. Strong verticality is preserved, however, by the *śṛṇgas*, which extend directly and continuously from these rounded *rathas* onto the lower levels of the main *śikhara*.

The Lakṣmaṇa temple emphasizes verticality primarily, and in spite of its monumentality, lacks the massiveness of the Rājarāni. Yet verticality is not conveyed by the continuity of lower *rathas* and *śṛṇgas*. Such continuity occurs only at the corners of the *prāsāda*. The lower walls are dominated instead by large ambulatory porches, which break up any potential vertical rhythmic pattern. Soaring verticality is attained, however, by the attenuated shape of the core *śikhara*, which narrows considerably at its summit.

It is in its sense of massive bulk, outward expansion, the vertical rhythms of *rathas* and *śṛṇgas*, and the way in which these elements cluster around or embed the core structure, that the Rājarāni differs most markedly from the Lakṣmaṇa temple.[32]

A central Indian temple with greater conceptual affinities to the Rājarāni is the Toteśvara Mahādeo temple in Kadwaha, Madhya Pradesh (fig. 180). Its lower walls are articulated in a way strikingly similar to the Rājarāni. In both temples, rounded *rathas* alternating with wide interstices create a rhythm of protrusions and recesses. These *rathas* are strongly divided into two "storeys" by bands of mouldings, a division further strengthened by the two-storey divisions of the *bhadra*.

Although the overall profiles of these temples are very similar, there are differences as well. The Rājarāni has a greater sense of massive bulk, whereas the Kadwaha temple seems less encumbered by mass, being slightly more attenuated in its proportions. Further, the rounded appearance of the *rathas* of the Rājarāni contributes both to the heaviness of the structure, and to the sense of outward expansion.

While the Rājarāni temple has some obvious affinities with central Indian architecture, it is more accurate to consider it as a distinctive Orissan variant within the widespread corpus of *śikhara*-cluster temples. It can be seen as the result of a development tracable through several Orissan temples, the major characteristic of this development being the stepped articulation and hence rounded appearance of the lower *rathas*, which are capped by miniature *śikharas*, and which exhibit a continuous verticality.[33]

This rounding of the *rathas*, and with it a greater sense of their independent structure, is seen in an early phase on the Mukteśvara temple, becoming more pronounced on the Gaurī, Vārāhī, and Rājarāni temples (see fig. 147). On the Mukteśvara the *pratibhadras* and *karṇas*, while clearly differentiated, are not as complexly articulated as those on the Gaurī. The faces of the *pratibhadras* in particular tend to be flat, whereas those on the Gaurī have advancing central parts. The corresponding *rathas* on the Vārāhī temple are even more complex, their faces having three step-like levels. This *ratha* articulation becomes most highly developed on the Rājarāni, where they stand practically as free-standing columns, with angular projections from the wall proper (which appears recessed), placed between them.[34]

The Orissan temple reaches a new degree of refinement in the Rājarāni. It successfully combines massive solidity with a sense of verticality (which would be more sweeping if the "core" *śikhara* were somewhat less stunted), conveyed through a narrowing and lengthening of forms, and by arranging them in a way calculated to produce uninterrupted vertical rhythms.

This elongation of architectural forms is also seen in the temple's sculpture (fig. 178). The long sinuous contours of the female figures particularly emphasize upward sweeping movement. Yet these tall, elegant figures are imbued with a full-bodied robustness which checks their attenuation, just as massive solidity checks the rising verticality of the temple as a whole. A delicate balance is maintained in that the figures function as integral with the architectural components (like the *rathas*, they are conceived as outwardly expanding and projecting forms), yet dynamically engaged with their surrounding space as well. The overall effect of *rathas* and figures together is altogether sculptural. In circumambulating the temple one experiences totally new imagery at every turn. The *ratha* figures seem almost to revolve, reacting either with space, or with the recessed wall areas. It is an effect that fully departs from the cubic conception of the Paraśurāmeśvara, preserved in part even in the Mukteśvara. Subsequent temple builders look back to the older monuments in order to attain buildings conceived more as self-contained masses, this being tempered by the forms of the *śikhara*-cluster temple.

THE MATURE STYLE

Temples of the next developmental phase of Orissan architecture, which will here be called the mature style, make a conceptual shift from the previous style. The earlier monuments' most characteristic elements—the round, column-like nature of the lower *rathas,* and the *śikhara*-clusters around the upper body of the temple—are rejected. Rather than developing these characteristics, seen from the Gaurī temple through to the Rājarāni, the mature style looks to the Mukteśvara as a prototype, though retaining certain elements which tradition seems to have made it impossible to reject.

SIDDHEŚVARA TEMPLE, BHUBANESWAR, ca. 1040

Several temples can be taken as representative of the initial phase of the mature style, the Siddheśvara temple being the most well known (fig. 181).[35] On the Siddheśvara a new surface treatment is introduced, while the temple also retains some characteristics seen on the Rājarāni.[36]

The two-storey division of the lower walls was by the time of the Siddheśvara an unalterable convention, necessitated further by a desire for monumentality. The central *bhadras* are flanked by *pratibhadras* and *karṇas* which bear motifs resembling miniature shrines, rendered in low relief and unfinished in detail. Those on the lower storey resemble the barrel-shaped superstructures of the Gaurī and Vārāhī temples, while the upper ones are modeled after the pyramidal roof of the *maṇḍapa.* Though formally very different, these miniature shrines seem to be inspired by those of the *pratibhadras* of the Mukteśvara, or even possibly of the Paraśurāmeśvara. They signal on the Siddeśvara a kind of archaizing, a looking back to older forms, resulting in the return to a more cubical architecture.

The treatment of the *śikhara* shows a rather tentative interest in the *śṛṅga.* While present on the lower levels of the superstructure, *śṛṅgas* are not given a high degree of emphasis. Carved in shallow relief, they do not dominate the surface of each *ratha,* the one on the *karṇa* covering only half of it.

A feature incorporated from the Rājarāni is the division of the two storeys of the lower wall by a string course of three mouldings. Also, the lower *rathas* are somewhat rounded, though not to the same degree as on the Rājarāni. It is as if a return to a flatter wall treatment (cf. the Mukteśvara temple) is being worked toward. This slight rounding of the *rathas* extends also to the pilasters flanking the *bhadra* niche, which also resembles the Rājarāni's. Finally, multi-coursed *varaṇḍikās* divide the lower wall from the main *śikhara,* serving also as bases for the *śṛṅgas.* Their use results in the uninterrupted vertical contour of wall and *śikhara.* On the Siddheśvara the wall, *varaṇḍikā,* and the *karṇas* and *pratibhadras* of the *śikhara,* all similarly rounded, together produce a unified surface, and a smooth unencumbered upward surge on the body of the temple. This is the main departure of the mature style from that of the Rājarāni. Rather than being broken up by *śṛṅgas,* the *prāsāda* returns to the continuous outline of the Mukteśvara, cancelling out that temple's interruption of verticality made by the *kaṇṭha* (horizontal recess) by replacing it with a moulded *varaṇḍikā.*

BRAHMEŚVARA TEMPLE, BHUBANESWAR, ca. 1050-55

The Brahmeśvara temple (figs. 181-183) is more important for this study in that it is securely datable.[37] It was dedicated ca. 1060, and so was probably begun five to ten years earlier. In general outline it closely resembles the Siddheśvara—it is, however, more monumental and more finished in its decorative details. The walls and *śikhara* of the *prāsāda* have five vertical divisions, with the lower walls divided into two storeys. Flat *śṛṅgas* are placed on the lower portions of the *rathas* of the *śikhara*.

Like the Siddheśvara, the Brahmeśvara rejects the sculptural conception of the Rājarāni, and the relative flatness of many of its architectural members seems to refer to the Mukteśvara. The pilasters flanking the Brahmeśvara's *bhadra* niche are wide rectangular members, resembling those of the Mukteśvara, though without figurative sculpture. The cubic nature of the Brahmeśvara's *bhadra* is further emphasized by the elements placed below the niche. Rather than the tall, *śikhara*-like niche base which is placed below the *bhadra* niche of the Rājarāni (seen also on the Siddheśvara), the Brahmeśvara has a single five-part base moulding flanked by two narrow decorated strips.

But while certain architectural members bear conceptual resemblance to the Mukteśvara, figurative sculptures on the Brahmeśvara are handled much differently. Sculpted niches, or rather, plaques, are placed on the *rathas* (as seen previously on the Siddheśvara). They are conceptually similar, in their resemblance to miniature shrines, to the *pratibhadra* niches of the Paraśurāmeśvara temple. These plaques bear iconically conceived cult images, female figures, and *mithunas*. The *pratikarṇas* bear figurative sculpture; *vyālas* on the lower storey, female figures on the upper. These "free standing" (rather than frame-enclosed) *pratikarṇa* figures recede into the wall, consistent with the temple's rejection of projecting and receding forms.

As mentioned in the discussion of the Mukteśvara, the Brahmeśvara finally works out the formal problems of the *maṇḍapa* roof. This fully developed roof supports the view that the Brahmeśvara's looking back to the Mukteśvara is a development later than the Siddheśvara. The aim of the builders seems to have been a pyramidal roof with a forty-five degree incline, capped by a *kalaśa*, and in an approximate one to two proportion with the *śikhara*. The eleven slabs of the Brahmeśvara's *maṇḍapa* roof incline upward in a strict forty-five degree angle. The roof, however, does not terminate in a point, for rather than several additional slabs, the "pyramid" is completed by a bell-shaped finial, about half the width of the finial slab. The bell is capped by an *āmalaka* stone, and this by a *kalaśa*. The bell-finial helps solve the formal problem of the Mukteśvara's curved *maṇḍapa* roof. All the horizontal slabs of the Brahmeśvara's roof retain a strictly geometric outline, without rising to a pyramidal apex, which would result in a proportionately too high and massive structure.[38]

LIṄGARĀJA TEMPLE, BHUBANESWAR, ca. 1065

The Orissan temple reaches full maturity with the Liṅgarāja (figs. 184-185).[39] That this monument represents a stage of resolution in the development of the Orissan temple is seen in that it becomes the formal paradigm for almost all Orissan temples built during the next 400 years.[40] The *prāsāda* is divided into five vertical divisions; a central niche, flanked on either side by wide *rathas*, with narrow *vyāla* (leogryph) pilasters between them. The major *rathas* consist of five-part *kumbha* mouldings, a wall section divided into two storeys by a string course, and a *varaṇḍikā*. This is surmounted by a curvilinear *śikhara*. This huge (180 feet) superstructure is proportionately balanced by the lower wall elements—the "base mouldings" (*vedibhanda*) are ten feet, eleven inches high, and the lower walls, forty-three and one half feet.[41]

The Liṅgarāja achieves a balance between the round *rathas* of the Rājarāni and the flat, squarish ones of the Brahmeśvara. This is attained by placing the shrine-niches upon narrow vertical wall sections, articulated in the receding step-like movement of the *rathas* of the Vārāhī temple at Chaurasi. The Liṅgarāja carries a suggestion of roundness, conveying a greater sense of energy than the flat, rather lifeless *rathas* of the Brahmeśvara, yet having their same architectural integrity.

The *śikhara* of the Liṅgarāja has its basis in the Siddheśvara and the Brahmeśvara, but introduces further advancements. It is innovative, first of all, by its height, the *karṇas* consisting of ten groups of horizontal mouldings divided by ten *bhūmi-āmalakas,* as opposed to five *bhūmi*-divisions on the Siddeśvara and Brahmeśvara. The *śikhara* is 120 feet higher than the Brahmeśvara's, and with finer articulation of its horizontal elements, is more refined and elegant in its proportions, and its curve toward the summit is more subtle. The use of *śṛṅgas* has also been modified. Rather than being placed all around the base of the *śikhara,* the *śṛṅgas* do not begin directly above the *varaṇḍikā*, but rather, at a distance of about one of their own lengths above it. Alternating with series of mouldings similar to those on the *karṇas*, the *śṛṅgas* are repeated four times along the length of the *pratibhadra*, reaching almost to the summit of the temple. They are in high relief, and seem to emerge from the wall (half the full from being visible) rather than appearing externally attached, as those of the Brahmeśvara.

This same sense of extended projections applies to the shrine-niches of the lower walls, which work as architectural elements, the final extensions of the *rathas,* rather than as flatly applied "plaques", as on the Brahmeśvara. And likewise, the figures in the recessed areas between the major *rathas* are placed on rounded, rather than planar platforms, and take much more vigorous and dynamic poses (cf. figs. 184, 186). It is as if a compromise (or a synthesis) has been reached between the sculptural dynamism of the Rājarāni and the cubic regularity and stability of the Brahmeśvara.

Several features—the step-curved walls which contribute to a more rounded plan, the continuous contour of wall and *śikhara,* the refined treatment of the course of the *śikhara's rathas*—all show a stylistic advancement from the Brahmeśvara. A synthesis of architectural forms developed and refined in the Mukteśvara, Rājarāni, and Brahmeśvara temples, the Liṅgarāja serves a primary model for later Orissan temples, and marks the last stage of a vigorously experimental architectural movement.

NOTES

1. This analysis owes much to observations made by Stella Kramrisch in two articles, "Kalinga Temples", JISOA, 2.1 (1934), pp. 43-60; and "The Walls of Orissan Temples", JISOA 15 (1947), pp. 178-96.

2. Kramrisch, "Kalinga Temples", p. 45.

3. *Ibid.*, pp. 50-51.

4. For the Paraśurāmeśvara inscription see ARB, pp. 56-58; for the Brahmeśvara inscription see below, note 37.

5. See M. F. Linda, "Medieval Kaliṅga Hindu Temples", Ph.D. thesis, University of California, Berkeley, 1986.

6. The Śiśireśvara and Mārkaṇḍeyeśvara temples are contemporary with the Vaitāl Deul and of the same style. The Vaitāl Deul is more accessible to study than either of these temples in terms of freedom of vantage point and state of preservation. For illustrations see HTAO, figs. 105-28 and 129-42.

7. The temple has been heavily, though with a good degree of accuracy, restored. For pre-restoration photographs see R. Chanda, *Bhañja Dynasty of Mayurabhañj and Their Ancient Capital Khiching* (Baripada?, 1929), p. 6.

8. Two other temples at Khiching bear certain similarities to the Kutai Tuṇḍi. The Khiñchakeśvarī is a modern reconstruction built from the remains of tenth through thirteenth century temples. For illustrations see HTAO, figs. 573-74. The Candraśekhara is a typical Bengali style temple, dating to the tenth to eleventh century (HTAO, figs. 590, 591). This style has strong conceptual relationships with Orissan architecture. For examples see D. Mitra, "Telkupi: A Submerged Temple Site in West Bengal", MASI, 76(1969).

9. The images in these niches seem to be modern, replacing the lost or detached originals.

10. The Dibbeśvara temple at Sarapalli and the Rājarājeśvarī temple at Jayati are part of the same Andhra tradition as the Someśvara and are close to it in date. For illustrations see HTAO, figs. 619, 620, 628-35.

11. A. de Lippe, *Indian Medieval Sculpture* (Amsterdam and New York, 1978), pl. 56.

12. D. R. Das, *Temples of Orissa: Study of a Substyle* (Delhi, 1982), pp. 39-40.

13. For example, the Hari-Hara temple at Osian (O. Viennot, *Temples de L'Inde Central et Occidentale* [Paris, 1976] pl. 108); the Kaśināth and Papanāth temples at Patadakal (P. Brown, *Indian Architecture* [Bombay, 7th reprint, 1976], pl. 52, fig. 2, and pl. 53, fig. 1).

14. For more details on the condition of this complex, see D. Mitra, "Pañca Paṇḍava Temple of Ganeswarpur", *J. N. Banerjea Volume* (Calcutta, 1960), pp. 292-97.

15. See above, note 13.

16. Also, for example, as at Gwalior, Barwa Sagar, Osia, Chitor, and Bhumdana. See Viennot, *Temples*, pls. 96-98, 108, 109, 201, 202, and *passim*.

17. The closest similarity in central India is in the niche decoration of the Toteśvara temple at Kadwaha (A.I.I.S. neg. no 428.72). The half-*gavākṣa* motif even here is not completely identical to the Mukteśvara's, and as this temple is generally considered to date from the 11th century, it may even have been influenced by the Mukteśvara itself.

18. Compare with the Sun temple at Mankheda (see note 12).

19. M. A. Dhaky, "The Genesis and Development of Māru-Gurjara Temple Architecture", P. Chandra, ed., *Studies in Indian Temple Architecture* (New Delhi, 1975), fig. 72.

20. Viennot, *Temples*, pl. 201.

21. M. W. Meister, "Phāṁsāna in Western India", AA, 38.2/3 (1976), fig. 23.

22. ARB (Calcutta, 1961), pp. 87-88; S. K. Saraswati, "Temples of Orissa", OHRJ, 1.4 (1953), pp. 233-53, V. Dehejia, *Early Stone Temples of Orissa* (New Delhi, 1979), pp. 139ff.; D. R. Das, "Early Bhadra Deuls of Orissa", J. Chakrabarti, ed., *Aspects of Indian Art and Culture* (*S. K. Saraswati Commemoration Volume*, Calcutta, 1983), pp. 182-92. Dehejia states further that in the Pataleśvara temple at Paikapada is found "an intermediate stage in the development of the pyramidal forehall roof". This roof, however, is a later reconstruction. See T. Donaldson, rev. of *Early Stone Temples of Orissa*, by V. Dehejia, JAS, 39.2 (Feb. 1980), pp. 383-84.

23. See J. M. Nanavati and M. A. Dhaky, *The Maitraka and Saindhava Temples of Gujarat* (Ascona, 1969), p. 43.

24. Also conceptually similar is the Ambikā temple, Jagat, Rajasthan. See Pramod Chandra, *On the Study of Indian Art* (Cambridge, Mass., 1983), fig. 1.

25. Temples also showing the influence of central Indian temples in the treatment of their forehalls, while also bearing various affinities with the Mukteśvara are the Kośaleśvara temple at Baidyanath and the Kapileśvara temple at Charda (Bolangir district), as discussed above. See D. R. Das "Kośaleśvara Temple at Baidyanath", AA, 38.4 (1976), pp. 297-307; and HTAO, pp. 203-07, and 209-12 (fig. 451-59, and 484-88).

26. For details of these elements see T. Donaldson, "Development of the *Vajra-mastaka* on Orissan Temples", *East and West*, 26.3-4 (1976), figs. 25, 27, 32, 33.

27. J. N. Banerjea, "The Vārāhī Temple at Chaurasi", *V. V. Mirashi Felicitation Volume* (Nagpur, 1965), pp. 349-54; D. Mitra, "Four Little-Known Khākharā Temples of Orissa", *Journal of the Asiatic Society*, 2.1 (1966), p. 3; Dehejia, *Stone Temples*, pp. 125-28. Donaldson dates the temple to the first quarter of the tenth century (HTAO, p. 247).

28. There are also *nāga*-pillars on the architecturally simple Marīci Kuṇḍa, a well next to the Mukteśvara temple.

29. For a plan of the Chaurasi temple see A. Volwahsen, *Living Architecture: Indian* (New York, 1969), p. 171.

30. Other square-shrine temples of this type in Bhubaneswar are the Dākrā Bhīmeśvara and the Ekāmbareśvara. A corpus of early *śikhara*-cluster temples has not been assembled, yet this would shed light on the problems of the origins and development of this particular temple type. Enough evidence exists, though, to suggest that small *śikharas* grouped around the base of the main one have their origin in western India (Gujarat and Rajasthan), this practice spreading, with regional variations, throughout western and central India. See Nanavati and Dhaky, *Temples*, p. 29 (Bileśvara temple), pl. 25 (temple no. 2, Bhanasara), pl. 33 (old temple, Pindara), but especially p. 51 (temple no. 1, Miyanai), and pl. 49 (Bhīma Devala, Praci).

31. See T. Donaldson, "Decorative Program of the Superstructure of the Orissan Rekha-Deul", M. N. Das, ed., *Sidelights on the History and Culture of Orissa* (Cuttack, 1977), pp. 584-85. S. Kramrisch discusses very generally the central Indian influence on the relationship with the Rājarāni in "Kaliṅga Temples", pp. 54-55; and "Walls", pp. 188-91.

32. The Kuladeo temple at Khajuraho, which dates more closely to the Rājarāni, shows the same conceptual differences. Although the large porch areas do not exist here, and the lower wall *rathas* are capped by *śṛṅgas*, their number is multiplied to five between each *bhadra*, creating a horizontal rhythm to counteract the lower walls' verticality, a verticality that is one of the Rājarāni's strongest features.

33. See also Saraswati, "Temples", pp. 243-44.

34. For full ground plans see Volwhasen, *Living Architecture*, p. 171 (Vārāhī temple), p. 146 (Rājarāni).

35. See also the Navakeśvara, Rāmeśvara, and Kedareśvara Gaurī temples, all in Bhubaneswar.

36. Donaldson gives it a date of ca. 1200, stating that it is part of conservative trend, "though exhibiting some of the experimental solutions achieved on the Brahmeśvara and Liṅgarāja" (HTAO, pp. 20, 390).

37. The Brahmeśvara temple bore a dedicatory inscription (now lost) dated in the 18th regnal year of Uddyotakeśarī, ca. 1058. K. C. Panigrahi has convincingly established a chronology for the Somavaṁśī dynasty, with the reign of Uddyotakeśarī dating ca. 1040-65. [K. C. Panigrahi, *Chronology of the Bhauma-karas and Somavaṃśīs of Orissa* (Madras, n.d. 1961?)], p. 17. See also ARB, pp. 43, 118, 248. The inscription was first published by John Prinsep, *Journal of the Royal Asiatic Society of Bengal*, 7 (1838), p. 557. For a translation see R. L. Mitra, *Antiquities of Orissa* (Calcutta, reprint, 1961), vol. 2, pp. 150-52.]

38. For an elevation drawing see Volwhasen, *Living Architecture*, p. 151.

39. K. C. Panigrahi has dated the Liṅgarāja slightly earlier than the Brahmeśvara, a beginning date of ca. 1040, which is unacceptable on stylistic grounds. His dating is based upon a "current tradition in Bhubaneswar", that the temple was built by Yayāti Keśarī and Lalatendu Keśarī, tenuously equated with Yayāti II and Uddyota Keśarī respectively (ARB, pp. 164-67).

40. For example the Megheśvara temple, Ananta Vāsudeva temple, and the Yameśvara temple, all in Bhubaneswar.

41. Measurements are from M. M. Ganguly, *Orissa and Her Remains: Ancient and Medieval* (Calcutta, 1912), pp. 130-32.

CONCLUSION

This Study has attempted to place the Mukteśvara temple in several contexts, historical, architectural, and iconographical. While the historical evidence is insufficient to assign precise dates for most of the monuments discussed here, a detailed study of temples marking a sequential development toward the mature Orissan style allows the important role of the Mukteśvara to be identified in greater detail than before.

We have seen that after 800, a development begins which moves the Orissan temple style out of its archaic phase, exemplified by the Paraśurāmeśvara temple. A continually developing subtlety of expression can be perceived through analyses of the Vaitāl Deul, the Siṁhanātha temple, the temples of Gandharadi and the Mukteśvara. Patterning becomes less bold, taking on a flowing linearity, particularly in that on the *prāsāda*, the treatment of lower walls begins to flow into a sweeping continuity with the *śikhara* (compare with the Paraśurāmeśvara, where the central *bhadra* continues vertically along up to the summit, but otherwise displays complete lack of continuity in the surface pattern of the lower walls and *śikhara*).

The Mukteśvara temple is the best example of this linear continuity between lower and upper portions. The recessed, horizontal *kaṇṭha* barely breaks the energetic sweeping lines of the individual *rathas* as they move from the base mouldings all the way to the temple's summit. There is here a consistency of pattern, evident in an earlier stage on the Vaitāl Deul, particularly in the treatment of the *bhadra*, conceived as a kind of attached *toraṇa* supported by pilasters on the lower walls. The real carriers of vertical continuity in the Mukteśvara, however, are the *pratibhadras*, which in both parts of the *prāsāda* are decorated with a continuous *gavākṣa*-net pattern. Even in a temple so close in conception to the Mukteśvara as the Siddheśvara at Gandharadi, there is a reluctance to include *gavākṣa*-nets on the lower walls, the *pratibhadras* being faced with offsets decorated with scroll work. The same is true at Ganeswarpur (Pañcayatana Viṣṇu temple), where the shrines are practically identical with the Mukteśvara except for this particular feature. The placing of *gavākṣa*-nets on the lower walls seems to be a feature brought in from central India—the Sūrya temple at Mankheda is an example. But even here, there is not the consistent continuity of pattern along the temple's entire length. With this feature, the Mukteśvara temple achieved uniqueness through eclecticism.

Emphasis on vertical continuity was a major factor in the transformation of the Orissan style. At the Gaurī temple, differentiation of lower and upper wall surface is negated not so much by continuity of pattern, but by giving greater three-dimensional articulation to the vertical *rathas* between the *bhadras*, which have the impression of massive colonnette-clusters. This treatment of *rathas* as attached columns is expressed most clearly at the Rājarāni temple, where with its greater monumentality, the rounded *rathas* almost take on an architectural life of their own. This treatment of the *rathas* combines with another feature of central Indian derivation, the *bhadra-śikharas* which seem to bulge outward from the "core" superstructure of the temple. That the Rājarāni is not quite yet a fully realized example of an Orissan "*śikhara*-cluster" temple is seen in the overly squat proportions of this core *śikhara*. The outermost *bhadra-śikhara* reaches to the middle of the *bhadra-śikhara* from which it ''emerges''. The *āmalaka* of this middle *bhadra-śikhara* should also terminate at the center of the main *śikhara,* which needs twice the area above the *bhadra-śikhara's āmalaka*, than it actually has. This lengthening of the superstructure would have created more elegant proportions in keeping with the more usual central Indian treatment of *śikhara*-cluster temples,[1] a treatment sometimes exaggerated at Khajuraho, where a few rather attenuated examples can be seen.

A fully developed *śikhara*-cluster temple is never realized in Orissa, and the use of *śṛṅgas* is severely curtailed after the Rājarāni. Modified usage is seen at the Brahmeśvara and Liṅgarāja temples. The Brahmeśvara seems almost staid in its rejection of the dynamic aspects of the Rājarāni's forcefully three-dimensional articulation of the *ratha* elements in favor of an arrangement of clearly angled vertical salients and recesses reminiscent of the Mukteśvara. Its lower walls even begin to recede inward again, though the overall sense of a smooth, continuous vertical outline, first achieved at the Mukteśvara, had by the time of the Brahmeśvara become firmly established. This is also true for the Liṅgarāja temple. The Liṅgarāja synthesizes with its monumentality the Mukteśvara's sense of decorative pattern, something of the Rājarāni's forceful articulation of the *rathas*, and the Brahmeśvara's forthright architectural integrity. It is the ideal point of departure for almost all subsequent temples in Orissa.

The Mukteśvara is of key importance in this chronological sequence because it makes certain stylistic "breakthroughs"—in its treatment of the *pratibhadras*, but also in its introduction of the pyramidal *maṇḍapa* roof. The overall result is a unique treatment of outside influences, and the temple seems to have appeared at a time particularly alive with experiment and new ideas. By presenting a minute description of the Mukteśvara temple, this monograph delineates its formal characteristics, and puts forth the components of its iconographical program.

The iconography of the Mukteśvara has two aspects, "orthodox" and tantric. The exterior perhaps only hints at the variety of religious concepts at work in Orissa at this time. If the temple was conceived as a *pañcamukhaliṅga*, by virtue of the *ākāśaliṅga* finial and the four *candraśālās* of the *śikhara*, temples as early as the Paraśurāmeśvara may have been built according to this same conception. The identification of the *yakṣiṇīs* as *ākarṣinīs* (attractions), placed in a continuous circular *yantra*-like fashion on the lower walls, may however come out of a generally tantric ambiance prevalent throughout northern India at this time. The unique three-part compositions of the *pratikarṇas*, the "lady at her door", meditating *yogin*, and divine face, repeated all along its surface, are perhaps less overtly "tantric". We may have here an almost narrative rendering of Indra's heaven, appropriately placed on the *śikhara*, where ascetic sages meditate in a pleasure garden populated with heavenly ladies. The female figures may, however, be considered as manifestations of Śakti, leading the aspirant to spiritual realization. Royal patronage is suggested by the images of kings (of the Somavaṃśī dynasty?) on the *śikhara* who, shown in close proximity with Śiva, are possibly conceived as gods (*devas*) themselves. The Mukteśvara, then, can also be seen as a visual proclamation of royal legitimacy.

The sculptural program of the interior, on the ceiling of the *maṇḍapa*, is almost unquestionably of a tantric nature, although on one level we have here a narrative-iconic tableau of Śiva with Pārvatī, Gaṇeśa, and Kārttikeya, this last deity accompanied also by his nurses, the Kṛttikās (in the guise of the Sapta Mātṛkās). On a deeper level, we have a *maṇḍala* image that may be interpreted as a depiction Śiva as *nāda* (primordial sound), with the Sapta Mātṛkās representing the concept of the *mantra-mātṛkās*, the first level of manifestation, from which in turn emanates the phenomenal plane of existence (indicated by the narrative reliefs of the Austerities of Pārvatī, and the music and dance scenes). That the tradition of Kashmir Śaivism evidently played a role in this symbolism shows that Orissa was hardly an isolated backwater, but was fully involved in a pan-Indian sphere of religious activity. As a center of Śaivism, it is completely feasible that Bhubaneswar/Ekāmra contains temples that can be interpreted in the light of major developments in Śaivite religious thought.

NOTE

1. For example the smaller Śiva temple, Kiradu (Rajasthan), Sasbabu temple, Nagoda (Rajasthan), Ambikā temple, Jagat (Rajasthan). Illustrated in M. A. Dhaky, "The Genesis and Development of Māru-Gurjara Temple Architecture", P. Chandra, ed., *Studies in Indian Temple Architecture* (New Delhi, 1975), figs. 35, 75, 76.

CHRONOLOGICAL TABLE

Antecedents

Vaitāl Deul, Bhubaneswar, ca. 800-25
Kutai Tuṇḍi temple, Khiching, ca. 825-50
Siṁhanātha temple, Baramba, ca. 850-75
Someśvara temple, Mukhaliṅgam, Andhra Pradesh, ca. 900

The "Somavaṃśī Style"

Kośaleśvara temple, Baidyanath, ca. early 10th century
Kapileśvara temple, Charda, ca. early 10th century
"Twin" temples, Gandharadi, ca. 950
Tīrtheśvara temple, Bhubaneswar, ca. 960
Pañcayatana Viṣṇu temple, Ganeswarpur, ca. 970
Mukteśvara temple, Bhubaneswar, ca. 970

Śikhara-Cluster Temples

Gaurī temple, Bhubaneswar, ca. 970-75
Three Śiva temples, Baudh, ca. 970-75
Vārāhī temple, Chaurasi, ca. 985
Rājarāni temple, Bhubaneswar, ca. 1030

The Mature Style

Siddheśvara temple, Bhubaneswar, ca. 1040
Brahmeśvara temples, Bhubaneswar, ca. 1050-55
Liṅgarāja temple, Bhubaneswar, ca. 1065

GLOSSARY

abhayamudrā	the gesture of reassurance
ācārya	teacher, especially of a Brahman
ahaṁkāra	philosophical term; the individuating principle, ego sense
ākarṣinis	"the attractions"; a group of manifestations of the Supreme Goddess, placed at the periphery of a *yantra* or on the walls of a temple
ākāśa	ether or space, the first elements of manifestation, pervading all other elements
ākāśaliṅga	"*liṅga* open to space", or "ether-*liṅga*", a temple finial having the shape of a *liṅga*
āmalaka	myrobalan; cushion-like crowning elements of Nāgara temple *śikharas* resembling the shape of this fruit
amṛta	water of life, nectar of immortality
amṛta kalaśa	"jar of the nectar of immortality"; finial in the shape of a jar
añjali	respectful gesture, made by joining the palms
āsana	a set; sitting posture
āvaraṇadevatās	"surrounding deities"; images in side niches of temples
bhadra	central projection on temple wall
buddhi (mahat)	"intelligence (great thing)", first produce of cosmic matter (*prakṛti*)
bhūmi	level, story
bhūmi-āmalaka	miniature *āmalaka* stone placed at intervals between series of mouldings on the *karṇas* of a *śikhara*, dividing it into "storeys"
bhūmisparṣa mudrā	"earth touching gesture"; made by the Buddha at the time of his enlightenment
candraśālā	prominent arched element on temple superstructure
ḍamarū	hourglass-shaped drum; and attribute of Śiva
devadāsī	"maidservant of the god"; a dancing girl
dharma	righteousness, order, established religion
dvārapāla	door guardian, image placed at the lower door jambs of temples
dhyāna	meditation, contemplation
dhyāna mudrā	"gesture of meditation"; the hands folded palms upward, placed on the lap
dikpāla	guardian of the direction
gandharva	celestial musician
gaṇa	spirit attendant of Śiva
garbhagṛha	"womb chamber"; inner sanctum of a temple
gavākṣa	"gable-window" motif

graha	"grasper"; a planet or astrological force
hasta mudrā	gesture made by Śiva dancing; the arm extends across the body and points downward
īsaścūḍa	finial with a *liṅga* as its upper form; same as *ākāśaliṅga*
jaṅghā	lower walls of a temple; area between base mouldings and superstructure
kalaśa	pot, jar
kaṇṭha	"neck"; recess between superstructure and lower walls
kapota	hand gesture with hands joined at the thumbs, top and bottom
kapotāli	upper level of four-part base moulding
karṇa	corner; corner wall division
karṇikā	projection between *kapotālis* on base mouldings
khura	"hoof"; lowest level base moulding
kīrttimukha	"face of glory"; composite animal head, issues strings of jewels from its mouth
kumbha	"pot", second part of typical Orissan base moulding
Kṛttikās	the Pleiades; wives of the seven sages and nursemaids of Skanda (Kārttikeya)
lakula	club; attribute of Lakulīśa
lalitāsana	relaxed seated posture, with the figure on a pedestal, one leg is drawn in, the other hangs down
liṅga	phallic emblem of Śiva; the main object of worship in Śiva temples
liṅga pīṭha	*liṅga* placed within a *yoni* (vulva)-shaped pedestal
makara	mythical aquatic animal
mālā	garland (of flowers of beads); rosary
manas	"mind"; the principle of cognition
maṇḍala	"circle"; geometrical diagram used to invoke a divinity, an image of the universe
maṇḍapa	hall before the sanctuary of a temple
mantra	ritual utterance; and essential sound; sacred invocation
mantra-mātṛkā(s)	"mothers of the *mantras*"; the primary emanations of primordial sound (*nāda*)
Mātṛkā	"Mother"; one of Seven Mother Goddesses (Sapta Mātṛkās)
mithuna	"couple"; propitious motif of man and woman together
mudrā	symbolic hand gesture
nāda	primordial, unheard sound
nāga	serpent divinity (male)

Nāgara	so-called "Northern" style of temple architecture; typified by curvilinear superstructure
nāginī	serpent divinity (female)
Navagrahas	"Nine Graspers"; the planetary deities
nāyikā	"heroine"; ideal female type in Sanskrit poetry
padmāsana	"lotus posture"; seated posture with the feet drawn up on the thighs, used in meditation
pañcamukhaliṅga	five-faced *liṅga*
pārśvadevatā	"accompanying deity"; images in central niches of temples
prakṛti	"nature"; cosmic matter, the uncaused cause of phenomenal existence
prāsāda	sanctum or sanctuary; houses the *garbhagṛha* and is surmounted by the *śikhara*
pratibhadra	wall projection between *bhadra* and *karṇa*; flanking *bhadra*
pratikarṇa	wall projection flanking *karṇa*
pūjā	ritual worship of an image of a deity with flowers, oblations etc.
Purāṇa(s)	"ancient lore"; class of Hindu religious texts
Puruṣa	Cosmic Man or Spirit; the ultimate principle
rāṣṭra	kingdom, realm, territory
ratha	vertical salient or recess on the walls of a temple
ṛṣi	sage, seer
Śaiva, Śaivite	pertaining to Śiva, as worshipper, etc.
śakti	"energy"; active power of deity, regarded as consort of a god
śālabhañjikā	woman embracing the *śāla* tree; female figure on temple walls
Sapta Mātṛkās	the Seven Mother Goddesses
siddhāsana	"adept's pose", seated posture for meditation
śikhara	superstructure above temple's sanctum
śilpa śāstra	text on art, architecture
śilpin	artisan, craftsman
śṛṅga	miniature *śikhara*; turret
śukanāsā	prominent arched element above the entrance to a *prāsāda*
Tantra(s)	body of religious texts emphasizing identity of the absolute and the phenomenal world; emphasis on *yoga*, meditation and secret ritual
toraṇa	ornamental gateway
tribhaṅga	"having three bengs"; curved standing posture
triśūla	"trident"; weapon attribute of Śiva
vāhana	animal vehicle of a deity
vairāgya	disgust, indifference; ideal detached attitude of the ascetic *yogin*

vajra-mastaka	"adamantine head"; term used in the *Śilpa Prakāśa* for *candraśālā/ śukanāsā*
varada mudrā	gesture of bestowing boons
varaṇḍikā	series of mouldings dividing lower walls and superstructure of a temple
vāstupuruṣamaṇḍala	"diagram of the Person of the site"; ideational plan of a site or building
vedibandha	base mouldings; lowest level of the wall of a temple
vidyādhara	celestial attendant of Śiva
vyāla	composite (lion, bird, elephant, etc.) animal
yakṣa	a terrestrial deity (male)
yakṣiṇī	terrestrial female divinity, associated with trees
yantra	"instrument"; and ideational geometric diagram, used in meditation as a means of identification with the deity
yoga	"union"; system of meditation, having as its goal union with God
yogāsana	seated posture of meditation
yogin	one who practices *yoga*
yogabandha, yogapaṭṭa	band of cloth used to hold the legs in a crossed position during meditation.

BIBLIOGRAPHY

Acharya, P.K. *A Summary of the Mānasāra*. Leiden, 1918.

———trans. *Architecture of the Mānasāra*. 8 vols. London, 1934.

Acharya, P.P. "Dikpālas and Their Śaktis in the Temples of Orissa." OHRJ, 11.2 (1962), pp. 312-15.

Agrawala, P.K. "The Early Indian Mother-Goddess Votive Discs." *East and West*, 29.1-4 (Dec. 1979), pp. 32-36.

———"Tetrad of Skanda Deities in a Relief at Bhubaneswar." *East and West*, 29.1-4 (Dec. 1979), pp. 157-61.

Agrawala, V.S., trans. *Devī Māhātmya*, Varanasi, 1963.

———*Studies in Indian Art*. Varanasi, 1965.

Arnot, M.H. *Report with Photographs of the Repairs Executed to Some of the Principle Temples of Bhubaneswar Between 1890 and 1903*. London, 1903.

Arya, V.B. "Chronology of the Temples of the Soma Dynasty." OHRJ, (1962), pp. 43-48.

Auboyer, J. *Le trône et son symbolisme dans l'Inde acienne*. Paris, 1949.

———"Le caractère royal et divin du trône dans l'Inde anciennne." *The Sacral Kingship*. Leiden, 1959.

Banerjea, J.N. *Development of Hindu Iconography*. 2nd ed. Calcutta, 1956.

———"The Vārāhī Temple at Chaurasi." *Dr. Mirashi Felicitation Volume*. Nagpur, 1965, pp. 349-354.

Banerji, R.D. "Antiquities of the Baudh State." JBORS, 15.1-2 (1929), pp. 64-81.

Basu, A. "Hindu Doctrine of Divine Kingship." *The Sacral Kingship*. Leiden, 1959, pp. 167-71.

Behera, K.S. "Palm Leaf Manuscript on the Architecture of Konark Temple." *Annals of the Bhandarkar Oriental Research Institute*, 57 (1976), pp. 175-80.

Bhardwaj, S.M *Hindu Places of Pilgrimage in India*. Berkeley, 1973.

Bhattacharya, A., V.K. Varma, and G.S. Rai, trans. *Kūrma Purāṇa*. Varanasi, 1972.

Biswas, D.K. "A Note on the First Sonpur Grant of Yayāti Mahāśivagupta I." *J.N. Banerjea Volume*. Calcutta, 1960, pp. 150-52.

Boner, A., and S.R. Śarmā. *Śilpa Prakāśa: Medieval Orissan Sanskrit Text on Temple Architecture*. Leiden, 1966.

———*New Light on the Sun Temple at Koṇārka*. Varanasi 1972.

Bose, N.K. *Canons of Orissan Architecture*. Calcutta, 1932.

Brown, P. *Indian Architecture: Buddhist and Hindu Periods*. Bombay, 7th reprint, 1976.

Brown, R. "The Four Stone Façades of Monastery I at Ratnagiri." AA, 40.1 (1978), pp. 5-28.

Brunner, H.. "Analyse du Kiraṇāgama." *Journal Asiatique*, 253 (1965), pp. 309-28.

Chand, R.P. "Explorations in Orissa." MASI, 44 (1934).

Chanda, R.P. "The Lingarāja, or Great Temple of Bhubaneswara." *Archaeological Survey of India Annual Report*, 1922-1924, pp. 119-22.

———"Note on the Ancient Monuments of Mayurbanj." JBORS, 13 (1927), pp. 131-36.

———*Bhañja Dynasty of Mayurbhanj and Their Ancient Capital Khiching*. Baripada (?), 1929.

Codés, G. "Le culte de la royauté divinisée, source d'inspiration de grand monuments du Cambodge ancien, "*Serie Orientale Roma*, vol.1 (1952) pp. 1-23.

Coomaraswamy, A.K. "Indian Architectural Terms." JAOS, 48 (1928), pp. 250-75.

———*Yakṣas,* New Delhi, reprint 1971.

———and G.K. Duggirala, trans. *The Mirror of Gesture, Being the Abhinaya Darpaṇa of Nandikeśvara.* Cambridge, Mass., 1917.

Cowell, ed., *The Jātakas or Stories of the Buddha's Former Births.* London, 1957.

———and A.E. Gough, trans. *Sarva-darśana-saṁgraha by Madhva Āchārya.* Varanasi, 1978.

Craven, R. *A Concise History of Indian Art.* New York, 1976.

Danielou, *A. Hindu Polytheism.* London, 1964.

Das, B. "Śaivism in Ancient Orissa." *Sidelights on the History and Culture of Orissa.* Ed. M.N. Das. Cuttack, 1977, pp. 337-43.

———*The Bhauma-Karas; Buddhist Kings of Orissa and Their Times.* Bhubaneswar, 1978.

Das, D.R. "Kośaleśvara Temple at Baidyanath." AA, 38.4 (1976), pp. 297-307.

———*Temples of Orissa: Study of a Sub-style.* Delhi, 1982.

Das, G. and K.C. Panigrahi "Taltali Plate of Dharma Mahādevī.'' IHQ, 21, (1945), pp 218-21.

Dehejia, V. *Early Stone Temples of Orissa.* New Delhi, 1979.

Devadhar, C.R. and N.G. Suria, ed. and trans. the *Abhijñānaśākuntala of Kalīdāsa.* Delhi, 1934.

Dhaky, M.A. "The Ākāśaliṅga Finial." AA, 36.4 (1974), pp. 307-15.

———"The Genesis and Development of Māru-Gurjara Temple Architecture." *Studies in Indian Temple Architecture.* Ed. P. Chandra. New Delhi, 1975.

Donaldson, "Propitious-Apotropaic Eroticism in the Art of Orissa." AA, 37.1/2 (1975), pp. 75-100.

———"Development of the *Vajra-Mastaka* on Orissan Temples." *East and West,* 26.3-4 (1976), pp. 419-33.

———"The Sculptural Program of the Orissan Rekha-Deul.'' *Sidelights on the History and Culture of Orissa.* Ed. M.N. Das. Cuttack, 1977, pp. 565-613.

———Review of *Early Stone Temples of Orissa,* by V. Deheja. JAS, 39.2 (Feb. 1980), pp. 383-84.

———T.E. *Hindu Temple Art of Orissa.* 3 vols. Leiden, 1985-87.

Eliade, M *Yoga: Immortality and Freedom.* Bollingen Series LVI. Princeton, 1969.

Fabri, C. *History of the Art of Orissa.* Calcutta, 1974.

Fergusson, J. *History of Indian and Eastern Architecture.* 2nd edn. Rev. and ed. by J. Burgess, London, 1910.

Gangooly, O.C. *Orissan Sculpture and Architecture.* Calcutta, 1956.

Ganguly, M.M. *Orissa and Her Remains: Ancient and Medieval.* Calcutta, 1912.

Gaston, A.M. *Śiva in Dance, Myth and Iconography.* Delhi, 1982.

Ghose, D.P. "The History of Orissan Hindu Temples." *Marg,* 8.4 (1955), pp. 34-36.

Ghose, M., trans. *Abhinaya Darpaṇa.* Calcutta, 1957.

Ghose, S. *The Original Yoga as Expounded in the Śiva Saṃhitā, Gheraṇḍa Saṃhitā and Patañjali Yogasūtras.* Delhi. 1980.

Gonda, J. "The Sacred Character of Ancient Indian Kingship." *The Sacral Kingship.* Leiden, 1959, pp. 172-80.

———"The Guru." *Change and Continuity in Indian Religion.* The Hague and London, 1965.

———*Ancient Indian Kingship from the Religious Point of View.* Lieden, 1966.

———*Viṣṇuism and Śivaism: A Comparison.* London, 1970.

———*Medieval Religious Literature in Sanskrit.* Wiesbaden, 1977.

Gupta, S., D.J. Hoens, and T. Goudriann. *Hindu Tantrism*. Leiden, 1979.

H.G. Review of *The Śilpa Prakāśa*, trans. A. Boner and S.R. Śarmā. JAOS, 88.2 (June 15, 1968), pp. 381-82.

Harper, K.A. "An Iconological Study on the Origins and Development of the Sapta Mātṛkās." Ph.D. thesis, University of California, Los Angeles, 1977.

Harza, R.C. *Studies in the Upapurāṇas*. Vol. 2. Calcutta, 1963.

Kielhorn, F "Ratnapur Stone Inscription of Jajalladepa." *Epigraphica Indica*, 1 (1892), pp. 30-40.

Kramrisch, S. "Kalinga Temples." JISOA, 2.1 (1934), pp.43-60.

———*The Hindu Temple*. 2 vols. Calcutta, 1946.

———The Image of Mahādeva in the Cave Temple on Elephanta Island." *Ancient India*, 2 (1946), pp. 4-8.

———"The Walls of Orissan Temples." JISOA, 15,(1947), pp. 178-96.

———"An Image of Aditi-Uttānapad." AA, 190 (1956), pp. 259-70.

———Review of *The Śilpa Prakāśa*, trans. A Boner and S.R. Śarmā. JAS, 27.2 (1968), pp. 408-09.

———"The Indian Great Goddess." *History of Religions*, 14.4 (1975), pp. 235-65.

———*Manifestations of Shiva*. Philadelphia, 1981.

———*The Presence of Śiva*. Princetorn 1981.

———"Wall and Image in Indian Art." B.S. Miller, ed., *Exploring India's Sacred Art: Selected Writings of Stella Kramrisch*. Philadelphia, 1983.

Krishnan, Y. "The Nāga Cult in Indian Art and Literature." *Oriental Art*, 13 (1967), pp. 180-92.

Kulke, H. "Der Devaraja-Kult. Legitimation und Herrscherapotheose im Angkor Reich." *Saeculum*, 25(1974). Trans. and reprint 95, Southeast Asia Data Program Paper, no. 118, Ithica, 1978.

———"Early State Formation and Royal Legitimation in Late Ancient Orissa." *Sidelights on the History and Culture of Orissa*. Ed. M.M. Das. Cuttack, 1977, pp. 104-14.

———"Early Royal Patronage of the Jagannātha Cult." CJRTO, pp. 104-14.

———"Jagnnātha as the State Deity under the Gajapatis of Orissa." CJRTO, pp 199-208.

———"Royal Temple Policy and the Structure of Medieval Hindu Kingdoms." CJRTO, pp. 125-37.

Lal, K. *Temples and Sculpture of Bhubaneswar*. Delhi, 1976.

Lehman, K. "The Dome of Heaven." *Art Bulletin* 27.4 (1945), pp. 1-27.

Linda, M.F. "Medieval Kaliṅga Hindu Temples". Ph.D. thesis,University of California, Berkeley, 1986.

de Lippe, A. *Indian Medieval Sculpture*. Amsterdam and New York, 1978.

L'Orange, H.P. *Studies on the Iconography of Cosmic Kingship in the Ancient World*. New Rochelle, New York, 1982.

Mahapatra, L.K. "Gods, Kings, and the Caste System in India." A Bharati, ed. *Ninth International Congress in Anthropological and Ethnological Sciences*. Chicago, 1973.

Mahtab, H. *History of Orissa*. Vol. 1, up to 1568 A.D. Cuttack, 1959.

Majumdar, R.C., ed. *History and Culture of the Indian People*. vols. 4 and 5. Bombay, 1951-69.

Mani, V. *Purāṇic Encyclopaedia*. New Delhi, 1975.

Marr, J.R. Review of *The Śilpa Prakāśa*, trans. A. Boner and S.R. Śarmā. *Bulletin of the School of Oriental and African Studies*, 27.2 (Feb 1968), pp. 408-09.

Masthanaiah, D. *The Temples of Mukhalingam*. New Delhi, 1978.

Maxwell, T.S. "The Five Aspects of Śiva in Theory, Iconography and Architecture." *Art International*, 25.3-4 (March, April, 1982), pp. 41-47.

Mazumdar, B.C. "Maranja-Mura Charter of Mahāśivagupta *alias* Yayāti." JBORS, 2.1 (1916), p. 53.

Michell, G. *The Hindu Temple: An Introduction to its Meaning and Forms.* New York, 1977.

Miller, B.S. *Bhartṛhari: Poems,* New York, 1967.

Mirashi, V.V. "The Śaiva Ācāryas of the Mattamayūra Clan." IHQ, 26.1 (March, 1950), pp. 8-16.

Misra, P.B. *Dynasties of Medieval Orissa.* Calcutta, 1933.

Mitra, D. "Pañcapaṇḍava Temples of Ganeswarpur." *J.N. Banerjea Volume.* Calcutta 1960.

———"Four Little-known Khākharā Temples of Orissa." *Journal of the Asiatic Society.* 4th series, 2.1 (1960-62), pp. 1-23.

———"Telkupi: A Submerged Temple Site in West Bengal." MASI, 76 (1969).

———*Bhubaneswar.* 7th ėd. New Delhi, 1977.

———"Ratnagiri." MASI, 80 (1981-83).

Mitra, R.L. *Antiquities of Orissa.* 2 vols. Calcutta, 1875-80.

Mukhopadhyaya, S.M., trans. *Vāmana Purāṇa.* Varanasi, 1968.

Nandi, R.N. *Religious Institutions and Cults in the Deccan (ca. A.D. 6000-A.D. 1000).* Delhi, 1973.

Nema, S.R. *Political History of the Somavaṁśī Kings of South Kosala and Orissa.* New Delhi, 1978.

O'Flaherty, W.D. *Hindu Myths.* Baltimore, 1975.

———*Śiva: The Erotic Ascetic.* London, 1981.

Panigrahi, K.C. "Sculptural Representations of Lakulīśa and other Pasupati Teachers." JIH, 38.3 (1960), pp. 653-63.

———*Archaeological Remains at Bhubaneswar.* Calcutta, 1961.

———*Chronology of the Bhauma Karas and Somavaṃśīs of Orissa.* Madras, n.d.. (1961?).

———*History of Orissa (Hindu Period).* Cuttack, 1981.

Pathak, V.S. "Ekāmra: Bhubaneswar in Inscriptions." OHRJ, 7.1 (April, 1958), pp. 47-50.

Pollock, S. "The Divine King in the Indian Epic." JAOS, 104.3 (1984), pp. 505-28.

Pirncep, J. "Inscription of the Brahmeśvara Temple, Bhubaneswar." *Journal of the Asiatic Society of Bengal,* 7 (1838), p. 557.

Rajaguru, S. "The Dasapala Copper Plate Grant of Ranaka Satrubhanja Deva, Samvat 198." OHRJ, 1.3 (1952), pp. 208-12.

———*Inscriptions of Orissa.* Vol. 4. Bhubaneswar, 1966.

Ramchandra Rao, P.R. *Bhubaneswar: Kalinga Temple Architecture.* Hyderabad, 1980.

Rao, T.A.G. *Elements of Hindu Iconography.* 4 vols. 1914-1916; reprint New Delhi, 1962.

Rath, B.K. *Cultural History of Orissa (A.D. 855-1110).* Delhi, 1983.

Roy, P.C., trans. *The Mahābhārata.* 12 vols. Calcutta, 1927-32.

Ryder, A.W. *Shakntala and Other Writings by Kalidasa.* New York, 1959.

Sah, A.H. *Life in Medieval Orissa.* Varanasi, 1976.

Sahu, J.K. "Śaivism in Orissa." *Sidelights on the History and Culture of Orissa,* Ed. M.N. Dass. Cuttack, 1976, pp. 329-30.

Sahu, N.K. "History of Kosala and the Somavaṃśīs of Utkala." OHRJ, 3.3 (Dec. 1956), pp. 127-36.

Sarma, B.K. *The History of Somavaṃśīs Rule in Orissa.* Calcutta, 1983.

Sarabhai, M. *The Eight Nayakas.* New York, 1965.

———*Longing for the Beloved: Songs to Siva in Bharata Natyam.* Ahmedabad, 1976.

Sarasvati, S.K. "Temples of Orissa." OHRJ, 1.4 (1953), pp. 233-53.

———"Orissan Temple Architecture." HCIP, Vol. 4, pp. 530-56.

Shastri, J.L. ed., and trans., "A Board of Scholars." *Śiva Purāṇa.* Ancient Indian Tradition and Mythology. Delhi, 1970.

———*Linga Purāṇa.* Ancient Indian Tradition and Mythology. Delhi, 1973.

Shastri, Pandit M.K. ed. *Mālinīvijayottara Tantram.* Srinagar, 1922.

Singh, J. trans. *Śiva Sūtras: The Yoga of Supreme Identity.* Delhi, 1979.

Singh T. "Some Reflections on Temple Architecture from Garuda Purāṇa." 22.1 (Feb. 1980) pp. 180-86.

———"Bhaviṣya Purāṇa and Bṛhatsaṃhitā on Temple Architecture: A Collātive Study." *Purāṇa,* 23.1 (Feb. 1981), pp. 62-72.

———"An Appraisal of the Data Regarding Temple Architecture Gleaned from Agni Purāṇa." 23.1 (July, 1981), pp. 188-200.

Sircar, D.C. "A Note on the Later Somavaṃśīs." IHQ, 22 (1946), pp. 300-07.

———"The Later Somavaṃśīs." OHRJ, 1 (1952), pp. 289-300.

———Review of *Chronology of the Bhuma-Karas and Somavaṃśīs,* by K.C. Panigrahi. JIH, 40.1 (1962), pp. 208-10.

———*Studies on the Geography of Ancient and Medieval India.* Delhi, 1971.

Sivaramamurti, C. *Chitrasutra of the Vishnudharmottara.* Delhi, 1981.

Smith, W. "The Ceiling of the Mukteśvara temple in Bhubaneswar." AA, 45.1 (1984), pp. 73-95.

———Review of *Hindu Temple Art of Orissa,* vols. 2 and 3, by T.E. Donaldson, JAS, 47.4 (1988), pp. 916-17.

Snellgrove, D. *The Hevajra Tantra: A Critical Study.* London, 1959.

Somasundaram Pillai, J.M. *The Great Temple at Tanjore.* Tanjore, 1958.

Soper, A. "The Dome of Heaven in Asia." *Art Bulletin,* 29.4 (1947), pp. 225-48.

Spellman, J.W. *Political Theory of Ancient India.* Oxford, 1964.

Subuddhi, U. *The Bhauma-Karas of Orissa.* Calcutta, 1978.

Sterling, A. "An Account, Geographical, Statistical, and Historical of Orissa Proper, or Cuttack (part III: Religion, Antiquities, Temples and Civil Architecture)." *Asiatic Researches,* 15 (1825), pp. 335-38.

A Taluqdar of Oudh, trans. *Matsya Purāṇa,* 2nd ed. 1917; reprint New Delhi, 1980.

Tucci, G. *The Theory and Practice of the Maṇḍala.* London, 1961.

Van Buitenen, J.A.B., trans. *The Mahābhārata.* Vol. 1. Chicago, 1978.

Viennot, O. *Temples de l'Inde central et Occidentale.* Paris, 1976.

Volwahsen, A. *Living Architecture: Indian.* New York, 1966.

Williams, J.G. *The Art of Gupta India.* Princeton, 1983.

Zannas, E., and J. Auboyer. *Khajuraho* 'S-Gravenhage, 1960.

Zimmer, H. *Myths and Symbols in Indian Art and Civilization.* New York, 1962.

INDEX

ILLUSTRATIONS

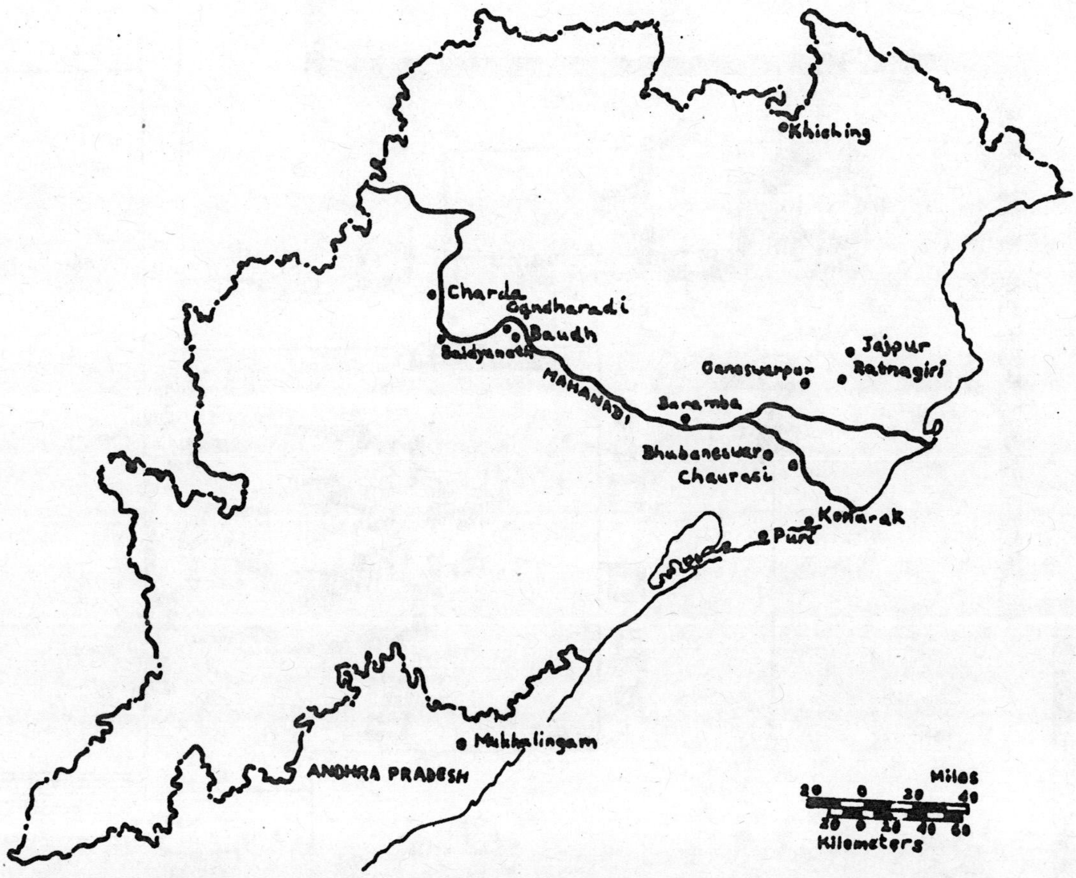

1. Map, Orissa, with modern district borders and archaeological sites.

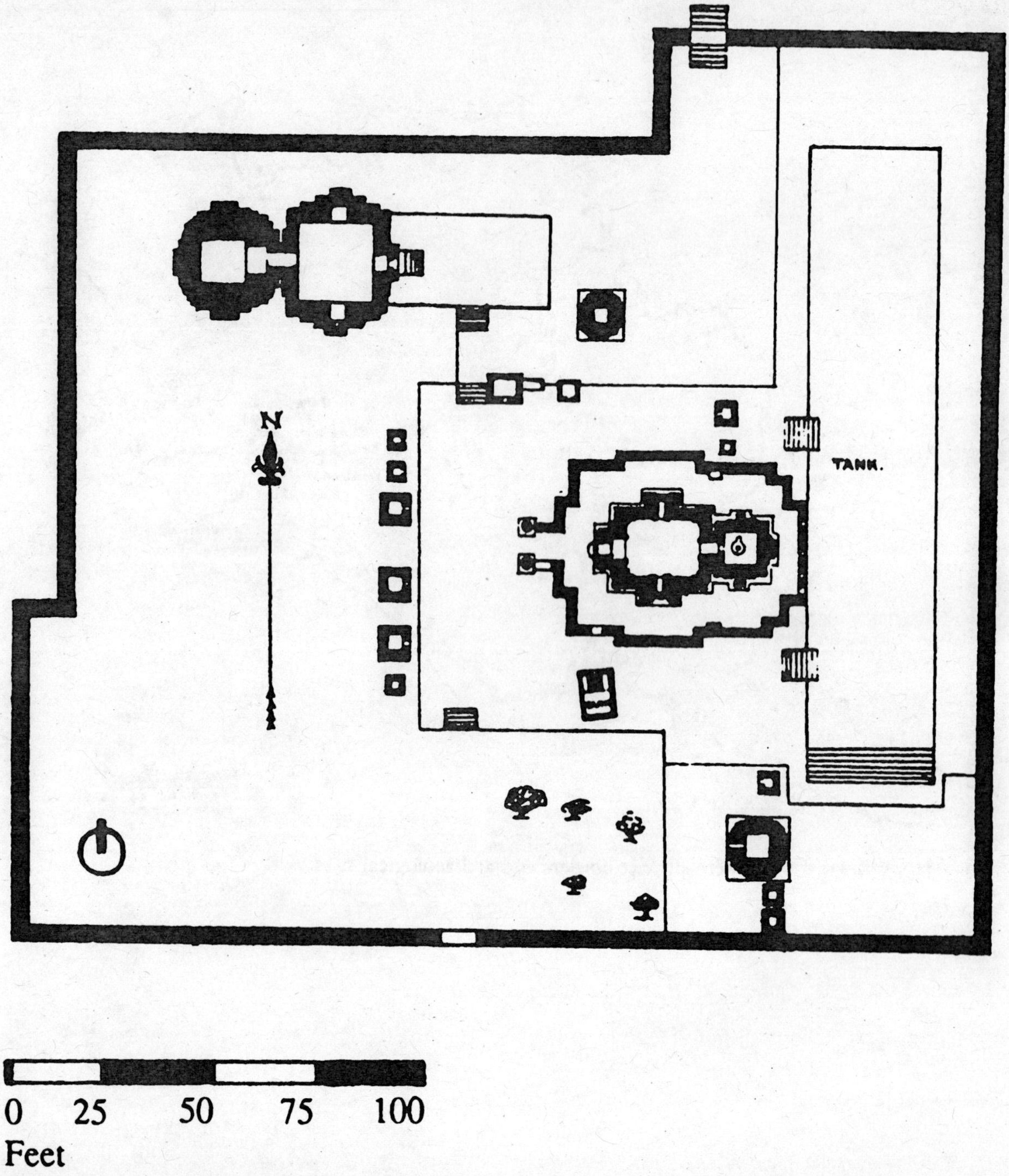

2. Muktesvara temple, Bhubaneswar, site plan. (M.M. Ganguly, *Orissa and Her Remains*).

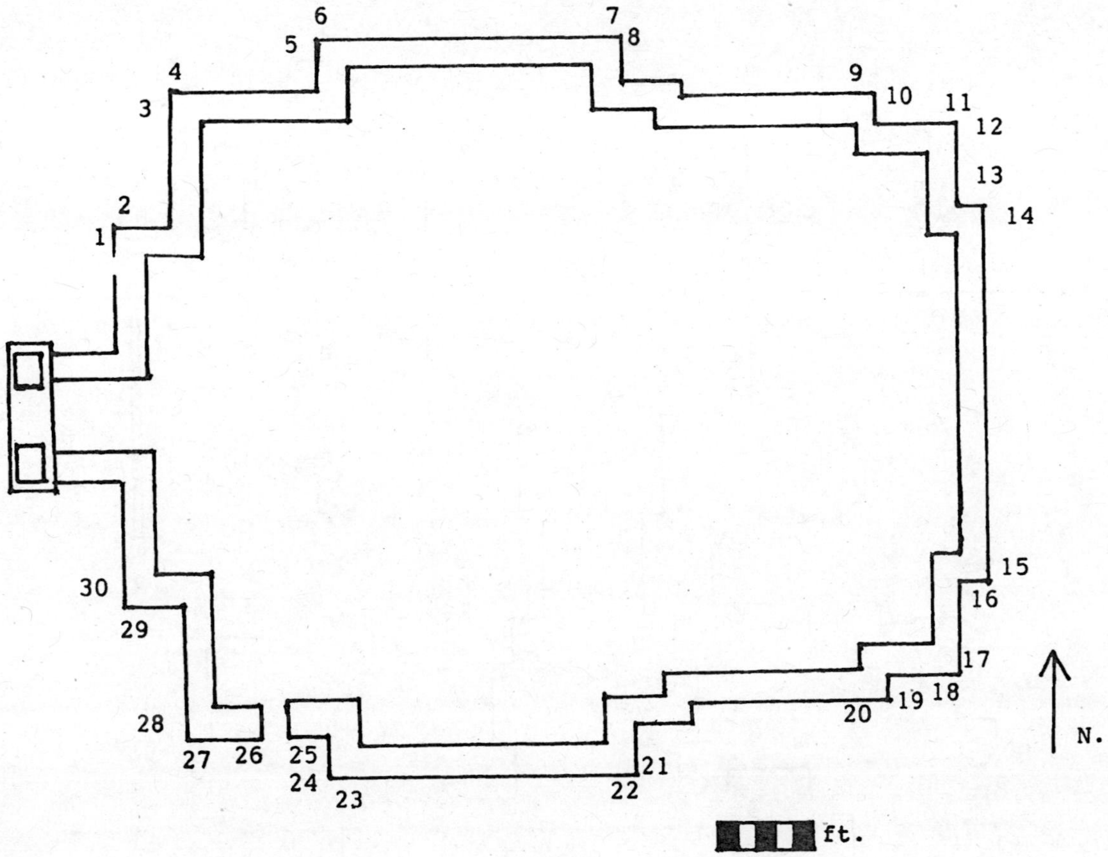

1. Avalokiteśvara
2. Yakṣa" (seated youth)
3. Lakulīśa
4. Yogin
5. Mātṛkā
6. Empty
7. Kārttikeya (?)
8. Sūrya
9. Yogin or king with disciples
10. Yogin
11. Empty
12. Empty
13. Sūrya
14. Ganeśa
15. Empty
16. Empty
17. Empty
18. Empty
19. Viṣṇu
20. Yogin or king with attendants
21. Sarasvatī
22. Composite figures
23. Vārāhī
24. Sarasvatī or celestial musician
25. Kārttikeya
26. Ganeśa
27. Śiva-Gajāsaṃharamūrti
28. Yogin (Lakulīśa?)
29. Goddess (Durgā?)
30. Composite figures

3. Mukteśvara temple, enclosure wall plan and list of corner images.

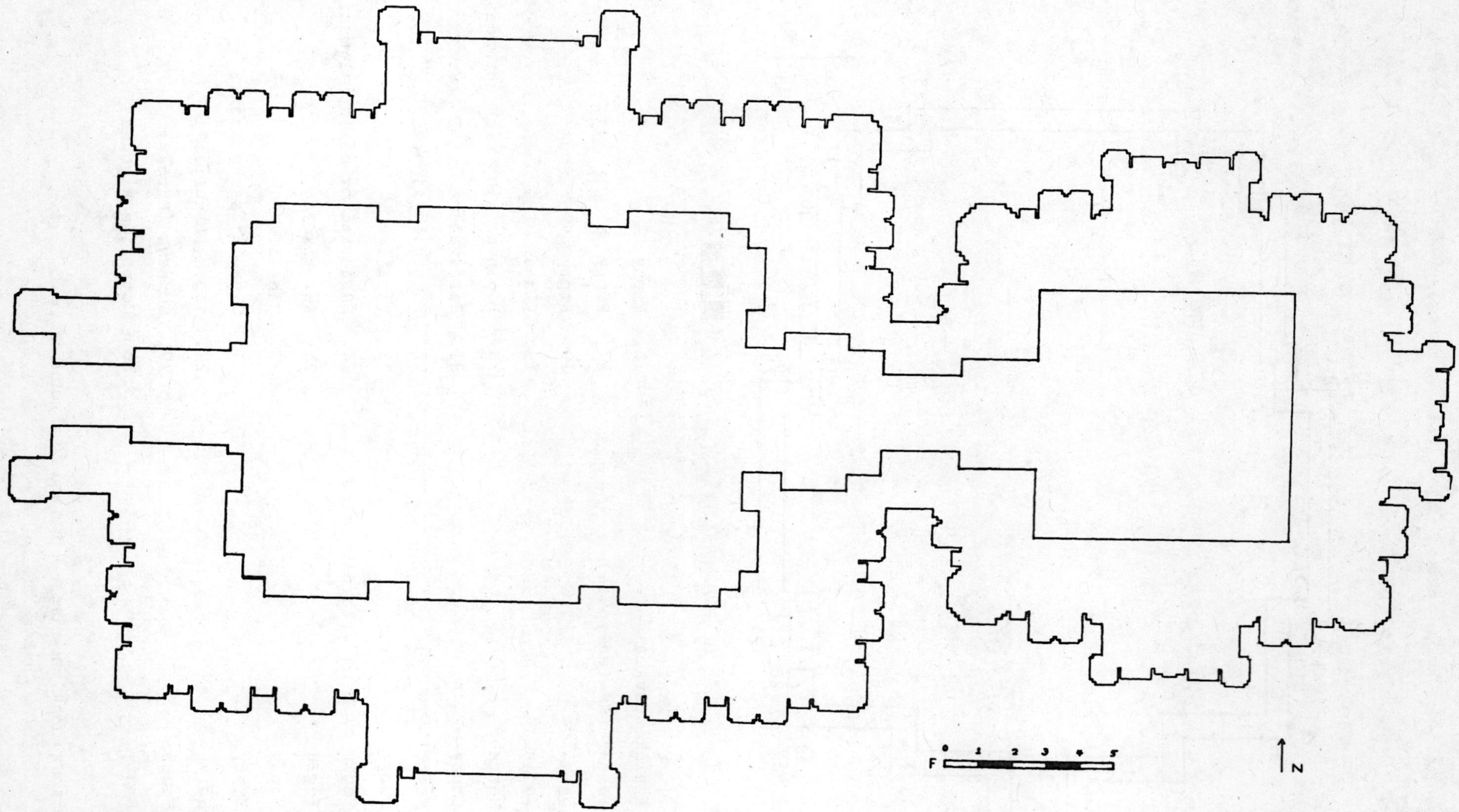

4. Plan, Mukteśvara temple.

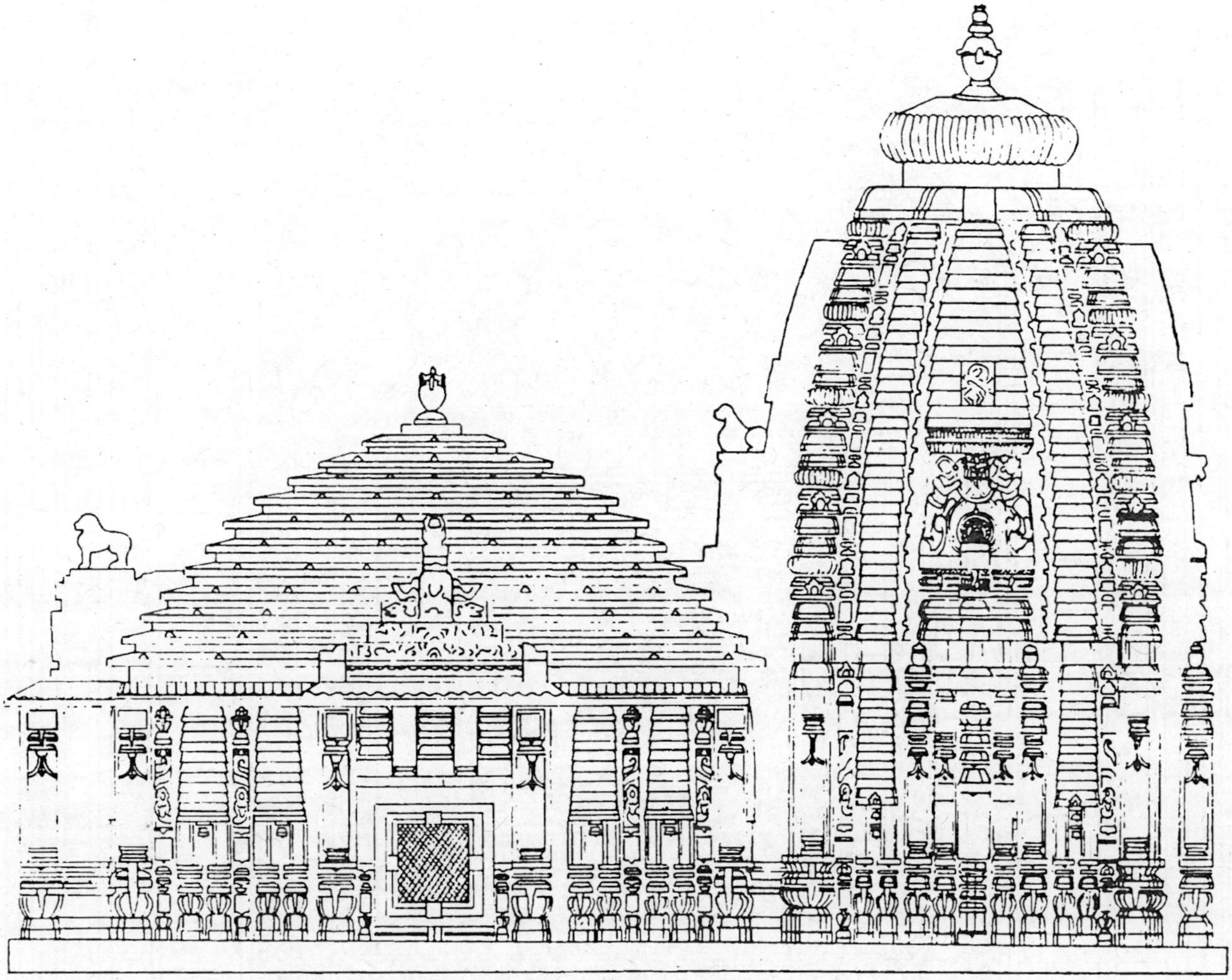

5. Mukteśvara temple, elevation. (Nancy Kipp Smith).

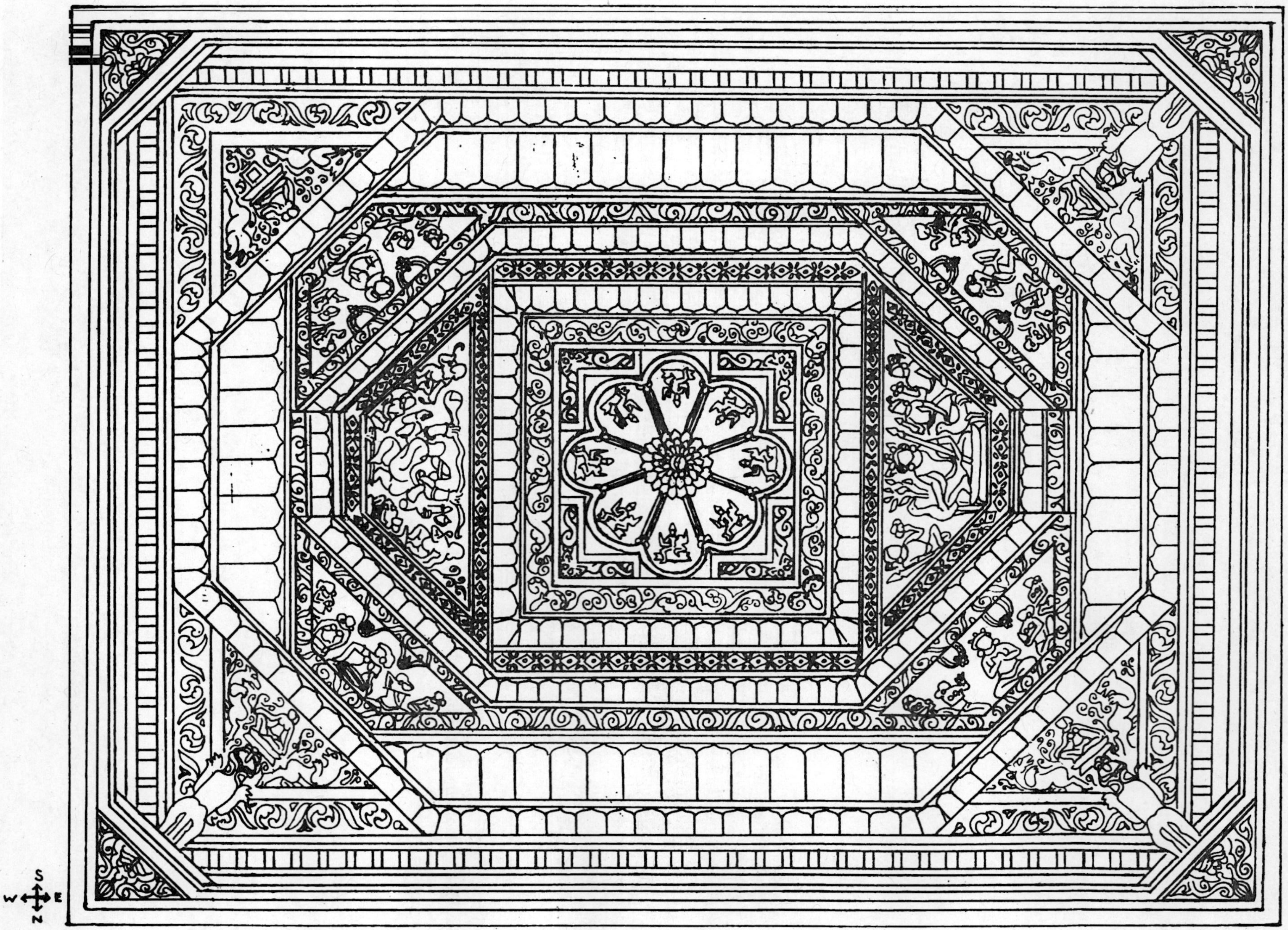

6. Mukteśvara temple, ceiling plan. (Nancy Kipp Smith, after R.L. Mitra, *Antiquities of Orissa*).

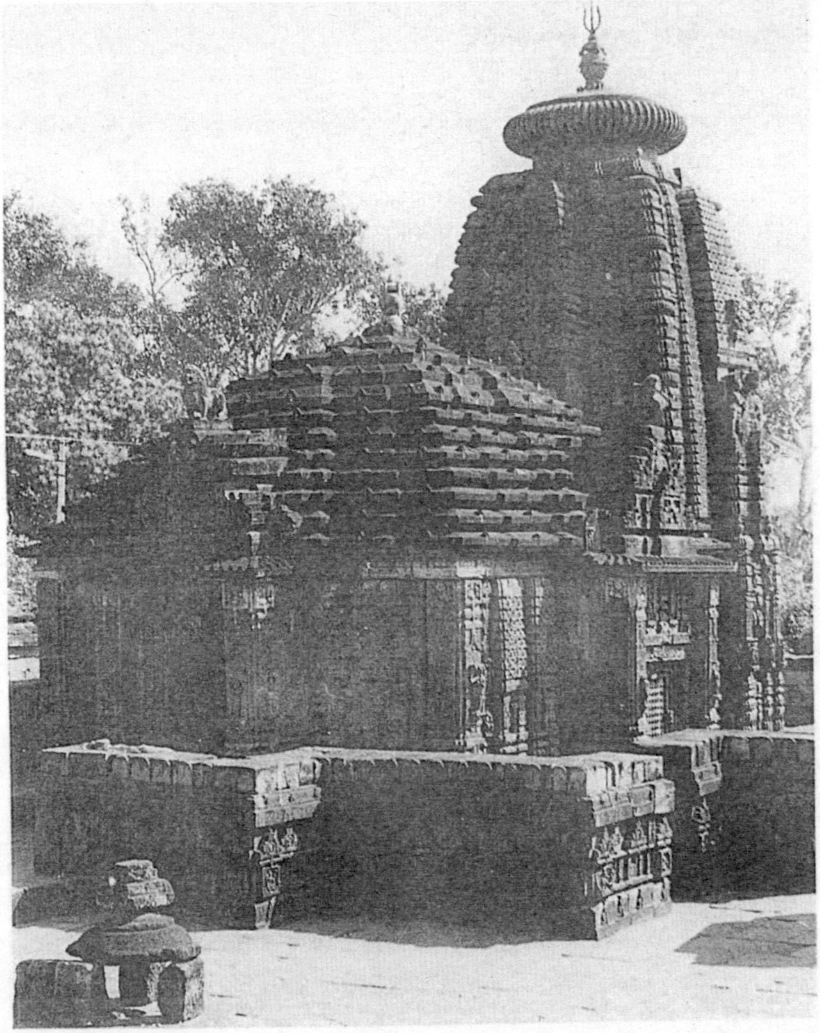

7. Mukteśvara temple, from southwest.

8. Mukteśvara temple, profile, from south.

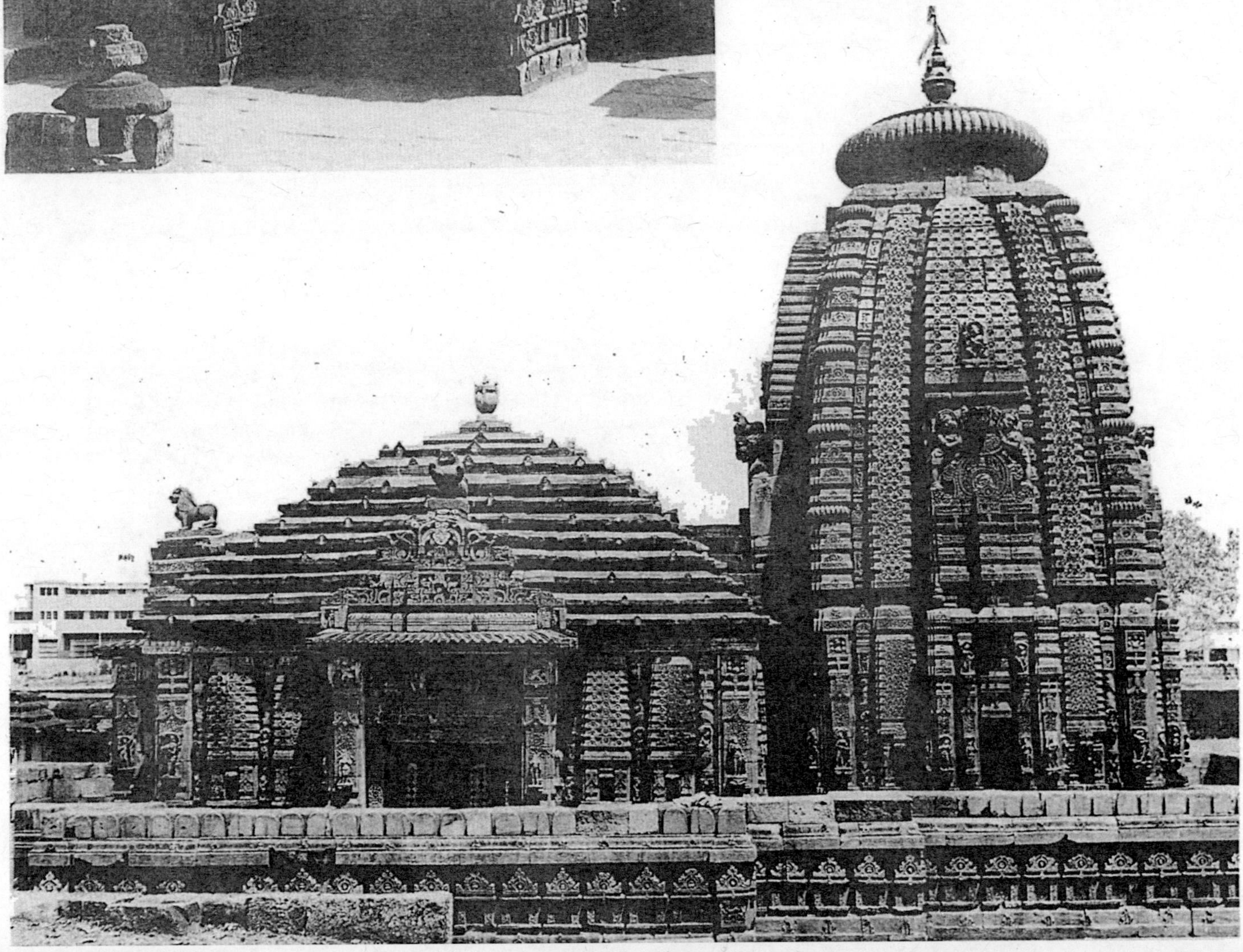

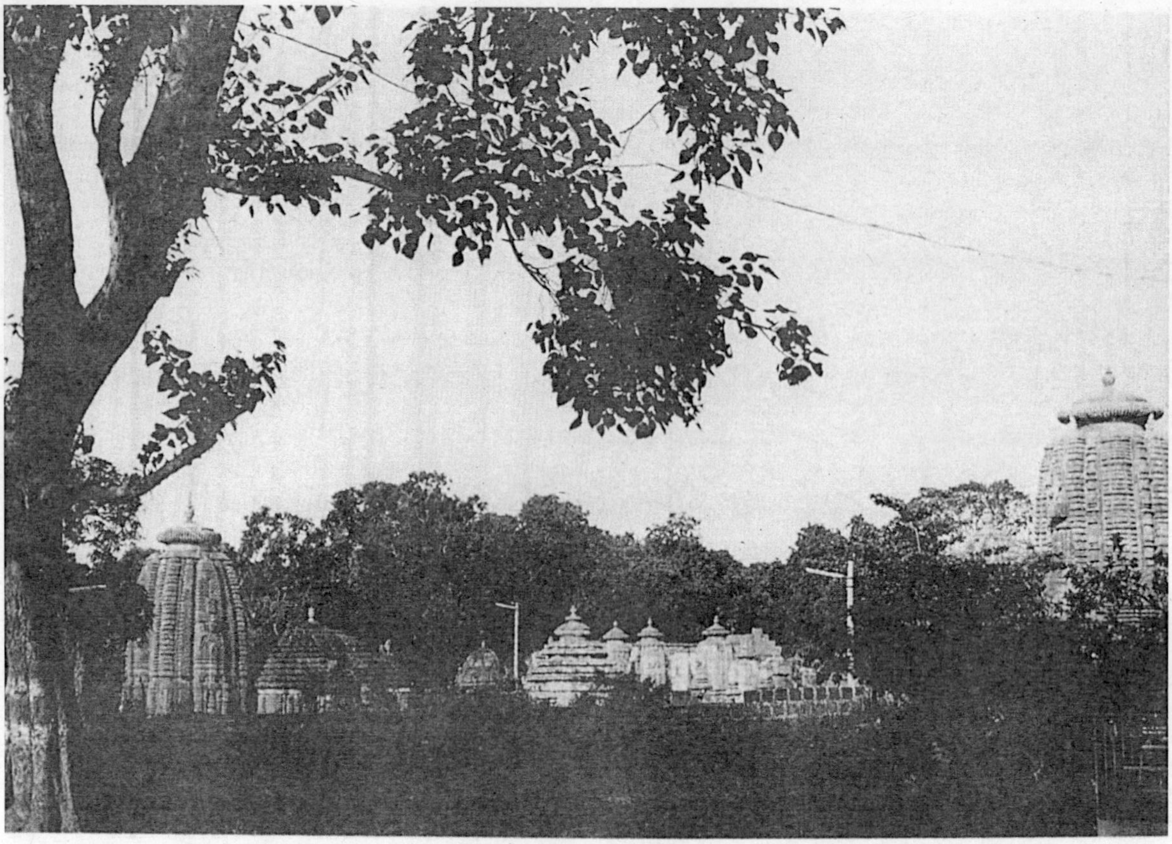

Mukteśvara temple compound, general view, from northeast.

10. Mukteśvara compound, miniature shrines west of entrance.

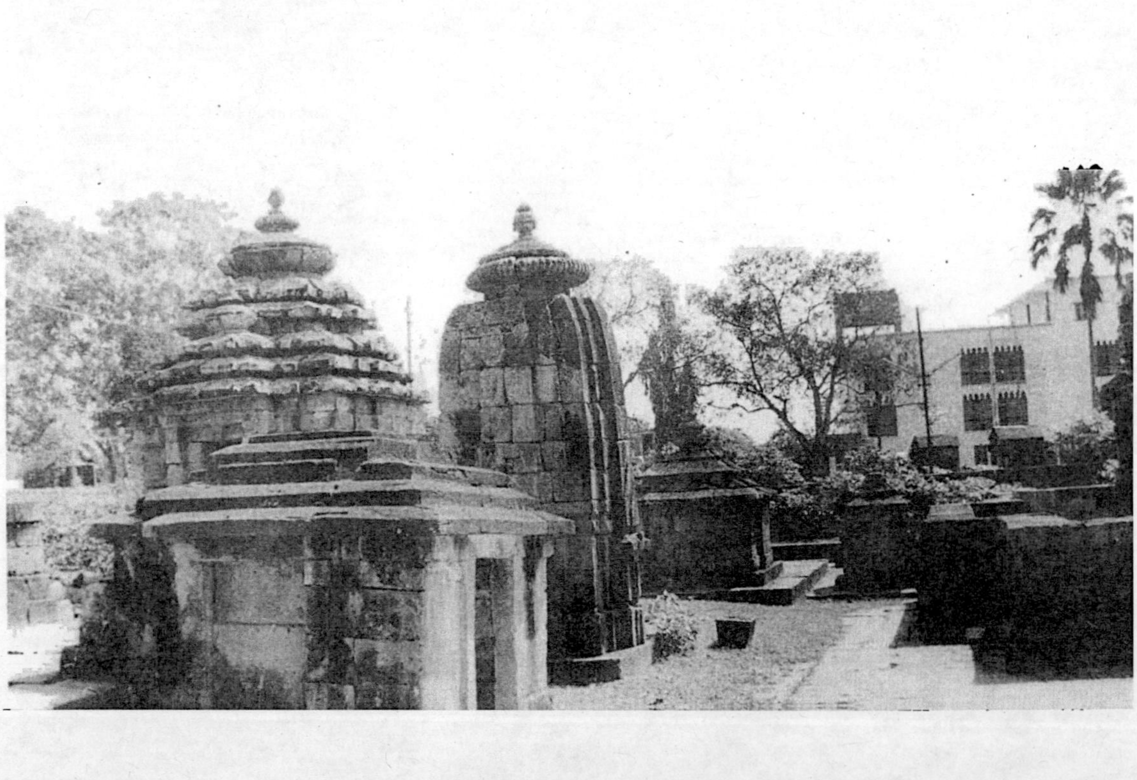

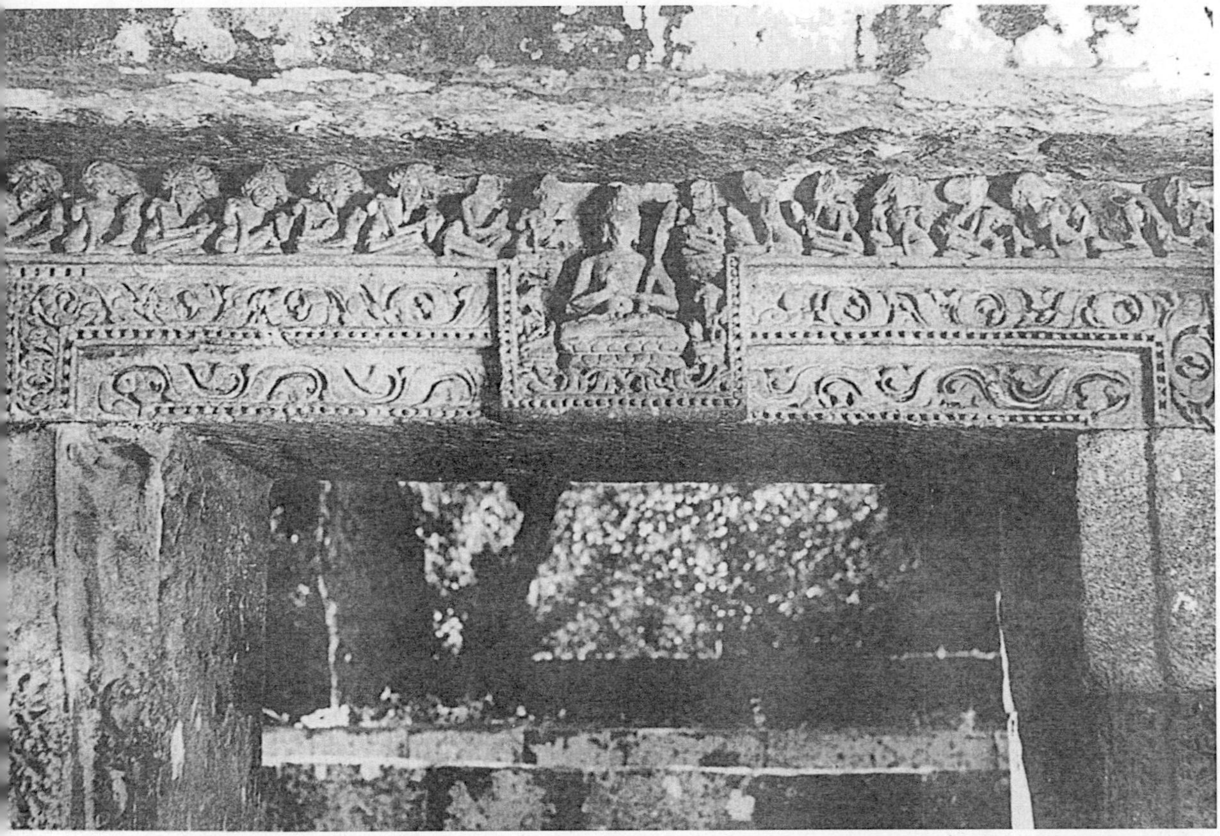

15. Marīci Kuṇḍa, lintel.

16. Mukteśvara temple, enclosure wall, from northeast.

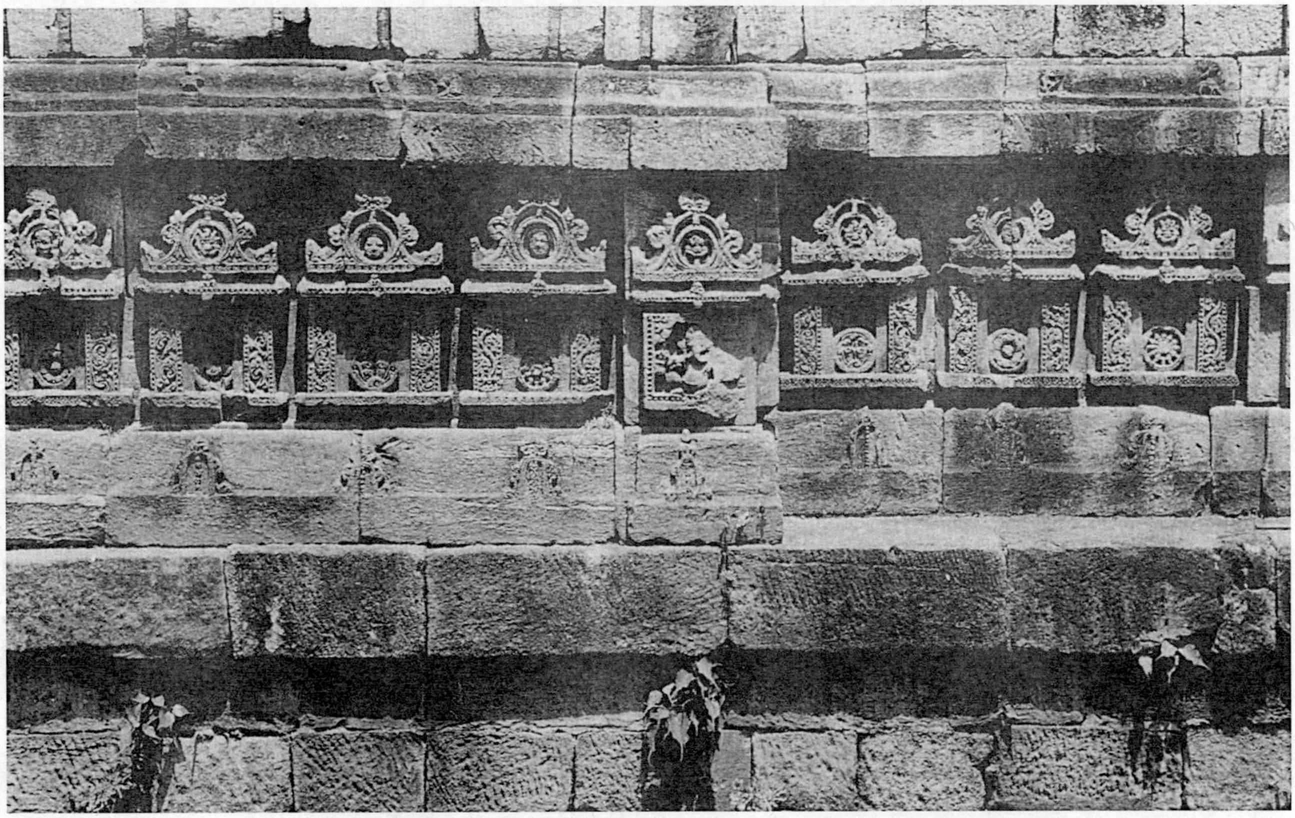

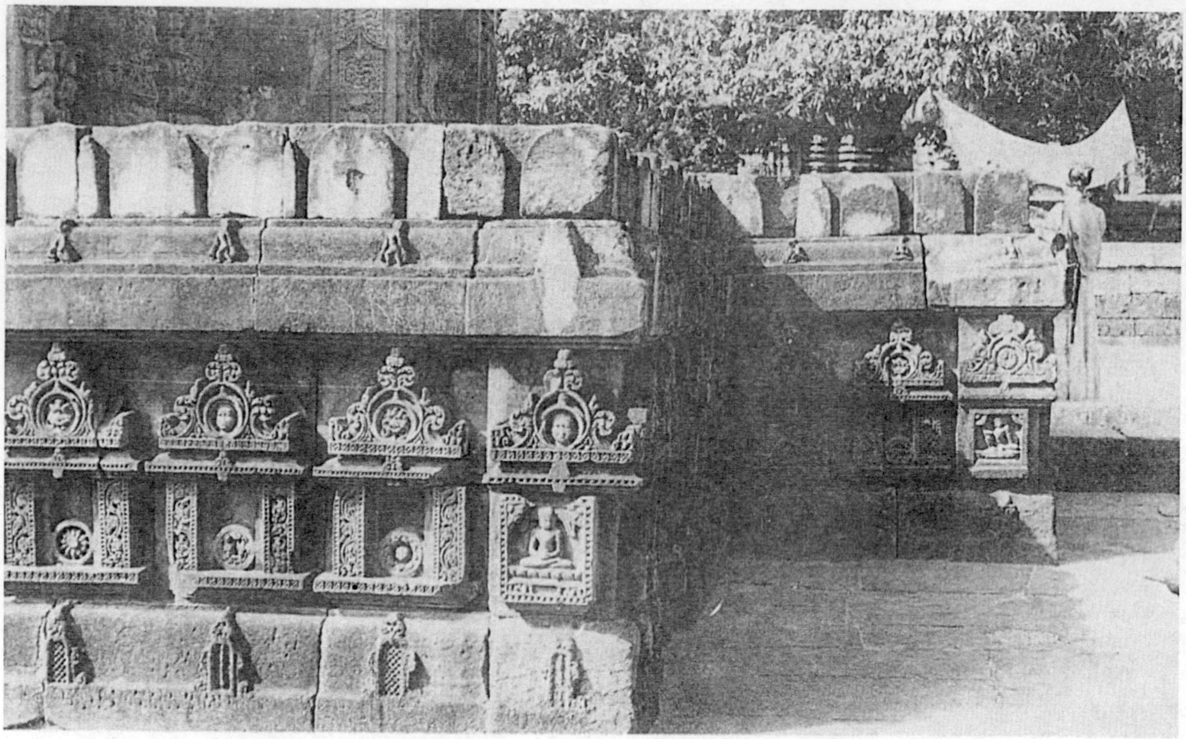

17. Enclosure wall, detail from northwest.

18. Enclosure wall, male figure.

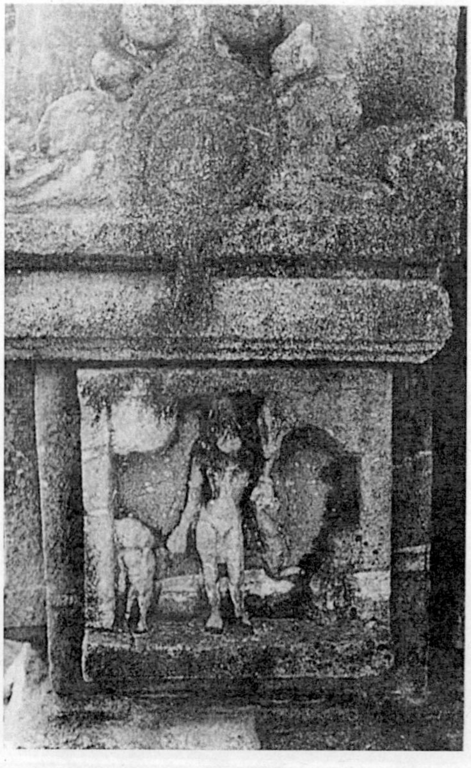

19. Enclosure wall, *yakṣa*.

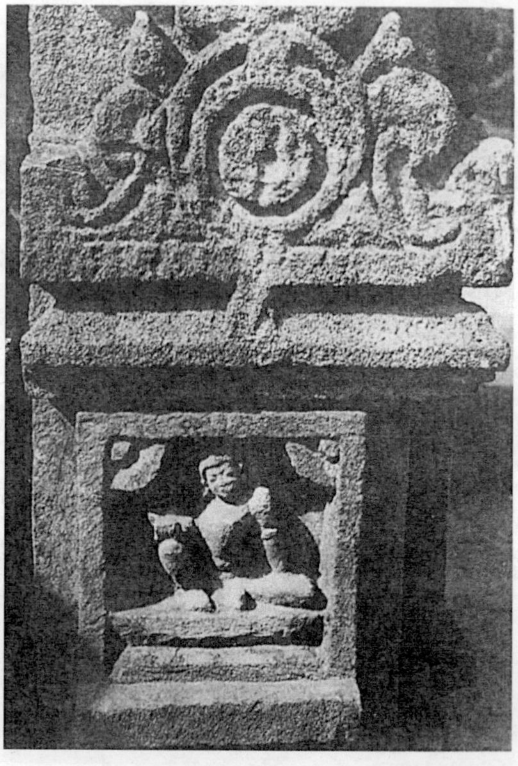

20. Enclosure wall, Lakulīśa.

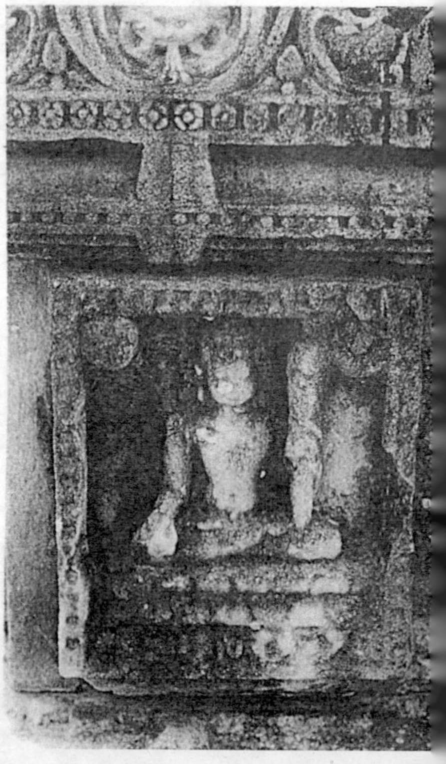

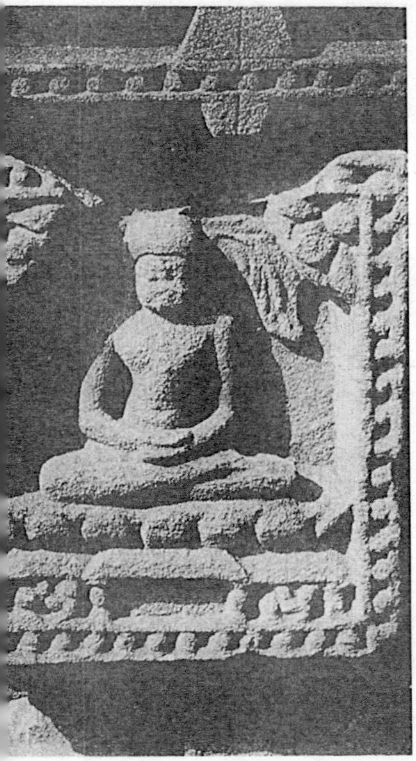

21. Enclosure wall, *yogin.*

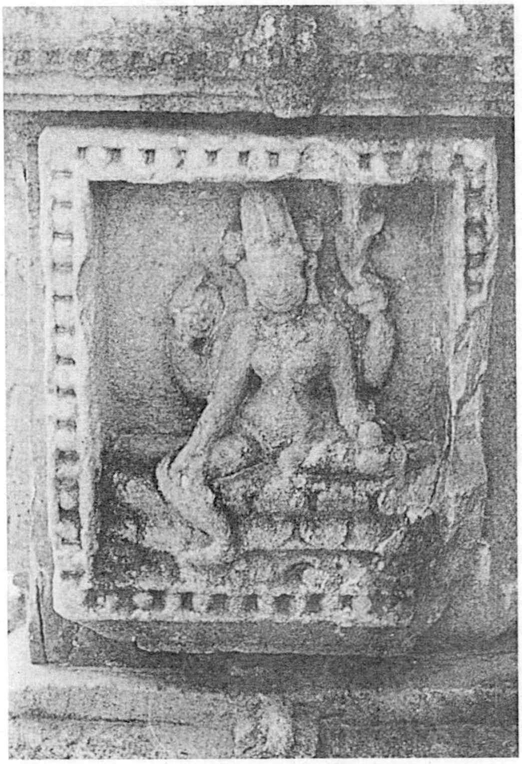

22. Enclosure wall, Mātṛkā.

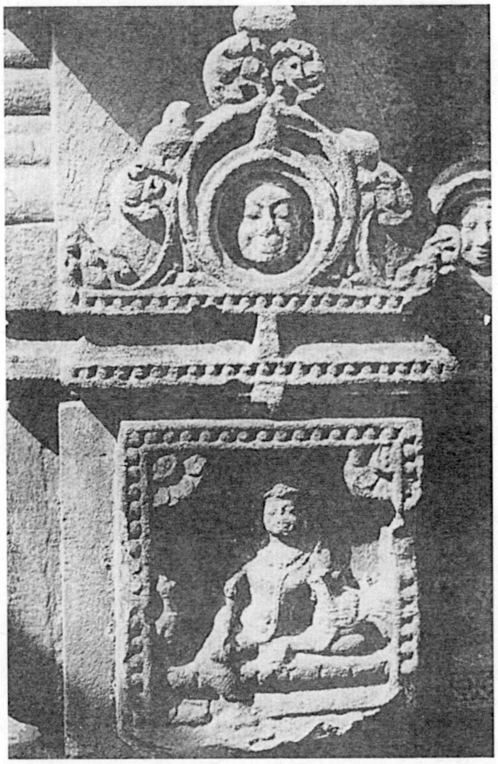

23. Enclosure wall, Kārttikeya(?).

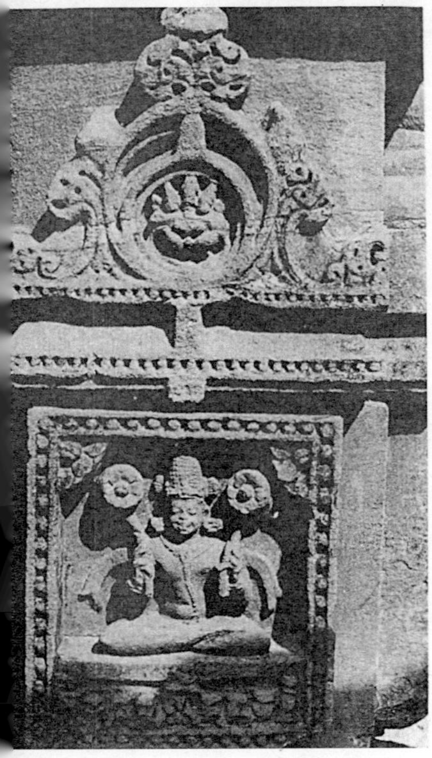

24. Enclosure wall, Sūrya.

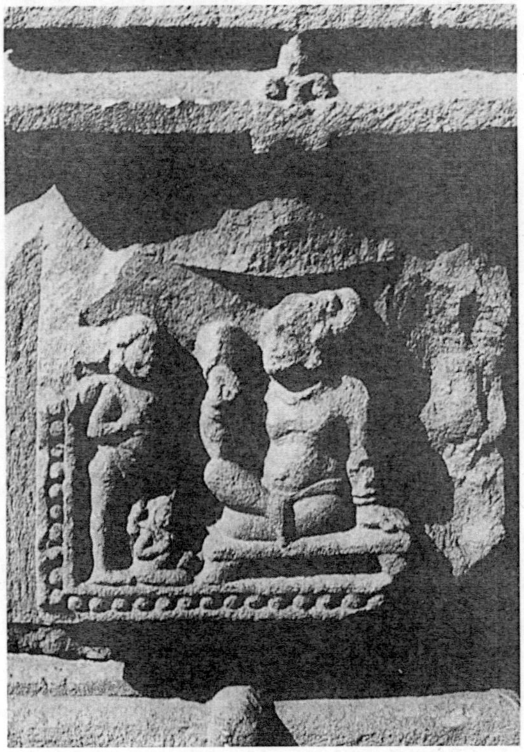

25. Enclosure wall, *yogin* with disciples.

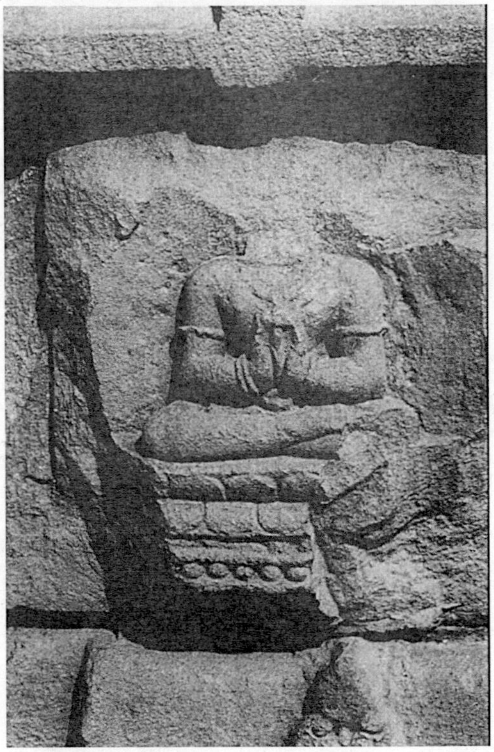

26. Enclosure wall, *yogin.*

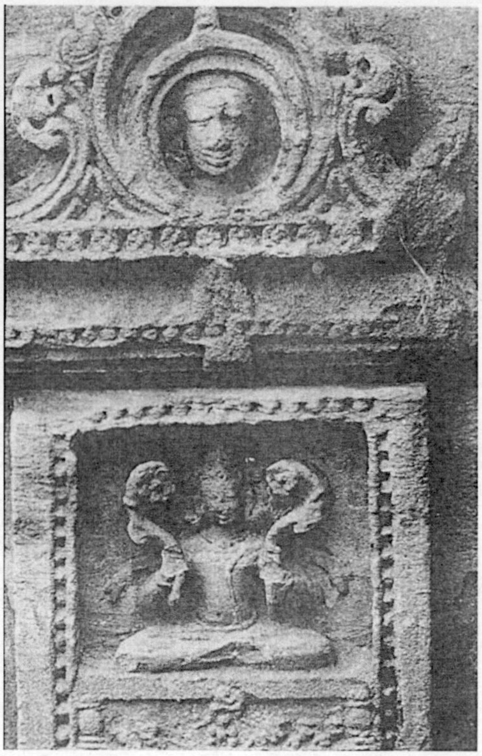

27. Enclosure wall, Sūrya.

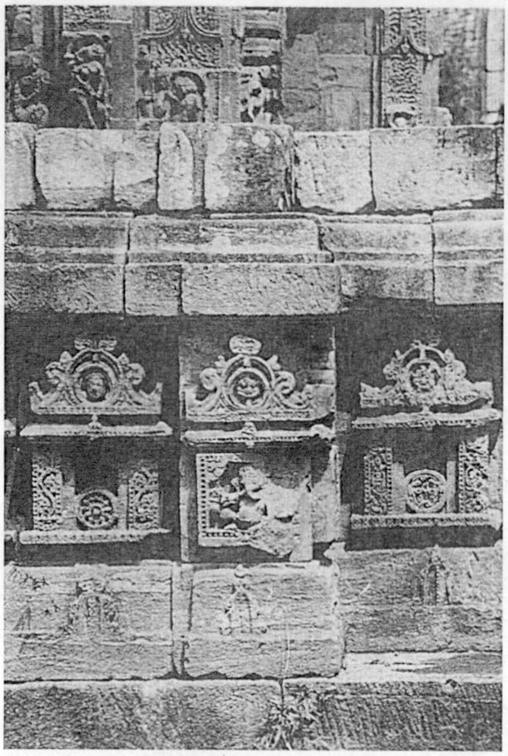

28. Enclosure wall, Gaṇeśa.

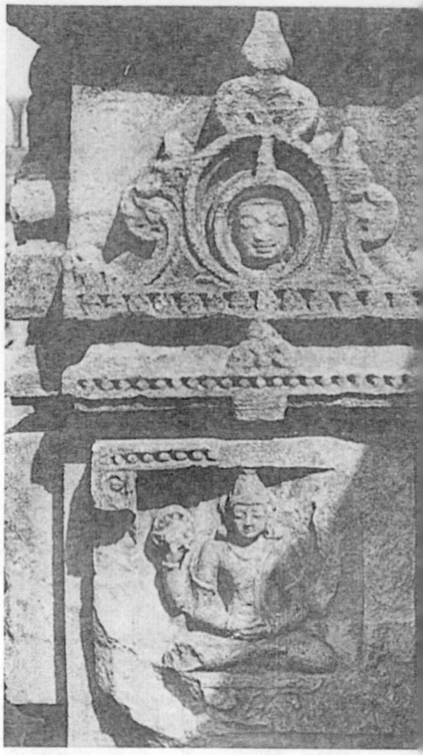

29. Enclosure wall, Viṣṇu(?).

30. Enclosure wall, royal figure(?).

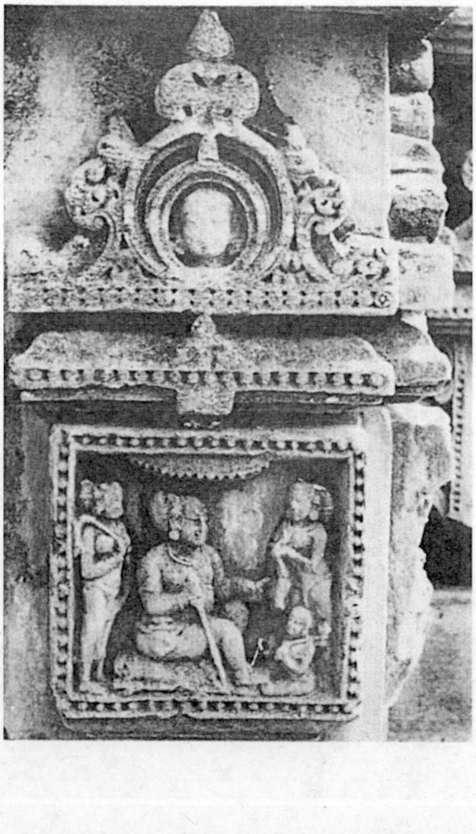

31. Enclosure wall, Sarasvatī.

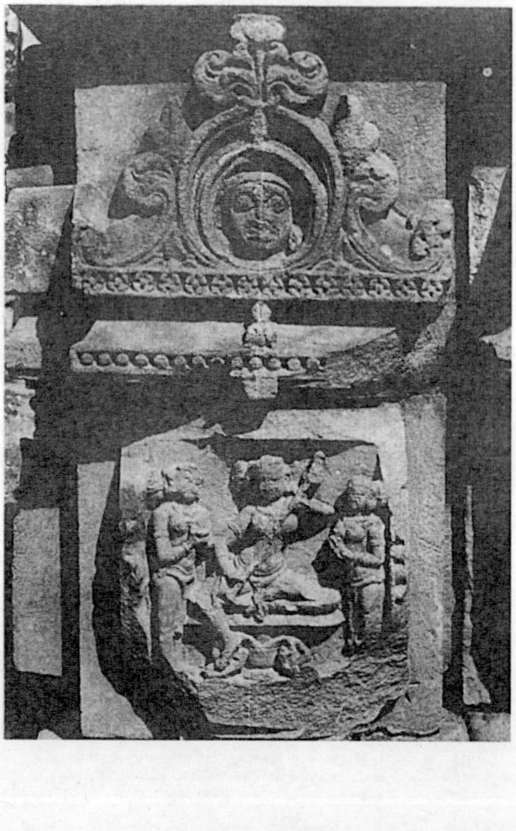

32. Enclosure wall, composite figure.

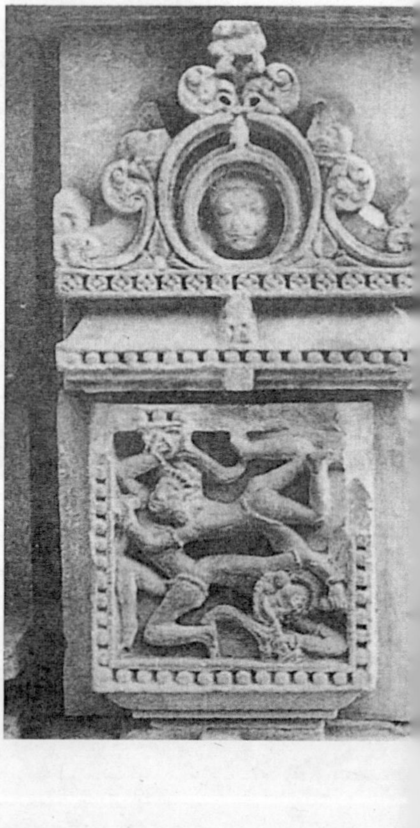

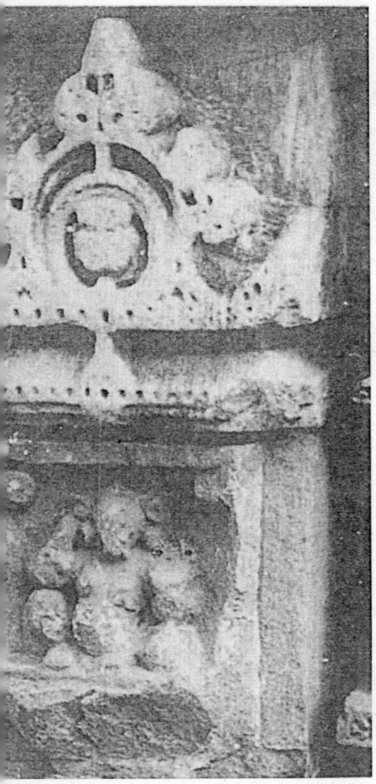

33. Enclosure wall, Vārāhī.

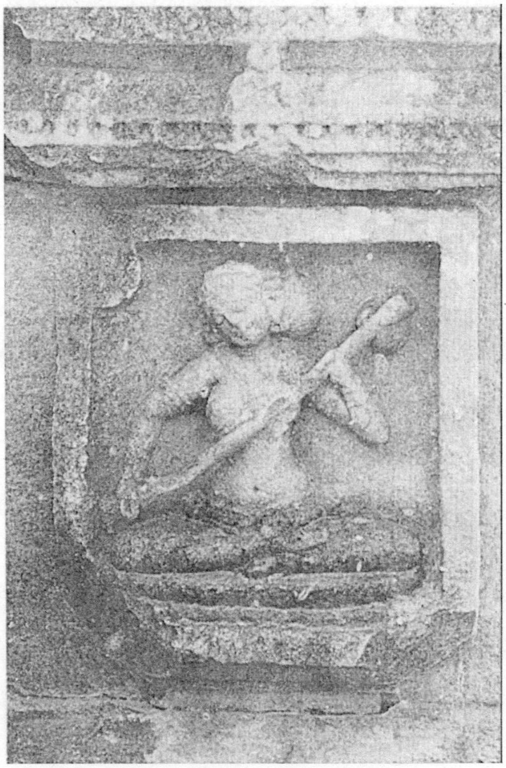

34. Enclosure wall, Sarasvatī celestial musician.

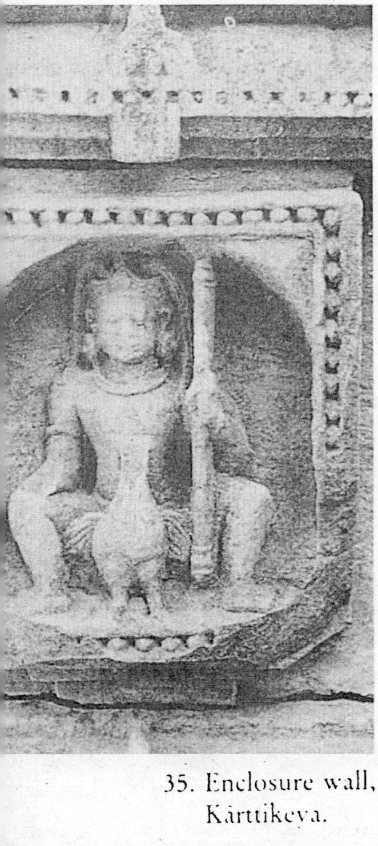

35. Enclosure wall, Kārttikeya.

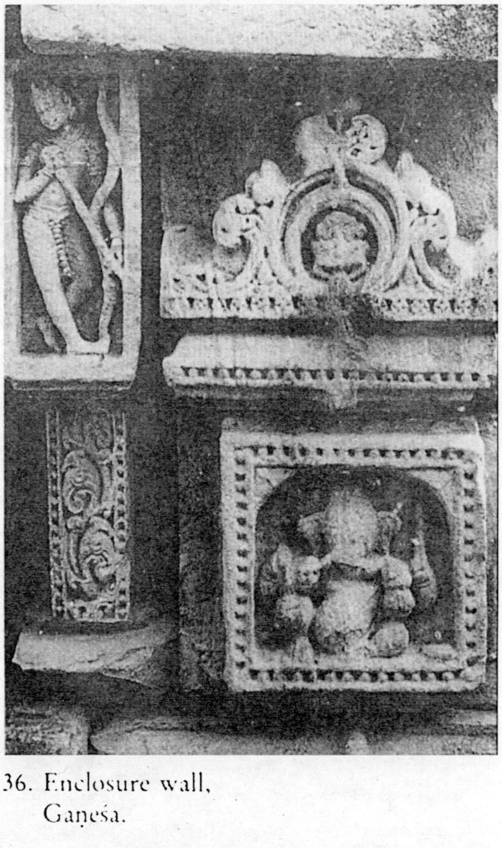

36. Enclosure wall, Gaṇeśa.

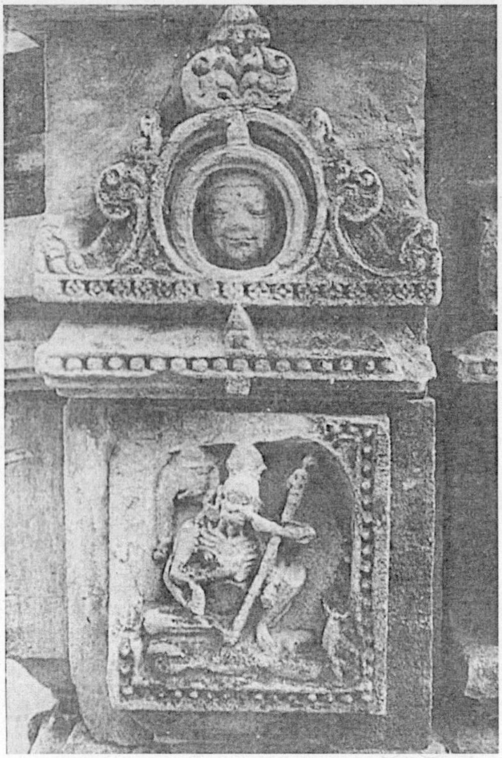

37. Enclosure wall, Śiva Gajāsurasaṁhāramūrti.

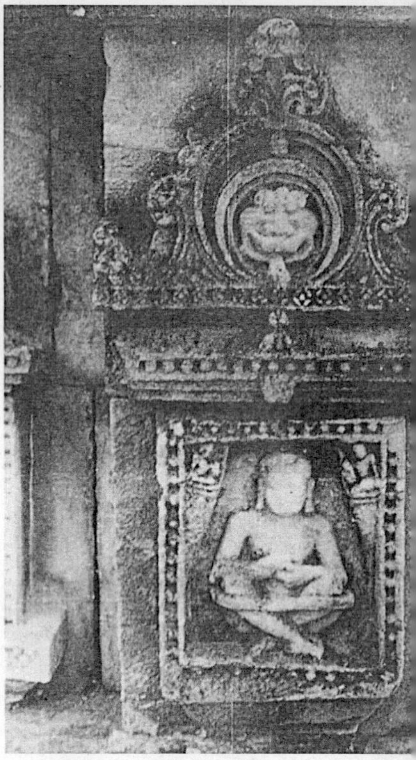

38. Enclosure wall, *yogin* (Lakulīśa?).

39. Enclosure wall, goddess.

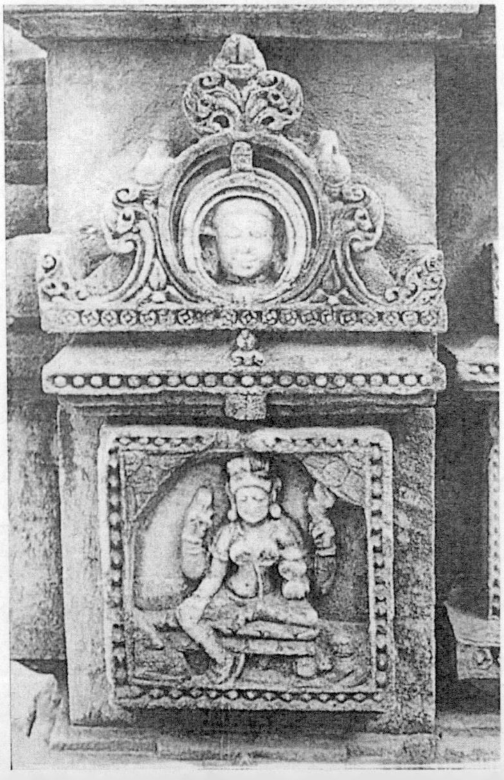

40. Enclosure wall, composite figure.

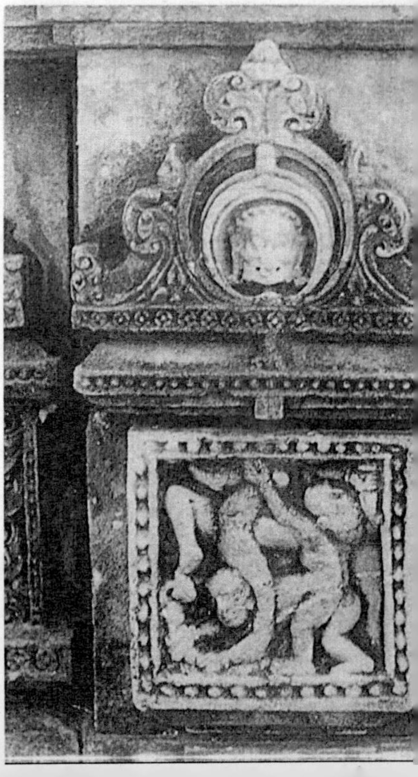

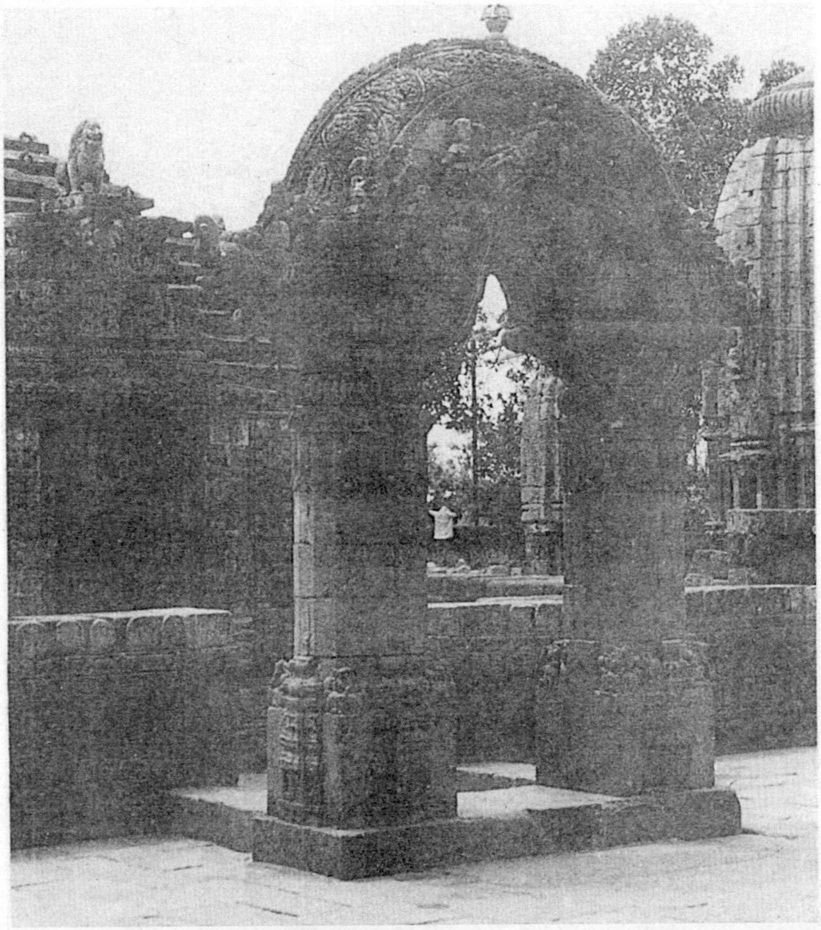

41. *Toraṇa*, from west.

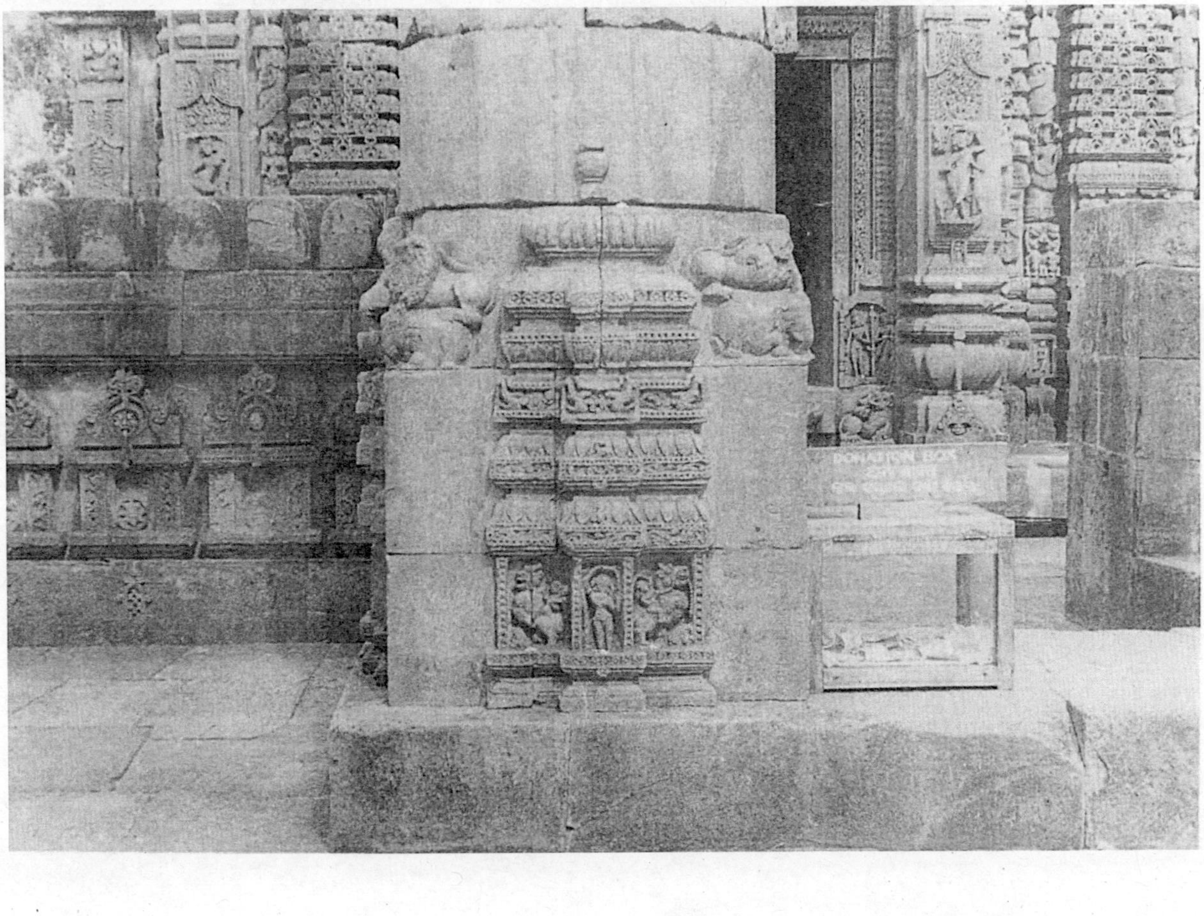

42. *Toraṇa*, detail of base.

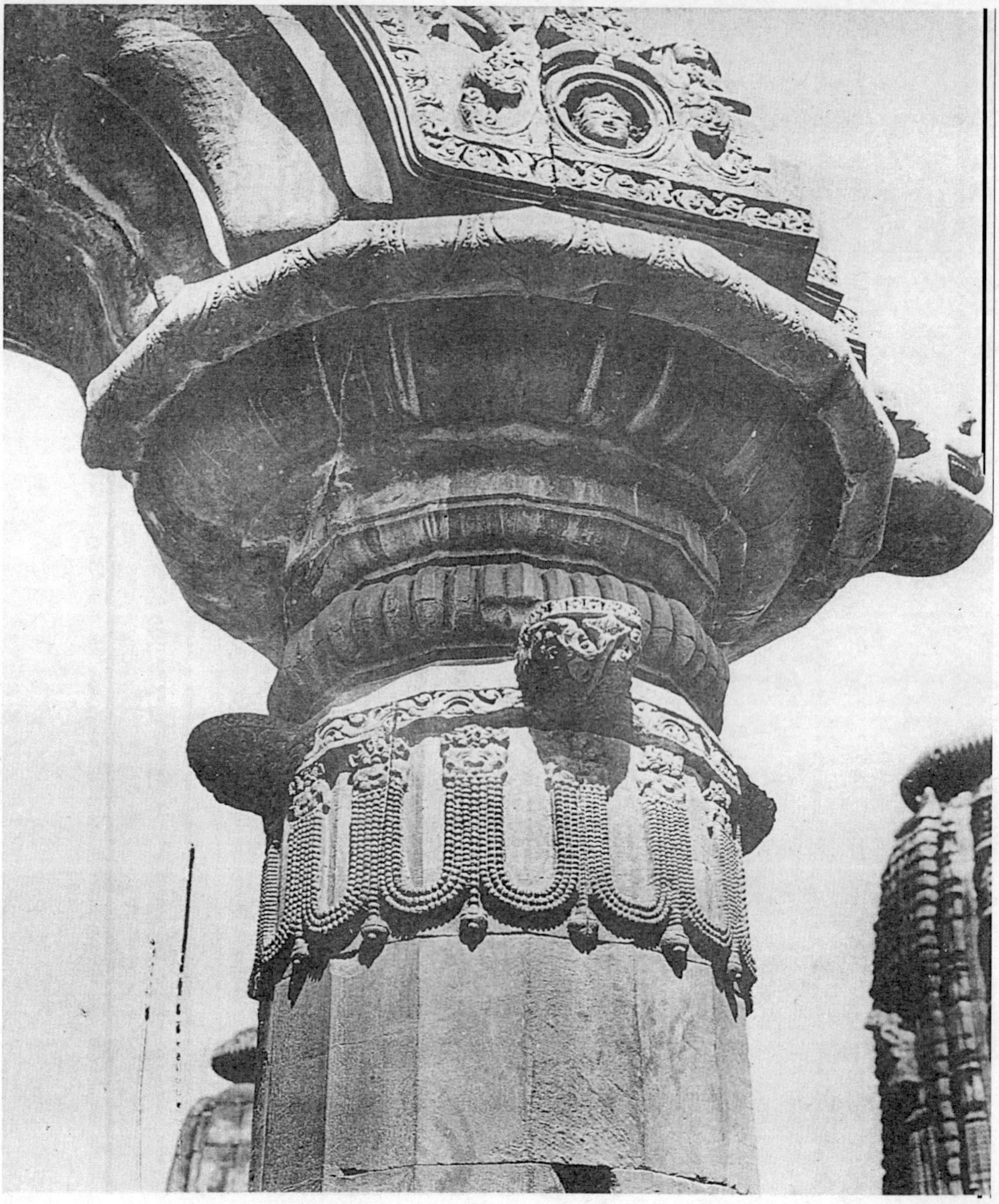

43. *Toraṇa*, detail of capital.

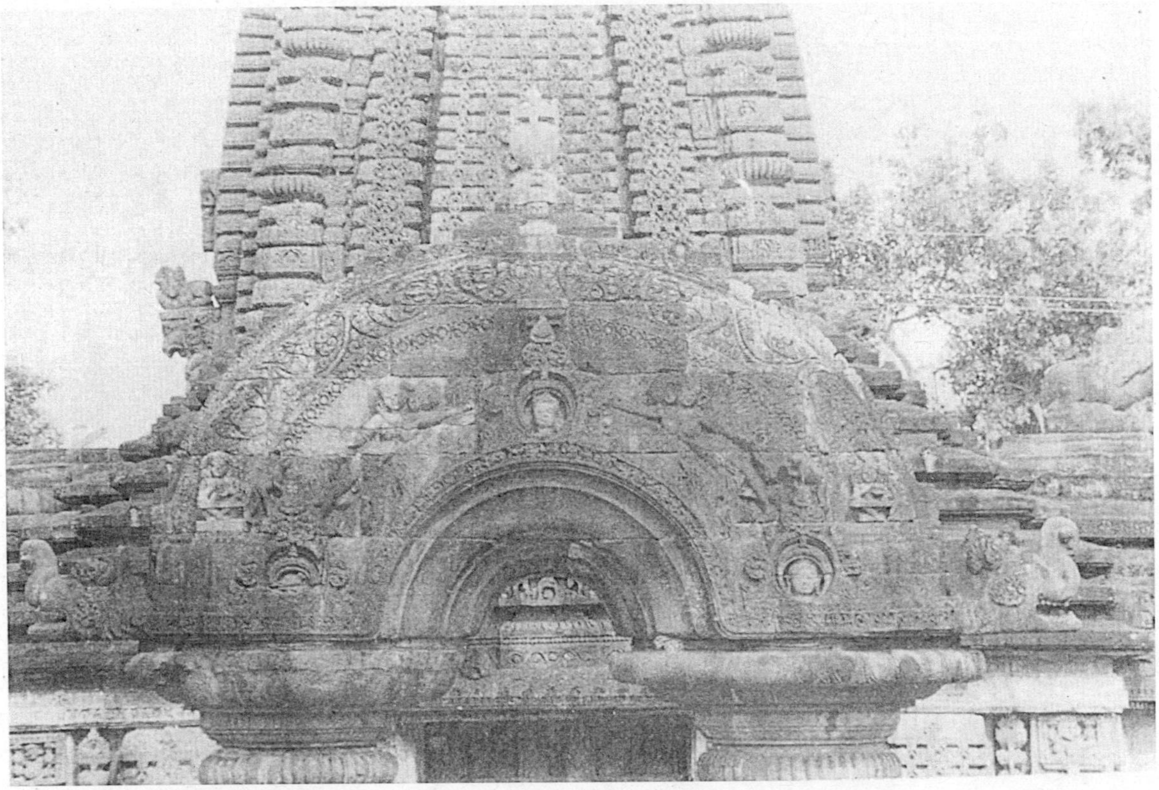

44. *Toraṇa*, arch from west.

45. *Toraṇa*, arch from east.

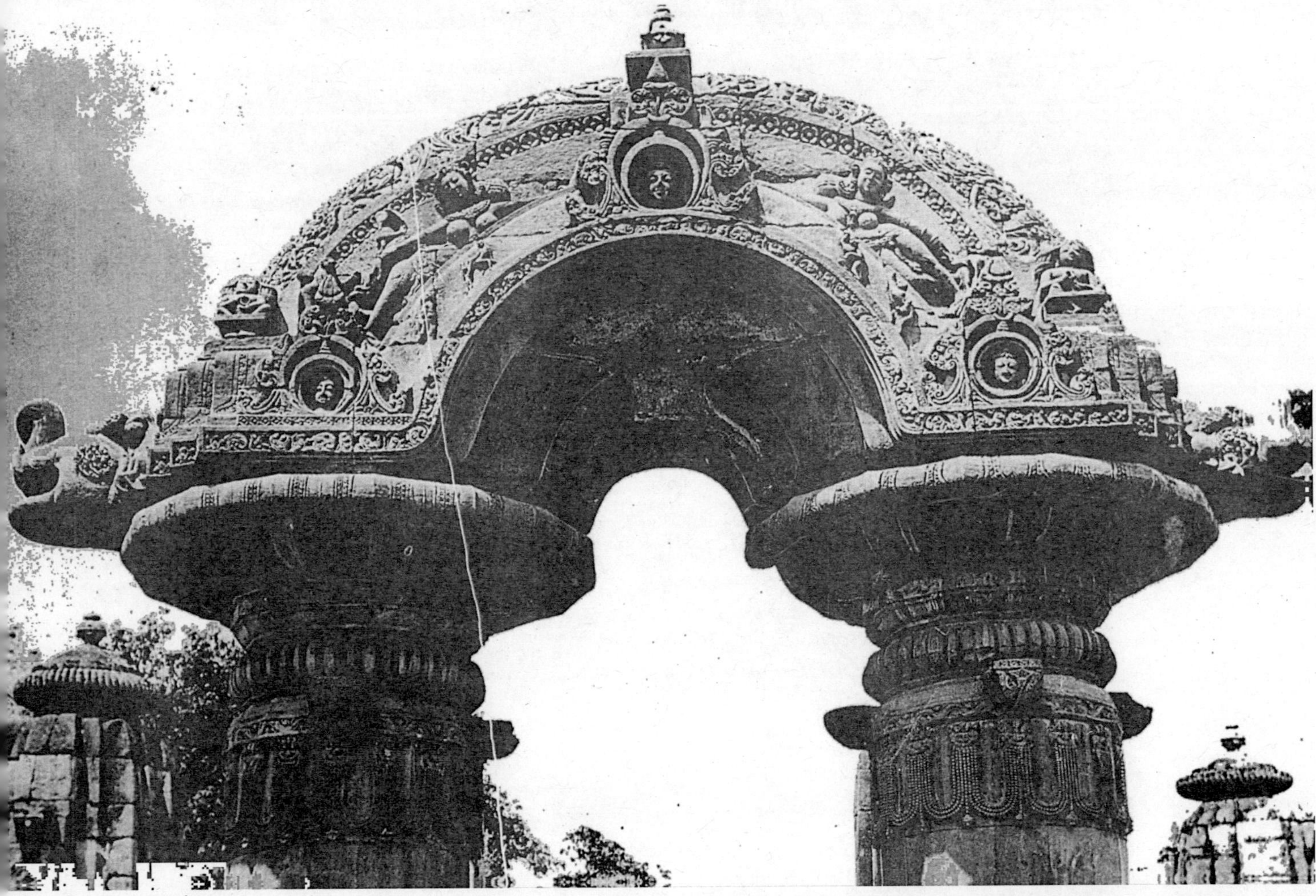

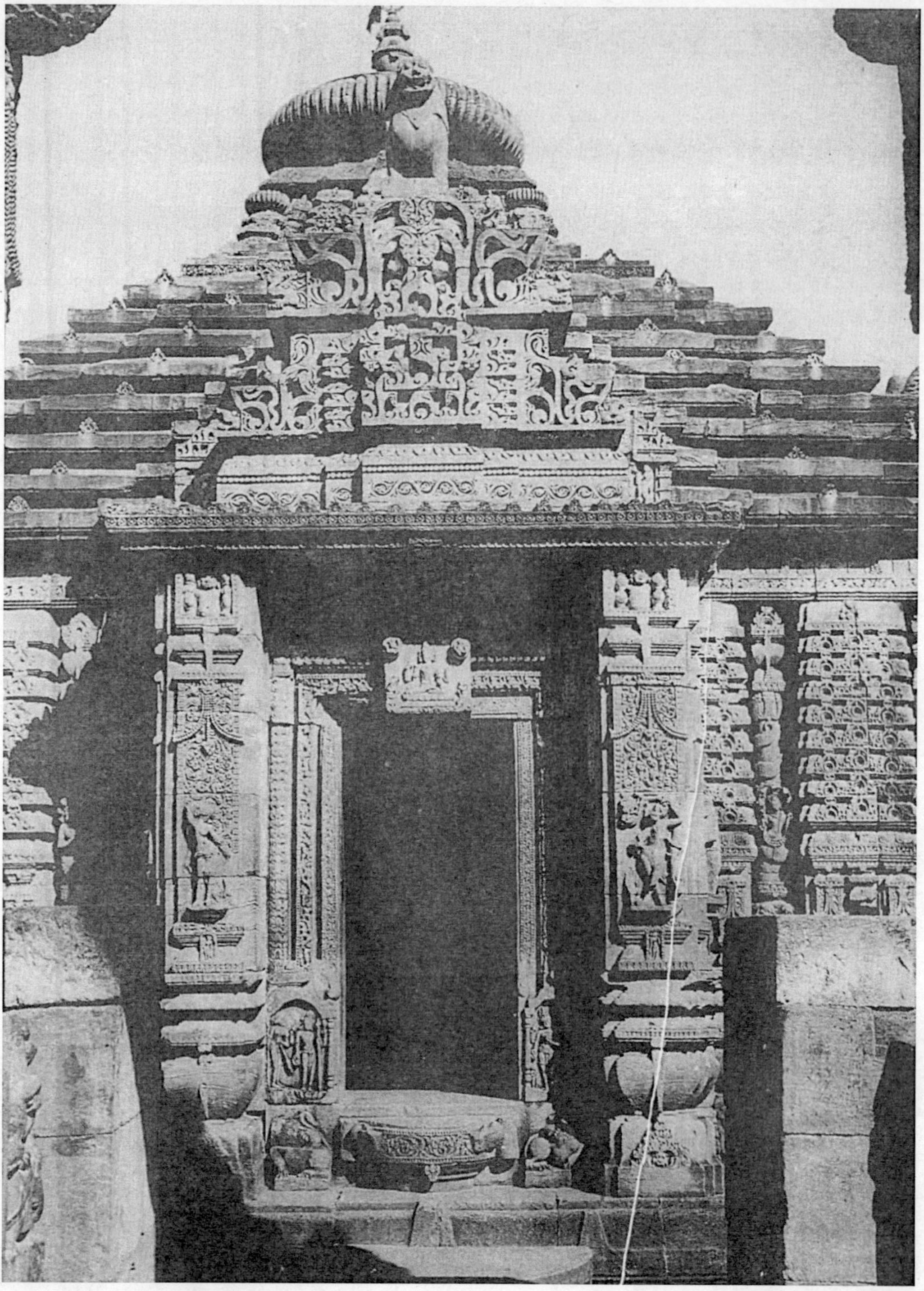

46. *Maṇḍapa*, entrance. (AIIS).

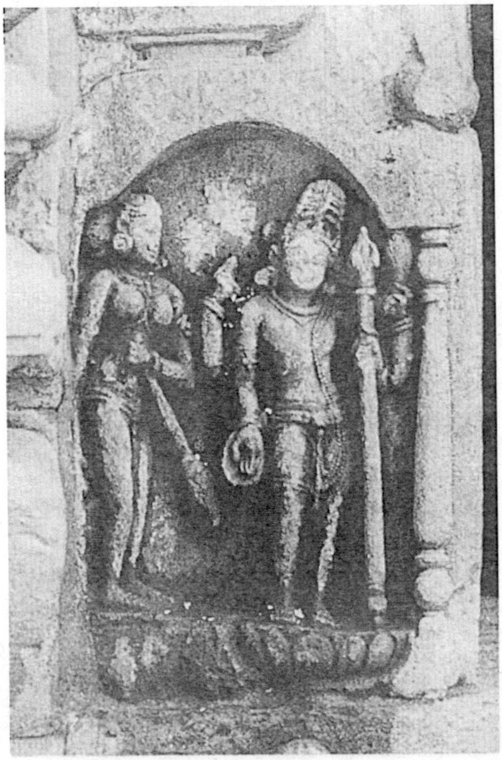

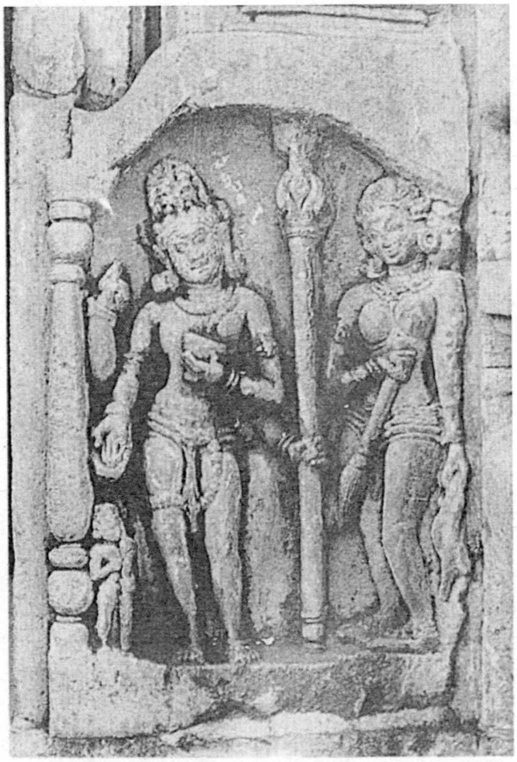

47. Entrance, left *dvārapāla*.

48. Entrance, right *dvārapāla*.

49. Entrance, detail of lintel.

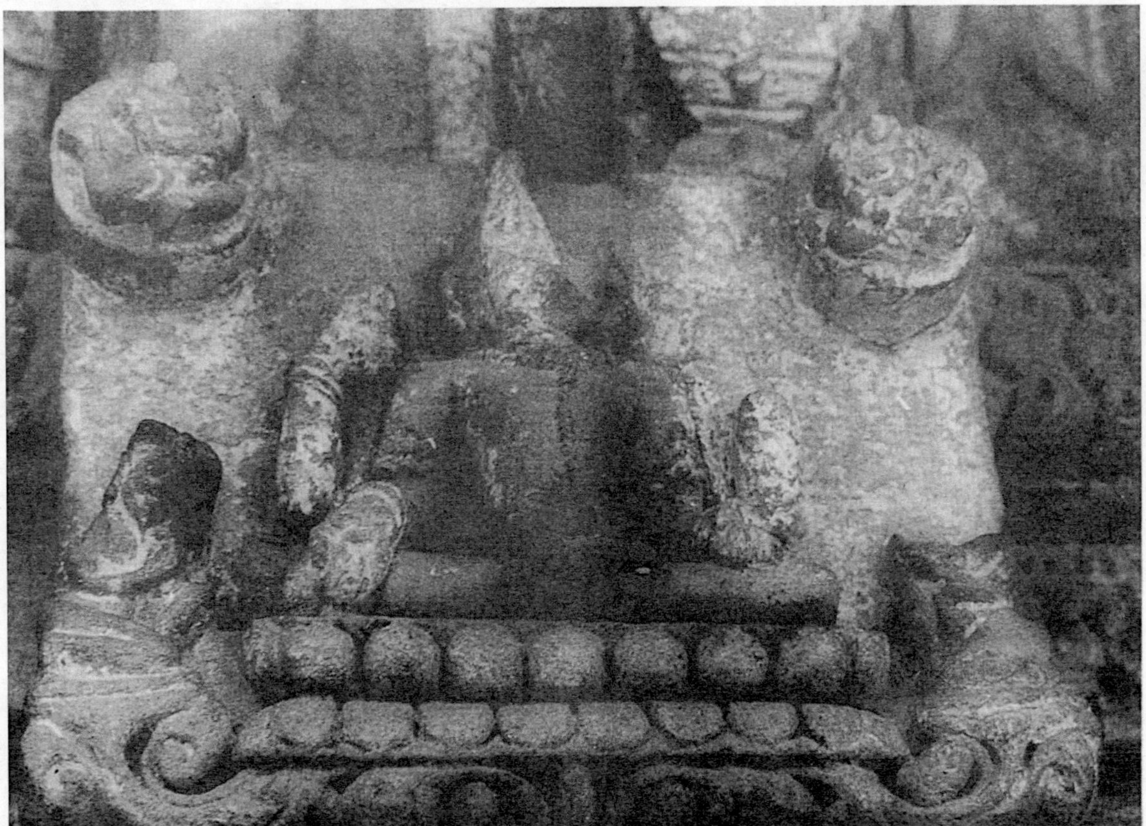

51. South wall, lattice window.

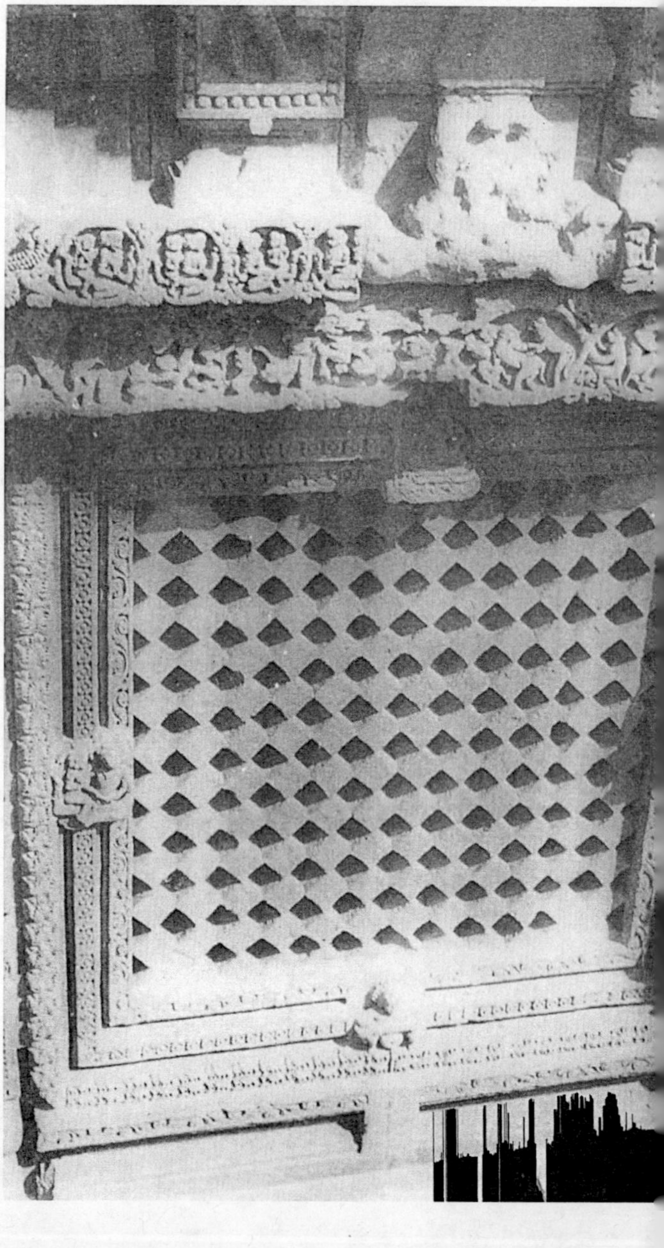

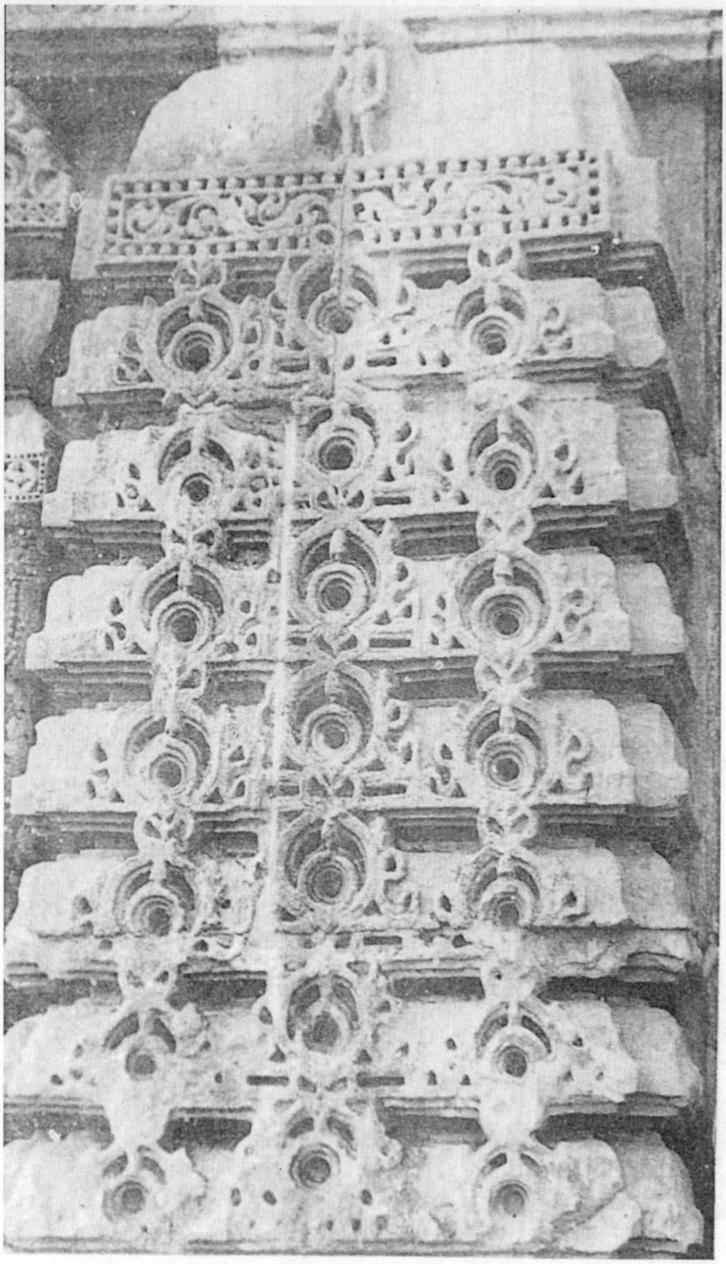

50. West wall, detail of *ratha*.

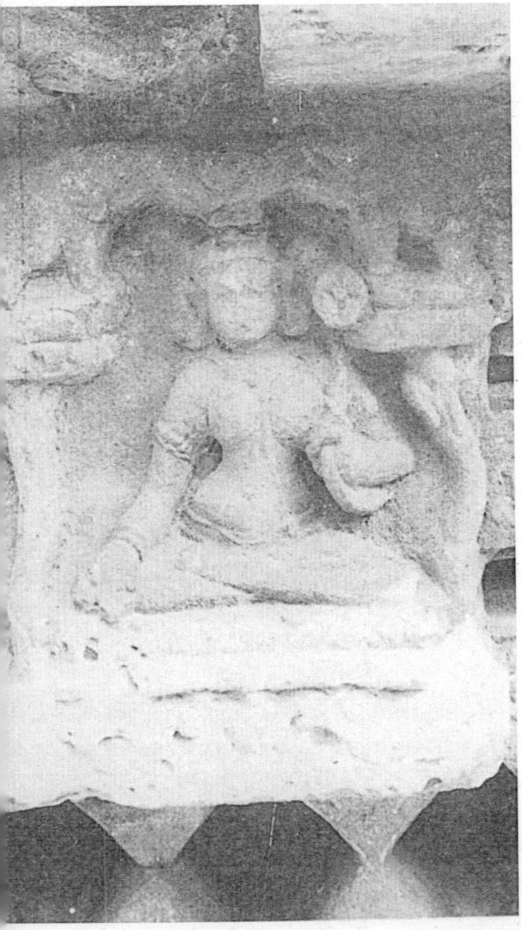

52. Lattice window, Gajalakṣmi.

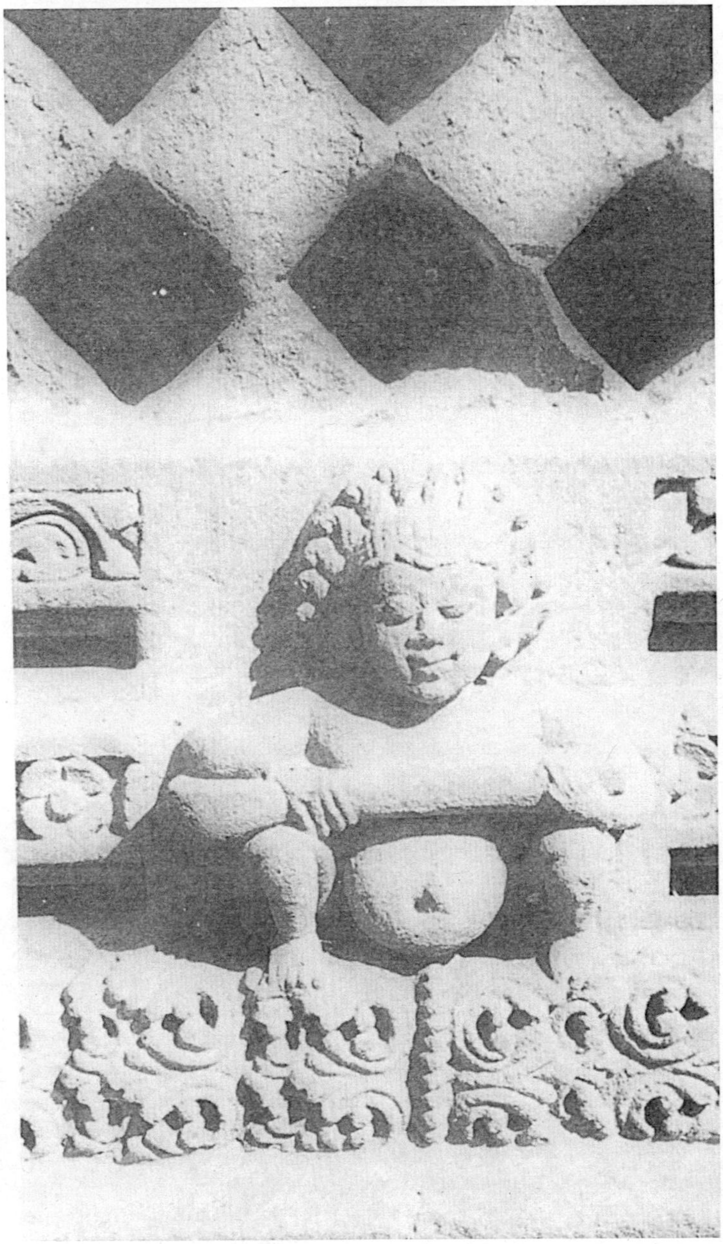

53. Lattice window, *gaṇa*.

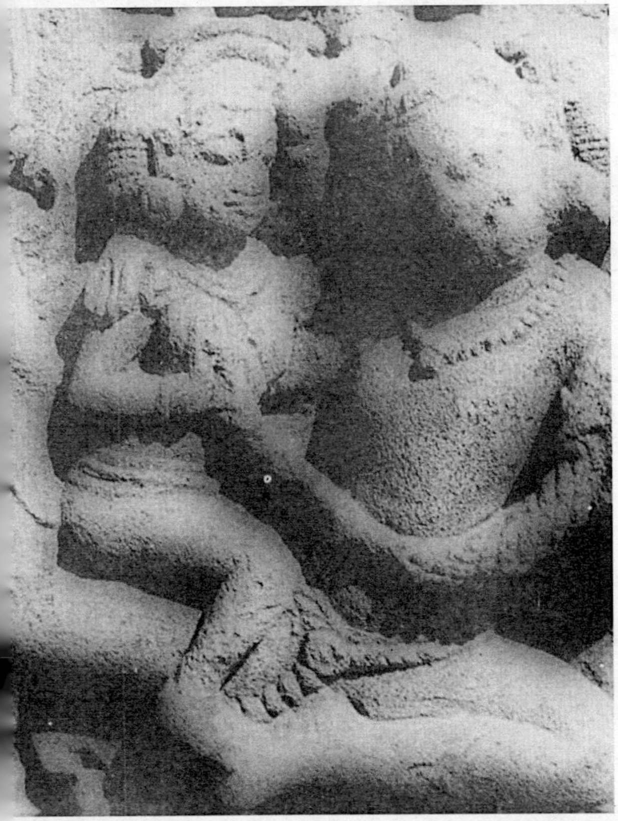

54. Lattice window, left side, *gandharva* couple.

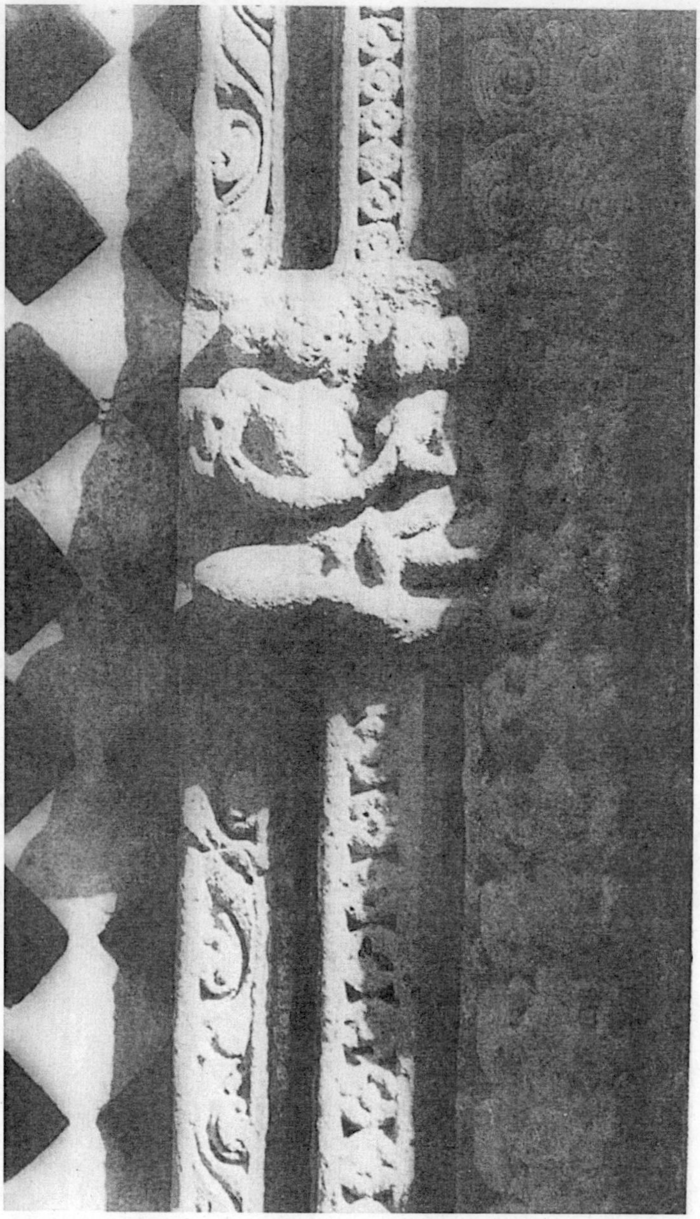

55. Lattice window, right side, *gandharva* couple.

56. Entrance, left pilaster, female figure.

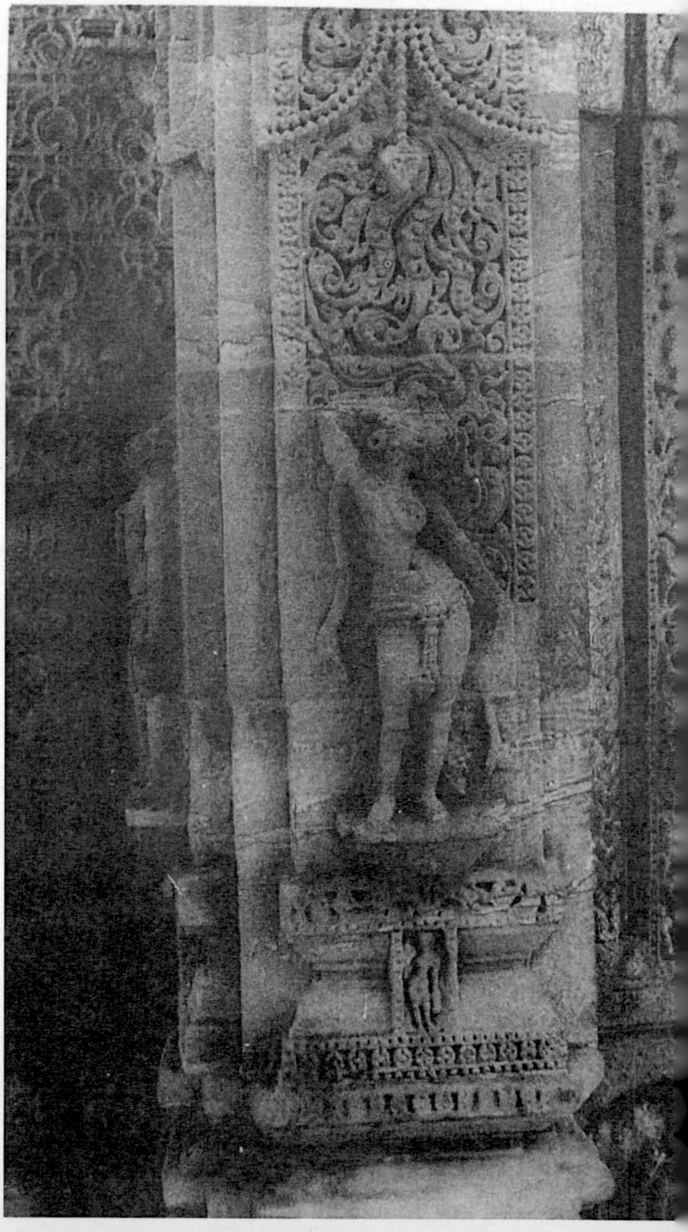

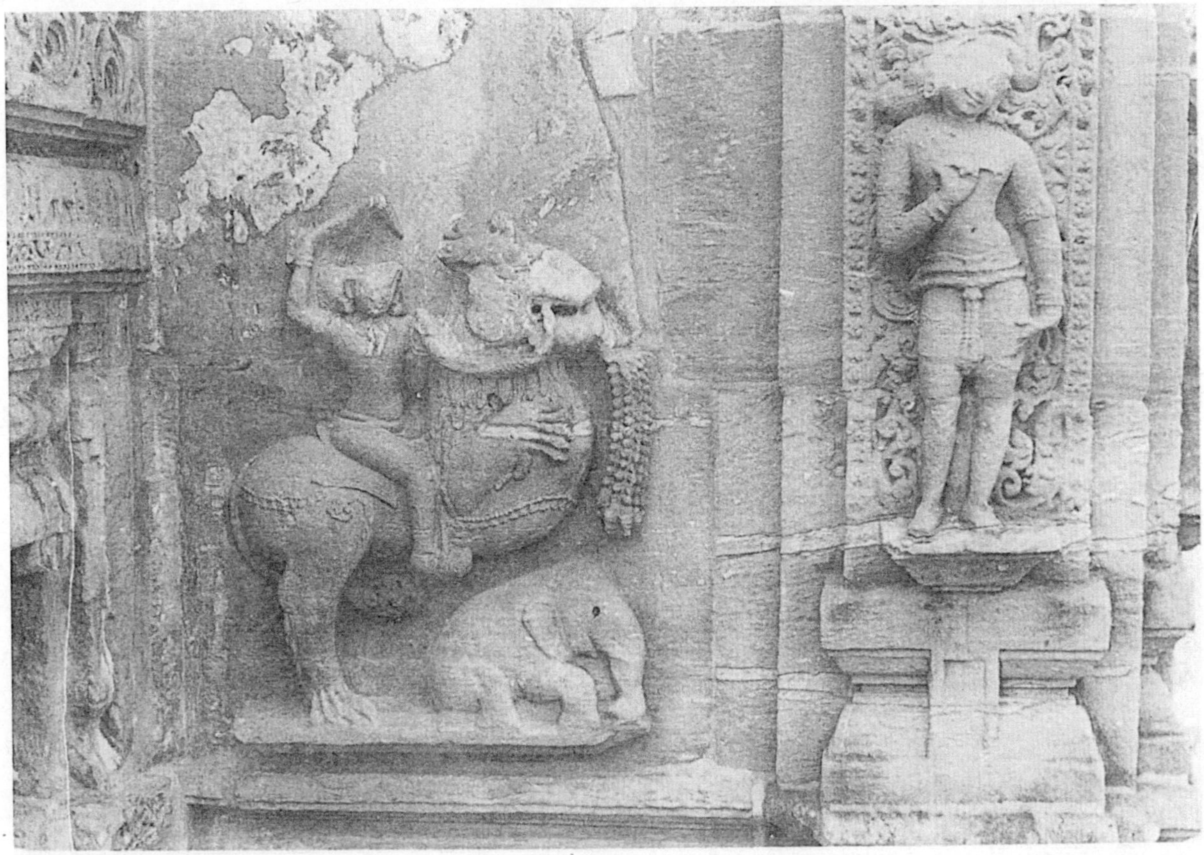

57. Entrance projection, north side, *vyāla* and male figure.

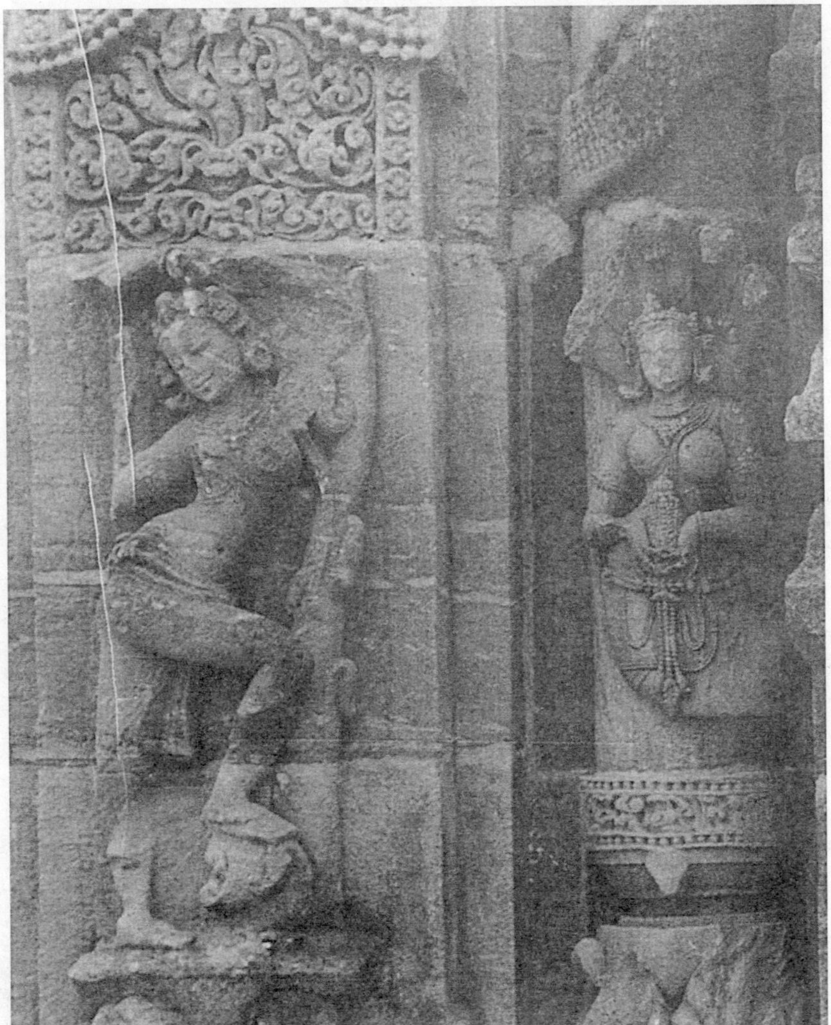

58. West wall (left of entrance), *nāga*-pilaster and *karṇa* figure.

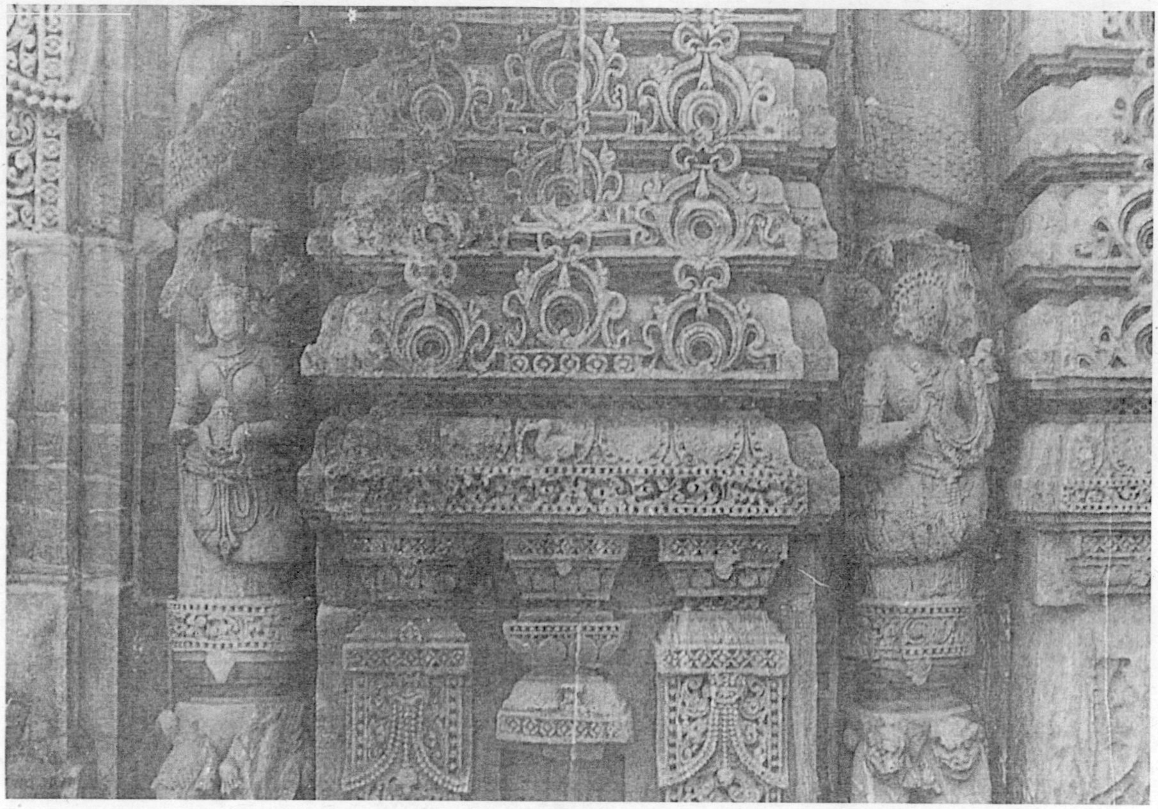

59. West wall (left of entrance), *nāga*-pilasters.

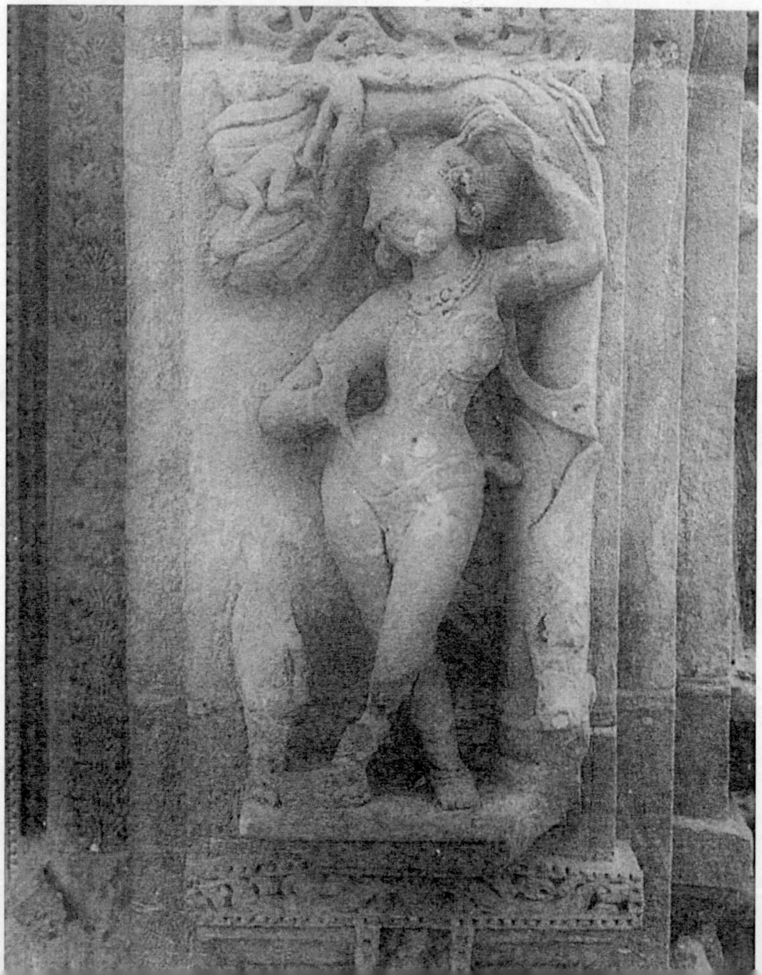

60. Entrance, right pilaster. *sālabhañjikā*.

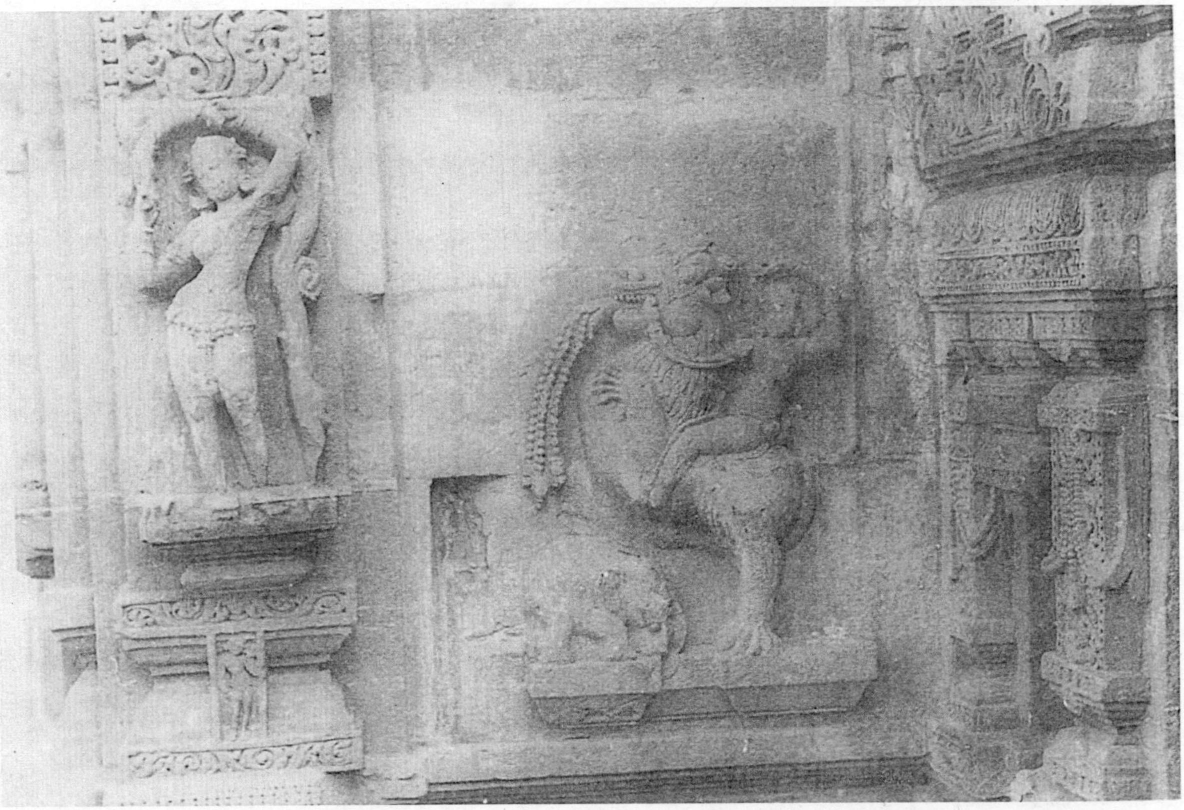

61. Entrance projection, south side, *śālabhañjikā* and *vyāla*.

62. West wall (right of entrance), *nāga*-pilasters and *karṇa* figure.

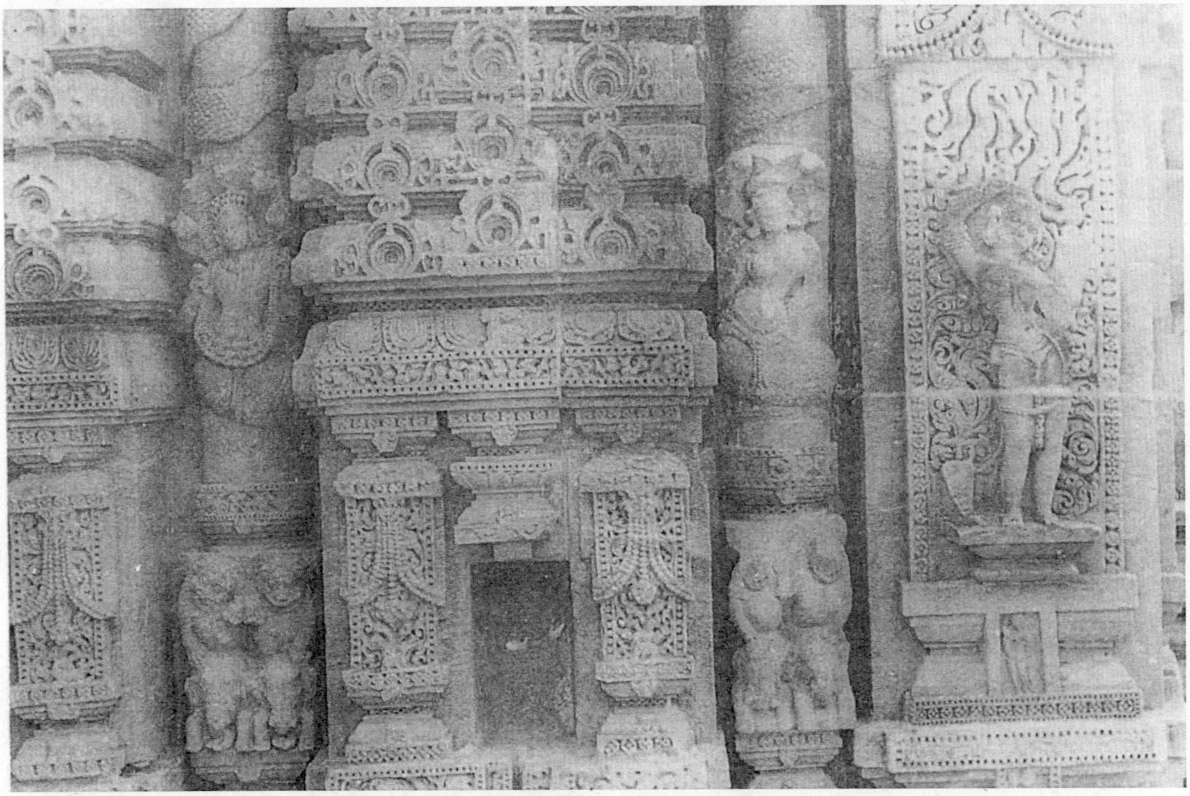

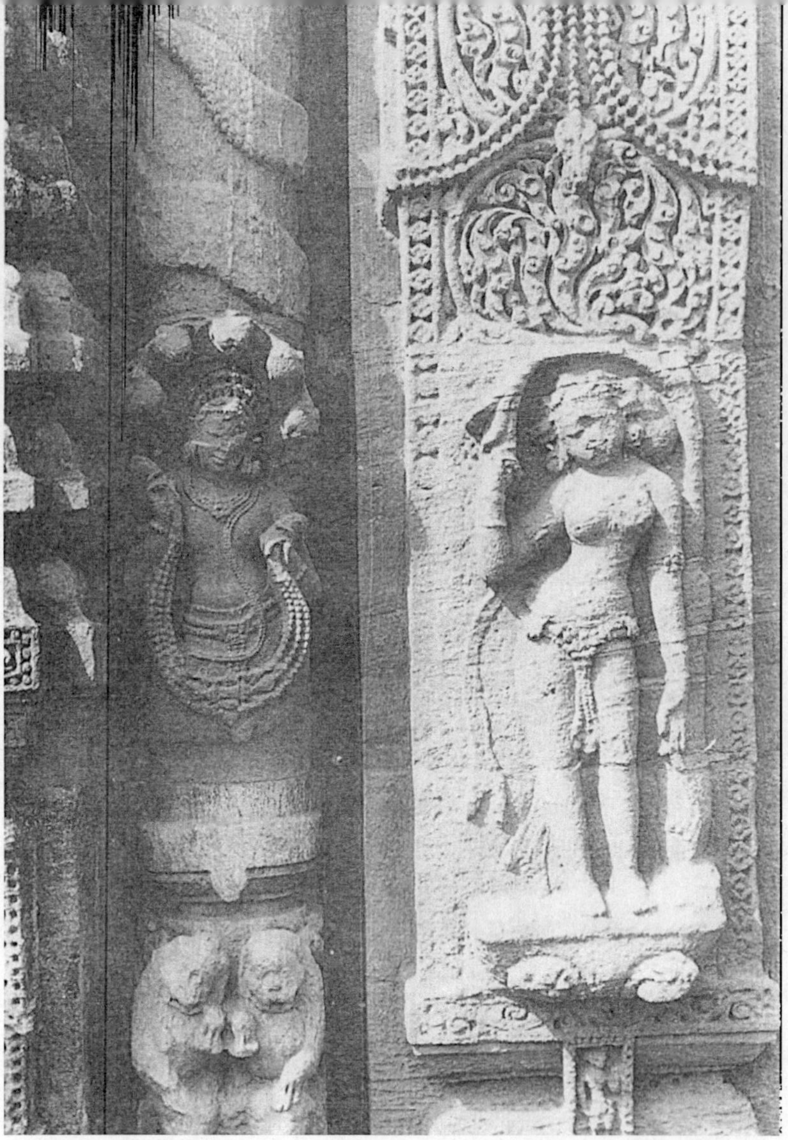

63. North wall, *karṇa* figure (*śālabhañjikā*) and *nāga*-pilaster.

64. North wall, *nāga*-pilasters.

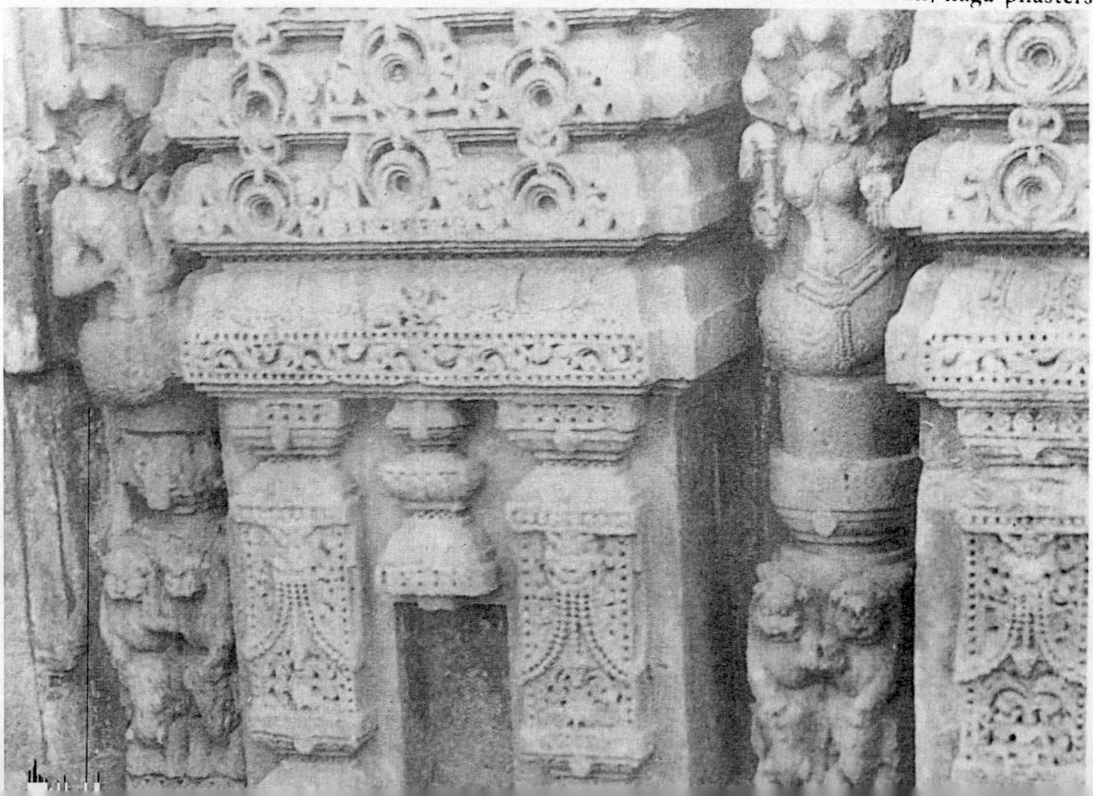

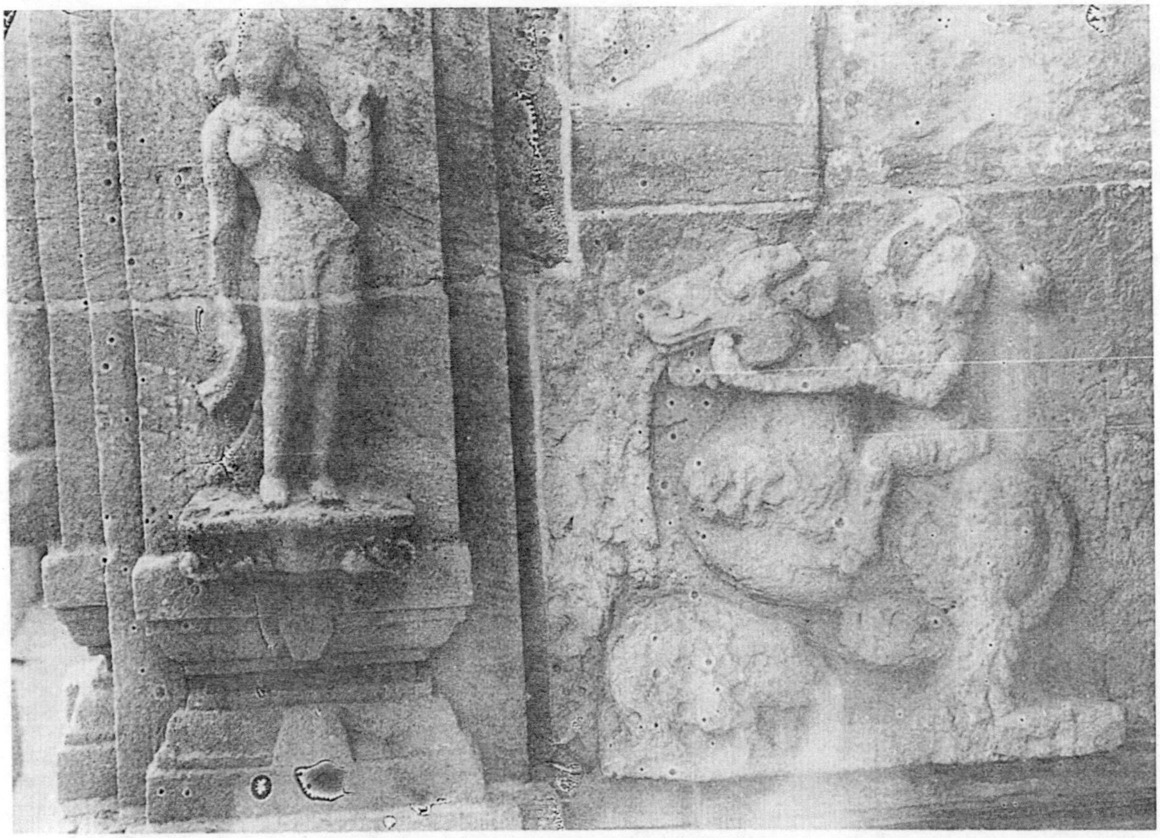

65. North wall, right side of projecting lattice window, *vyāla* and *karṇa* figure.

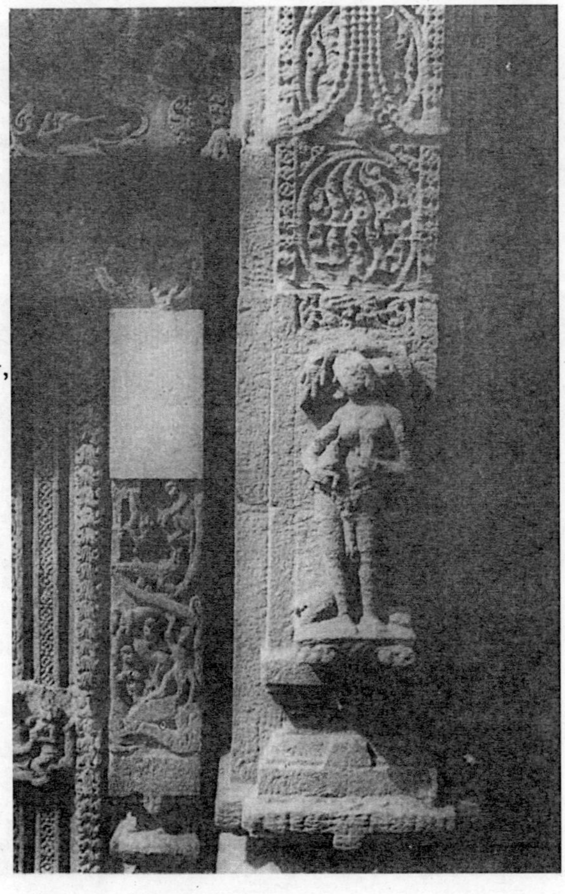

66. North wall, lattice window, right pilaster, ***śālabhañjikā***.

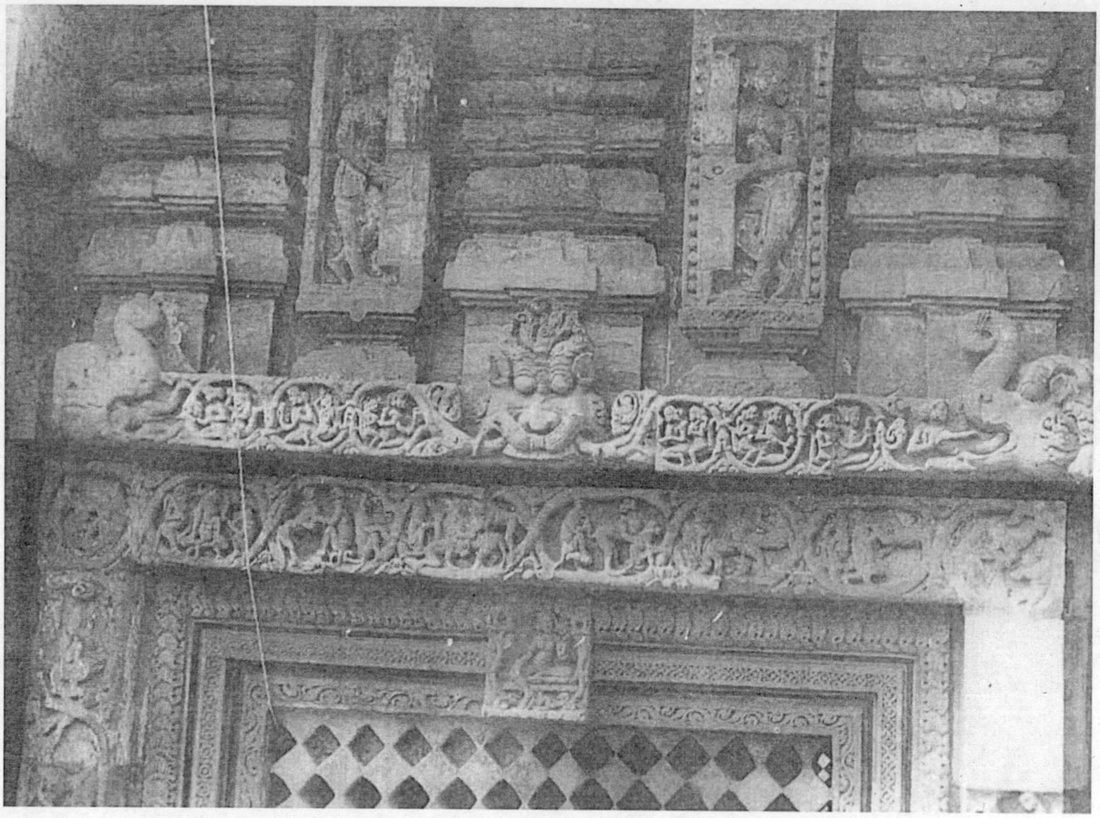

67. North wall, female figures above lattice windows.

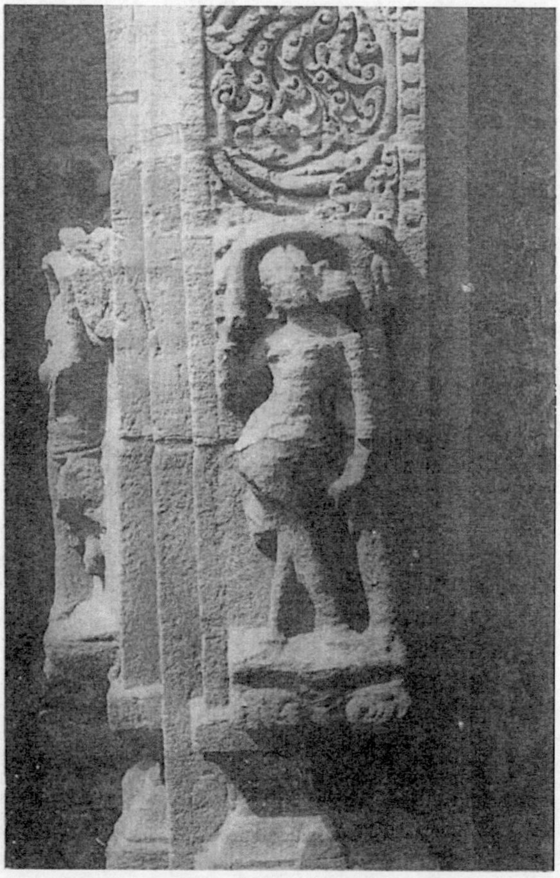

68. North wall, lattice window, left pilaster, *śālabhañjikā*.

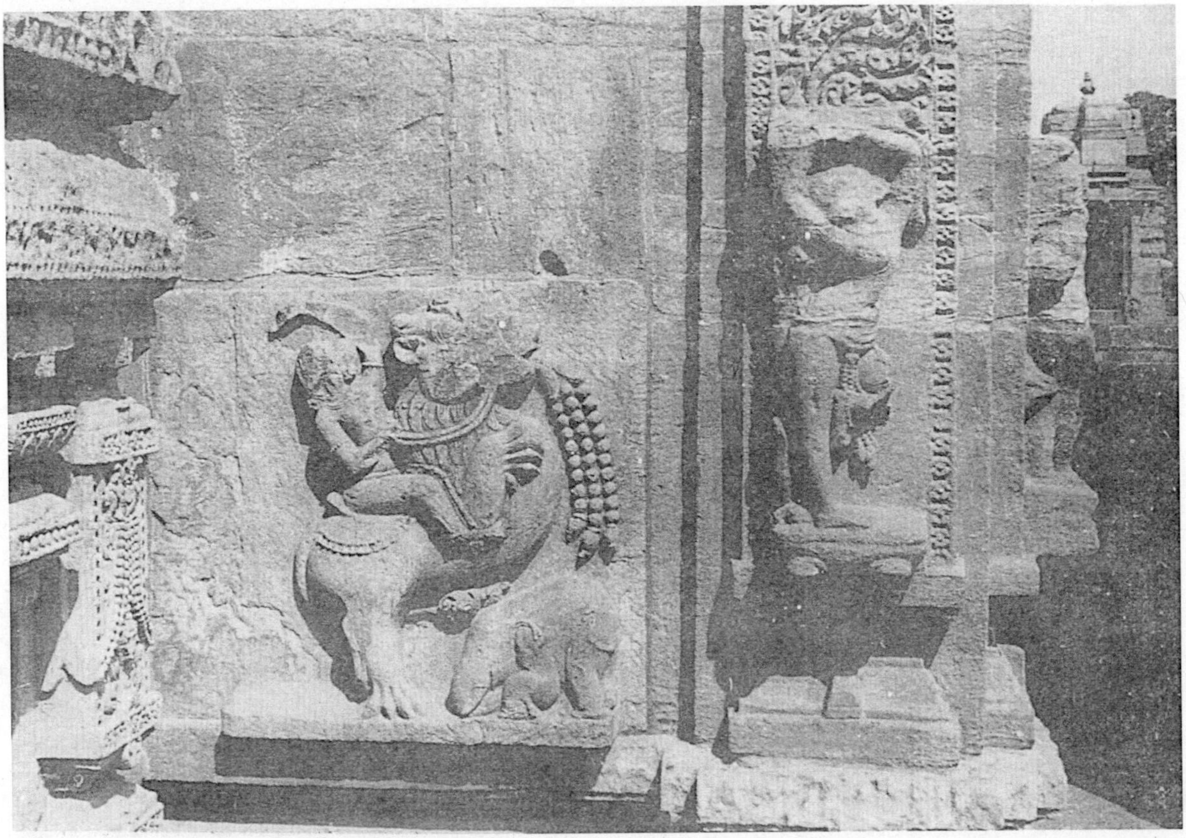

69. North wall, left side of projecting lattice window, *karṇa* figure and *vyāla*.

70. North wall, *nāga*-pilasters.

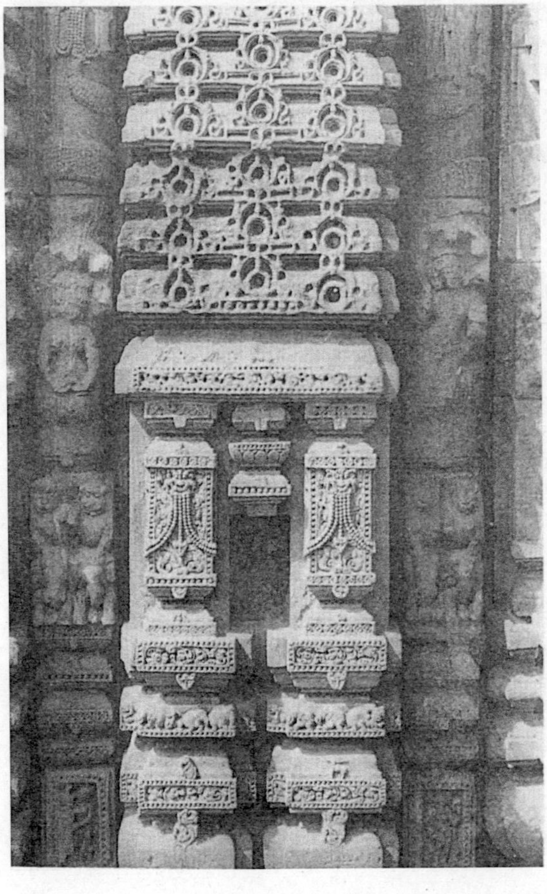

71. North wall, *karṇa* figure (*śālabhañjikā*) and *nāga*-pilaster.

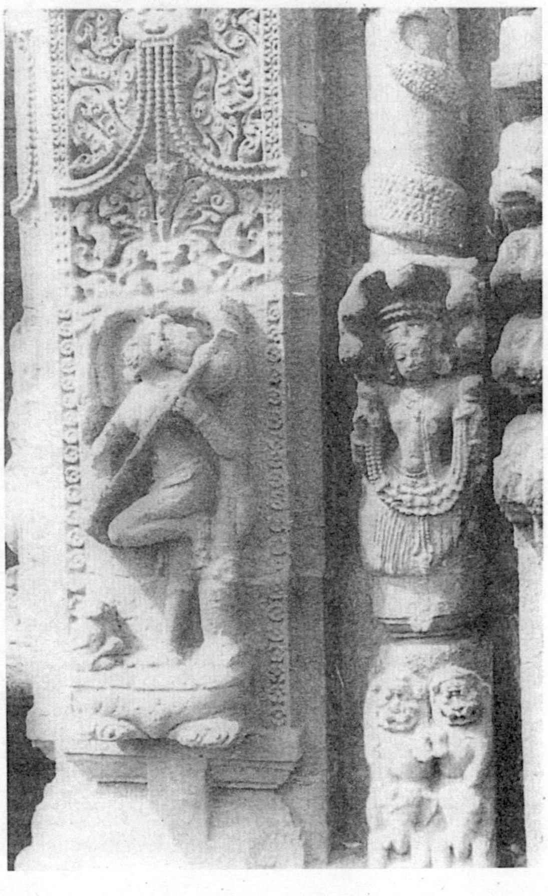

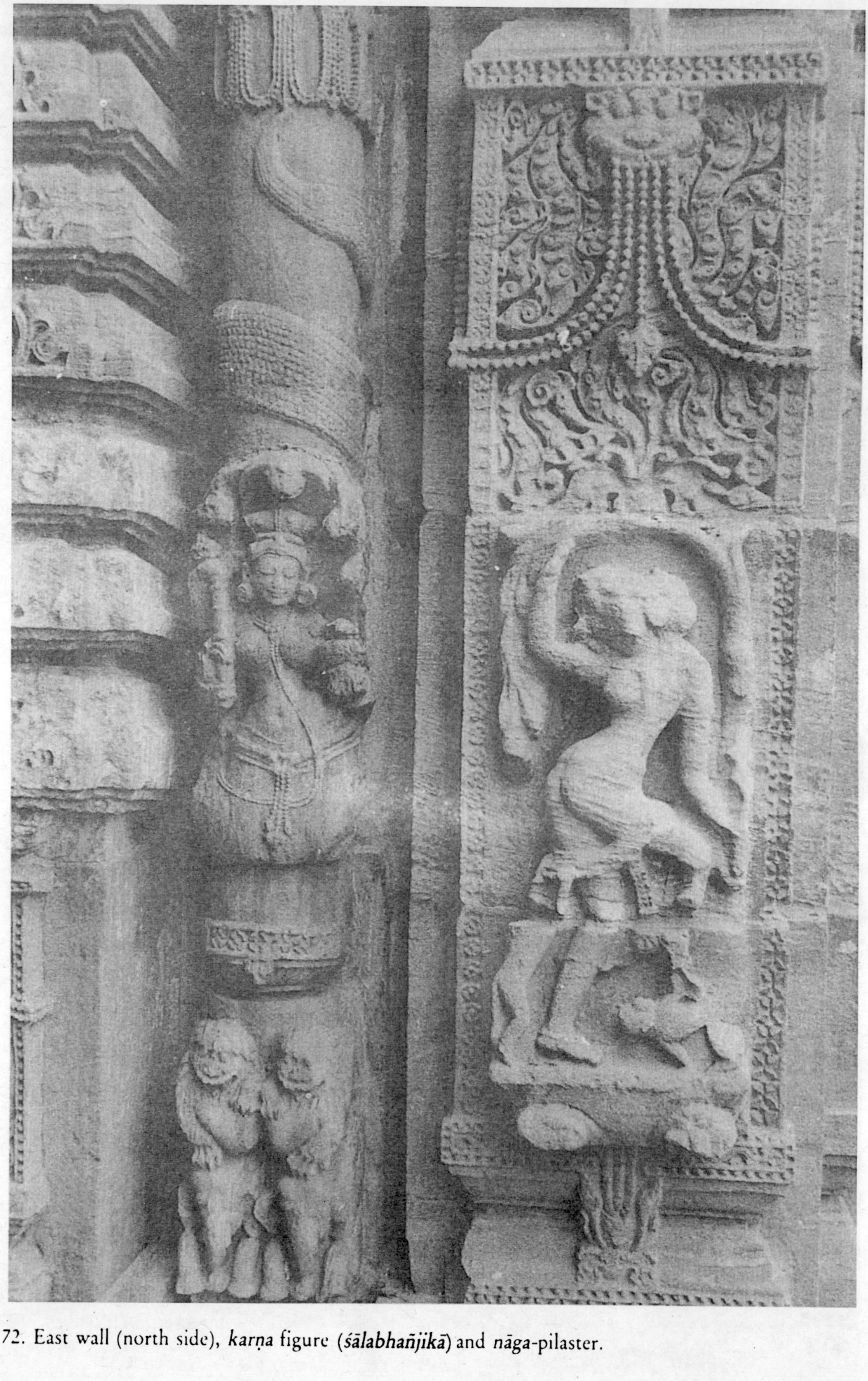

72. East wall (north side), *karṇa* figure (*śālabhañjikā*) and *nāga*-pilaster.

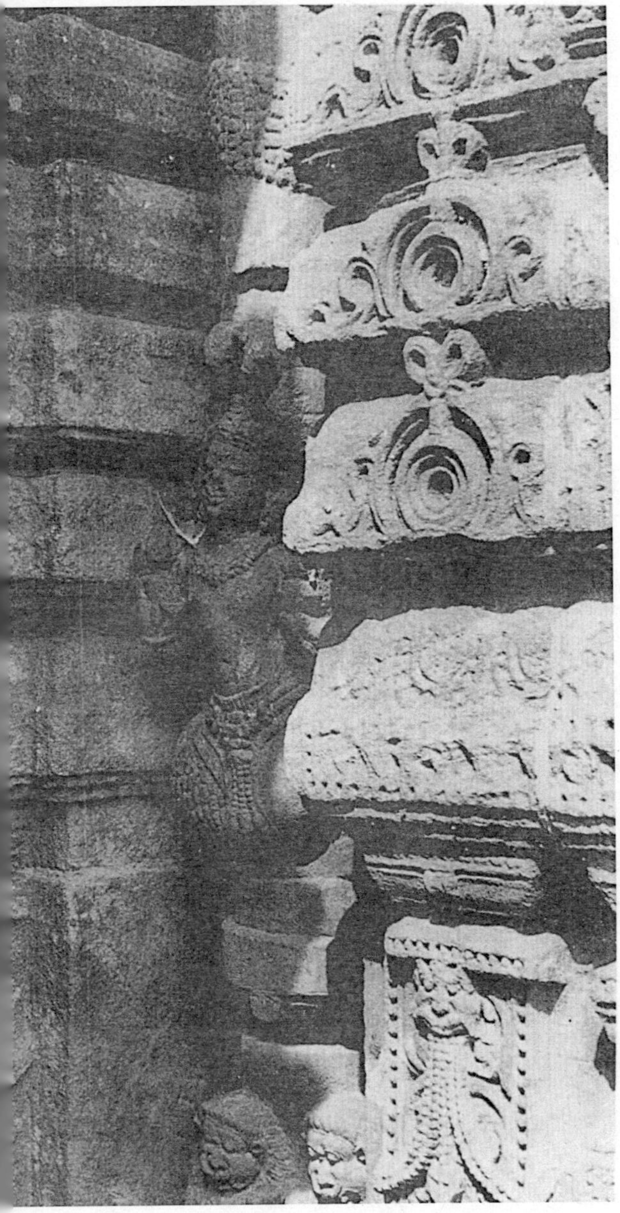

73. East wall, (north side), *nāga*-pilaster.

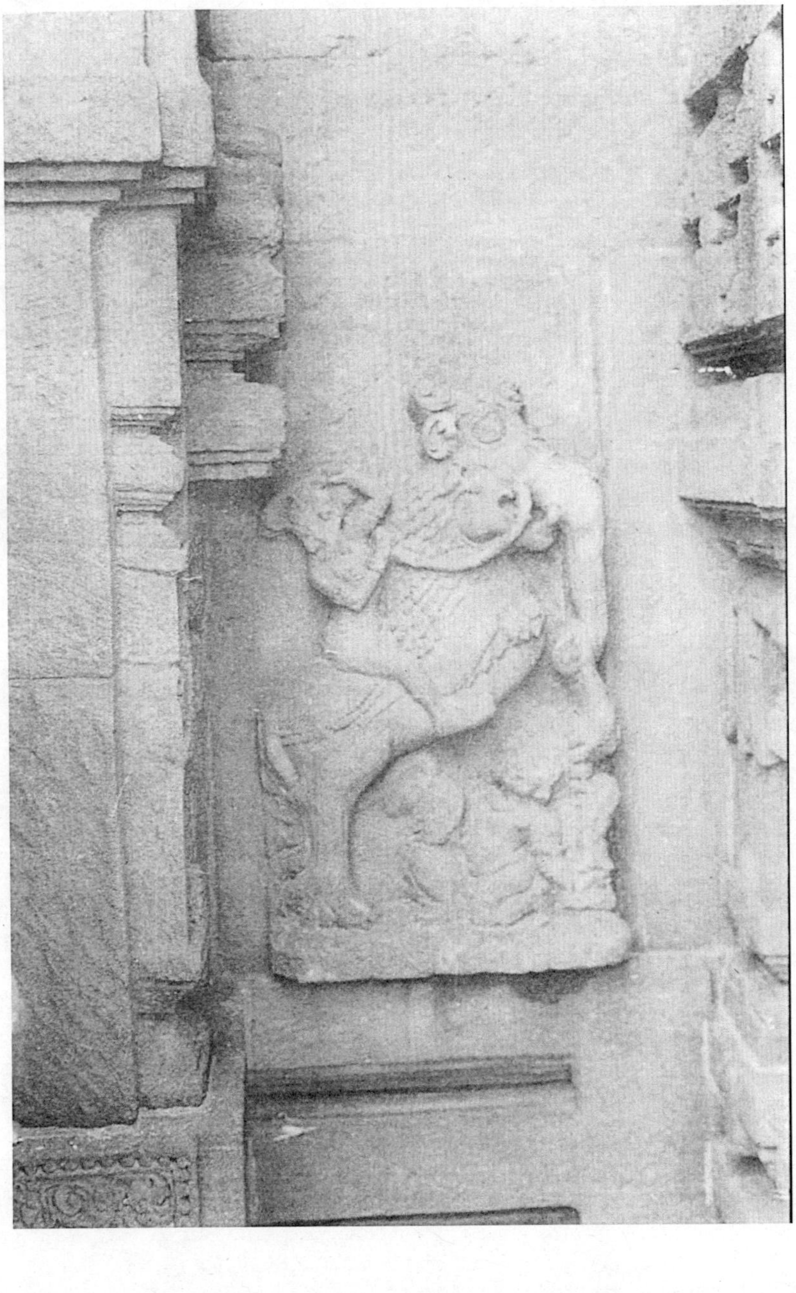

74. North buffer wall, *vyāla*.

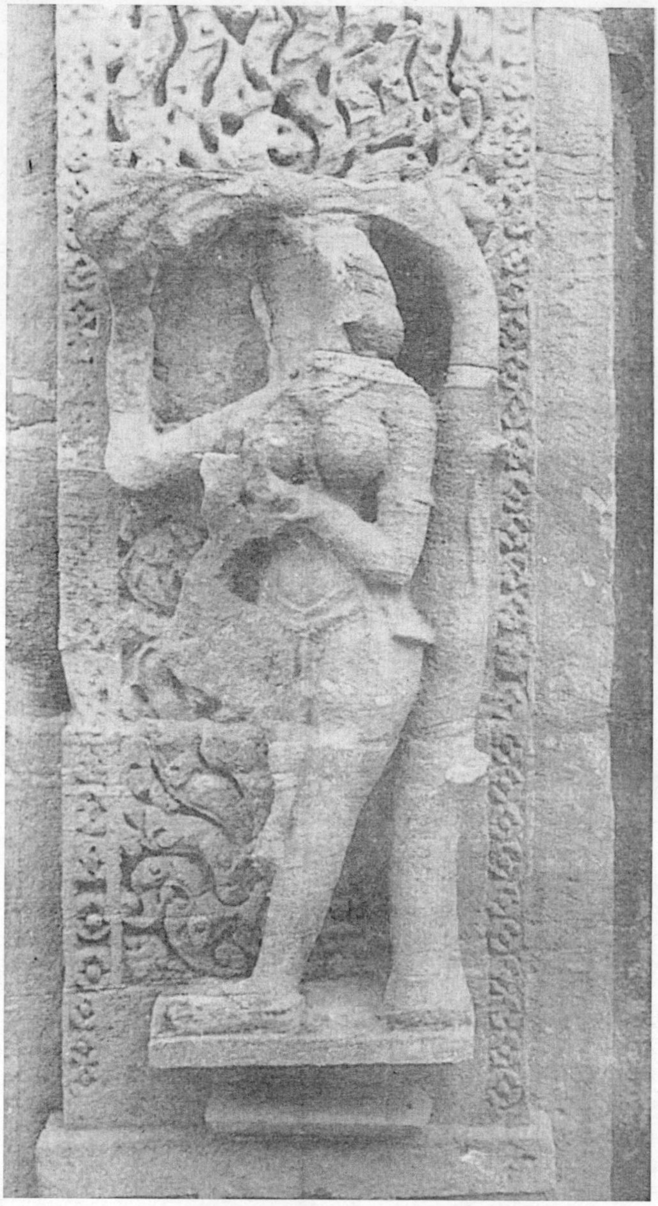

75. South wall, *karṇa* figure (*śālabhañjikā*) and *nāga*- pilasters.

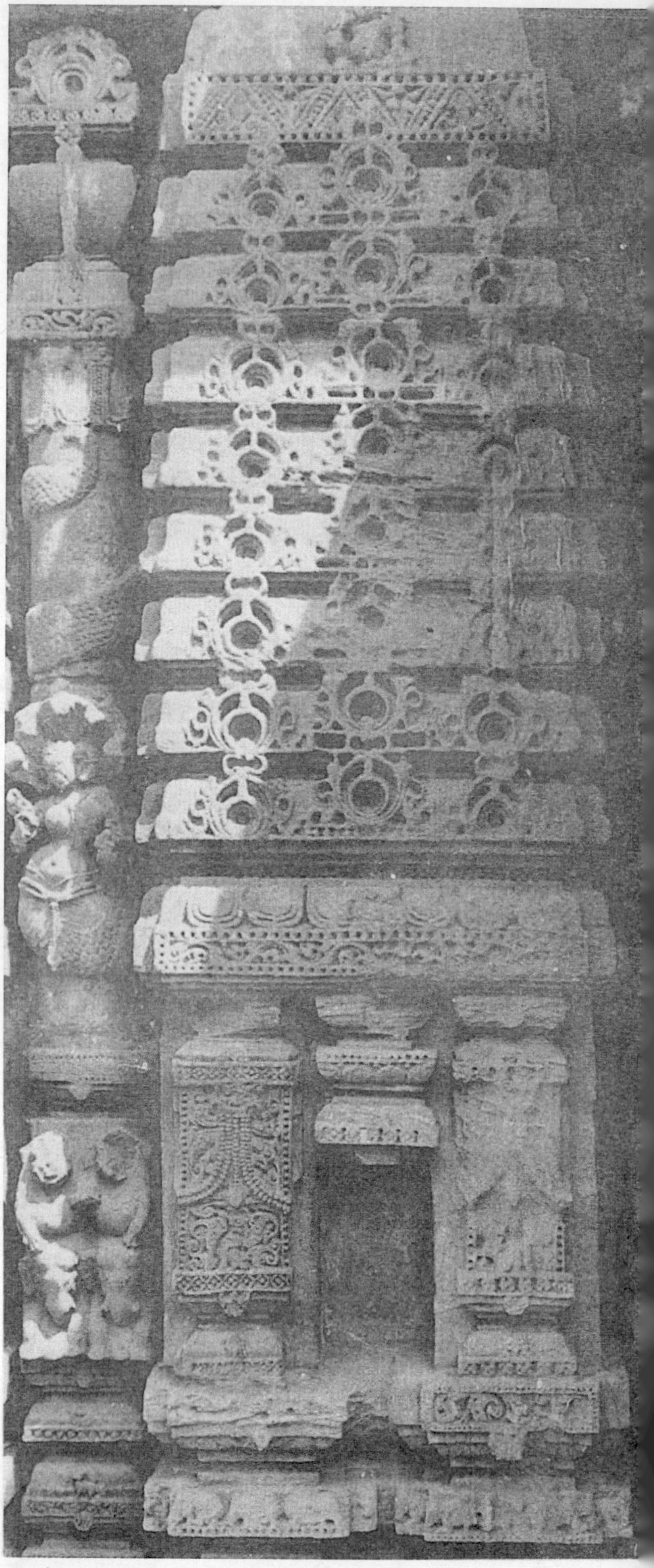

76. South wall, *nāga*-pilasters.

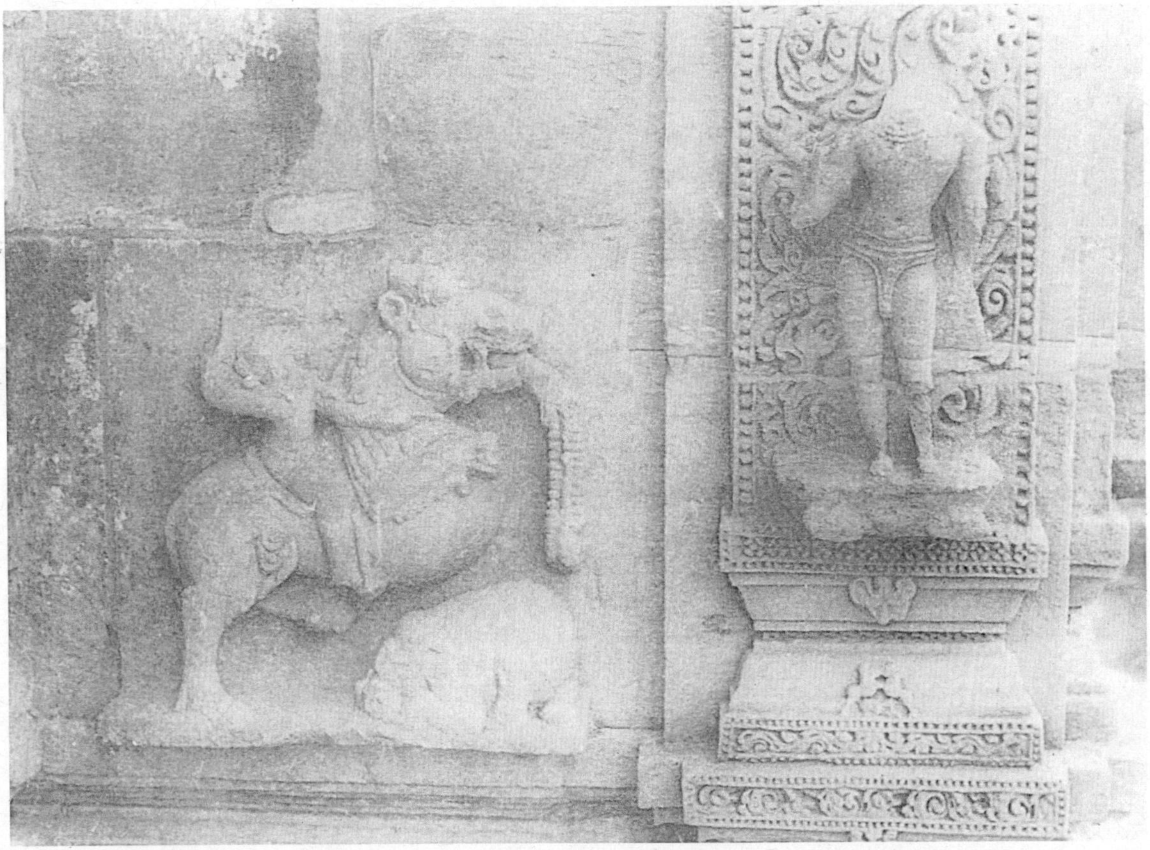

77. South wall, left side of projecting lattice window, *vyāla* and *karṇa* figure.

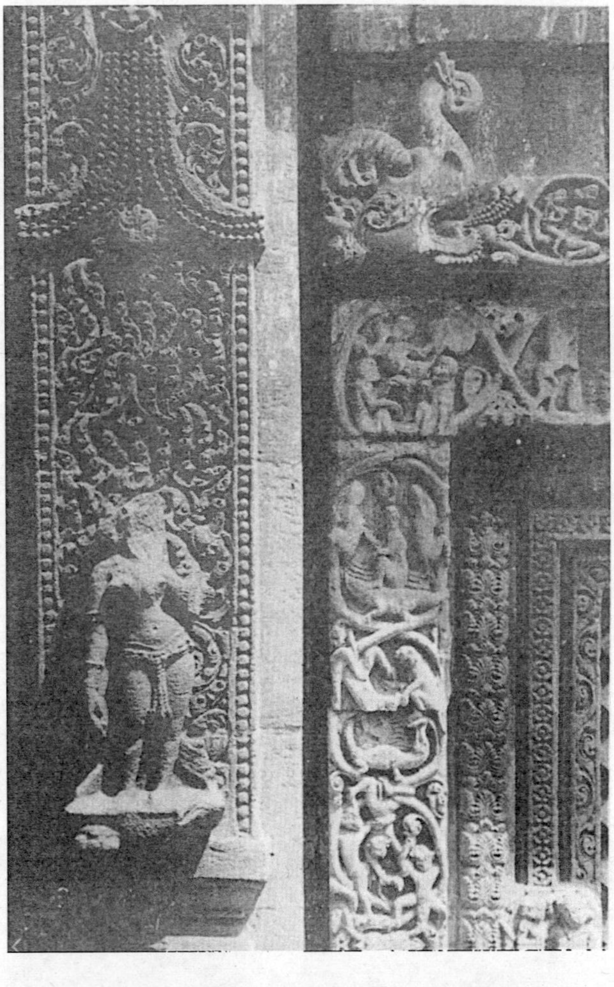

78. South wall, lattice window, left pilaster, female figure.

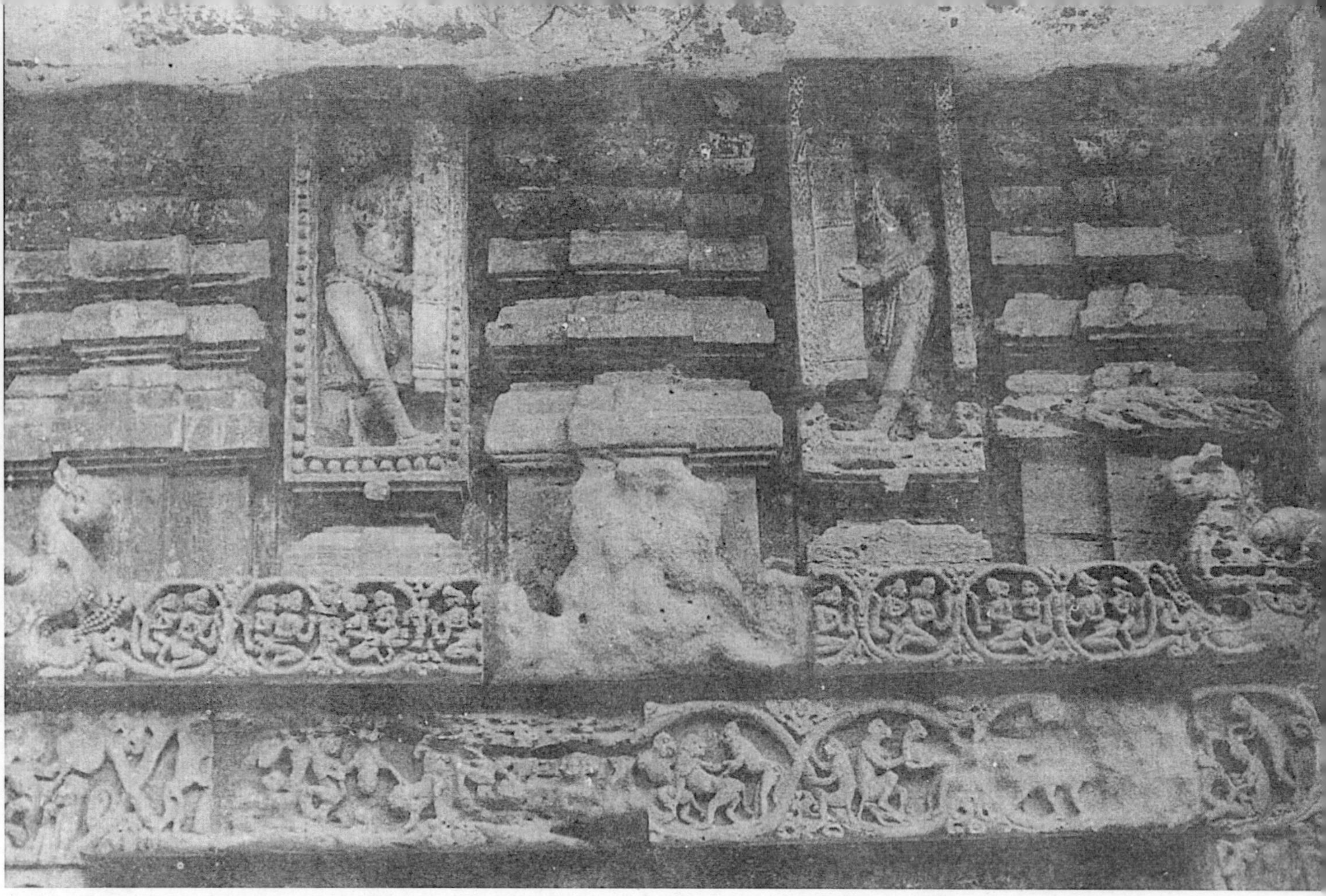

79. South wall, female figures above lattice window.

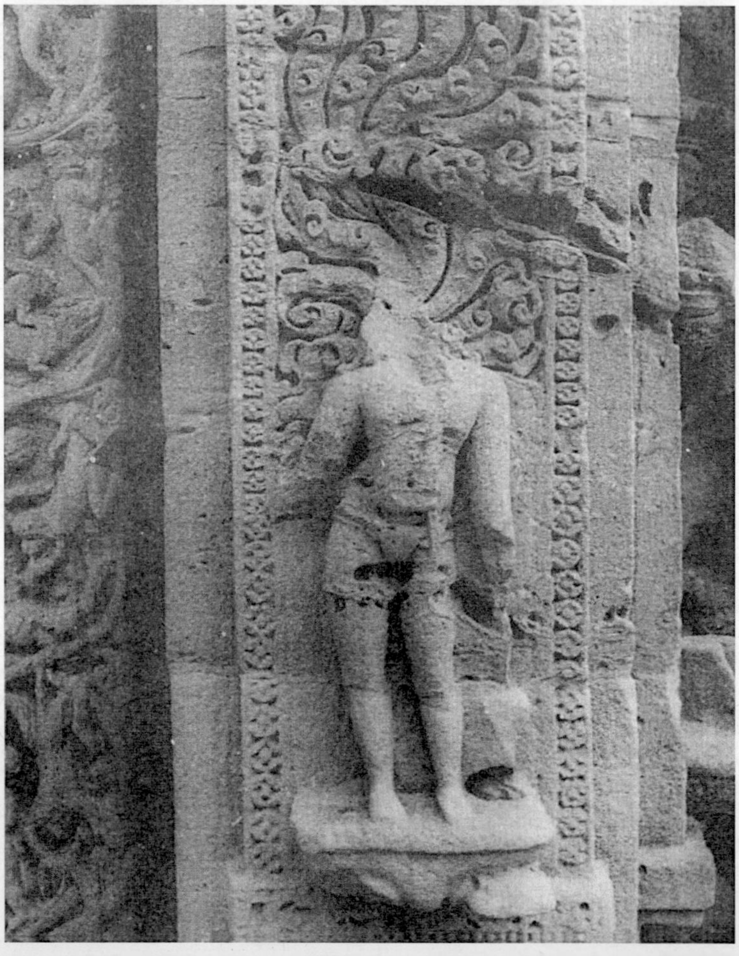

80. South wall, lattice window, right pilaster, male figure.

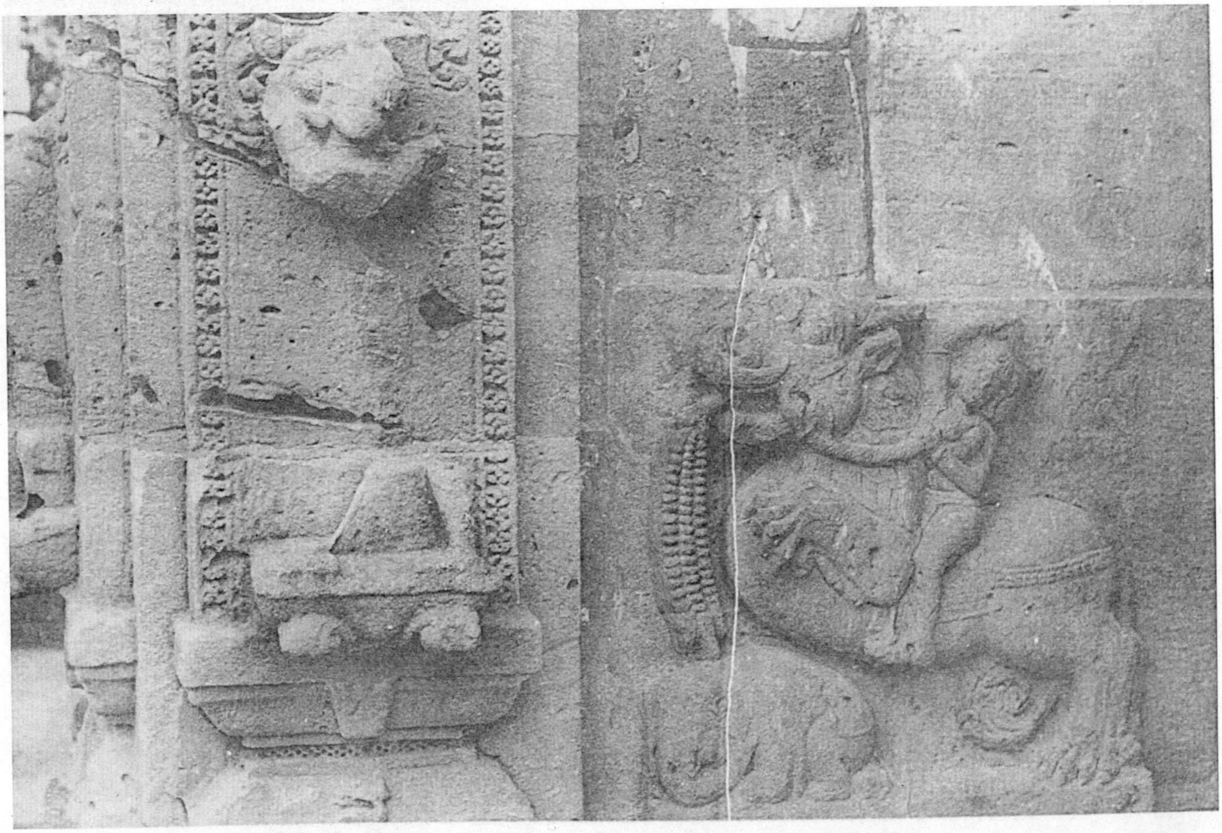

81. South wall, right side of projecting lattice window, female figure and *vyāla*.

82. South wall, *nāga*-pilasters.

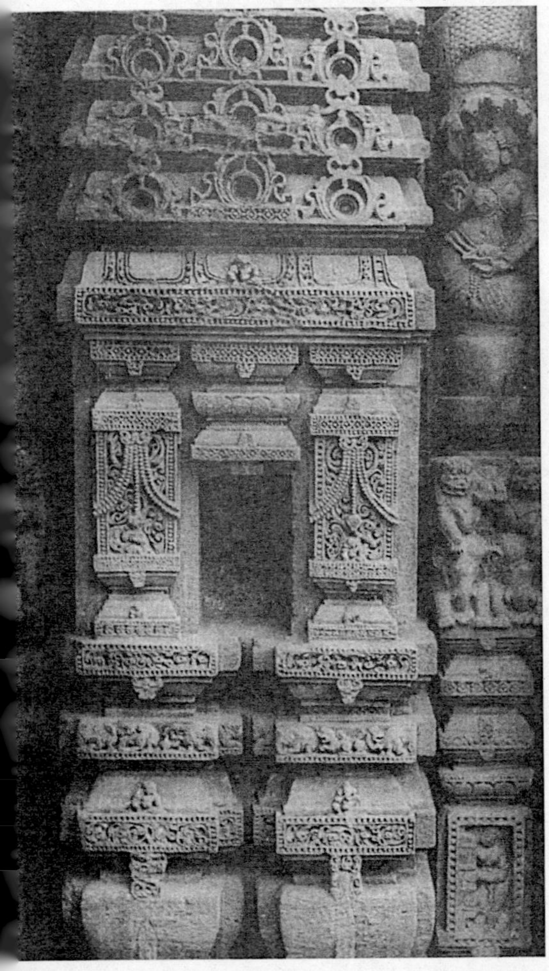

83. South wall, *karṇa* figure and *nāga*-pilaster.

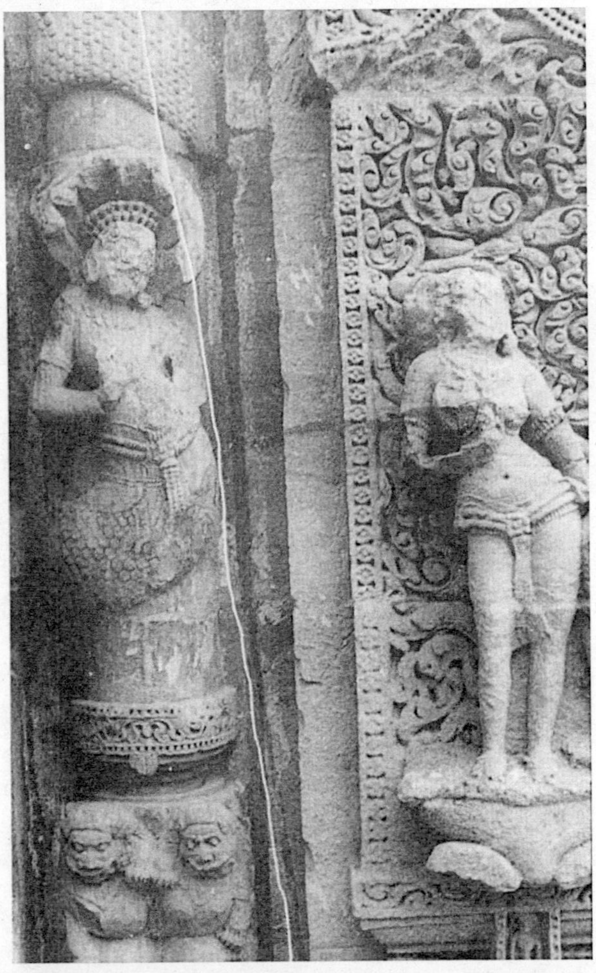

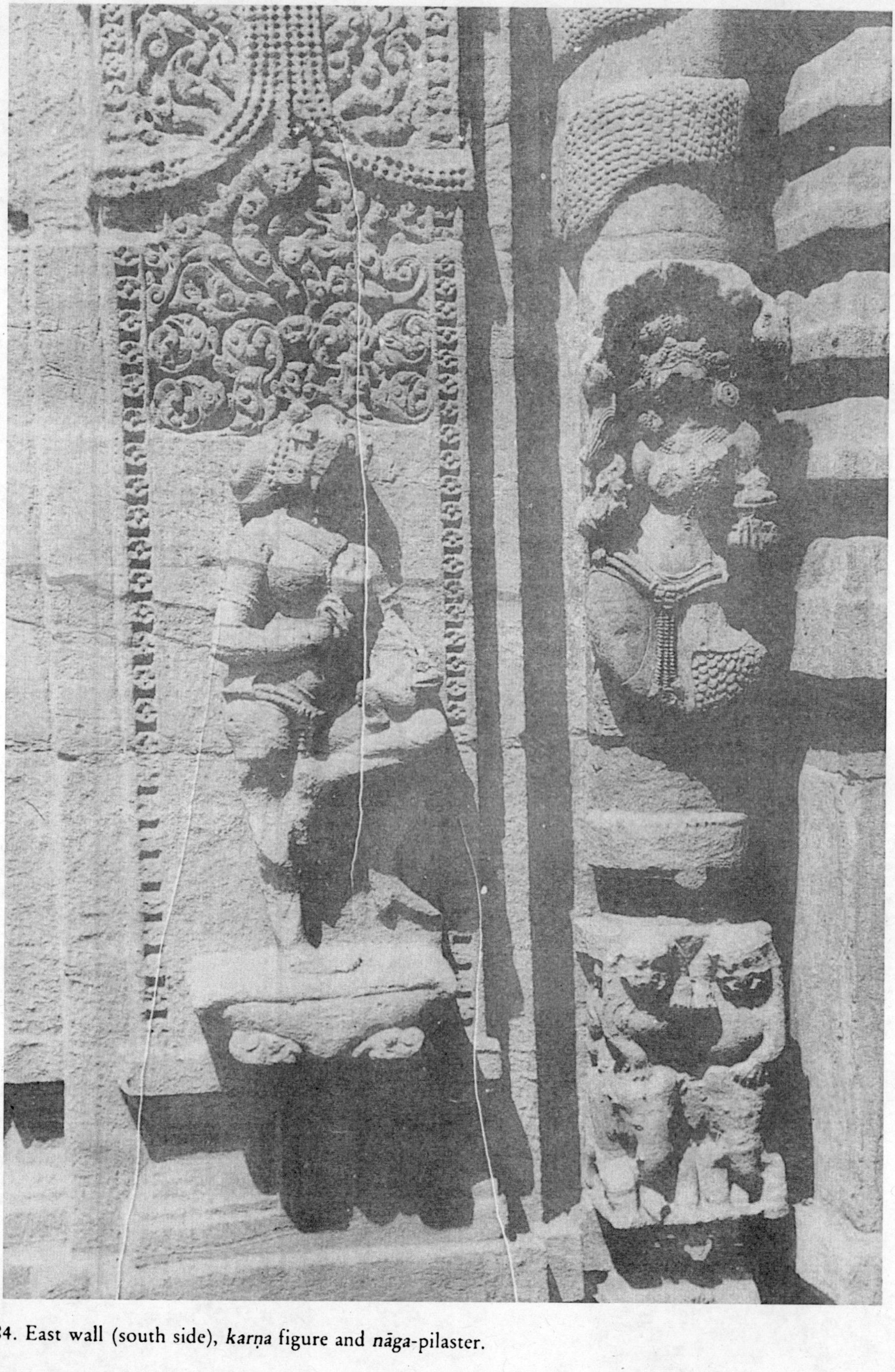

84. East wall (south side), *karṇa* figure and *nāga*-pilaster.

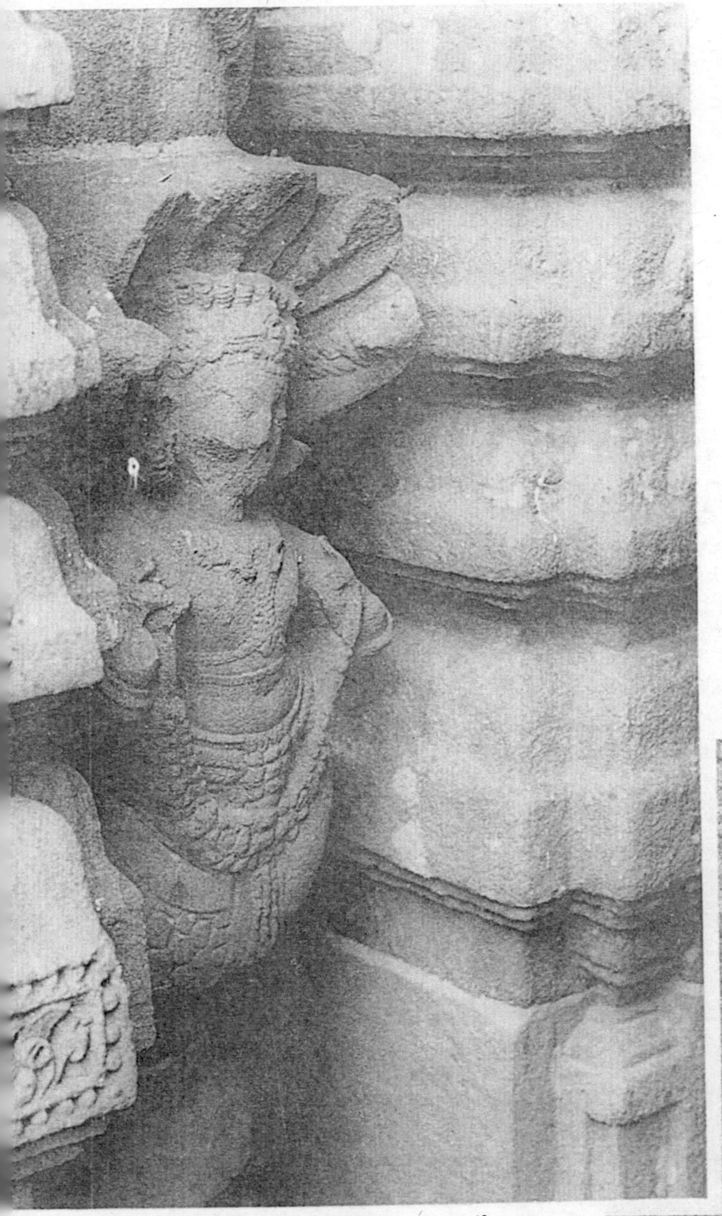

85. East wall (south side), *nāga*-pilaster.

86. South buffer wall, *vyāla*.

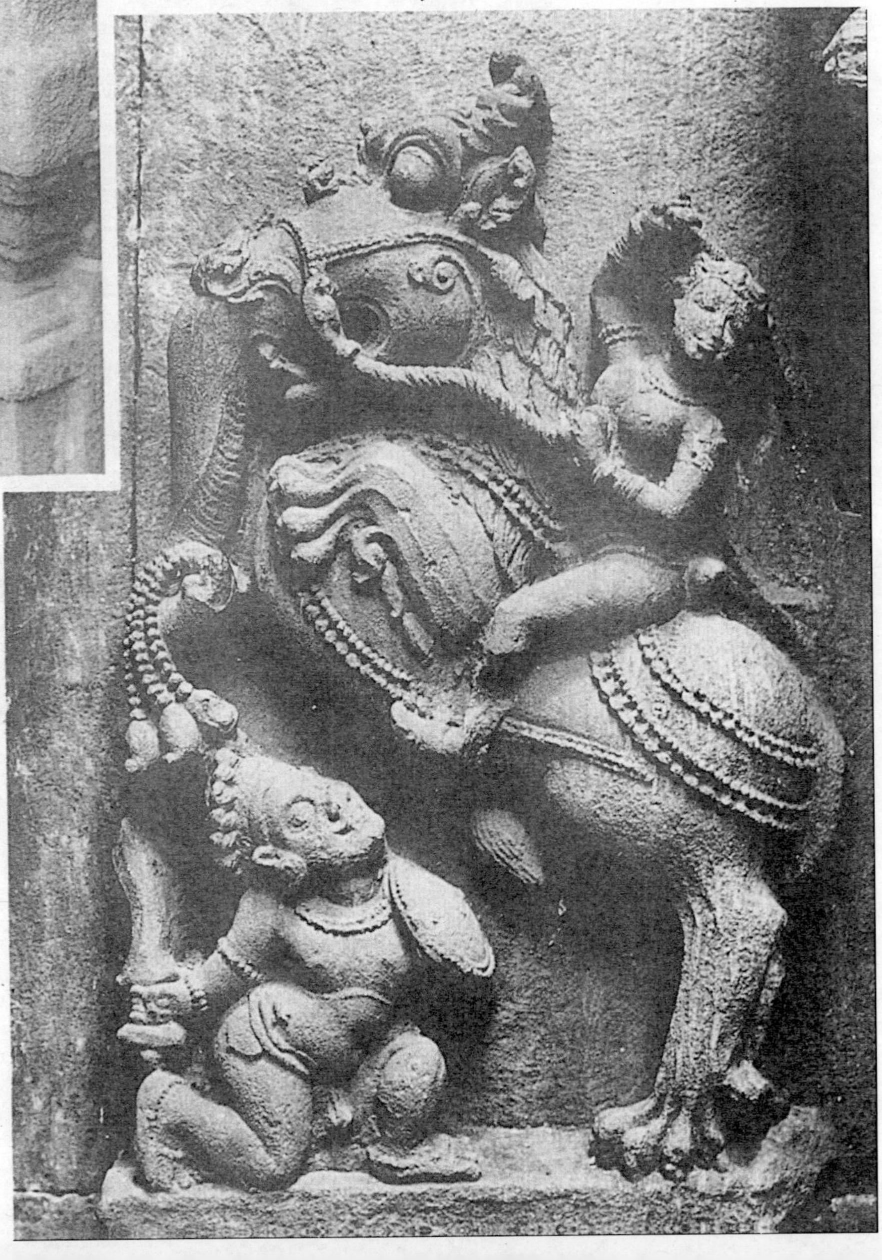

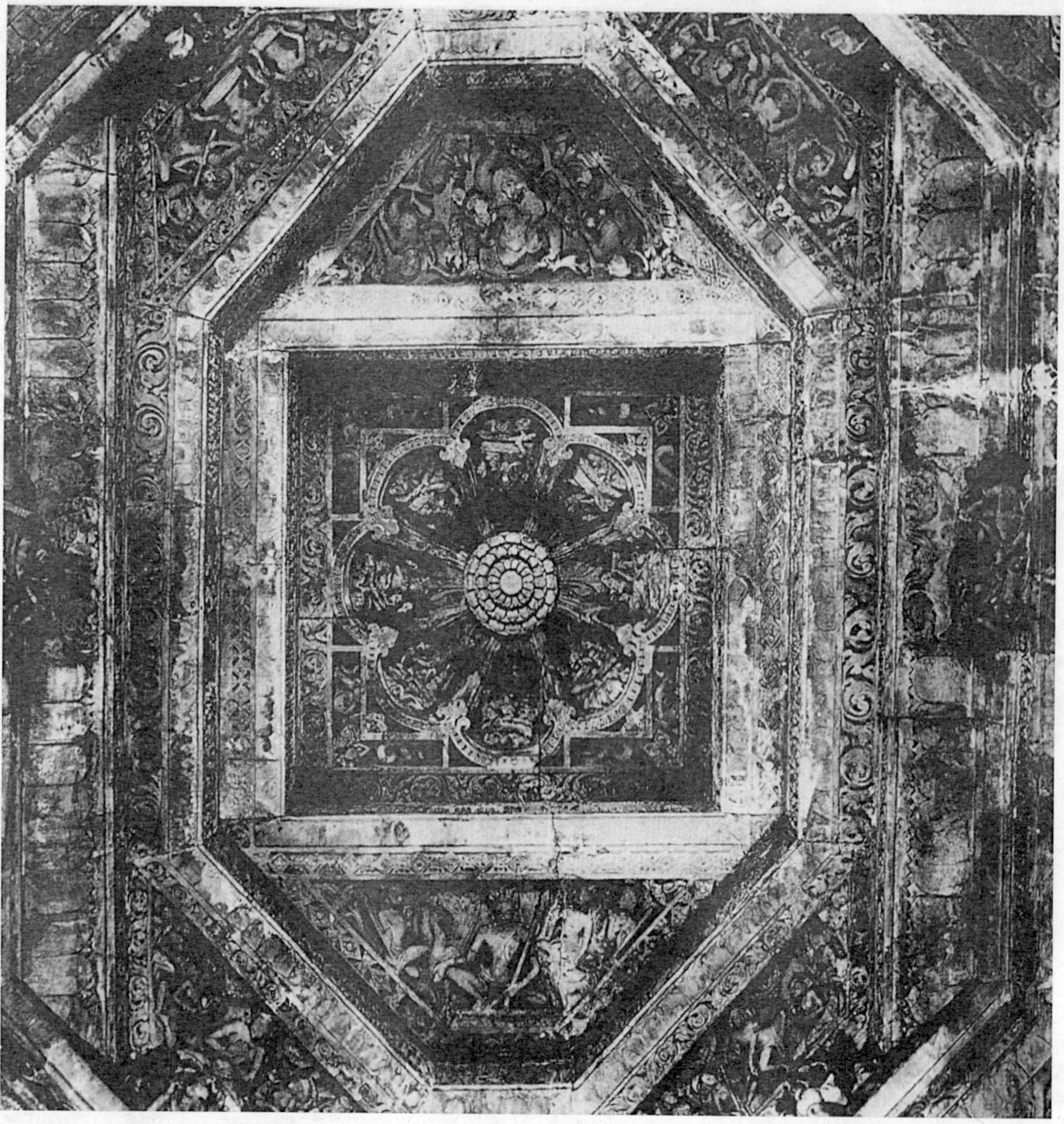

87. *Maṇḍapa* ceiling. (AIIS).

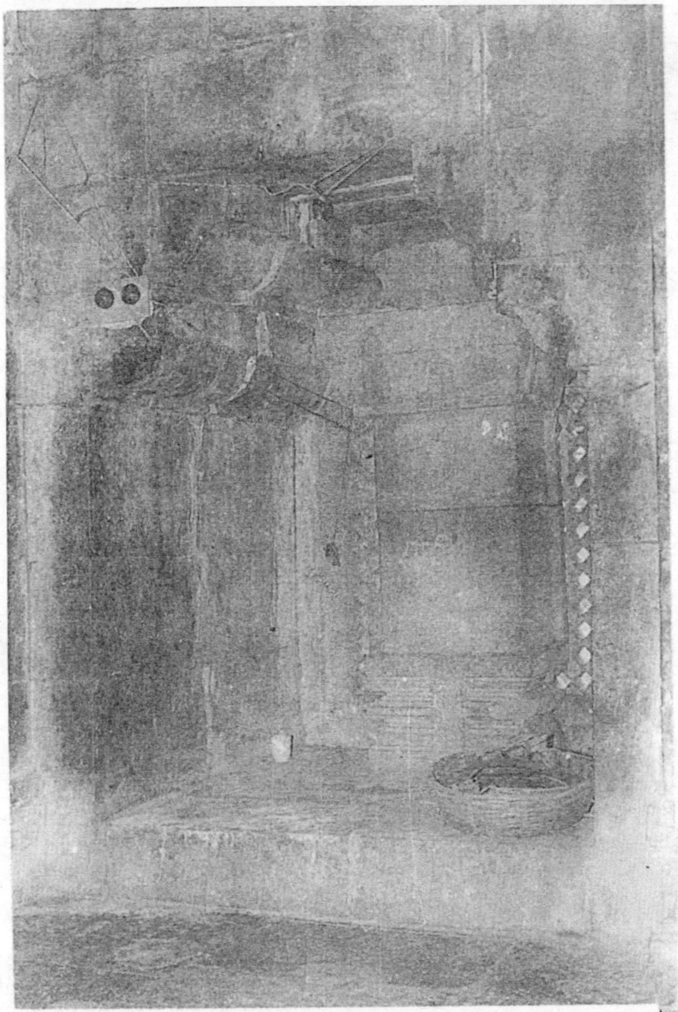

88. *Maṇḍapa*, interior, toward southeast, window.

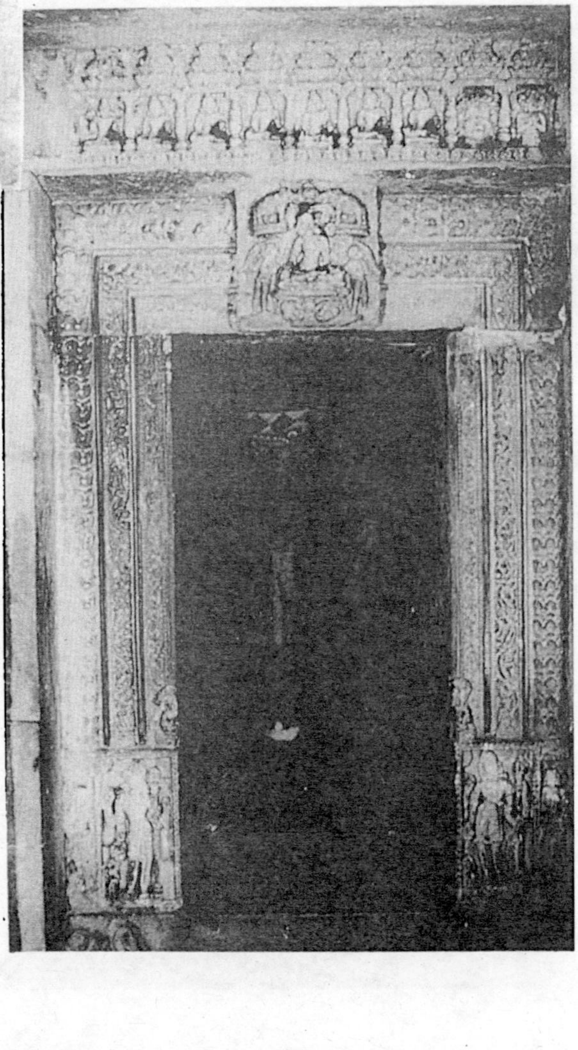

89. Entrance to *garbhagṛha*.

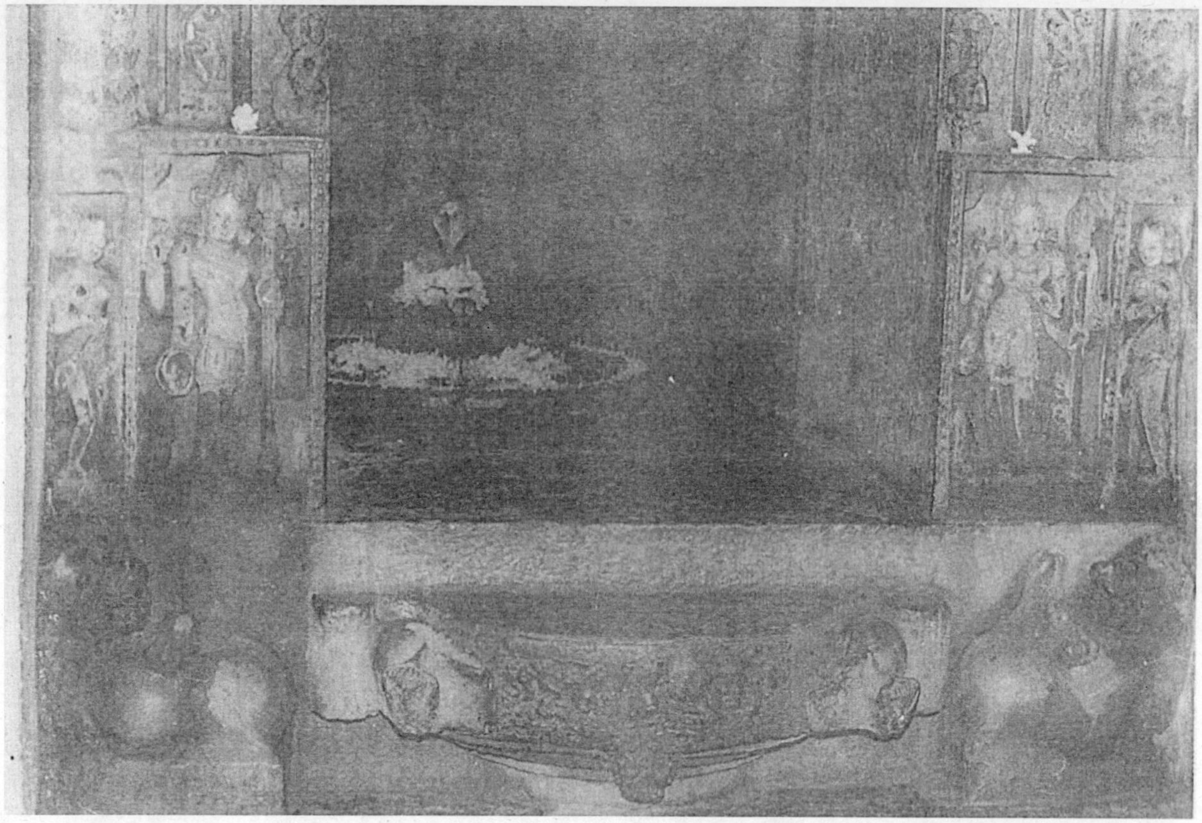

90. Entrance to *garbhagṛha*, *dvārapālas*.

91. Entrance to *garbhagṛha*, lintel.
(Asian Art Archives, University of Michigan).

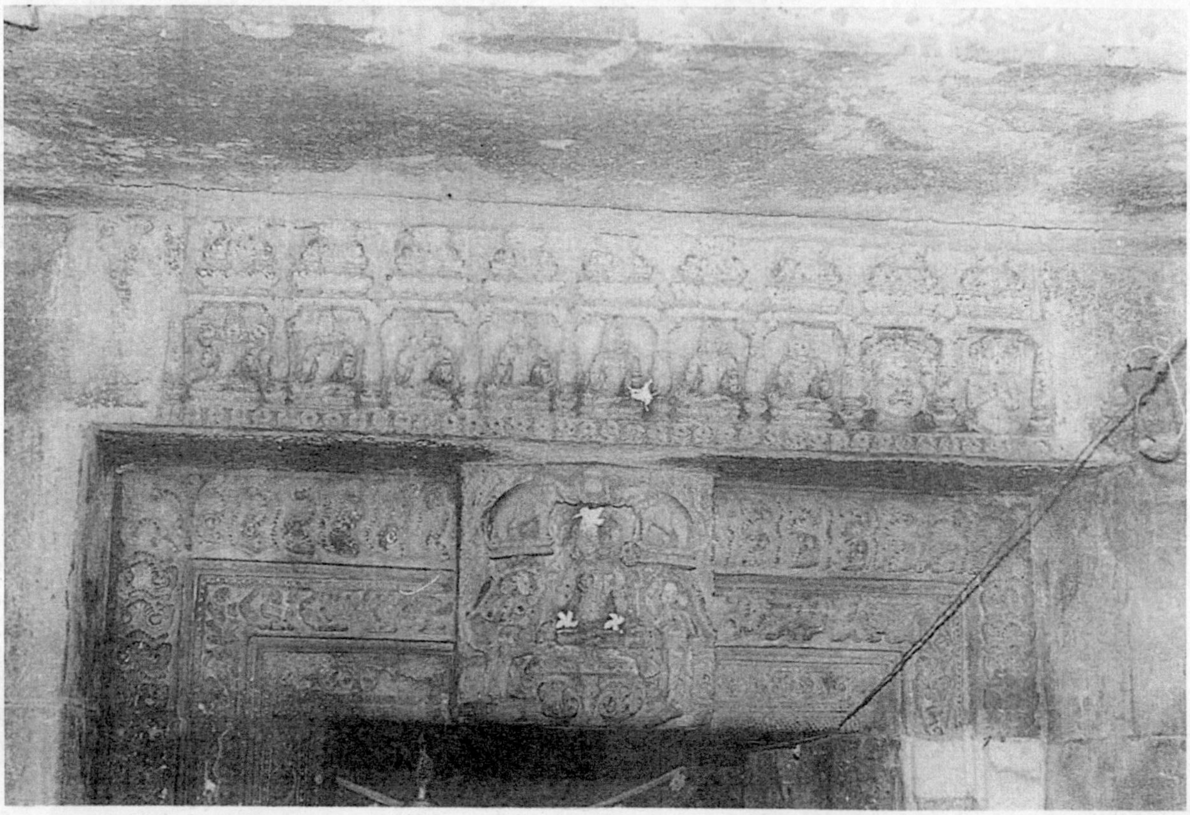

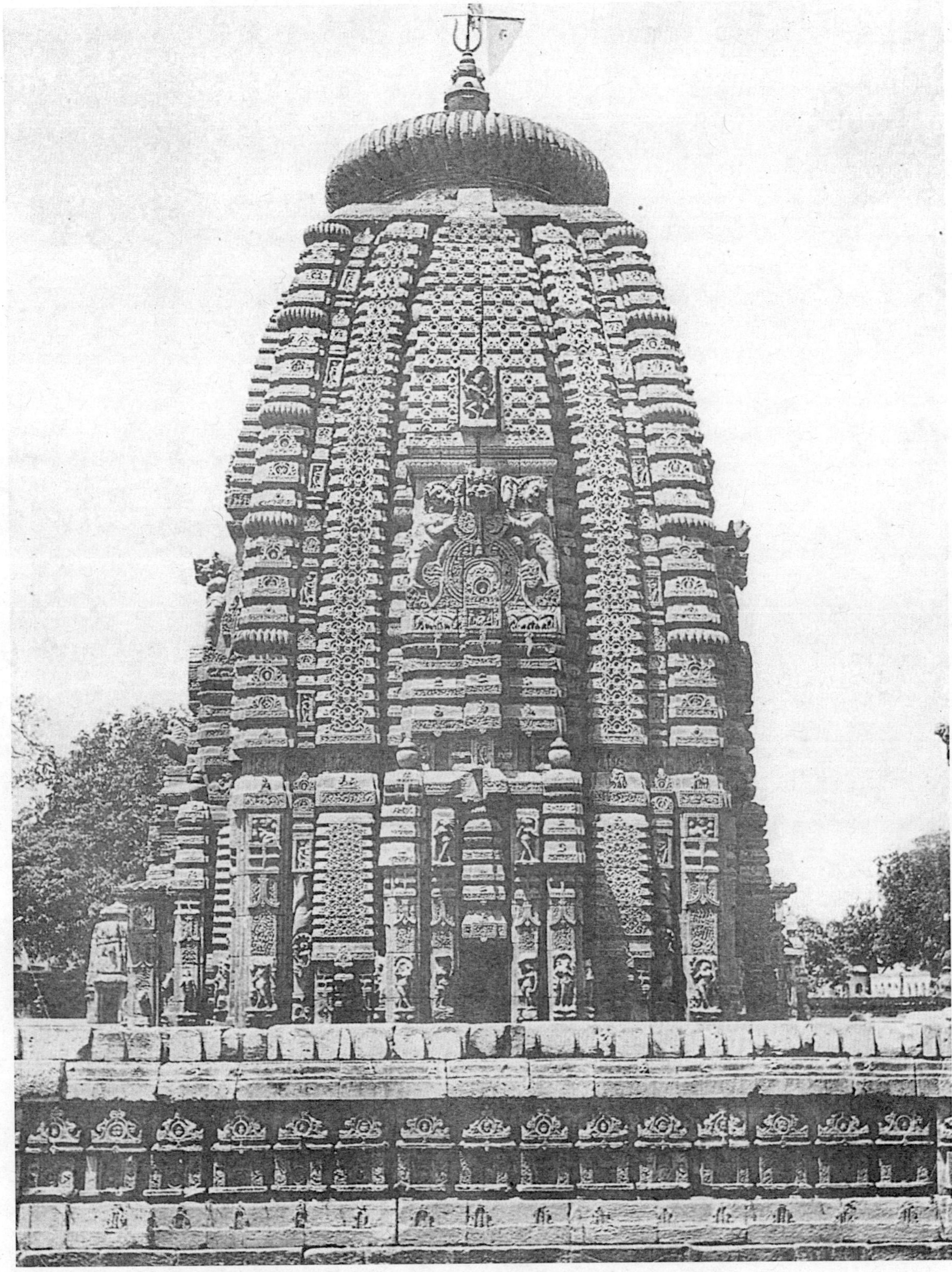

92. *Prāsāda*, from east.

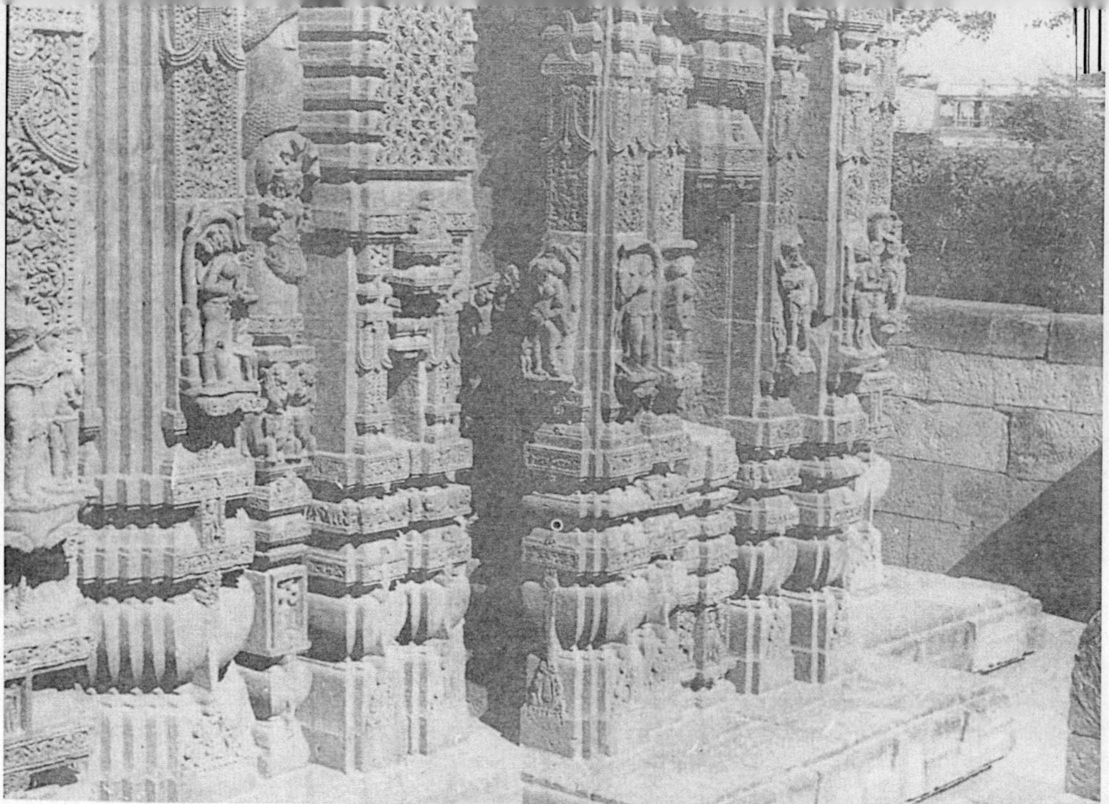

93. *Prāsāda*, lower walls, from southwest.

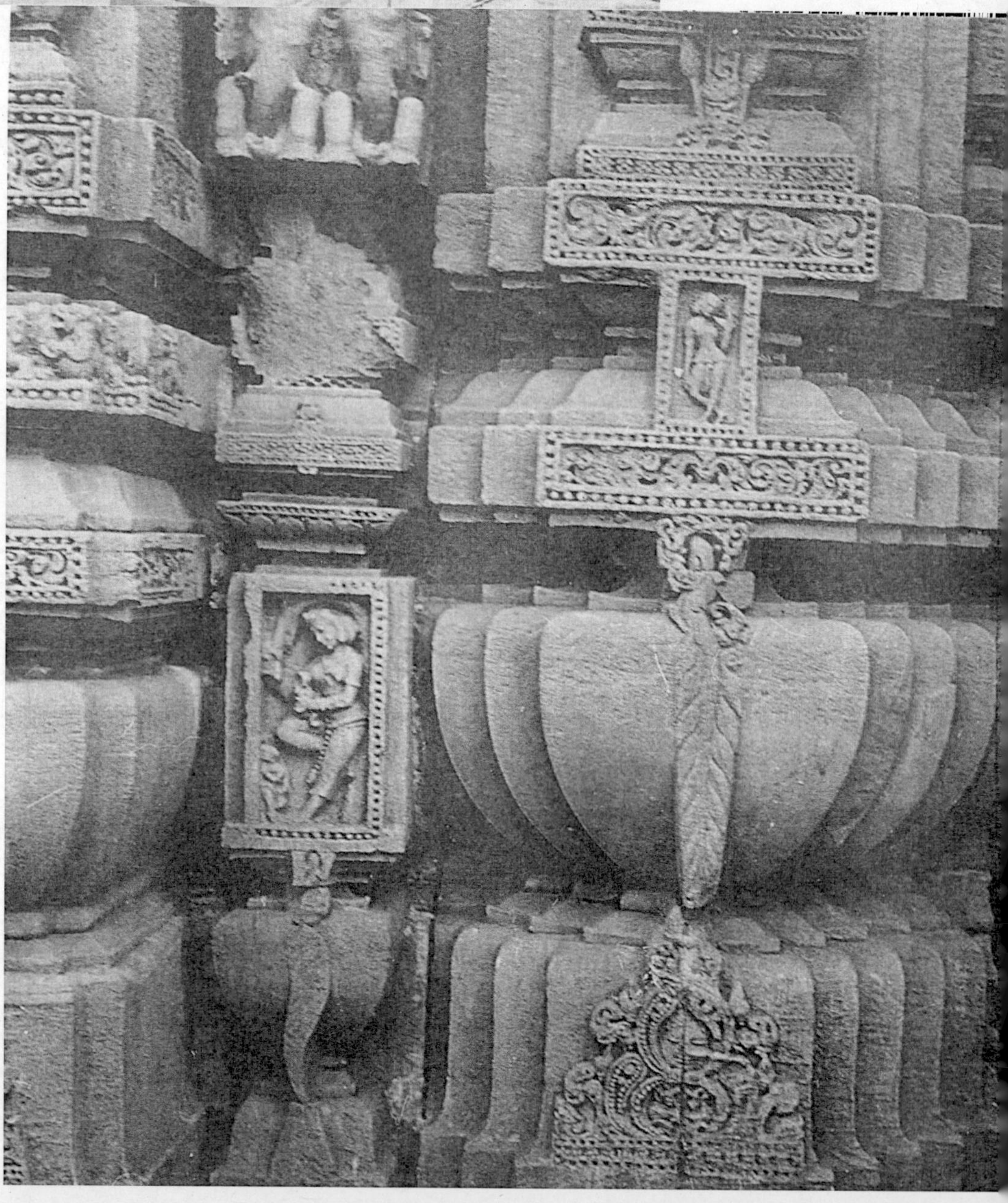

94. *Prāsāda*, detail of base mouldings. (AIIS).

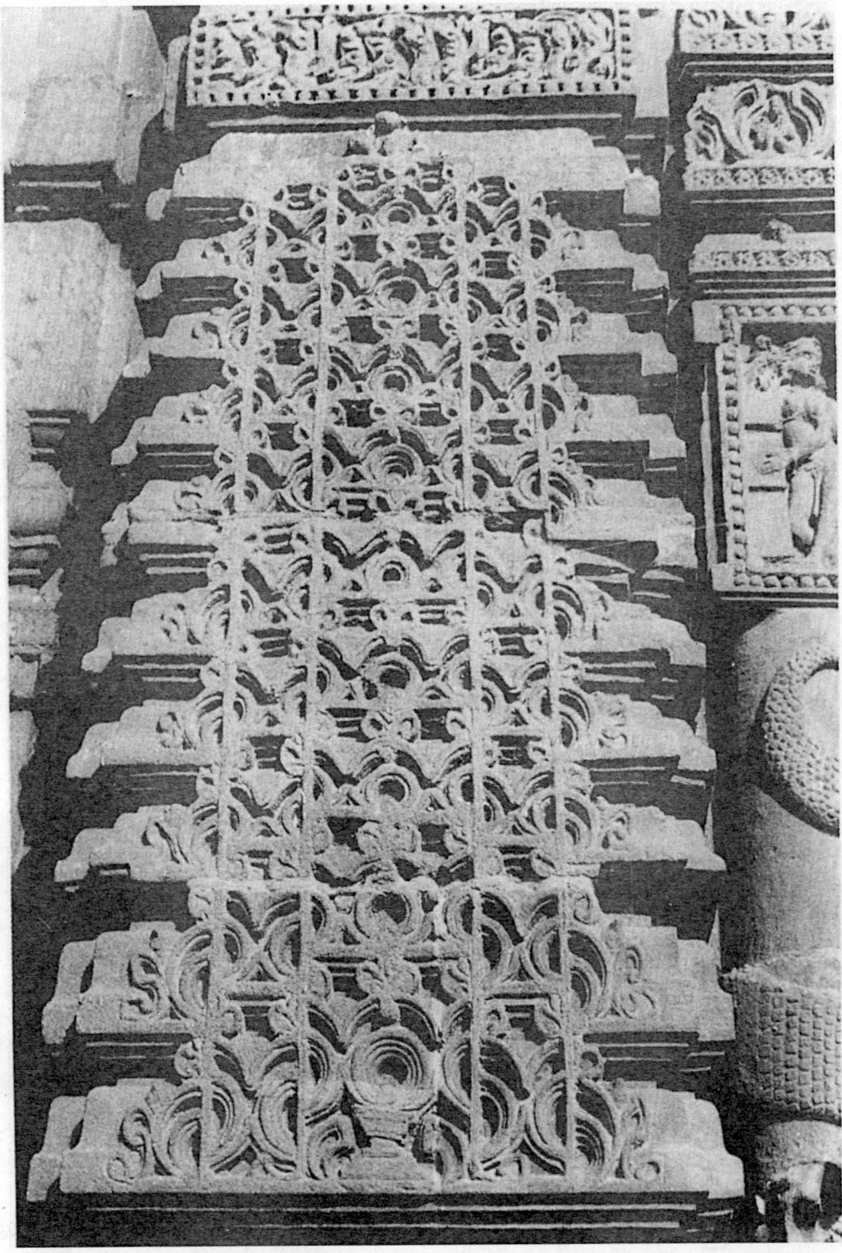

95. *Prāsāda*, detail of *pratibhadra*.

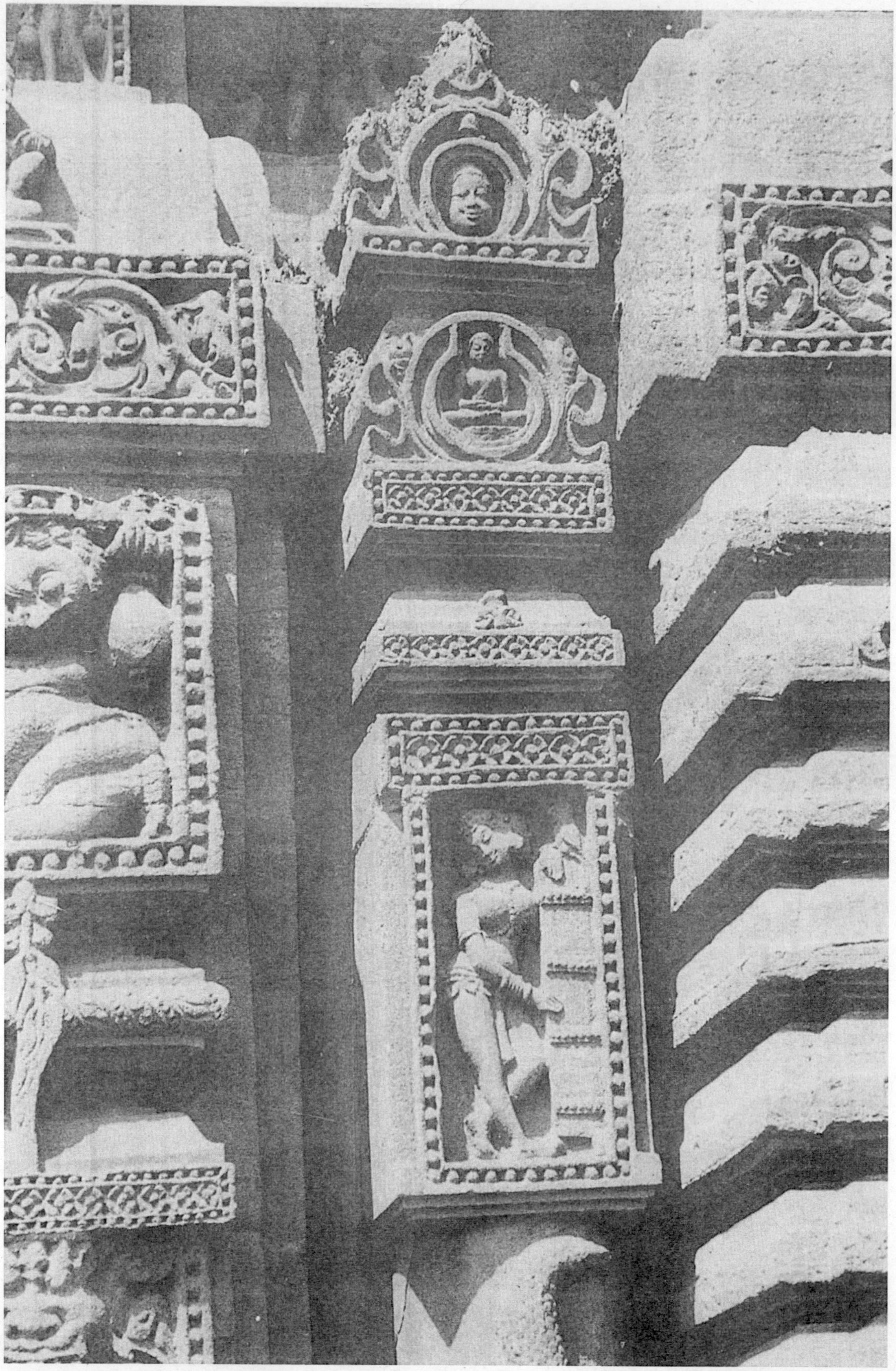

96. *Prāsāda*, detail of *pratikarṇa*.

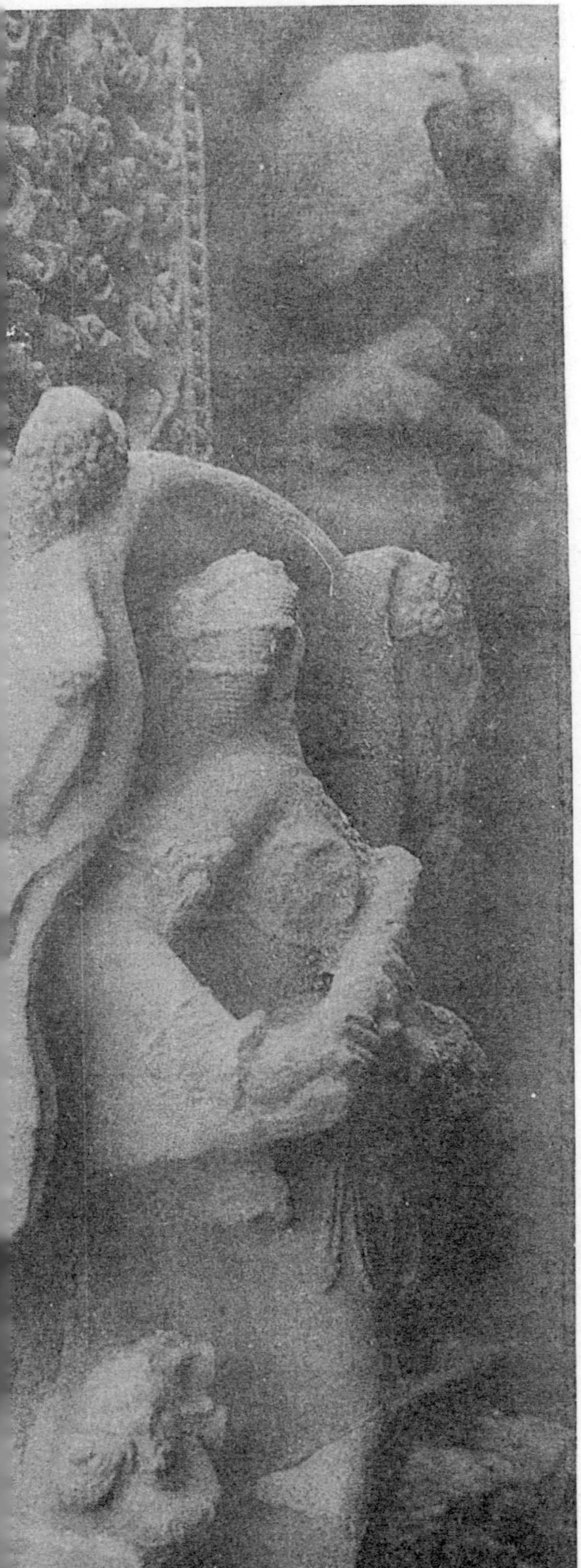

97. *Prāsāda*, west wall (north side), *karṇa* figure (*śālabhañjikā*) and *nāga*-pilaster.

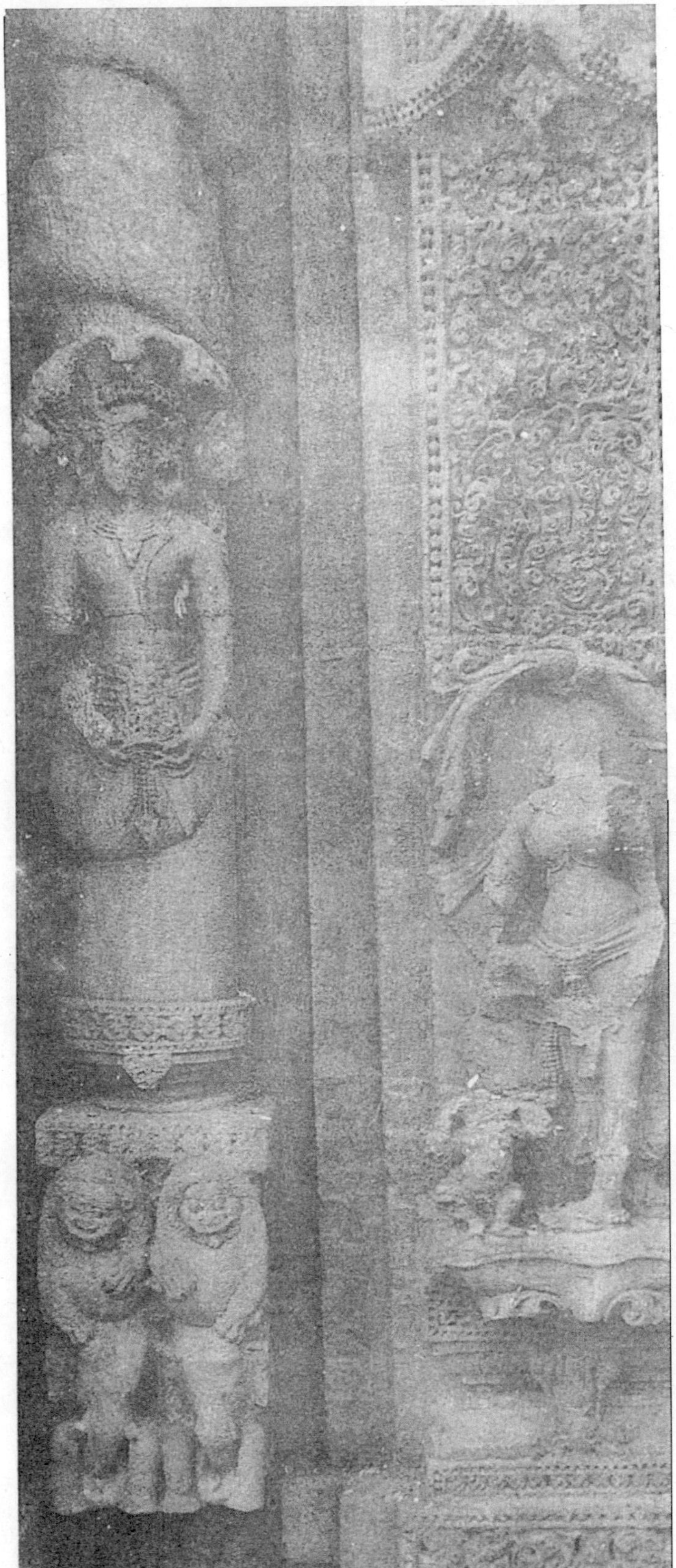

98. *Prāsāda*, north wall, *karṇa* figure (*śālabhañjikā*) and *nāga*-pilaster.

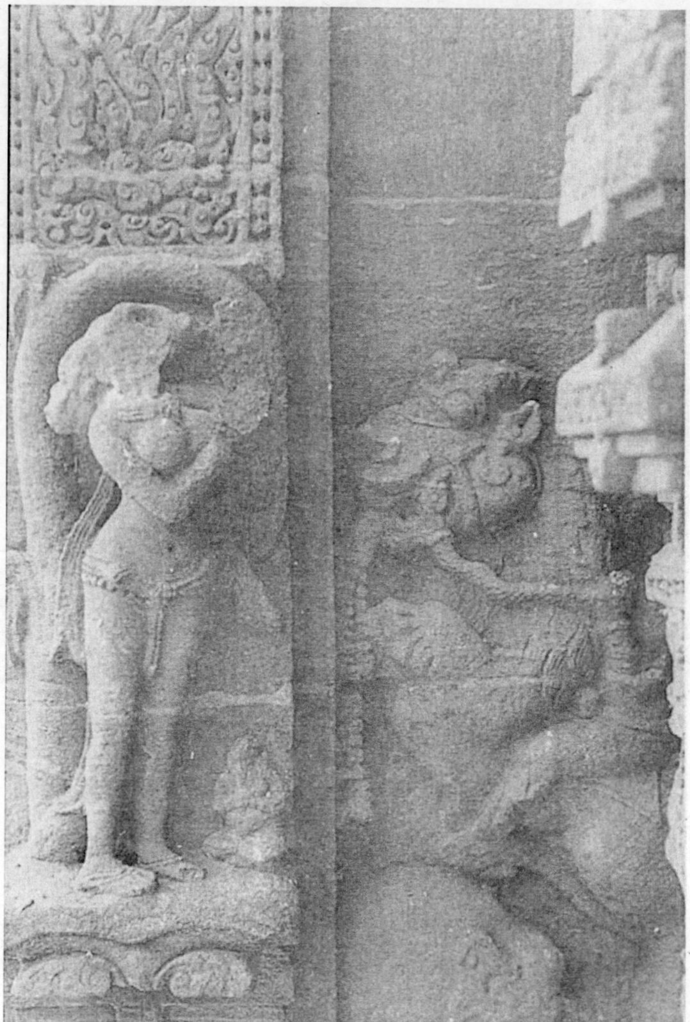

99. North wall, *bhadra*, right side, *śālabhañjikā* and *vyāla*.

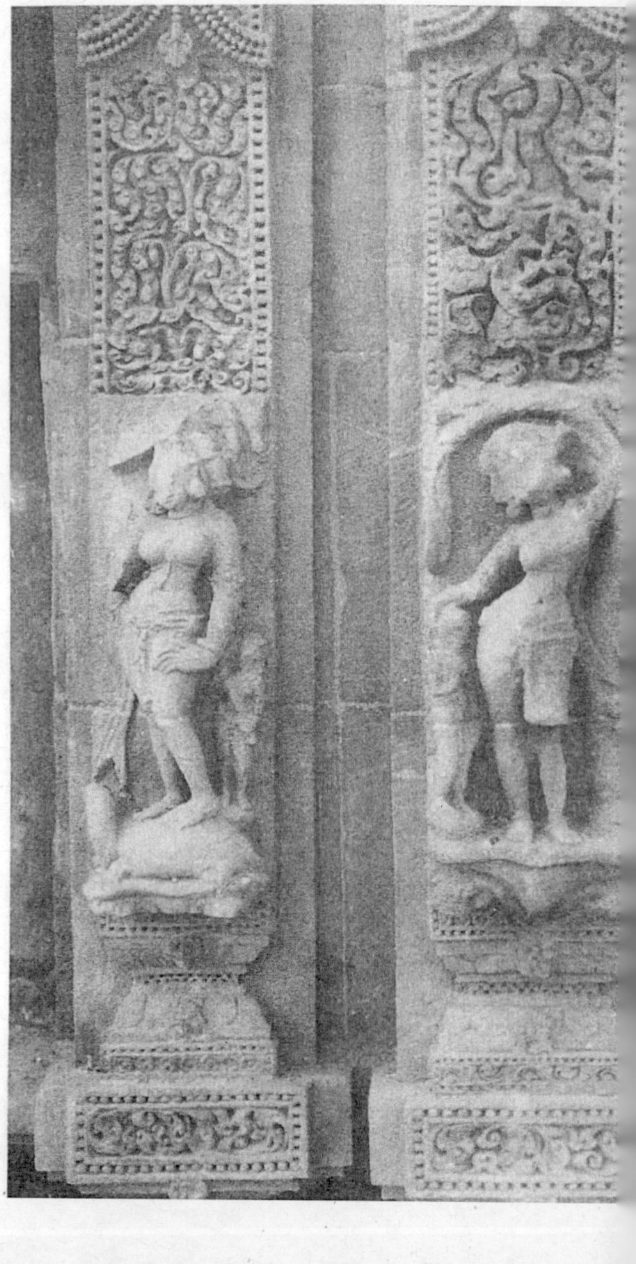

100. North wall, *bhadra*, right side, *śālabhañjikā* (right) and Yamunā.

101. North wall, *bhadra*, niche, left side, Gaṅgā (left) and *śālabhañjikā*.

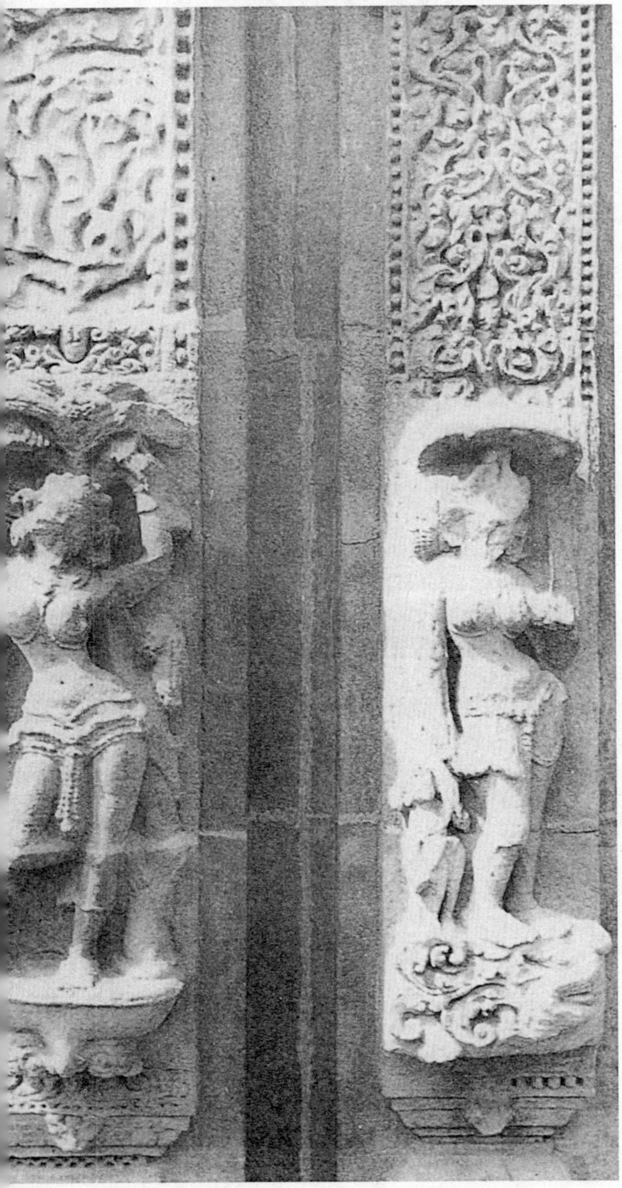

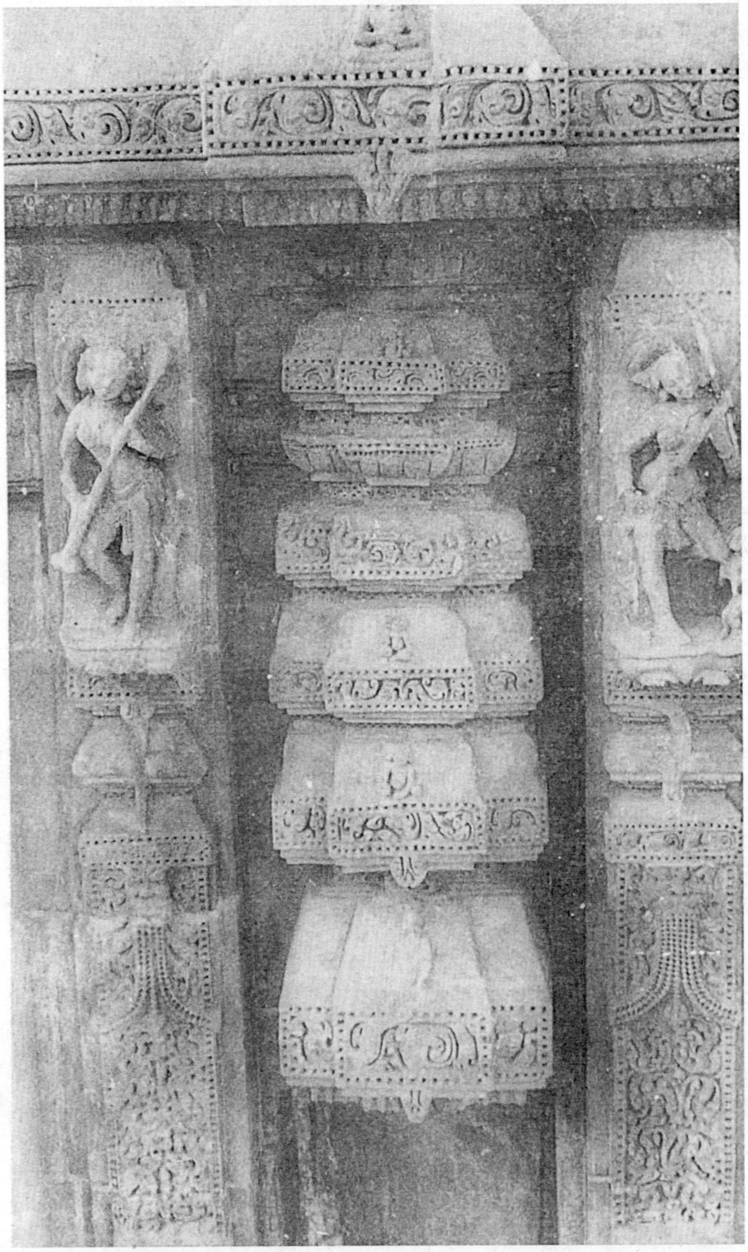

102. North wall, *bhadra*, female musicians above niche canopy

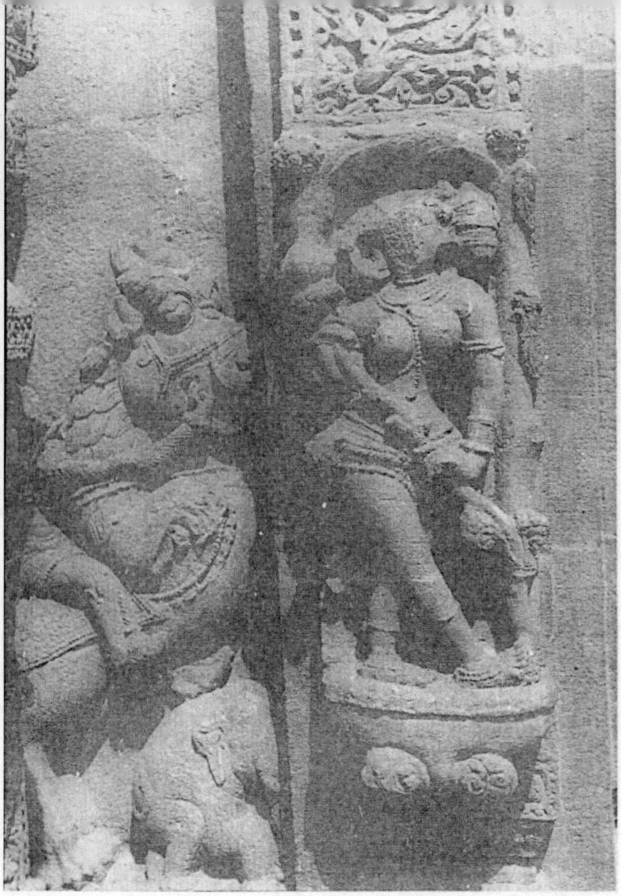

103. North wall, female, figure and *vyāla*.

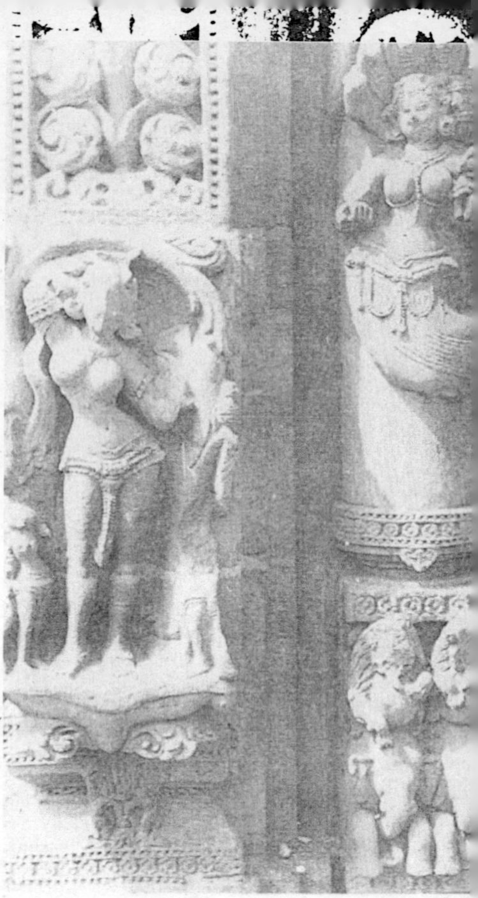

104. North wall, *nāginī*-pilaster and *karṇa* figure (*śālabhañjikā*).

105. East wall, *karṇa figure (śālabhañjikā)* and *nāga*-pilaster.

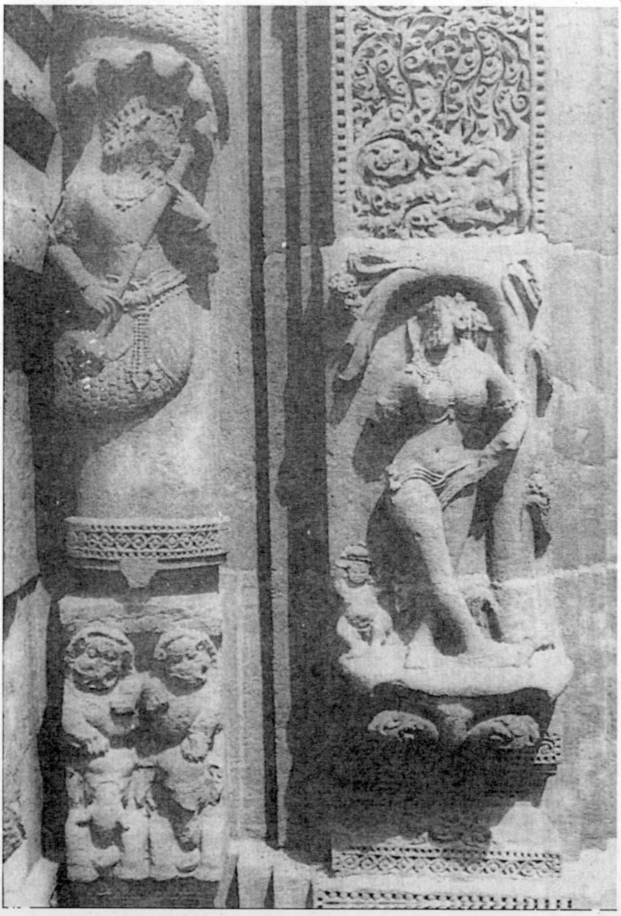

106. East wall, *bhadra*, right side, *vyāla* and male figure.

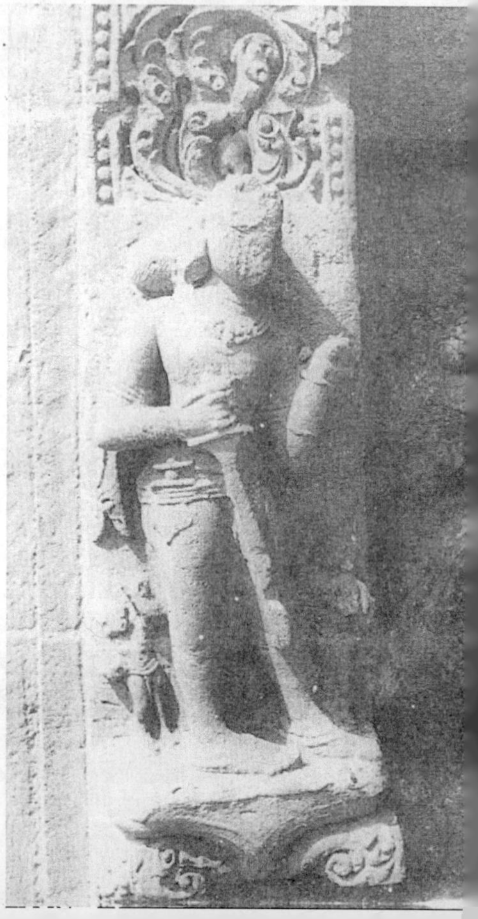

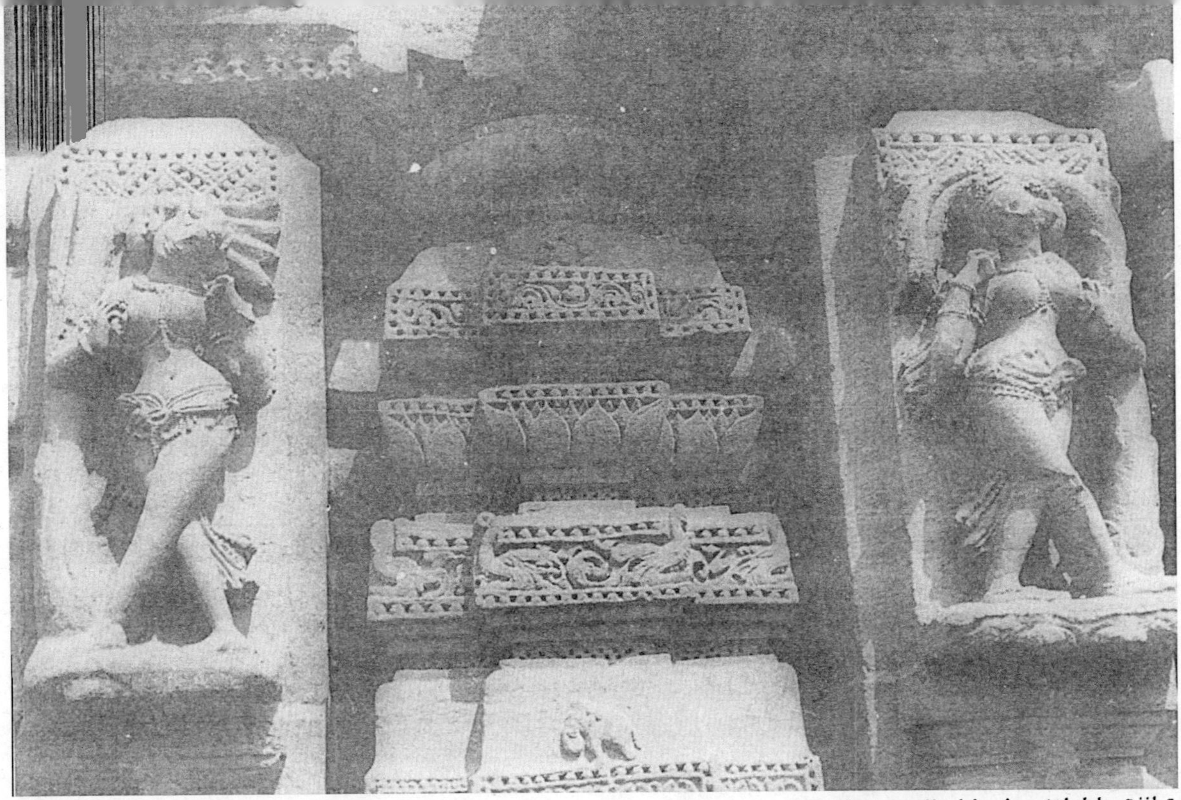

107. East wall, *bhadra śālabhañjikā* above niche canopy.

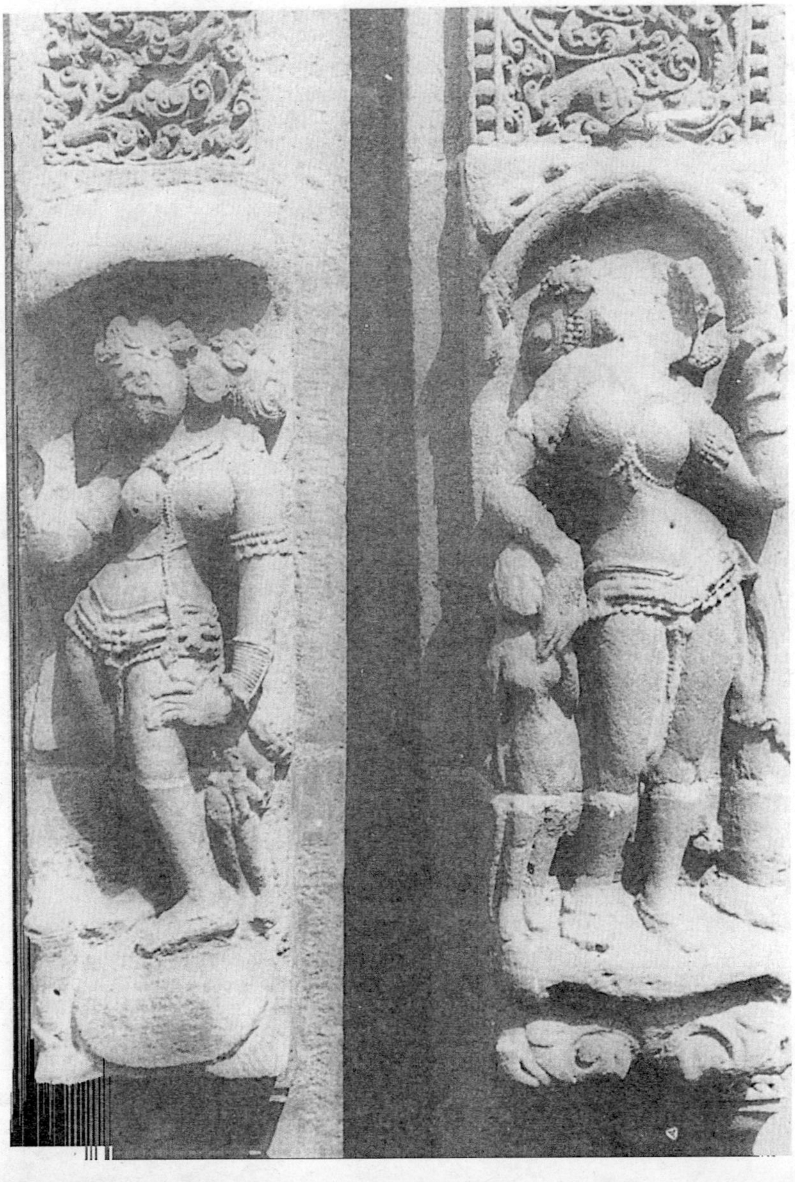

108. East wall, *bhadra* niche, right side *śālabhañjikā* (right) and Yamunā.

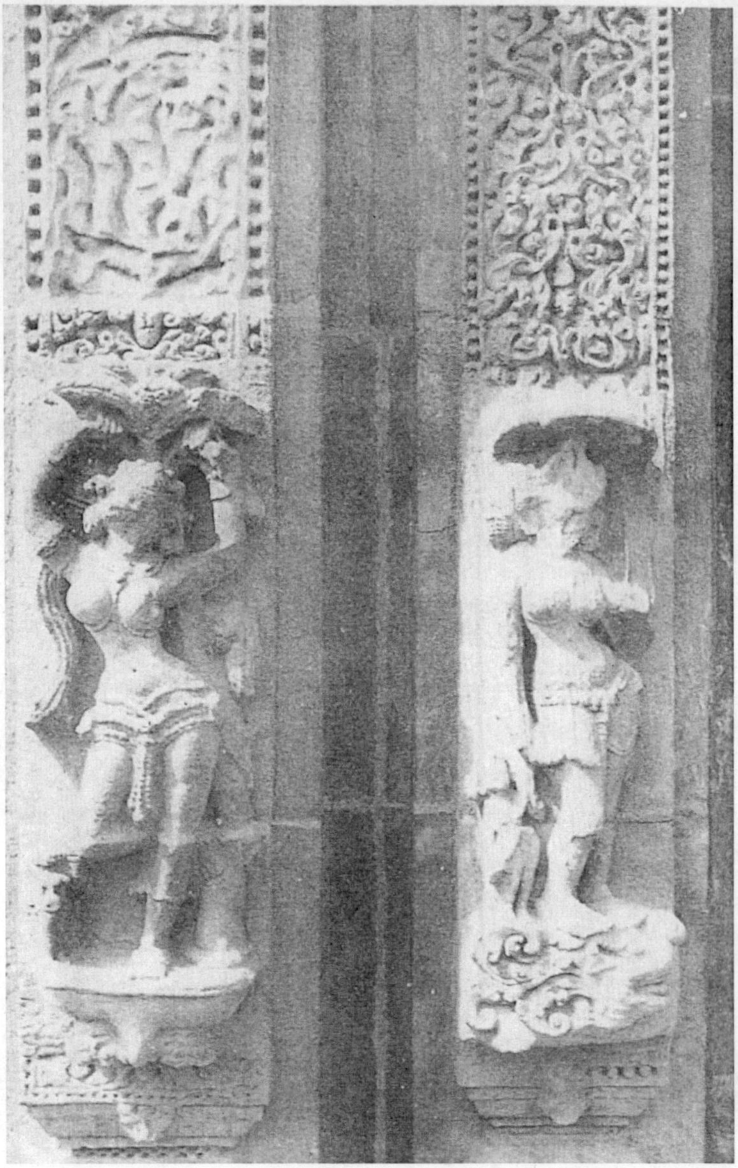

109. East wall, *bhadra* niche, left side, Gaṅgā (right) and *śālabhañjikā*.

110. East wall, *bhadra*, left side *śālabhañjikā* and *vyāla*.

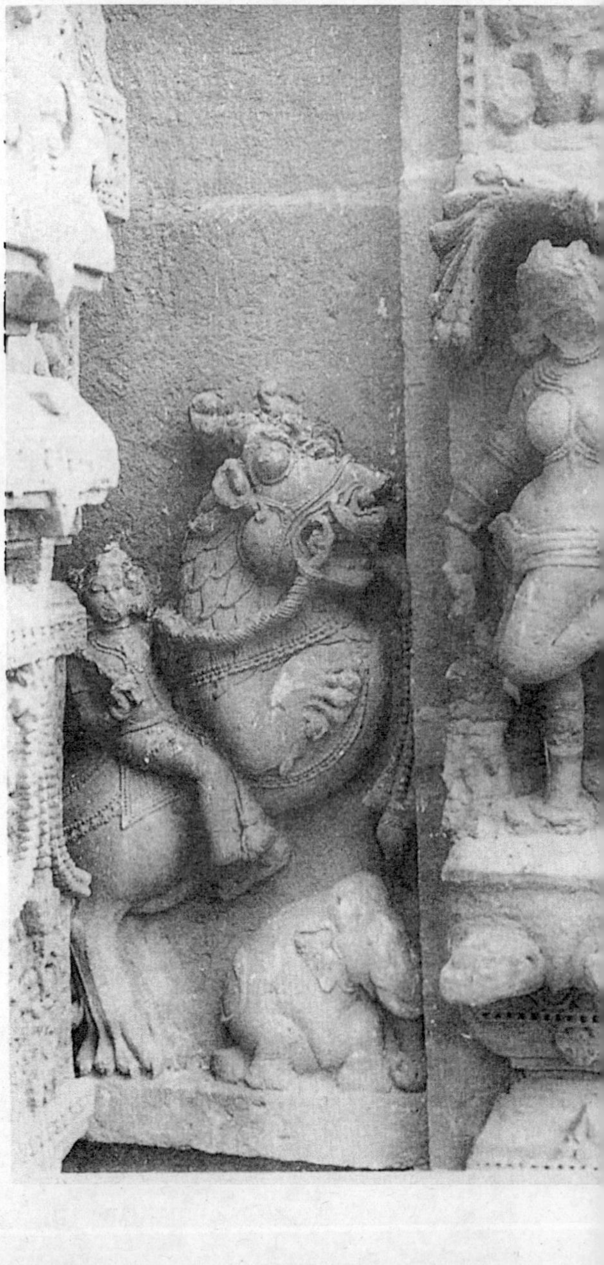

111. East wall, *nāginī*-pilaster and *karṇa* figure (*śālabhañjikā*).

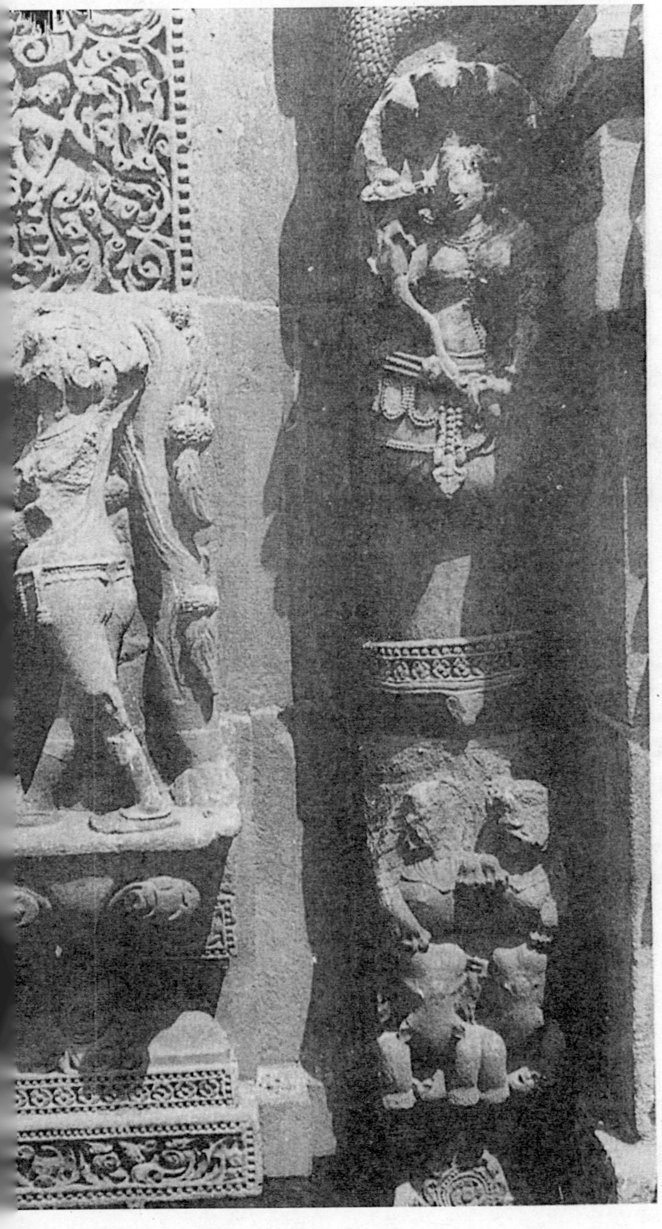

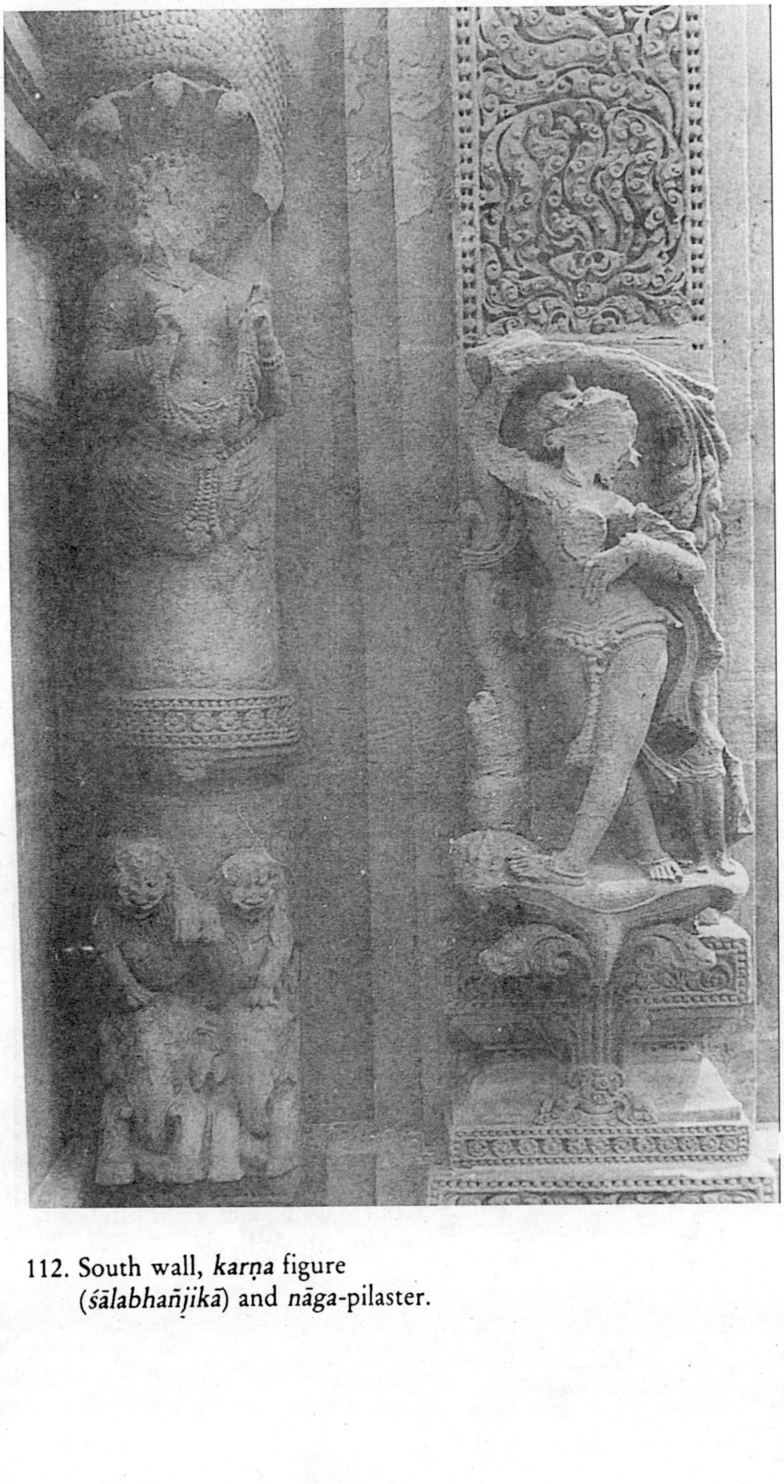

112. South wall, *karṇa* figure (*śālabhañjikā*) and *nāga*-pilaster.

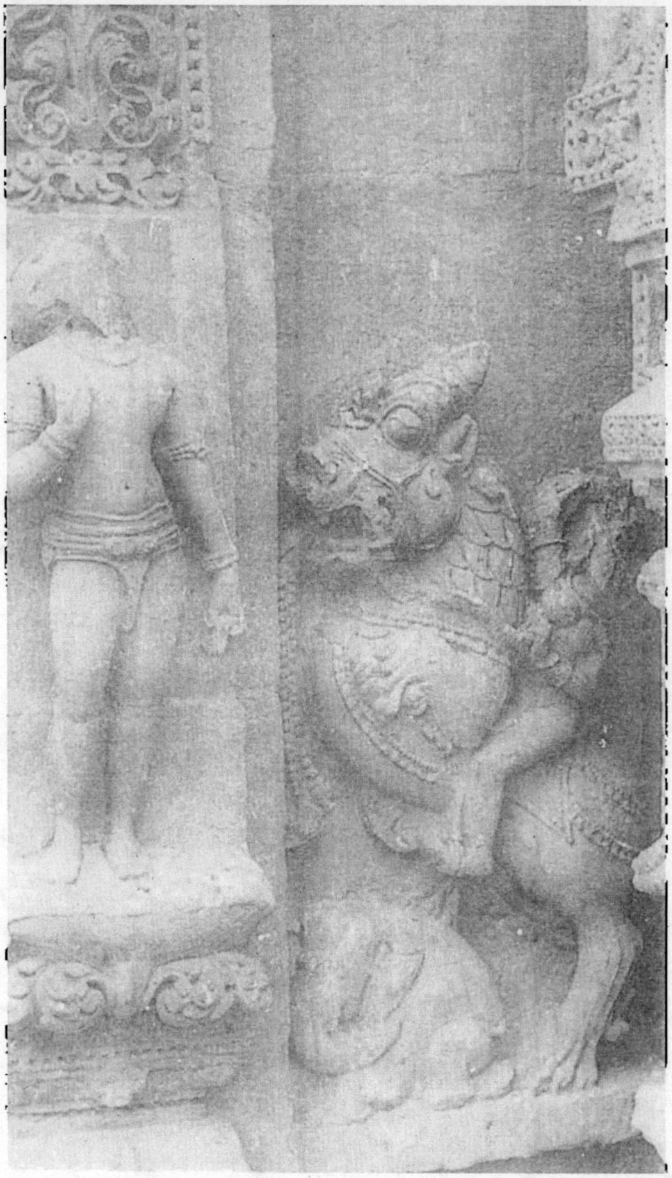

113. South wall, *bhadra*, right side, *vyāla* and male figure.

114. South wall, *bhadra*, right side, (*śālabhañjikā* (right) and Yamunā.

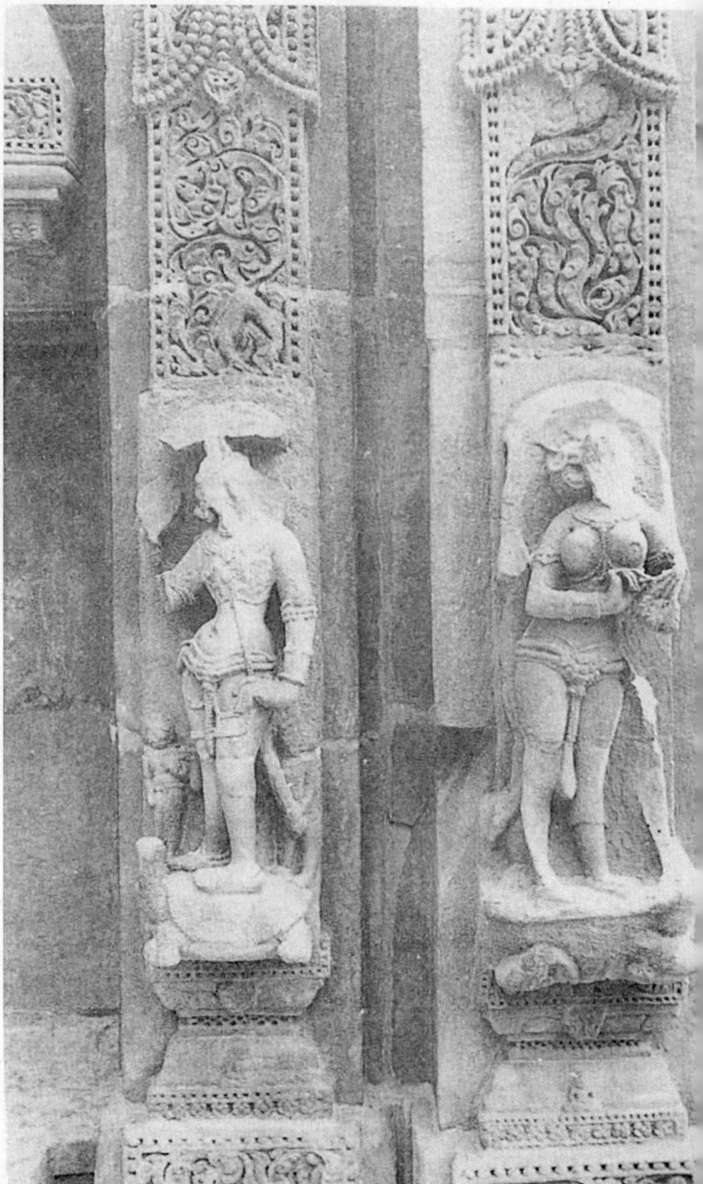

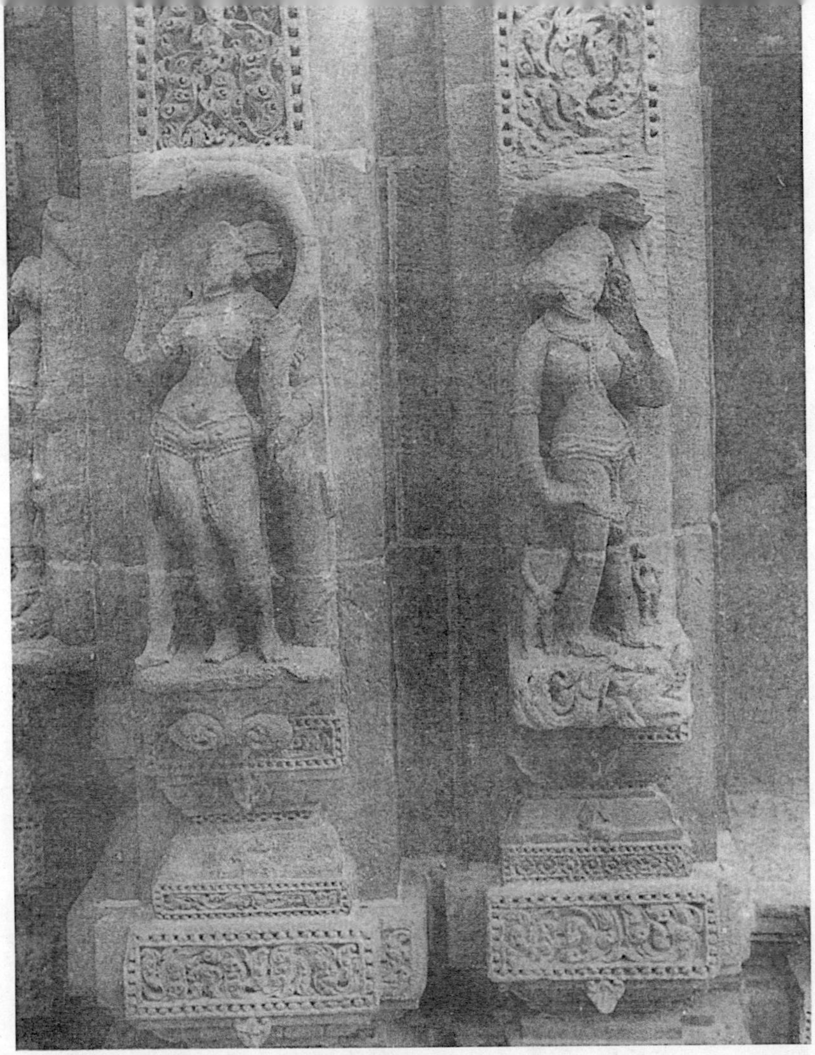

115. South wall, *bhadra* niche, left side, Gaṅgā (right) and *śālabhañjikā*.

116. South wall, *bhadra*, *śālabhañjikā*, above niche canopy.

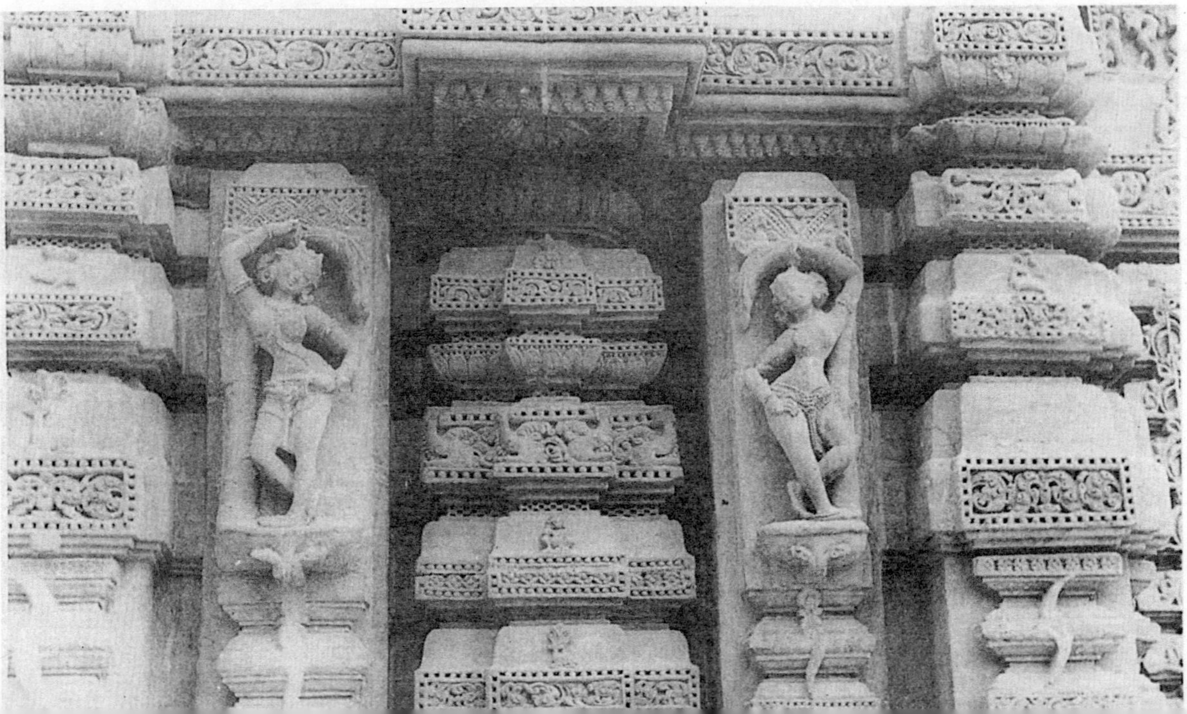

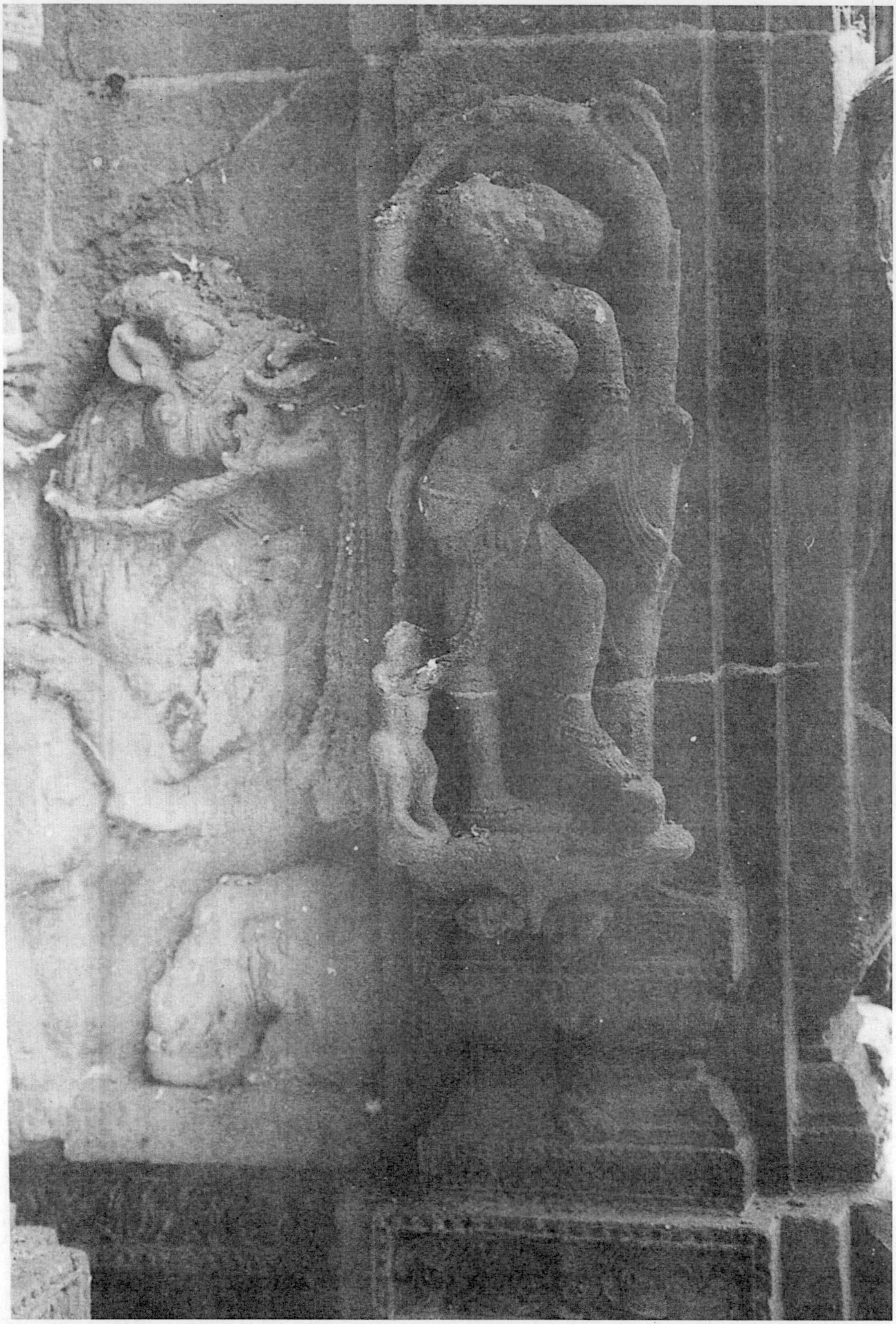

117. South wall, *bhadra*, left side, *śālabhañjikā* and *vyāla*.

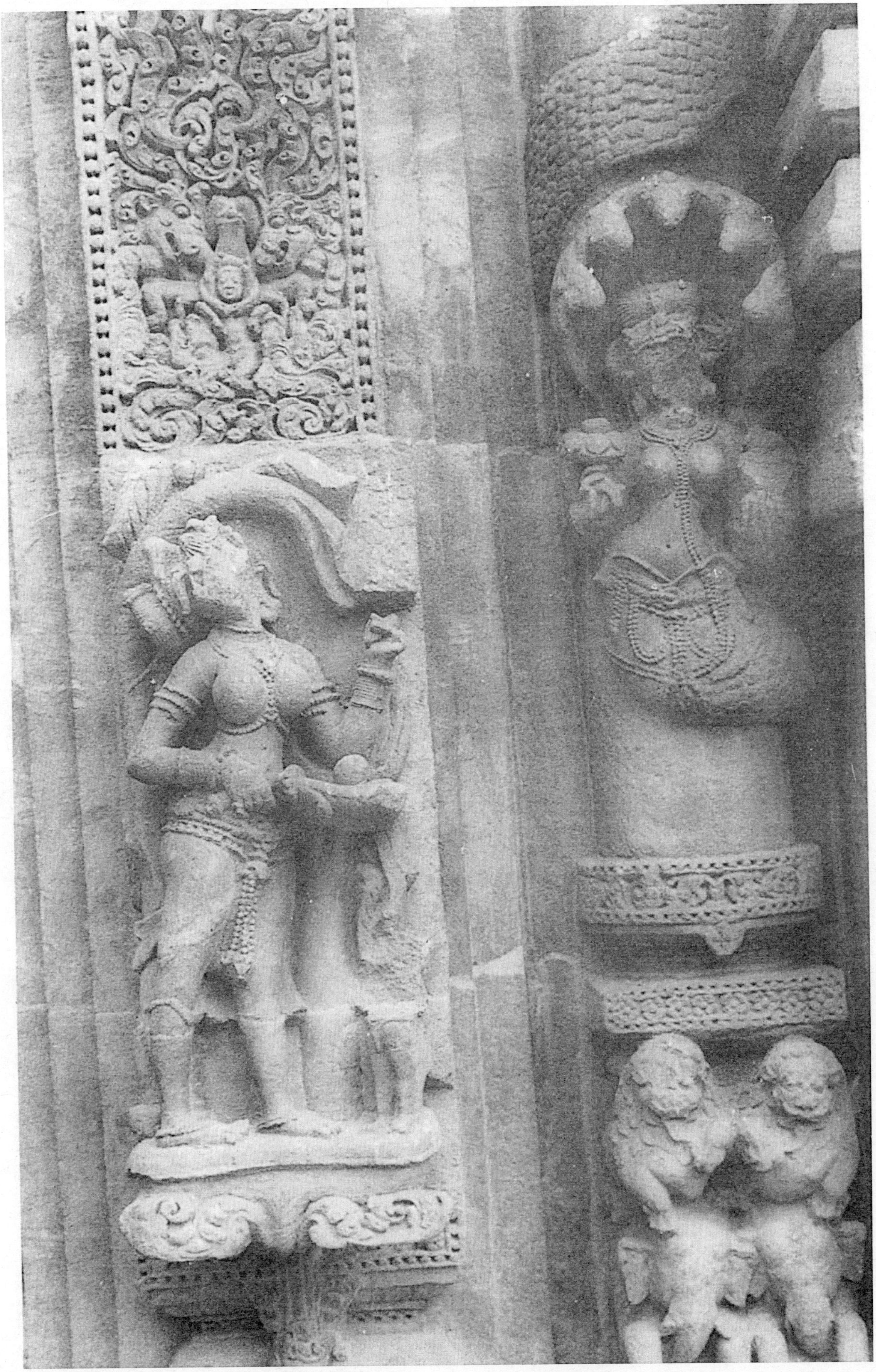

118. South wall, *nāgnī*-pilaster and *karṇa* figure.

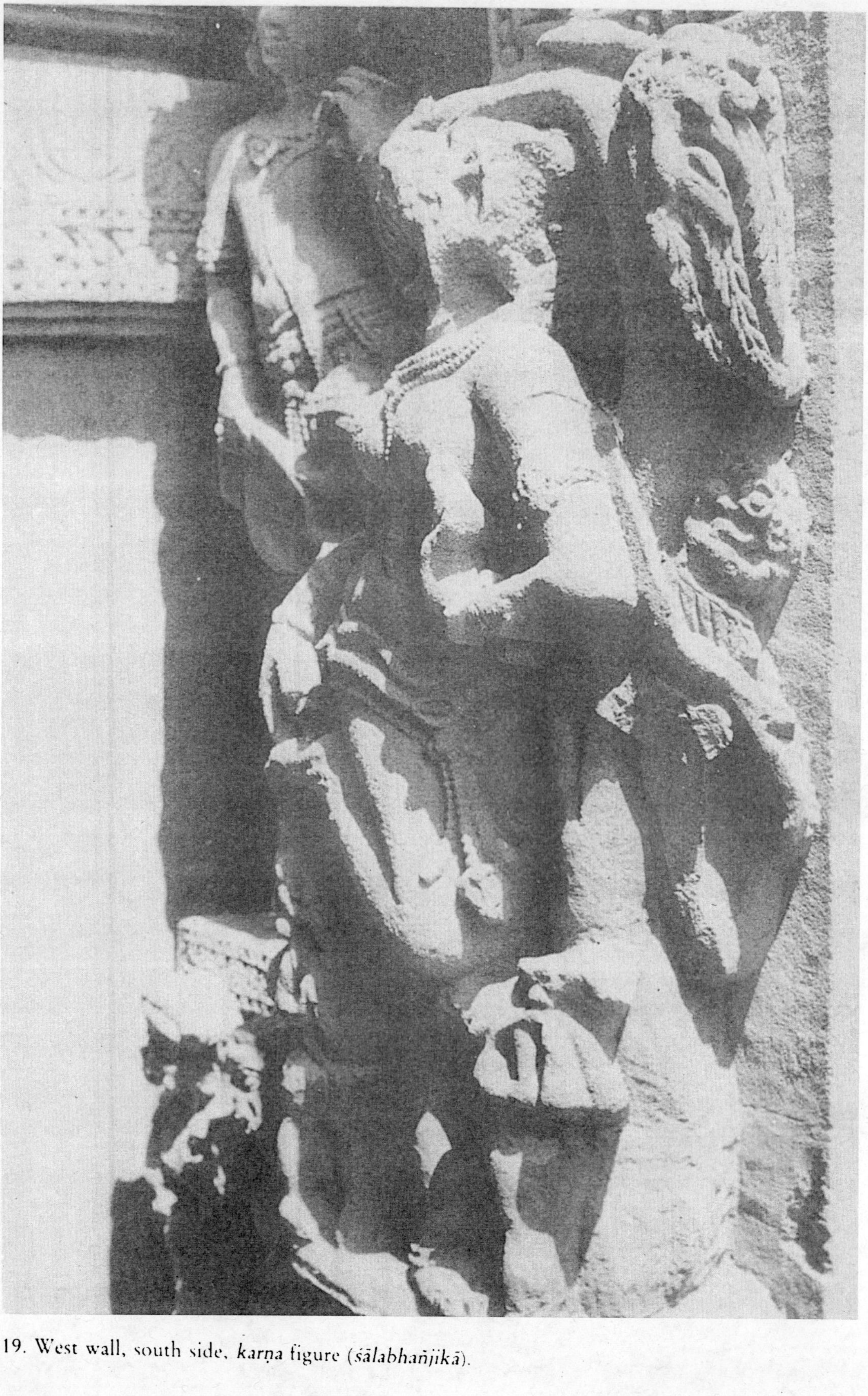

119. West wall, south side, *karṇa* figure (*śālabhañjikā*).

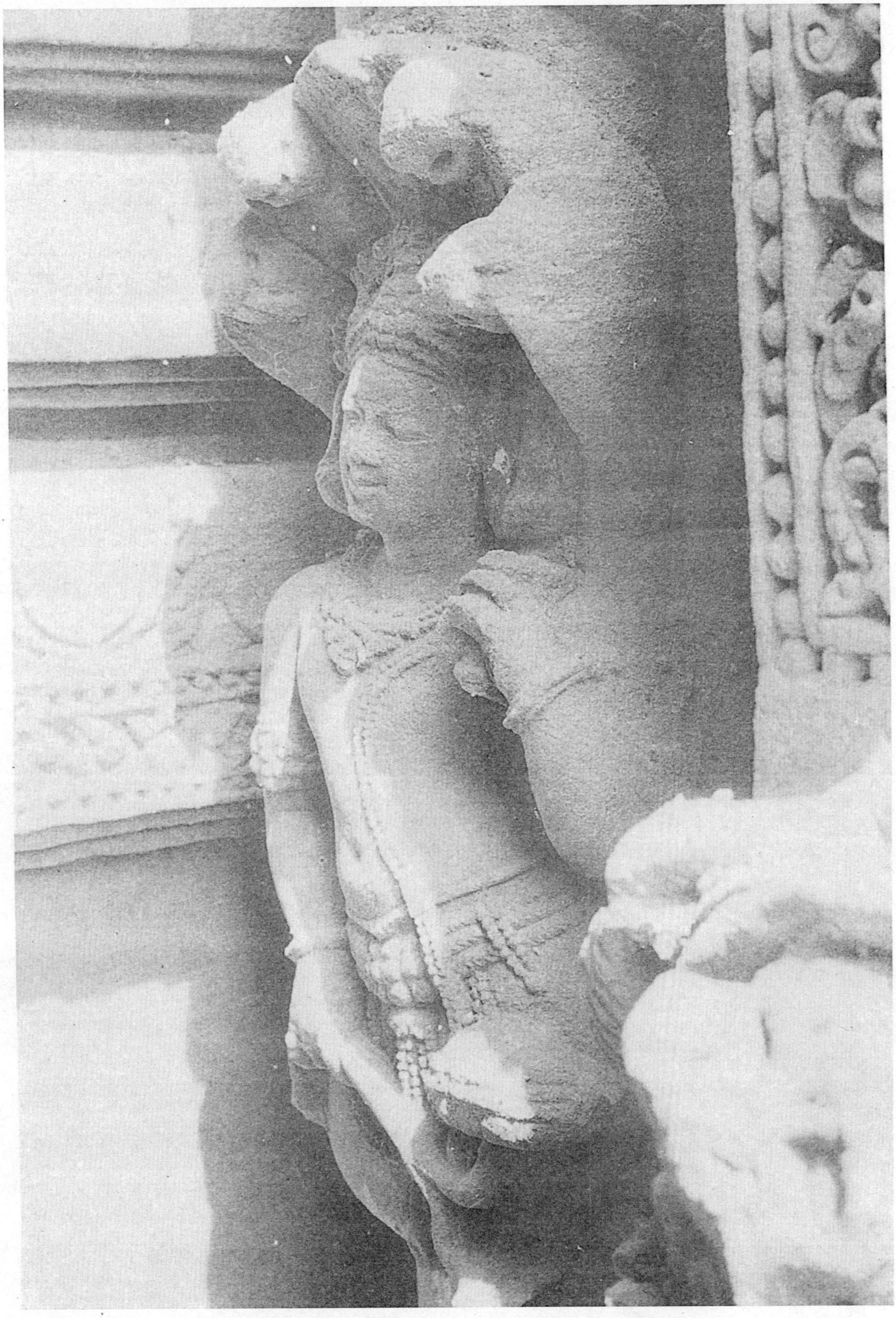

120. West wall, south side, *nāga*-pilaster.

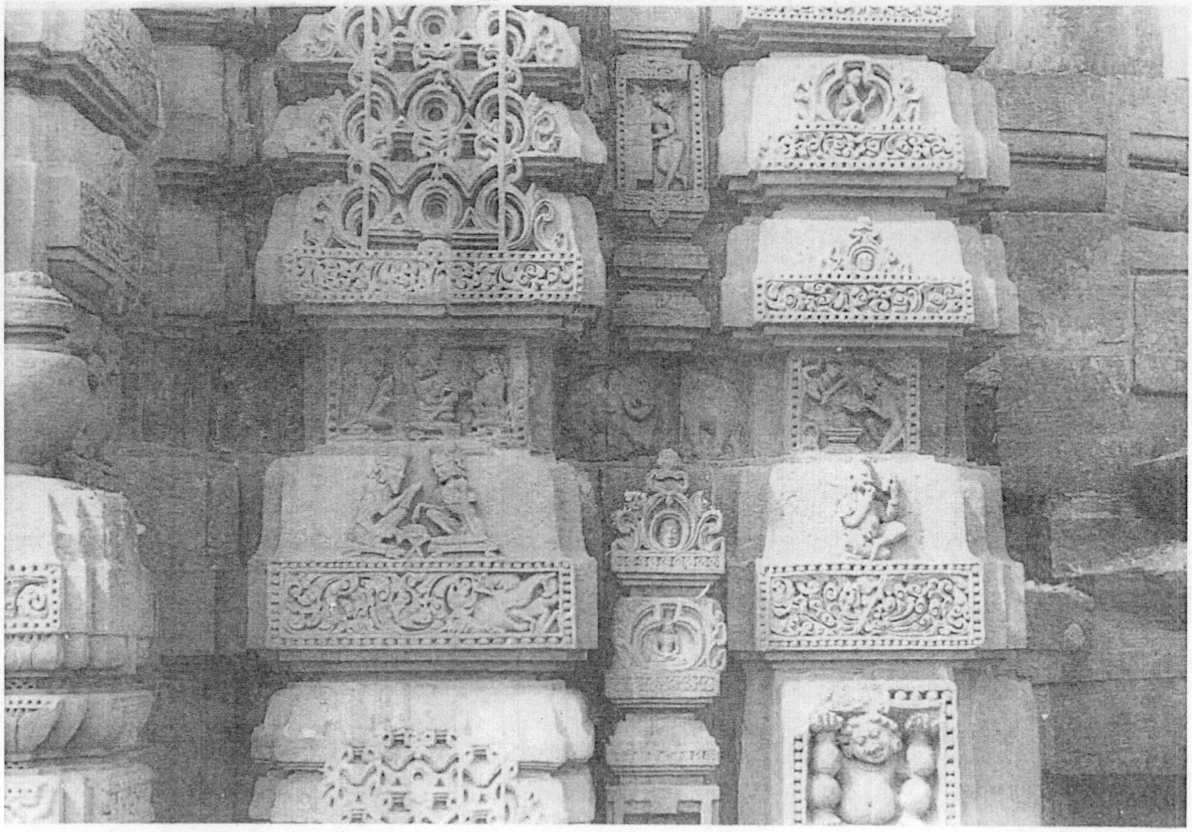

121. North wall, *kaṇṭha* reliefs (right of *bhadra*).

122. North wall, *kaṇṭha* reliefs (left of *bhadra*).

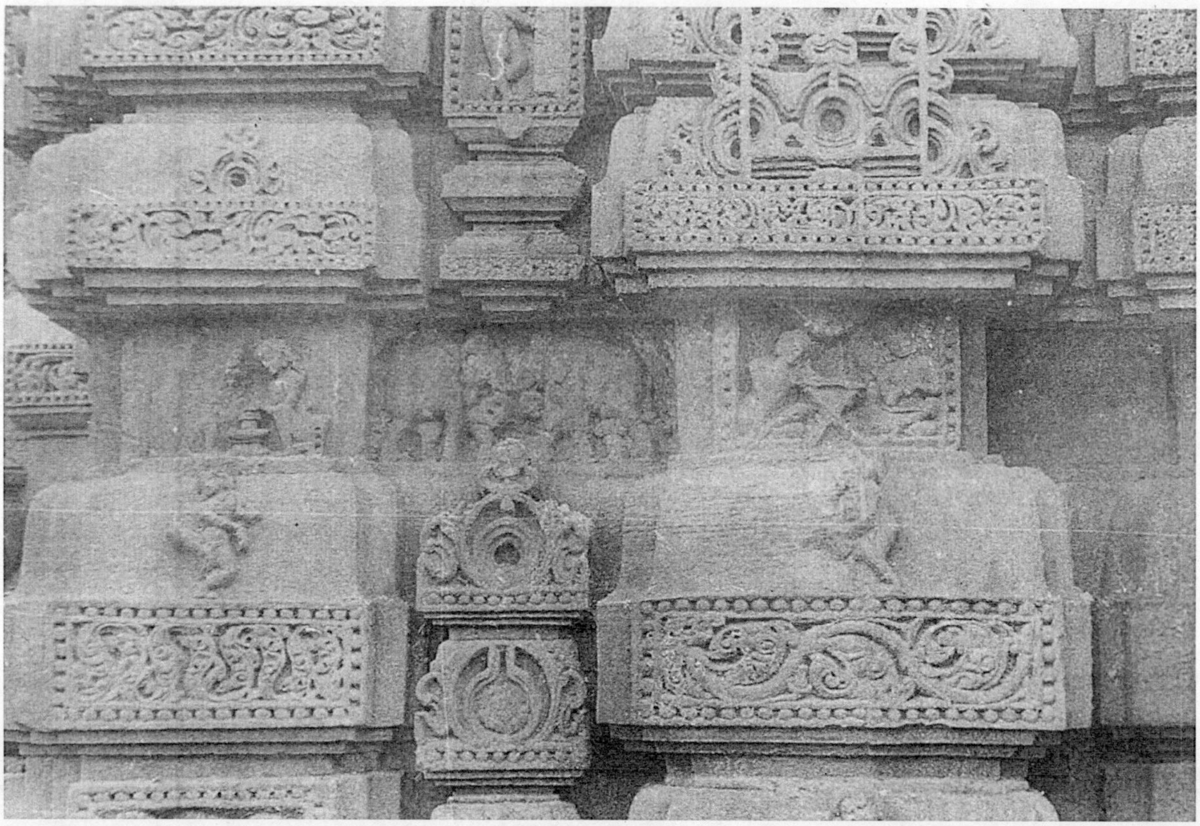

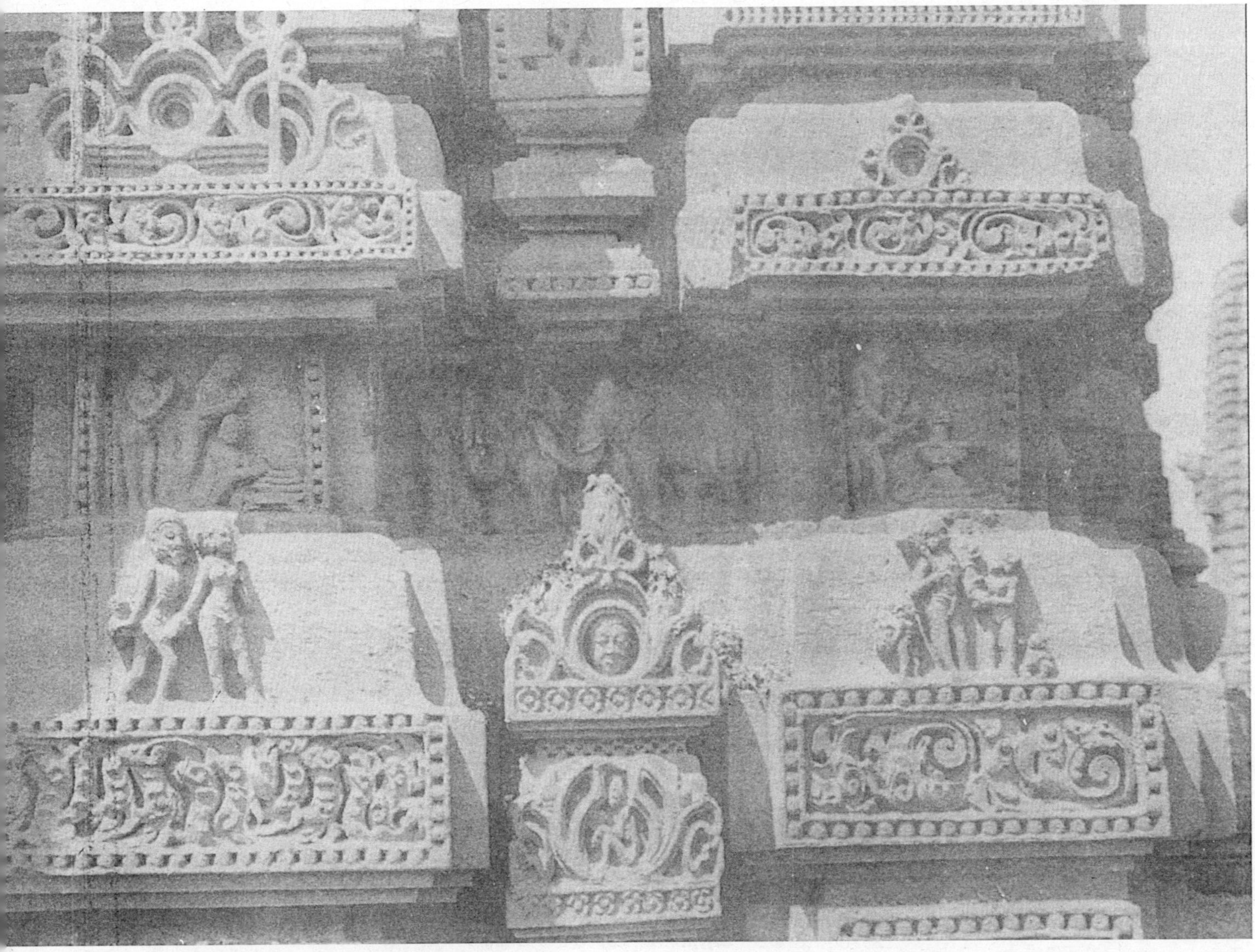

123. East wall, *kaṇṭha* reliefs (right of *bhadra*).

124. East wall, *kaṇṭha* reliefs (left of *bhadra*).

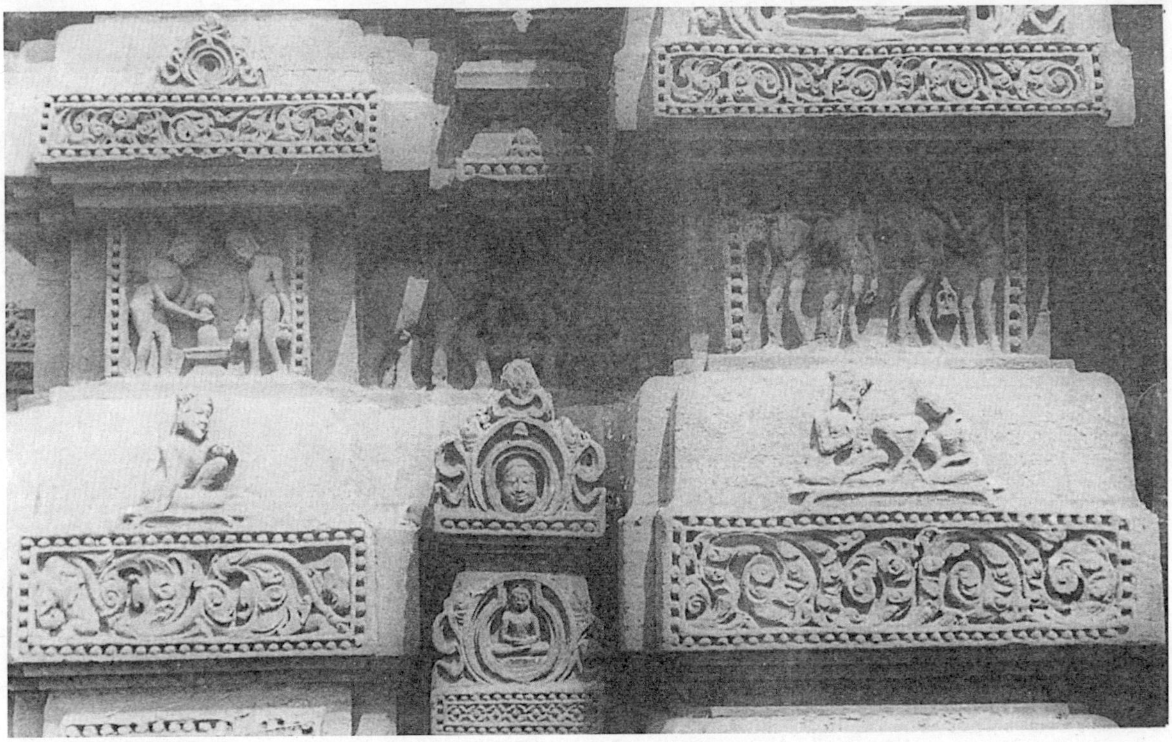

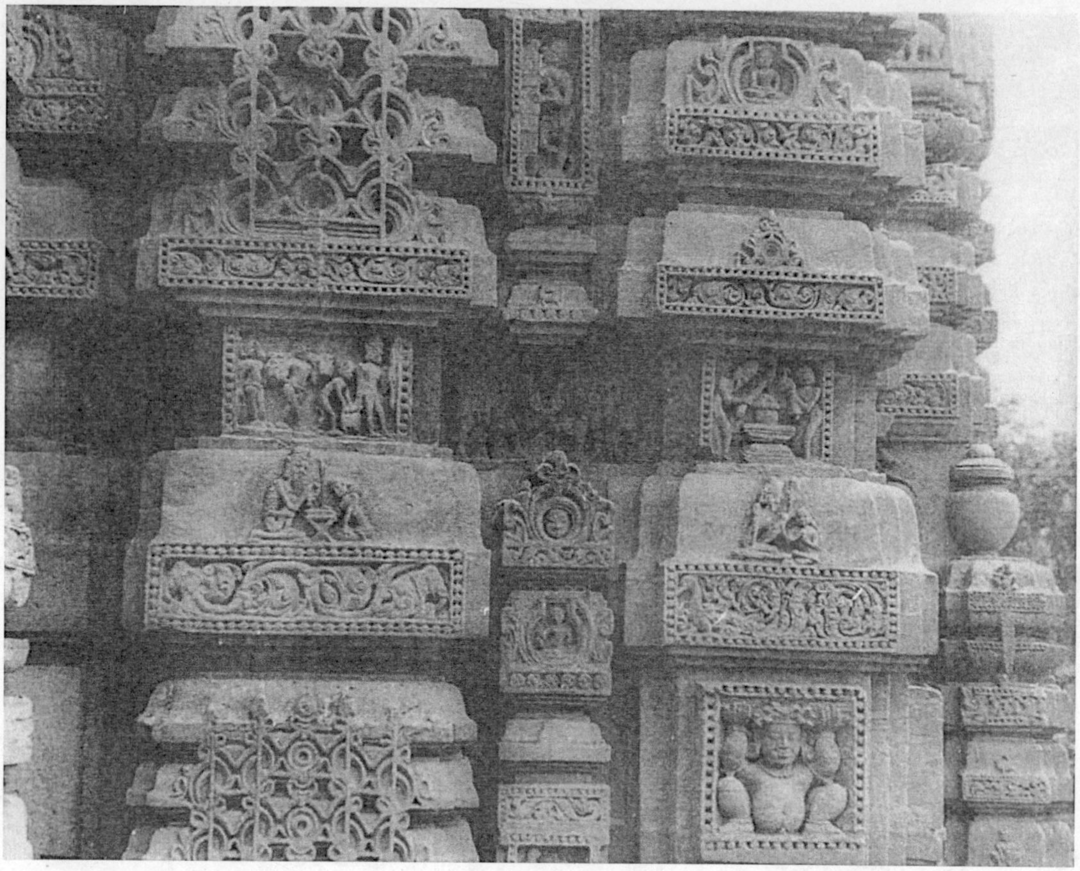

125. South wall, *kaṇṭha* reliefs (right of *bhadra*).

126. South wall, *kaṇṭha* reliefs (left of *bhadra*).

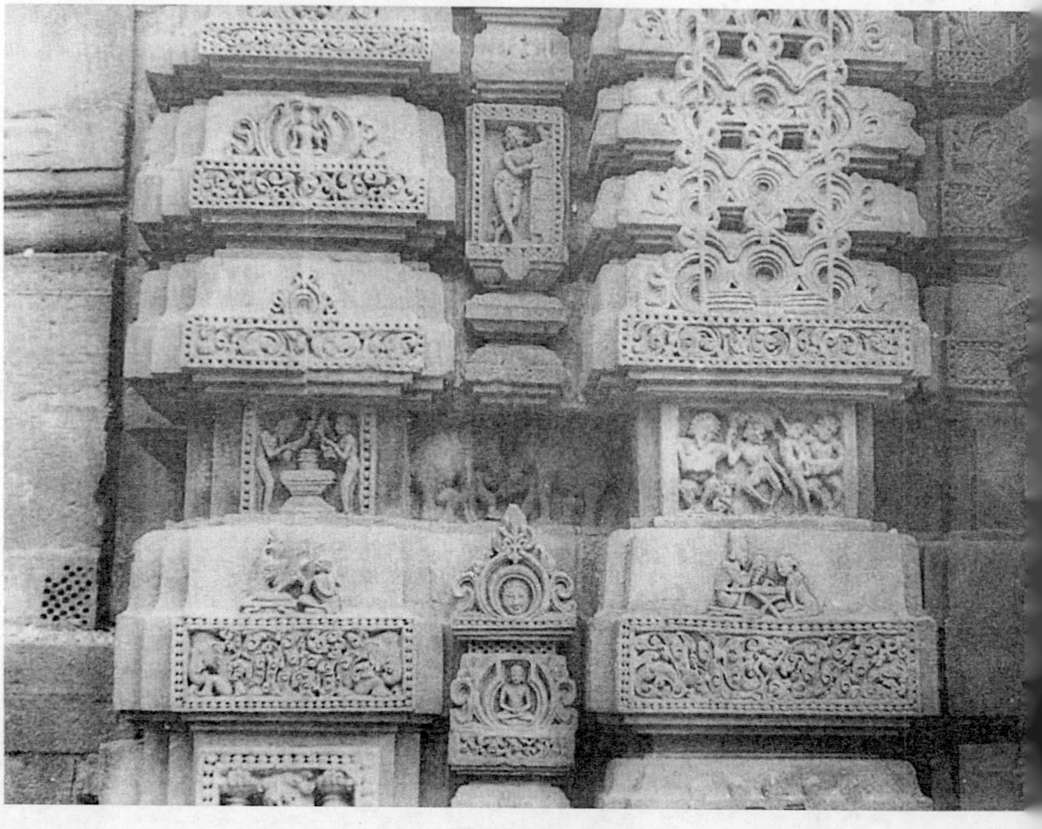

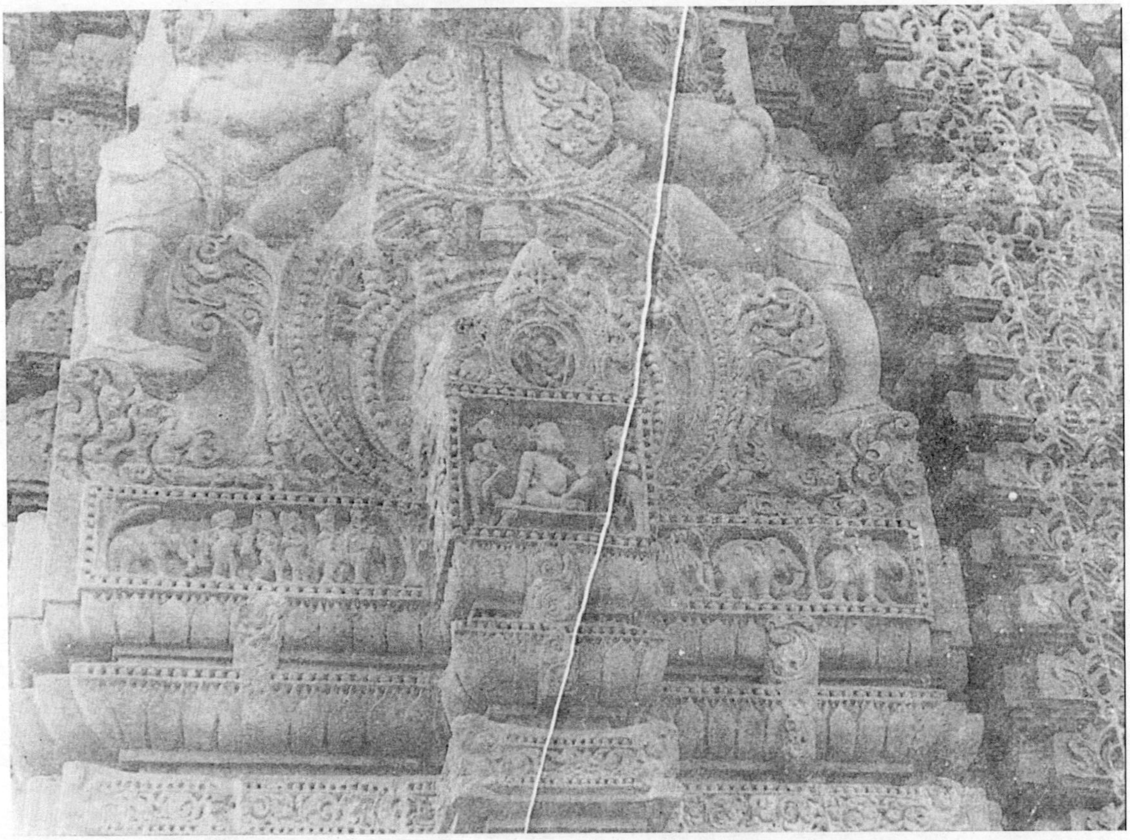

127. *Candraśālā*, north.

128. *Candraśālā*, north, detail.

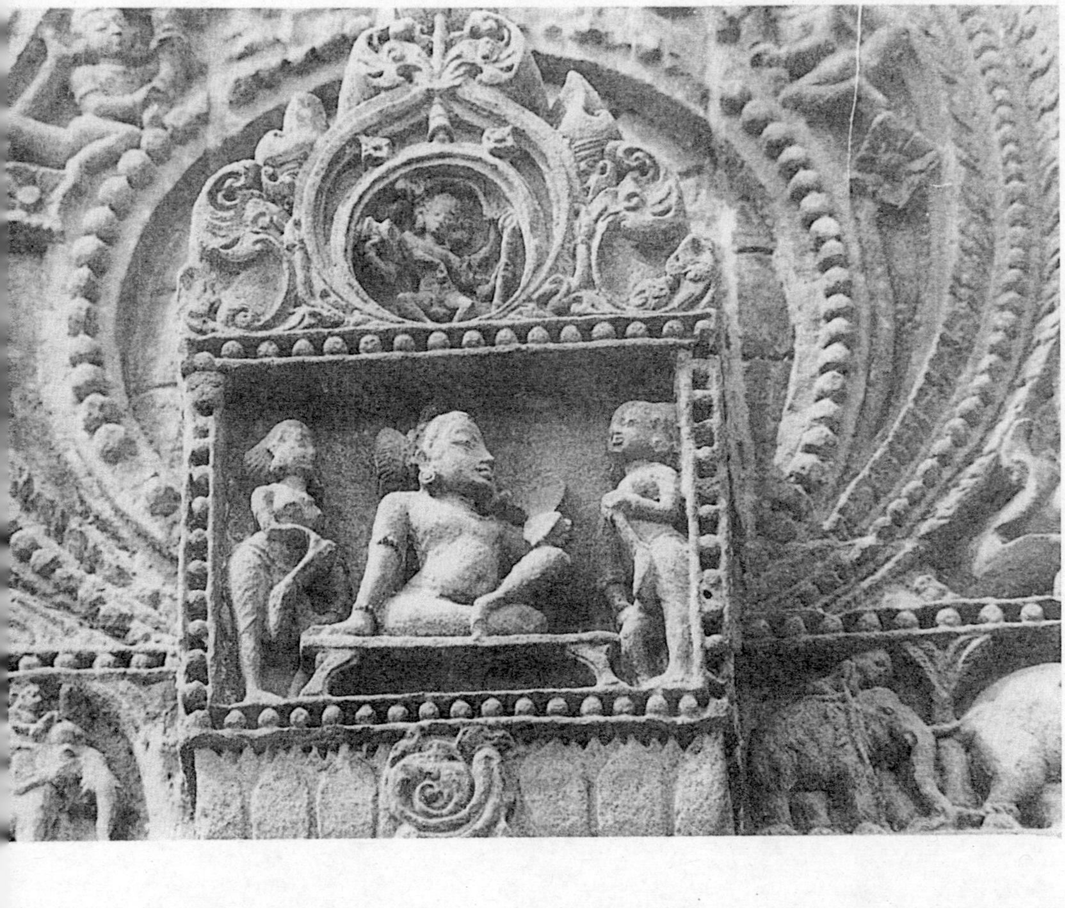

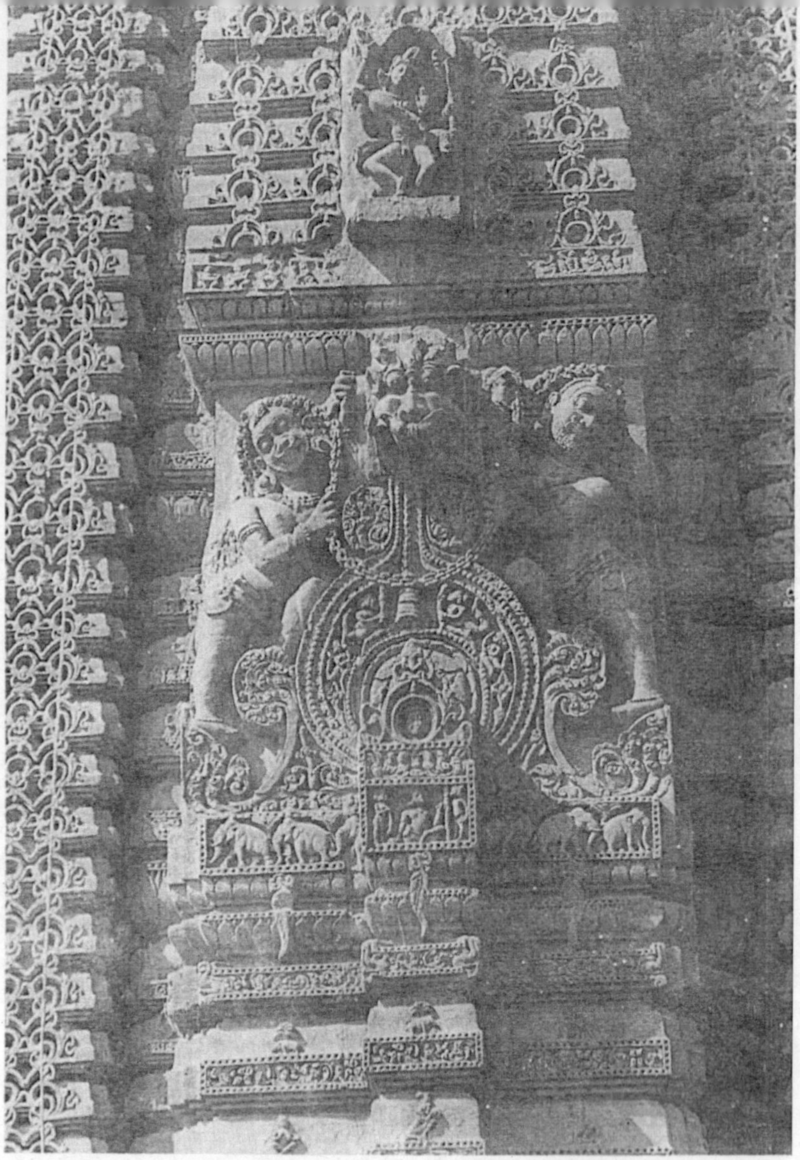

129. *Candraśālā*, east.

130. *Candraśālā*, east, detail.

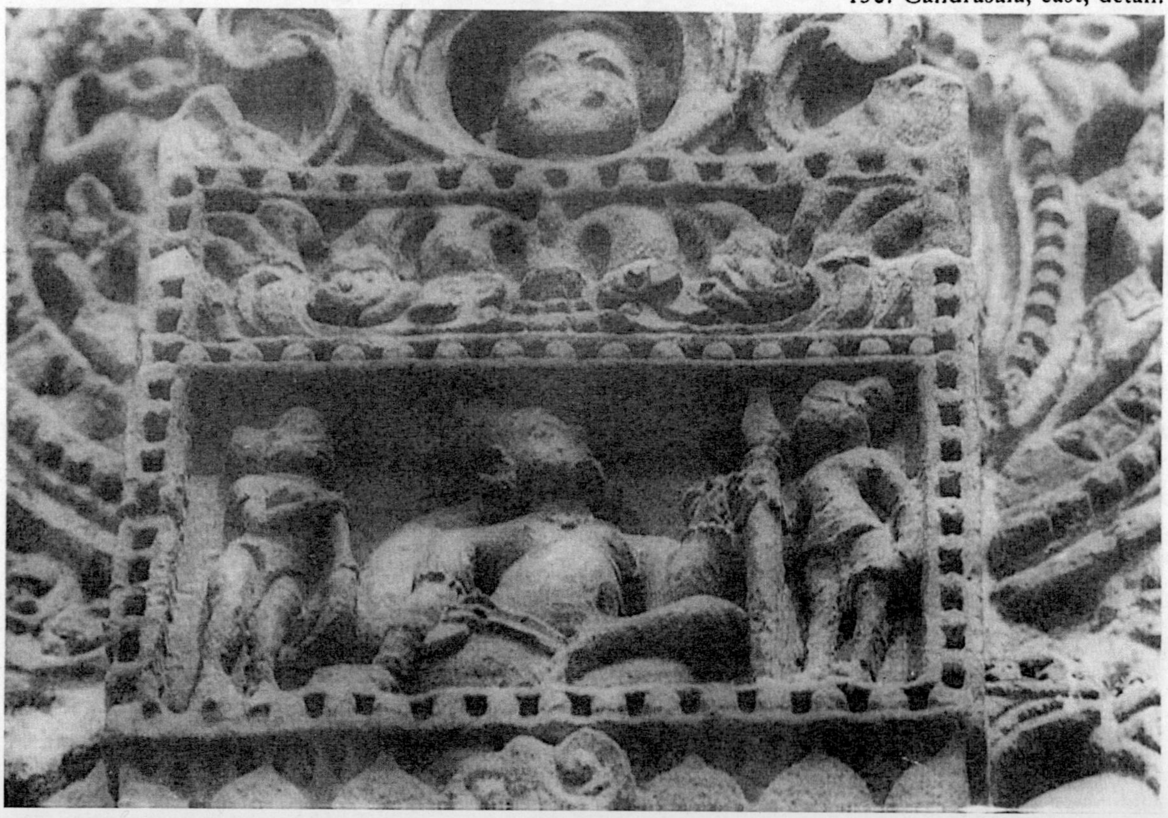

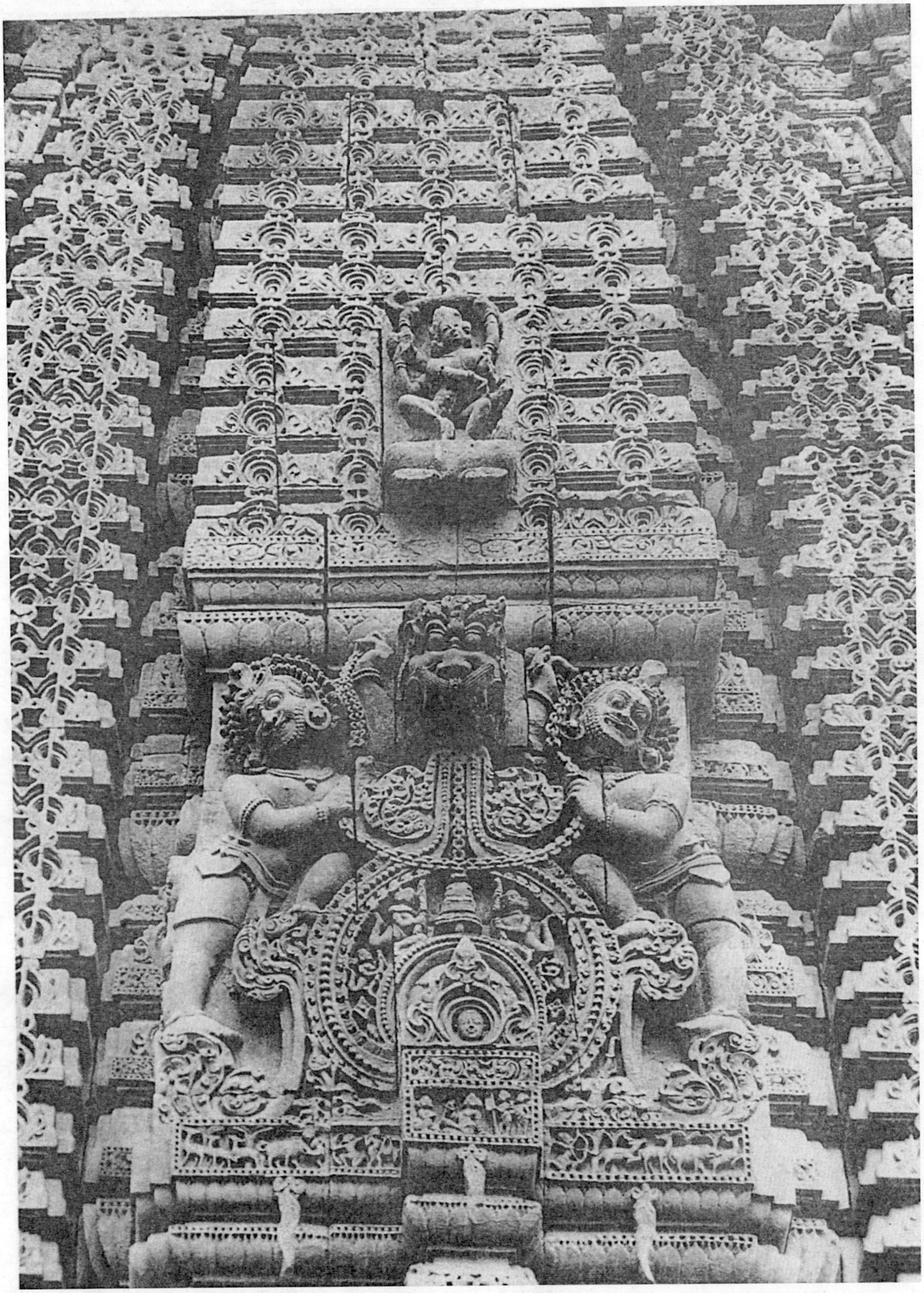

131. *Candraśālā*, south, (AIIS).

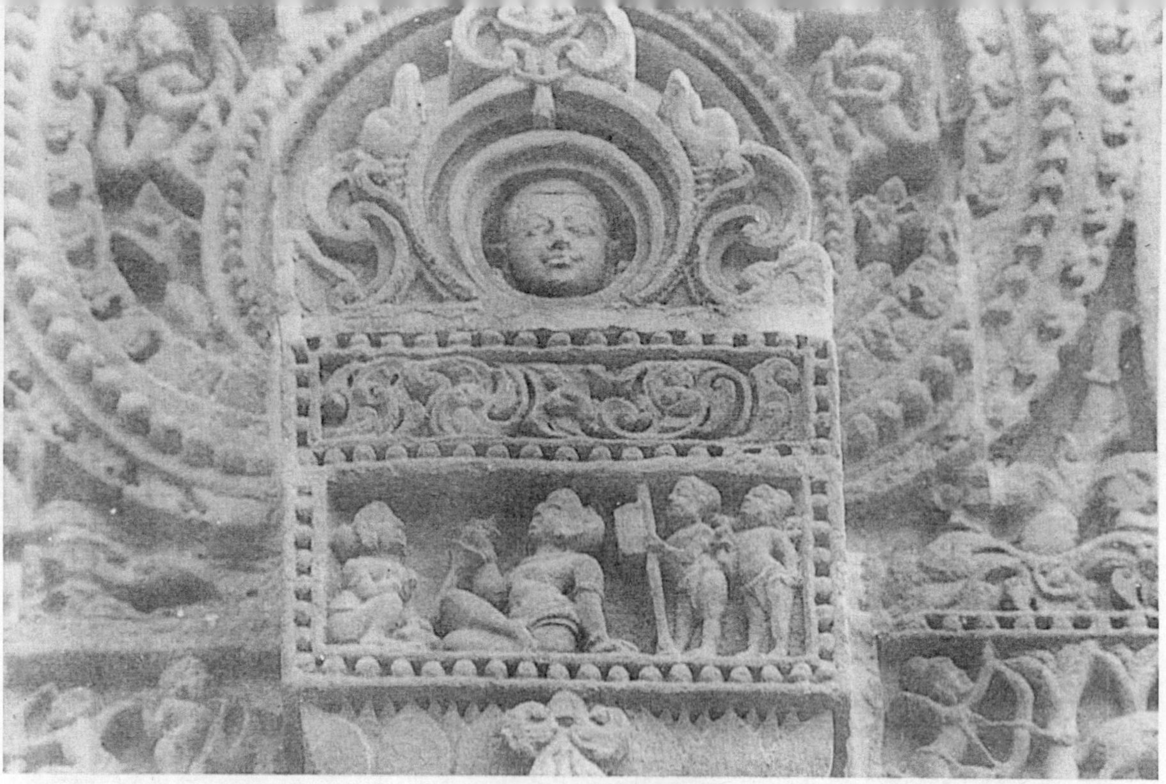

132. *Candraśālā*, south, detail.

134. *Śikhara*, north, Naṭeśa.

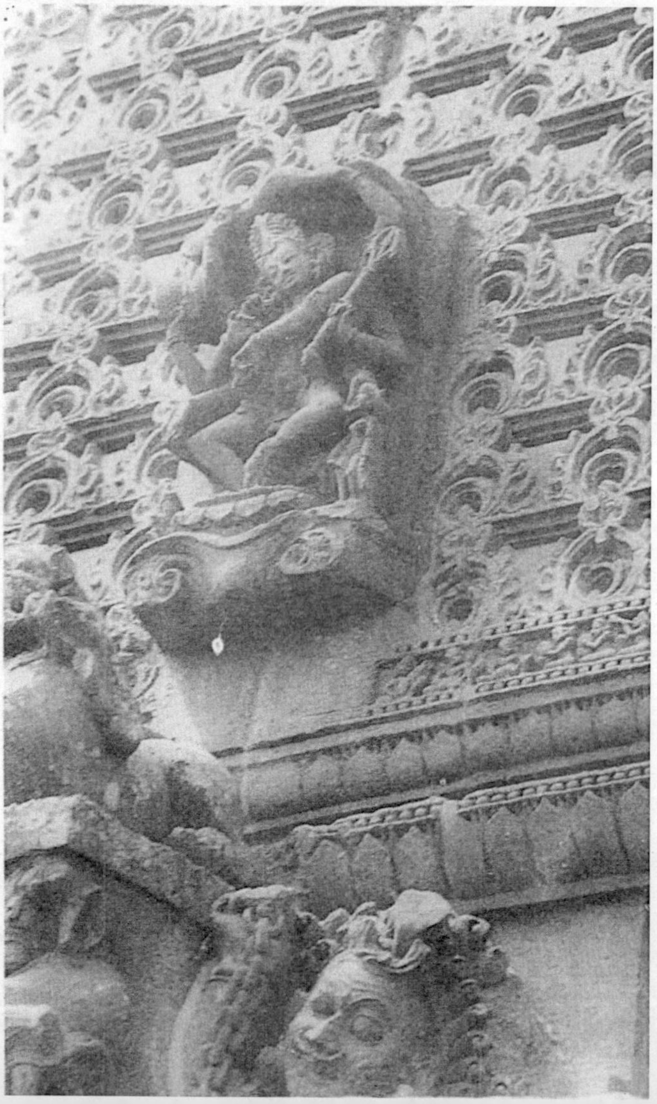

133. *Śukanāsa*, above entrance. (Asian Art Archives, University of Michigan).

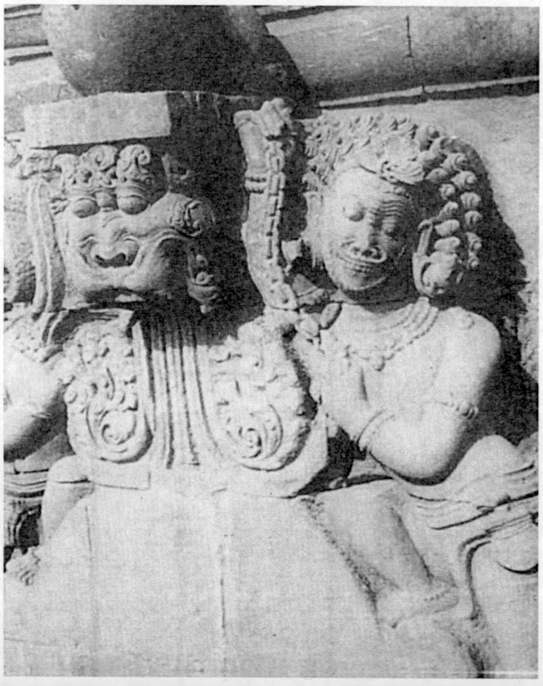

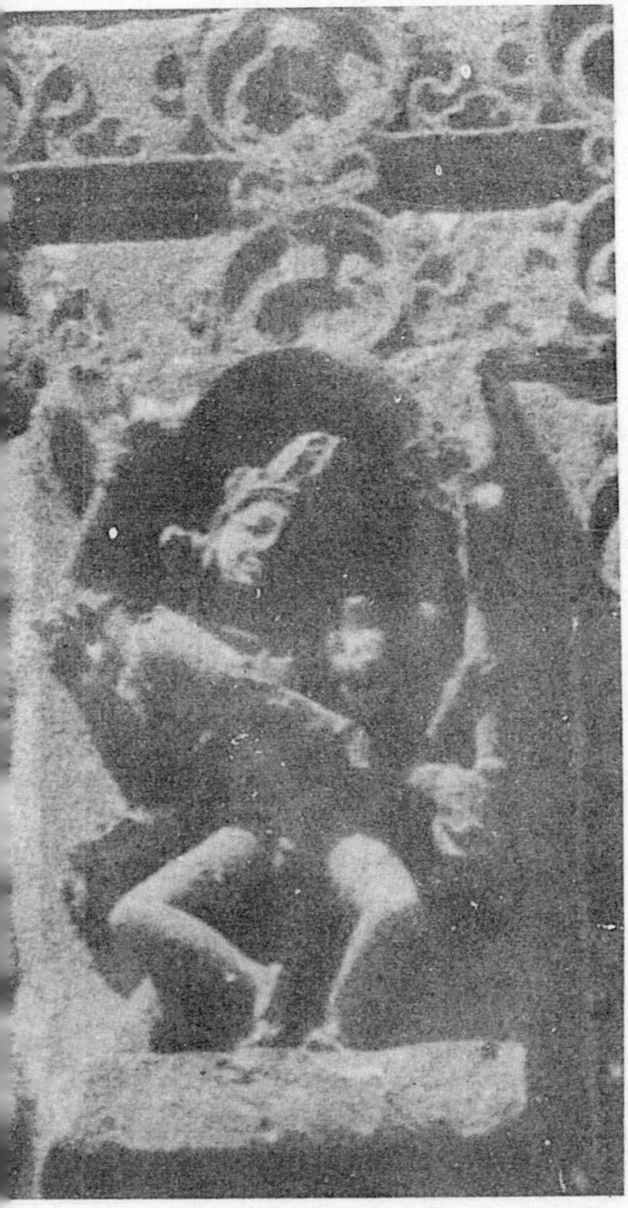

135. *Śikhara*, east, Naṭeśa.

136. *Śikhara*, south, Naṭeśa.

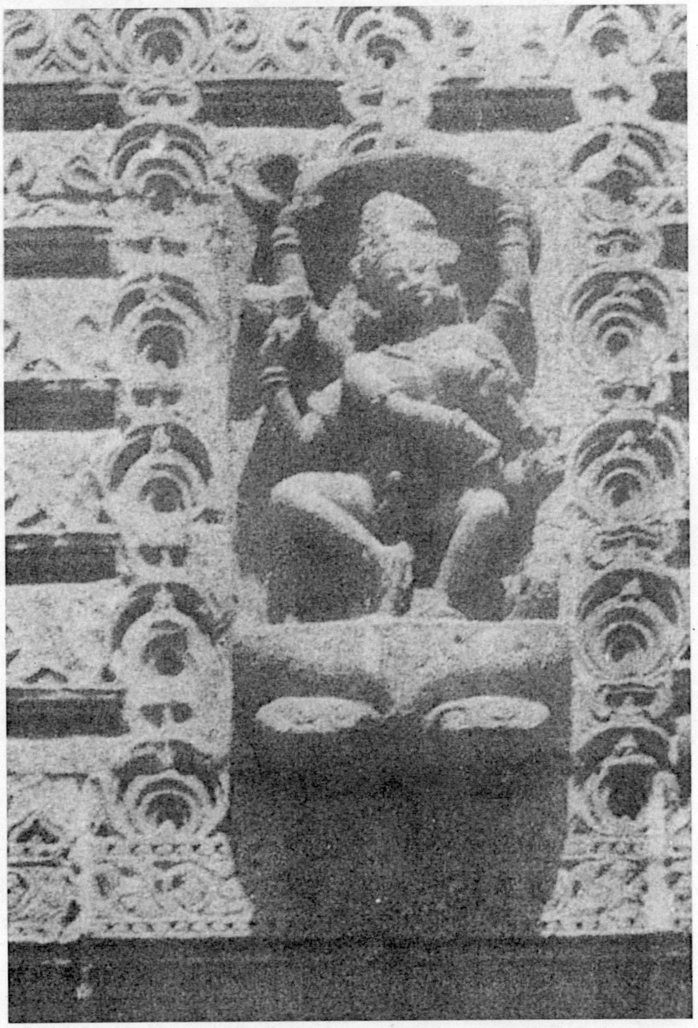

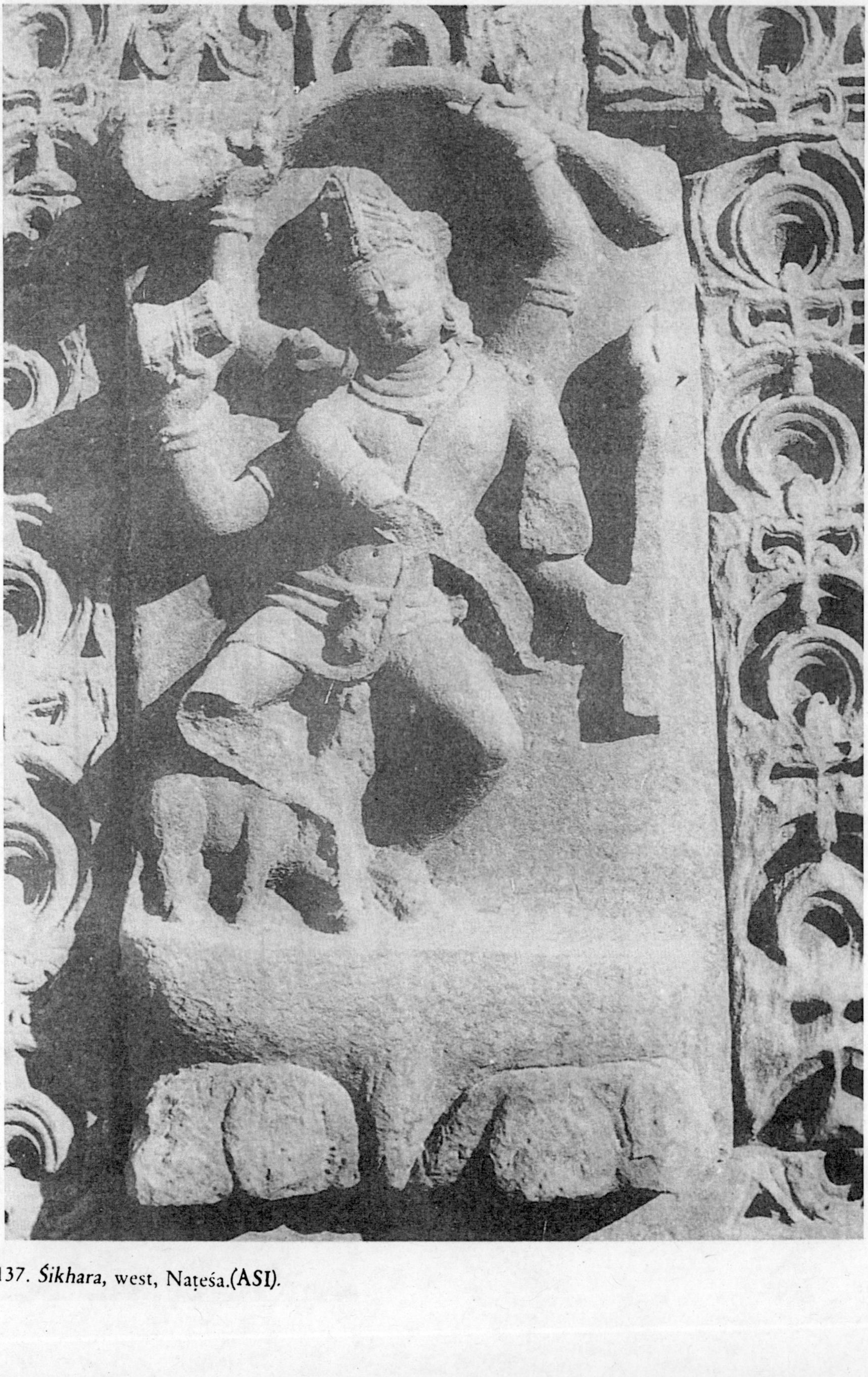

137. *Śikhara*, west, Naṭeśa.(ASI).

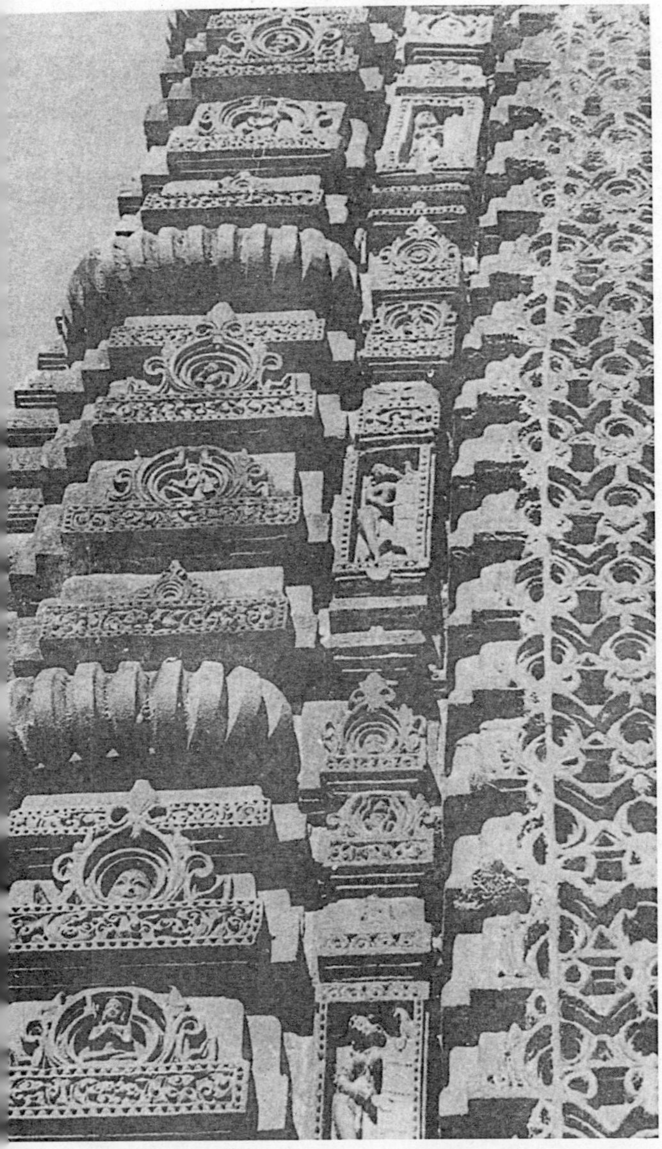

138. *Śikhara*, detail, *pratibhadra*, *pratikarṇa*, *karṇa*.

139. *Śikhara*, detail, *pratikarṇa*.

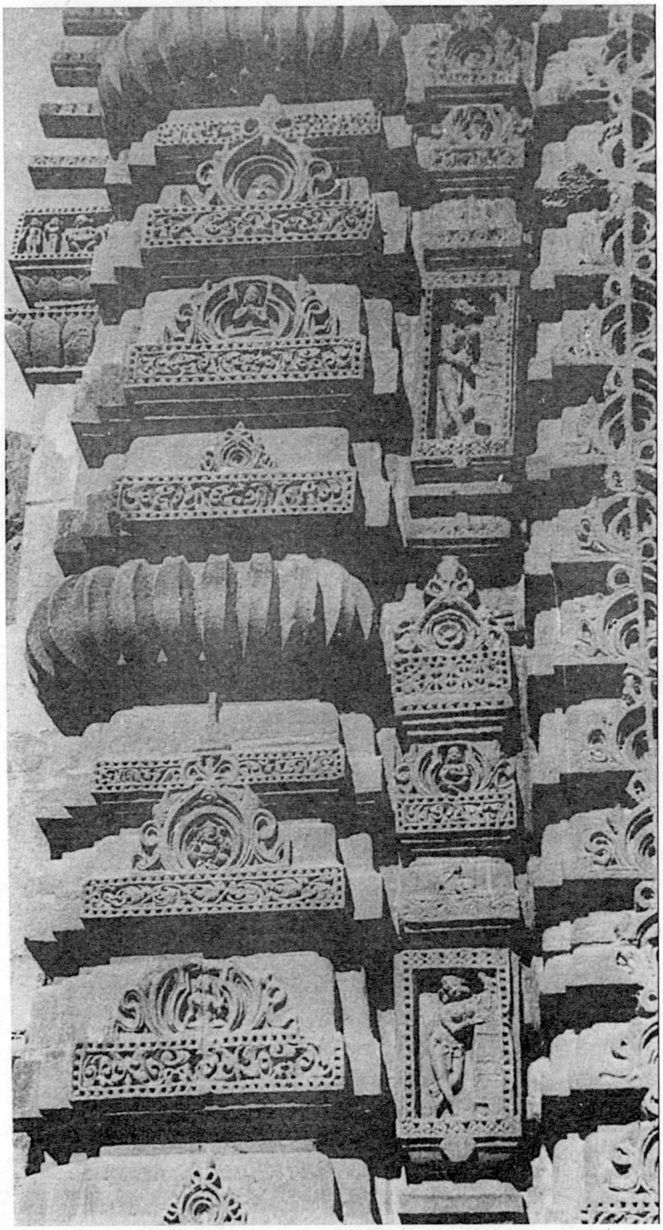

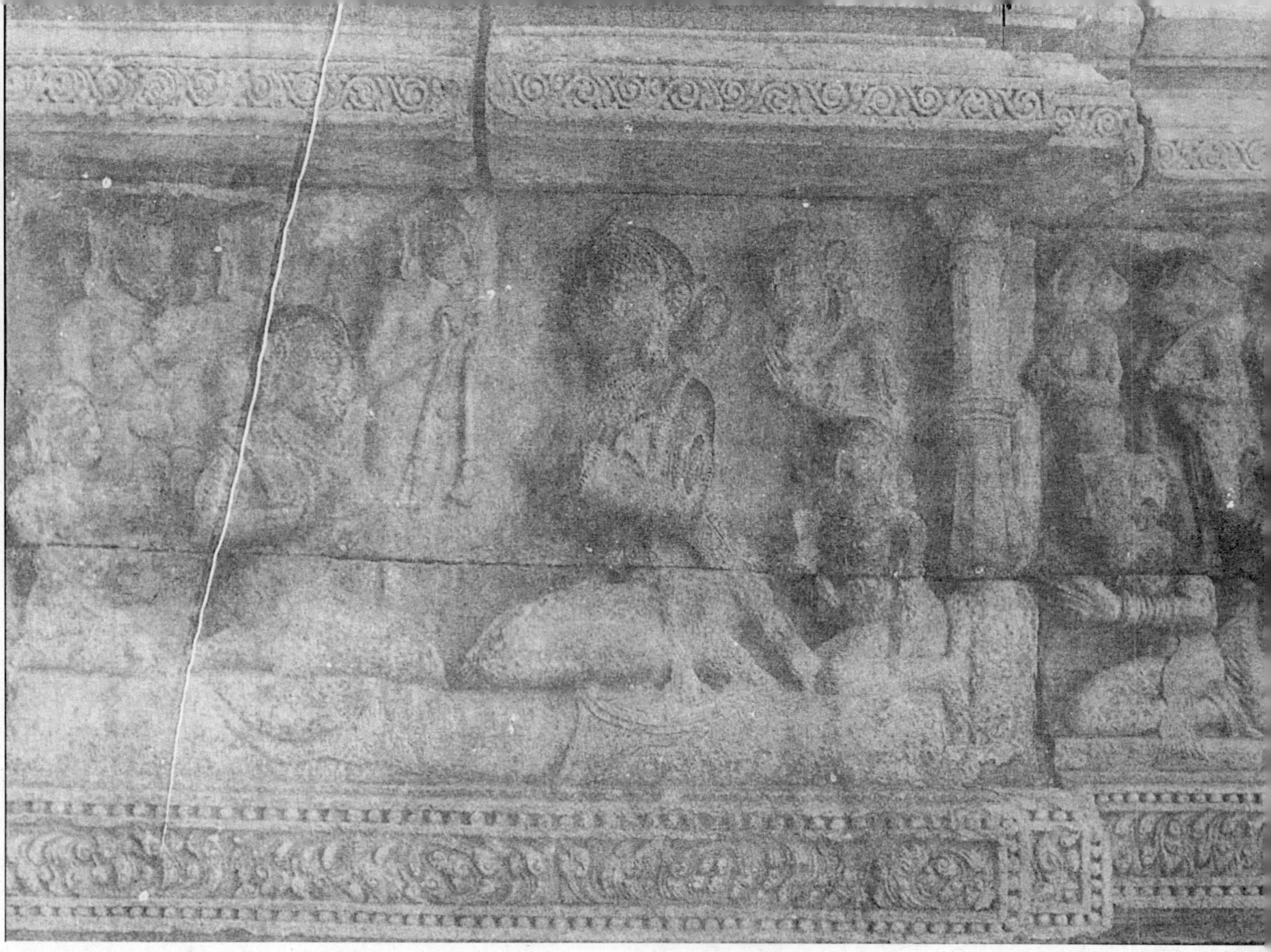

140. Konarak image pedestal from sanctum of Sūrya temple, 13th century.

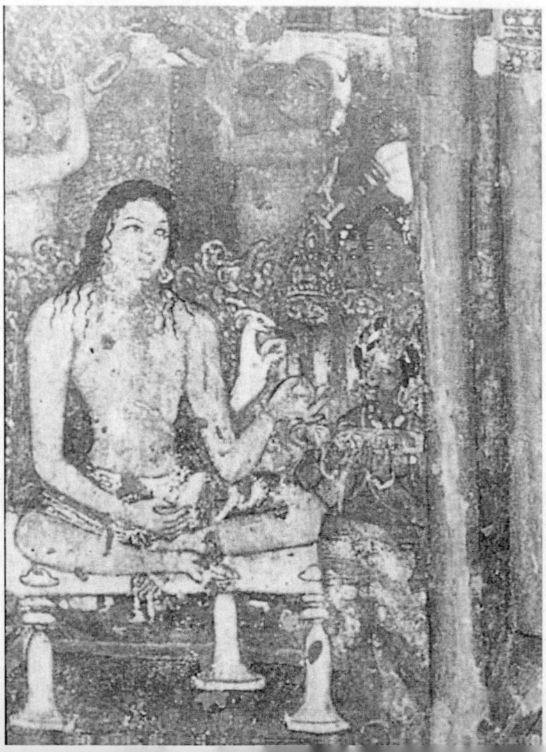

141. Ajanta, Mahājanaka Jātaka. 5th century. (from M. Singh, *Ajanta*).

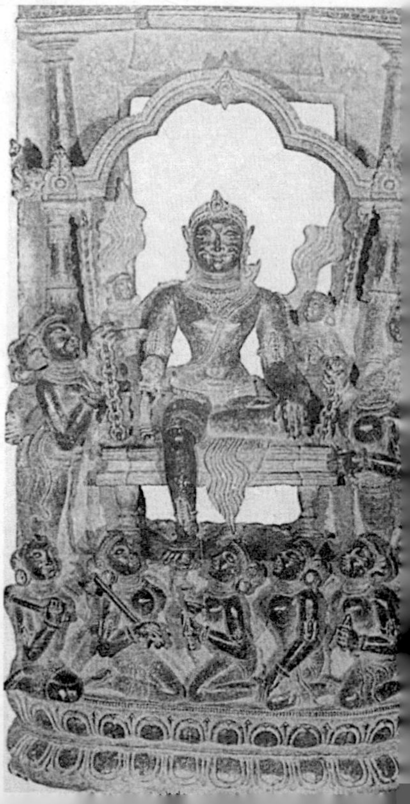

142. Konarak, King Narasiṁha on a swing. Ca 13th century.

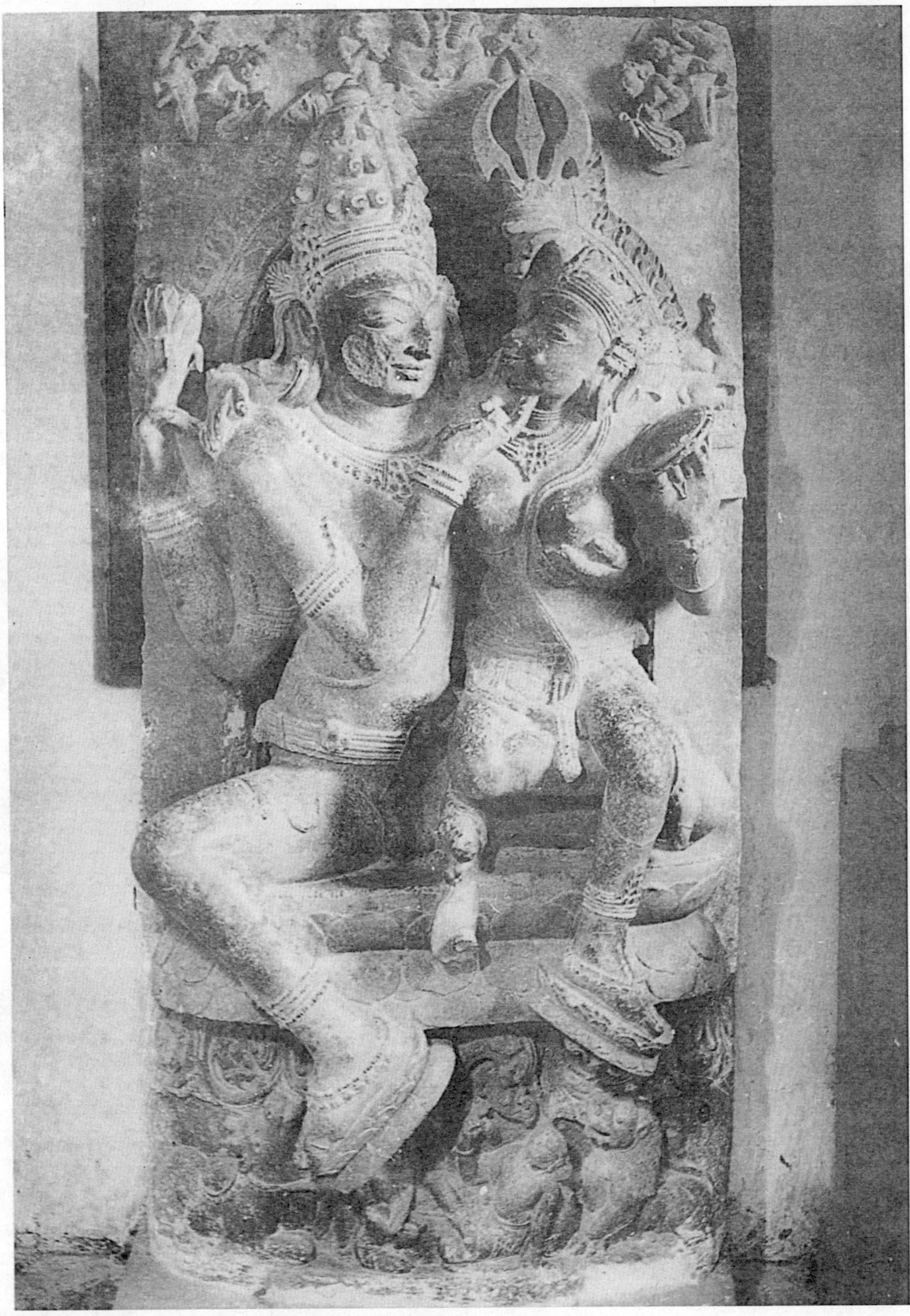

143. Khiching. Śiva and Pārvatī. Ca 13th century. (AIIS).

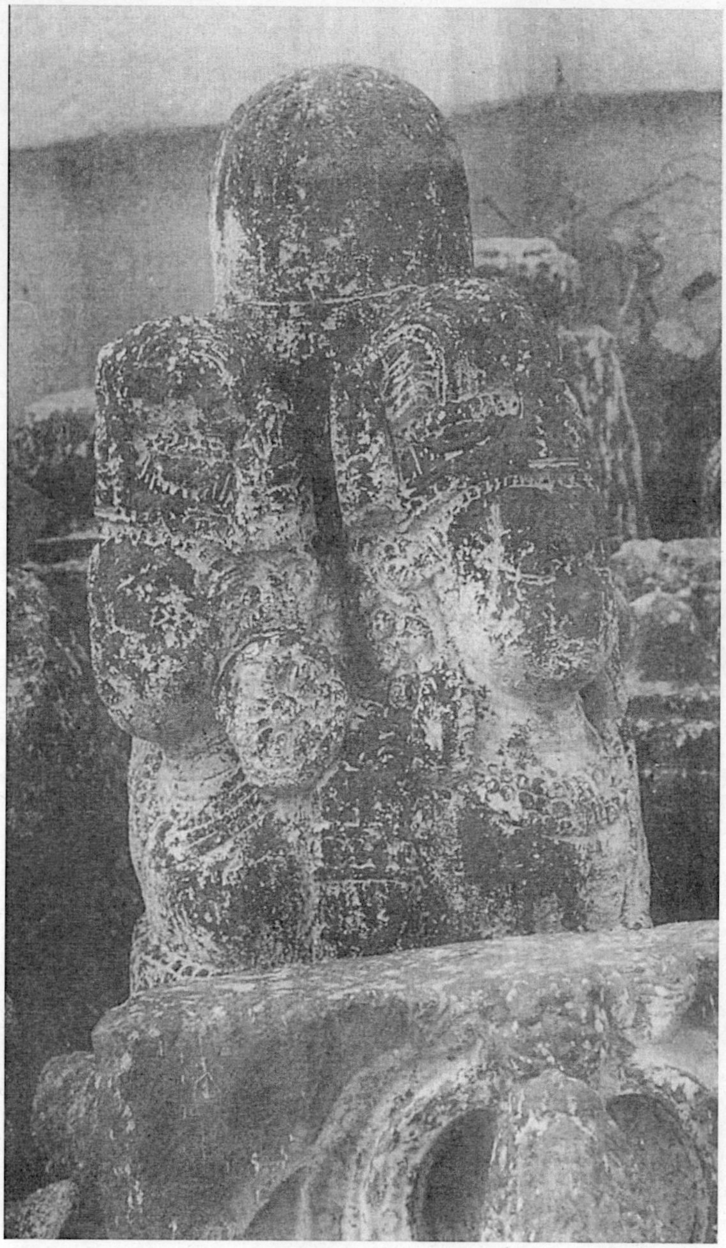

144. Bhubaneswar. Pañcamukhaliṅga. Ca 7th century.

145. Bhubaneswar. Paraśurāmeśvara temple, Candraśālā.

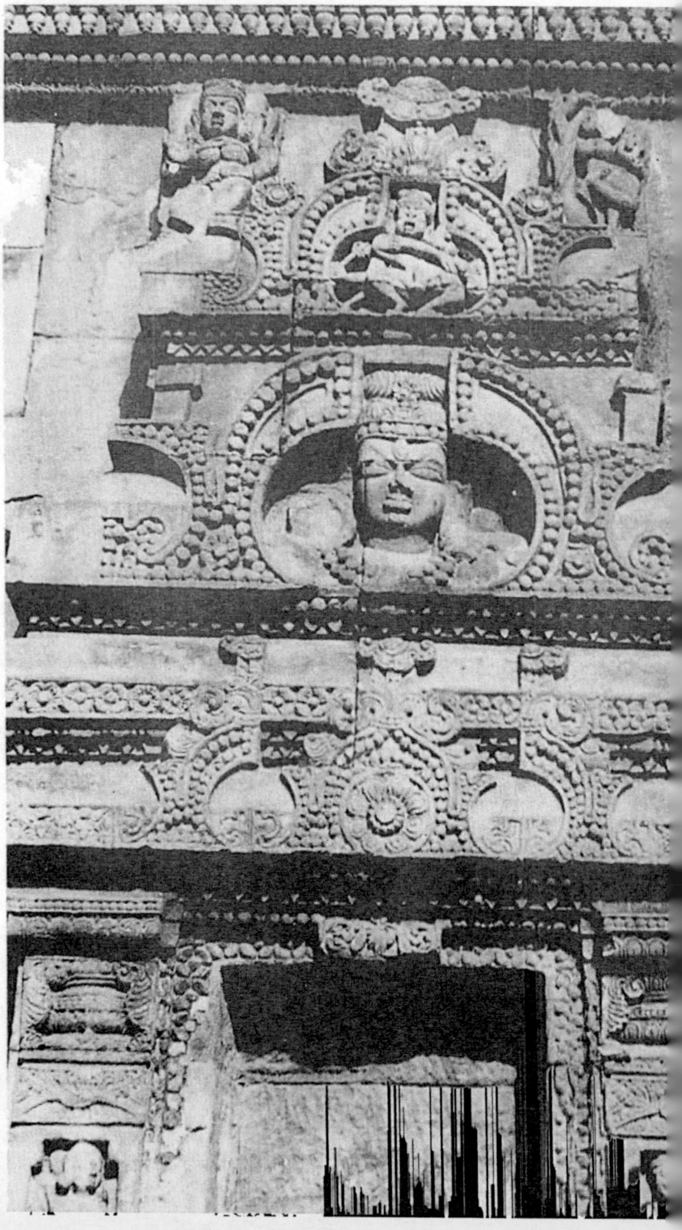

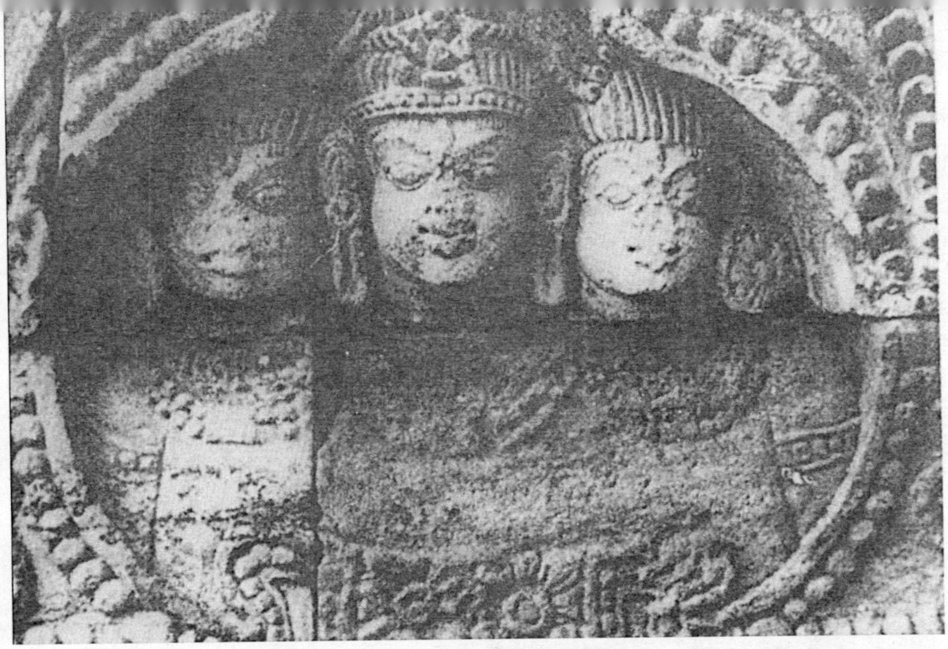

146. Paraśurāmeśvara temple. *Candraśālā* with Maheśamūrti.

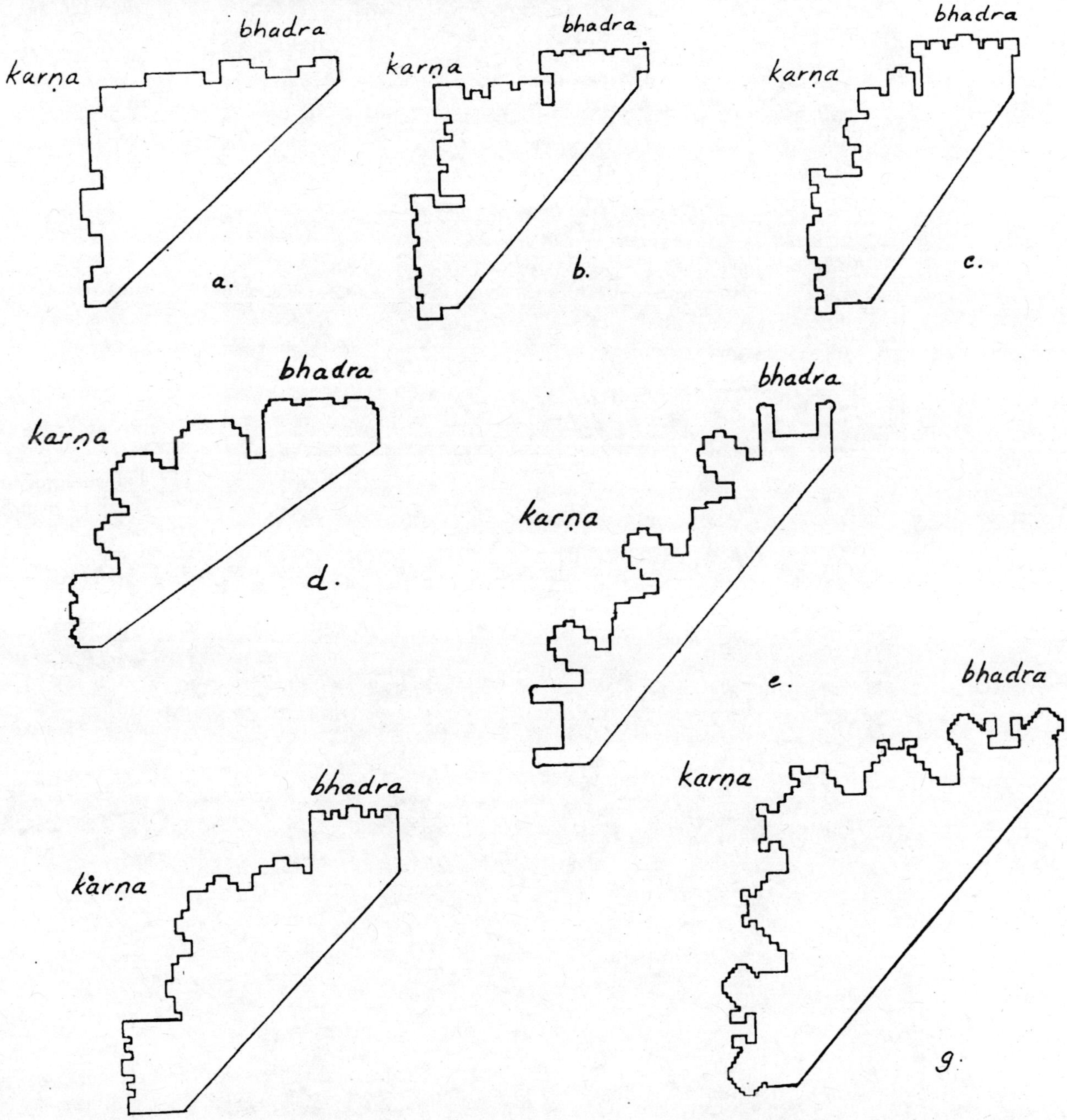

147. Sketches of temple wall plans.

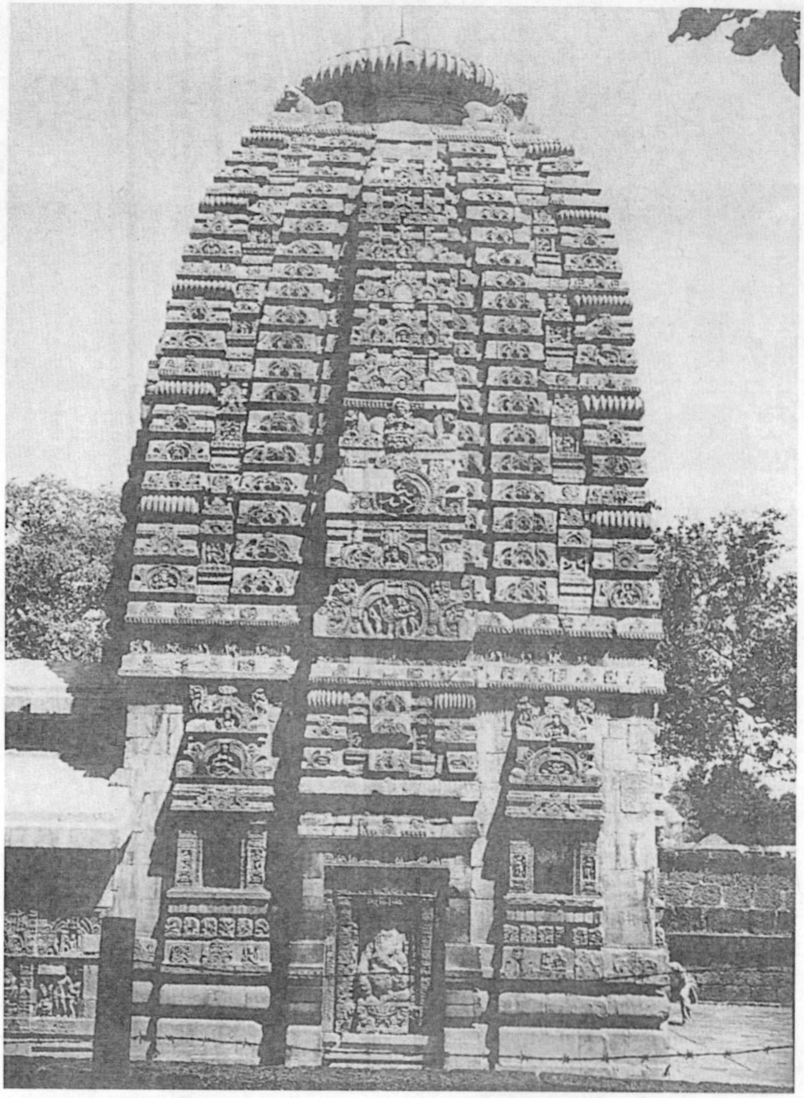

148. Paraśurāmeśvara temple

149. Paraśurāmeśvara temple
detail of *maṇḍapa*,
Śiva and Pārvatī.

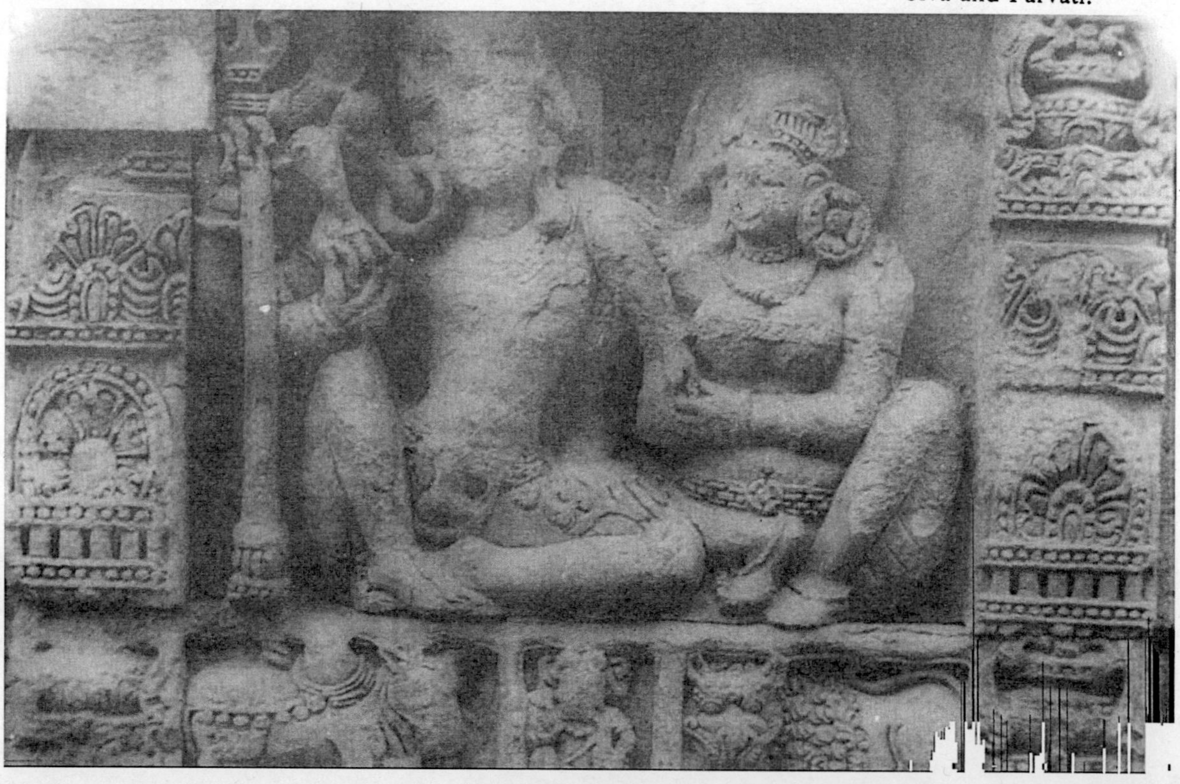

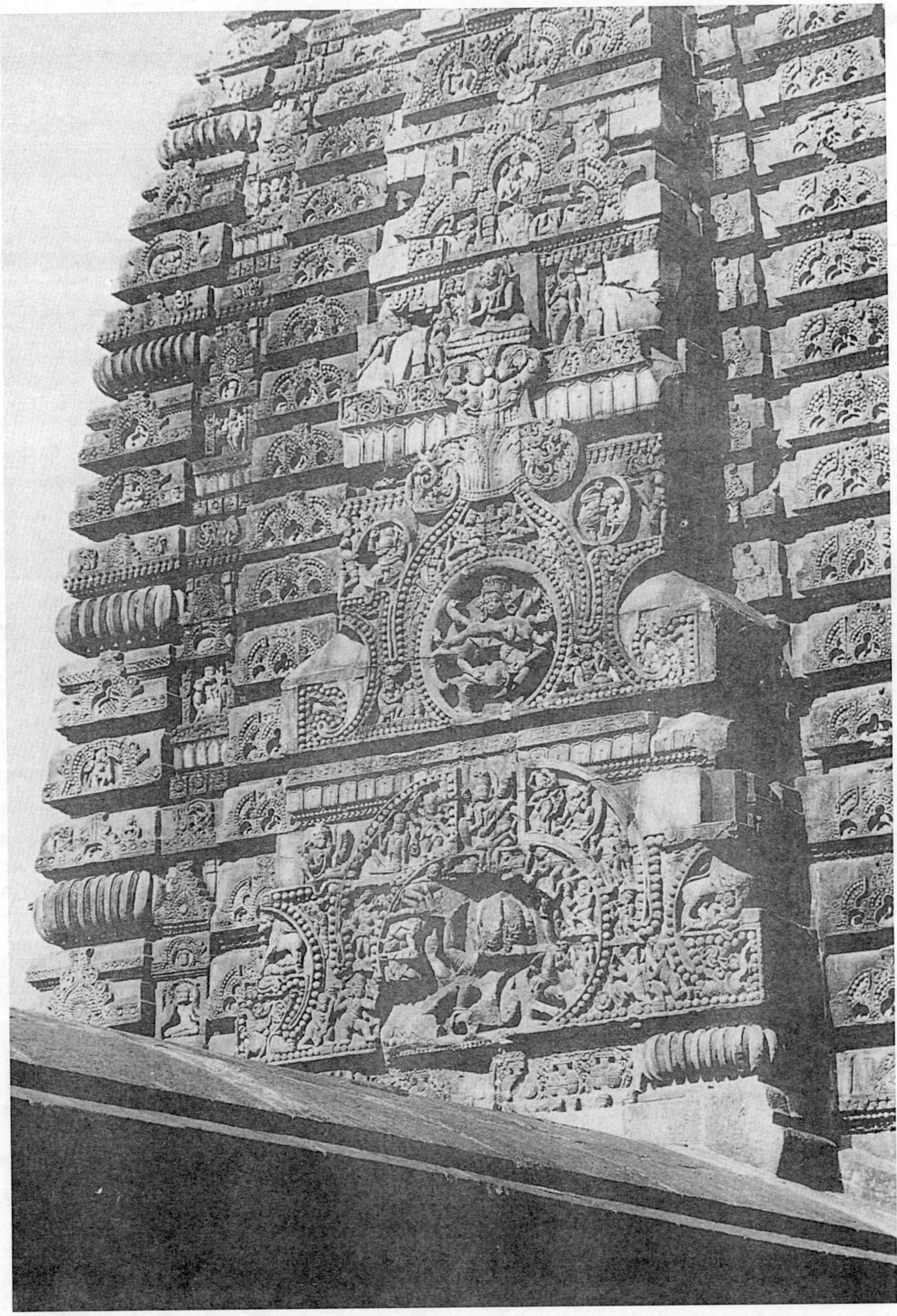

150. Paraśurāmeśvara temple,
śukanāsa.

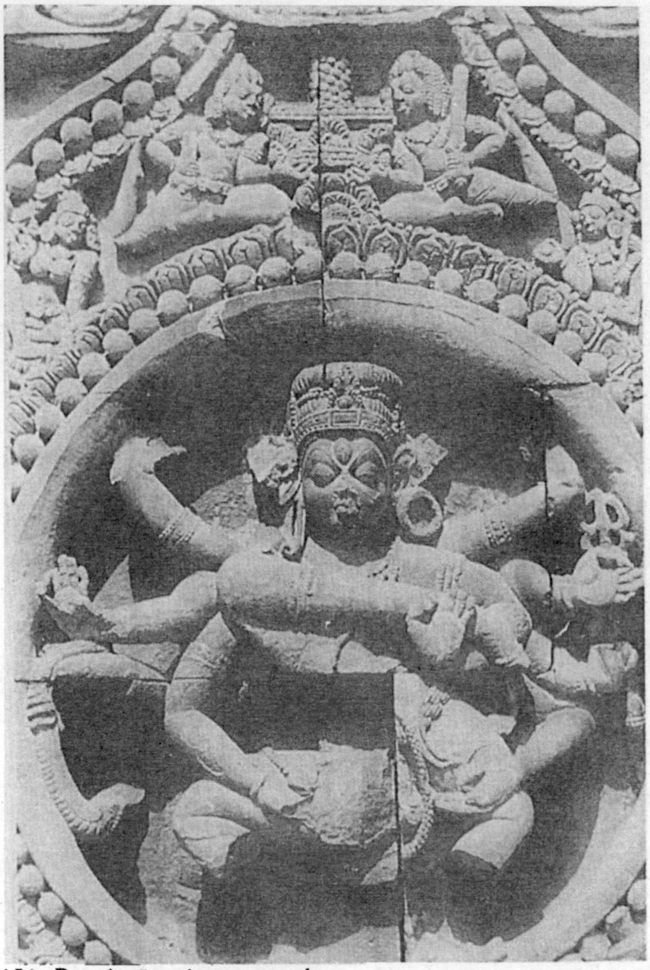

151. Paraśurāmeśvara temple,
detail of *śukanāsa*, Naṭeśa.

152. Bhubaneswar, Vaitāl Deul.

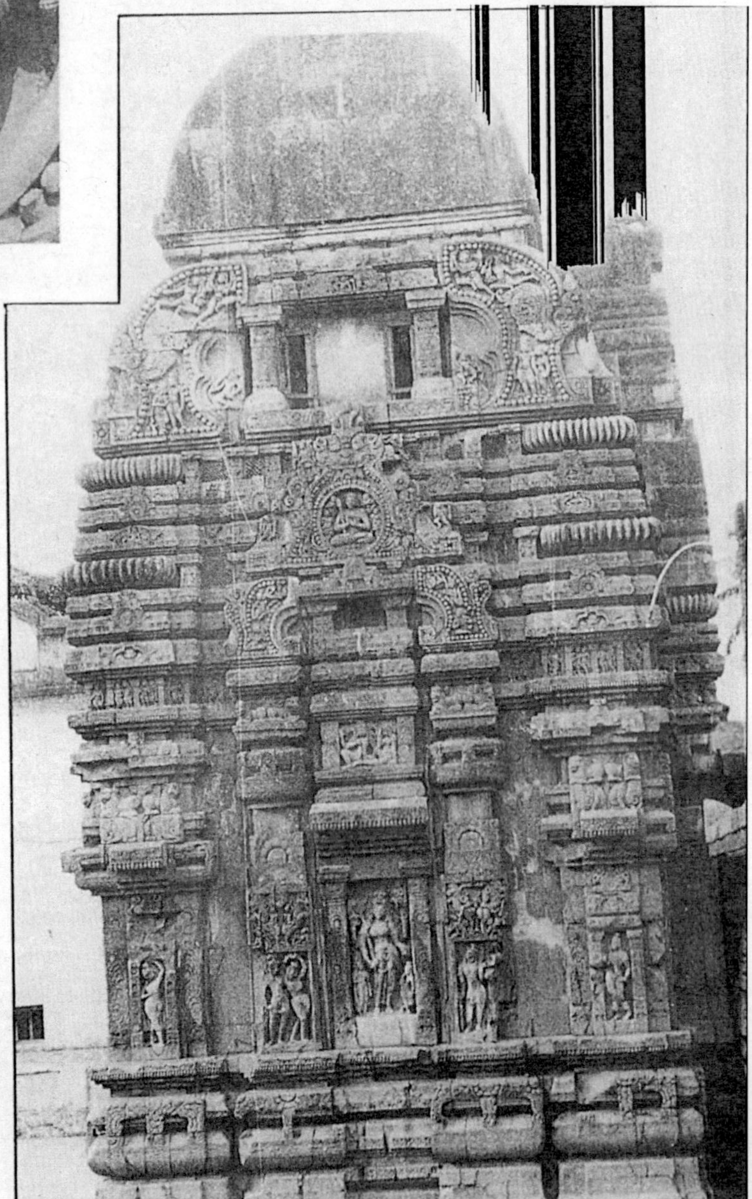

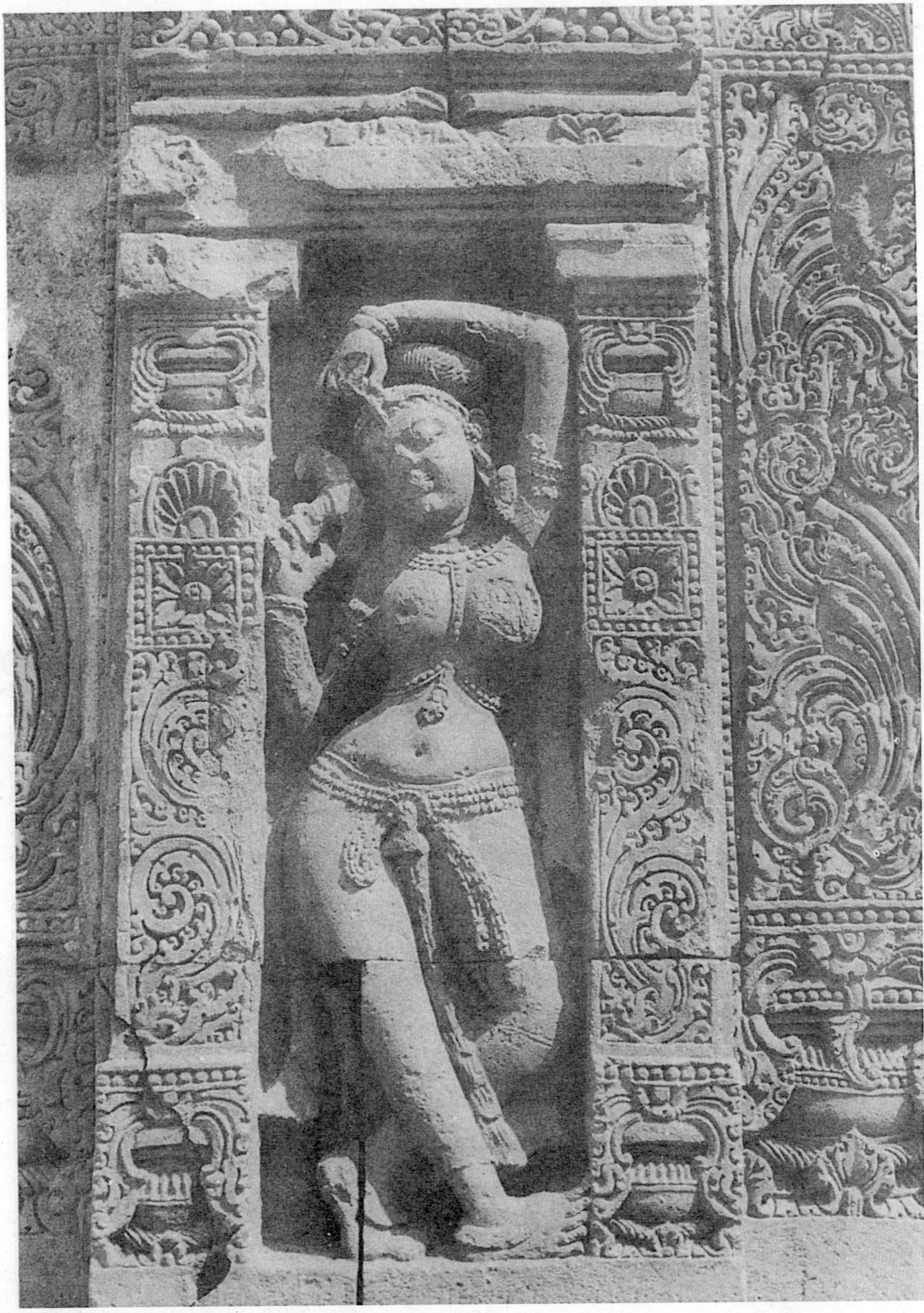

153. Vaitāl Deul. Female figure.

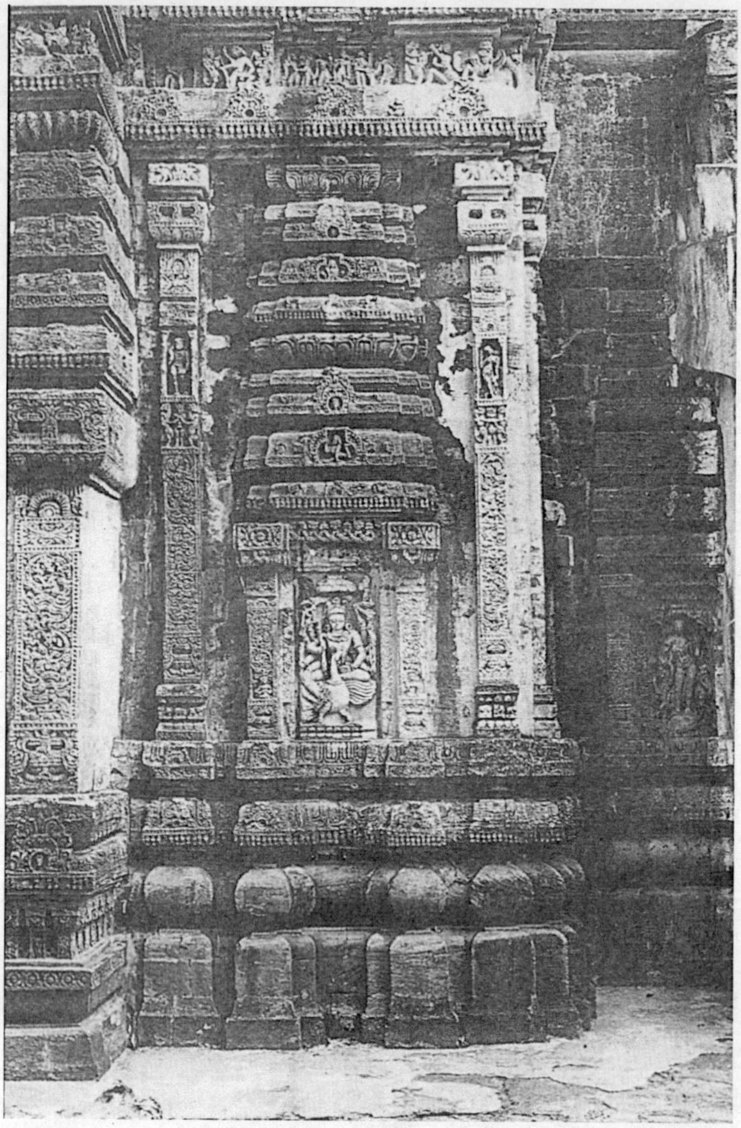

157. Simhanātha temple,
detail of lower walls. (AIIS).

158. Mukhalingam. Someśvara temple, from north. (AIIS).

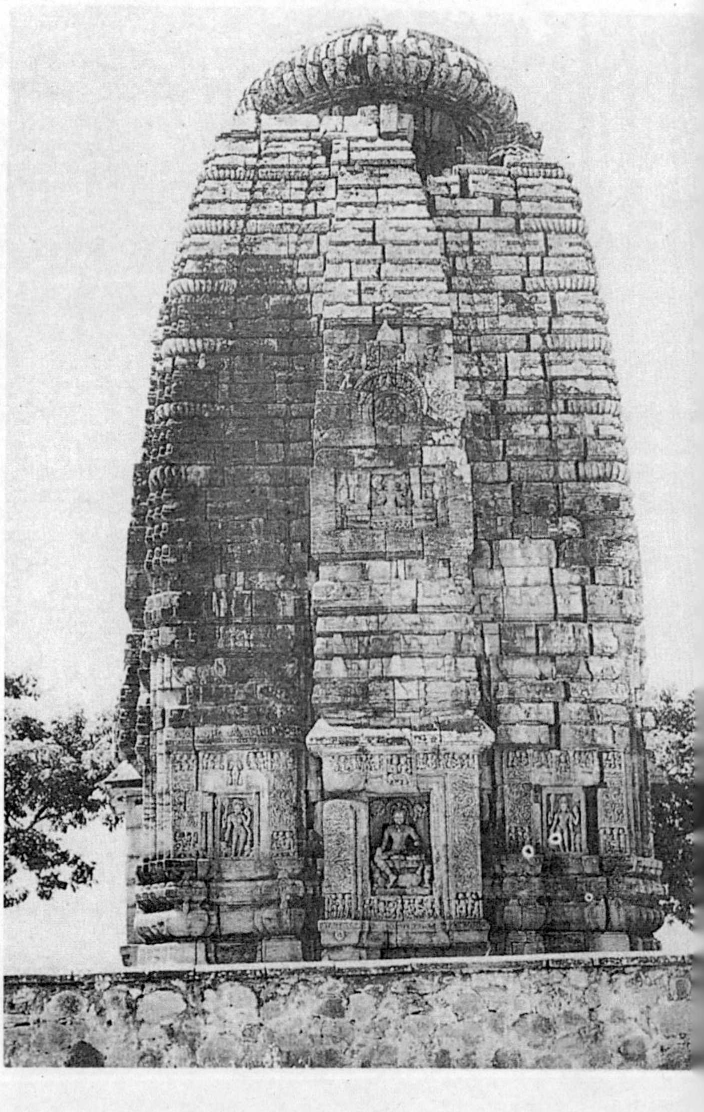

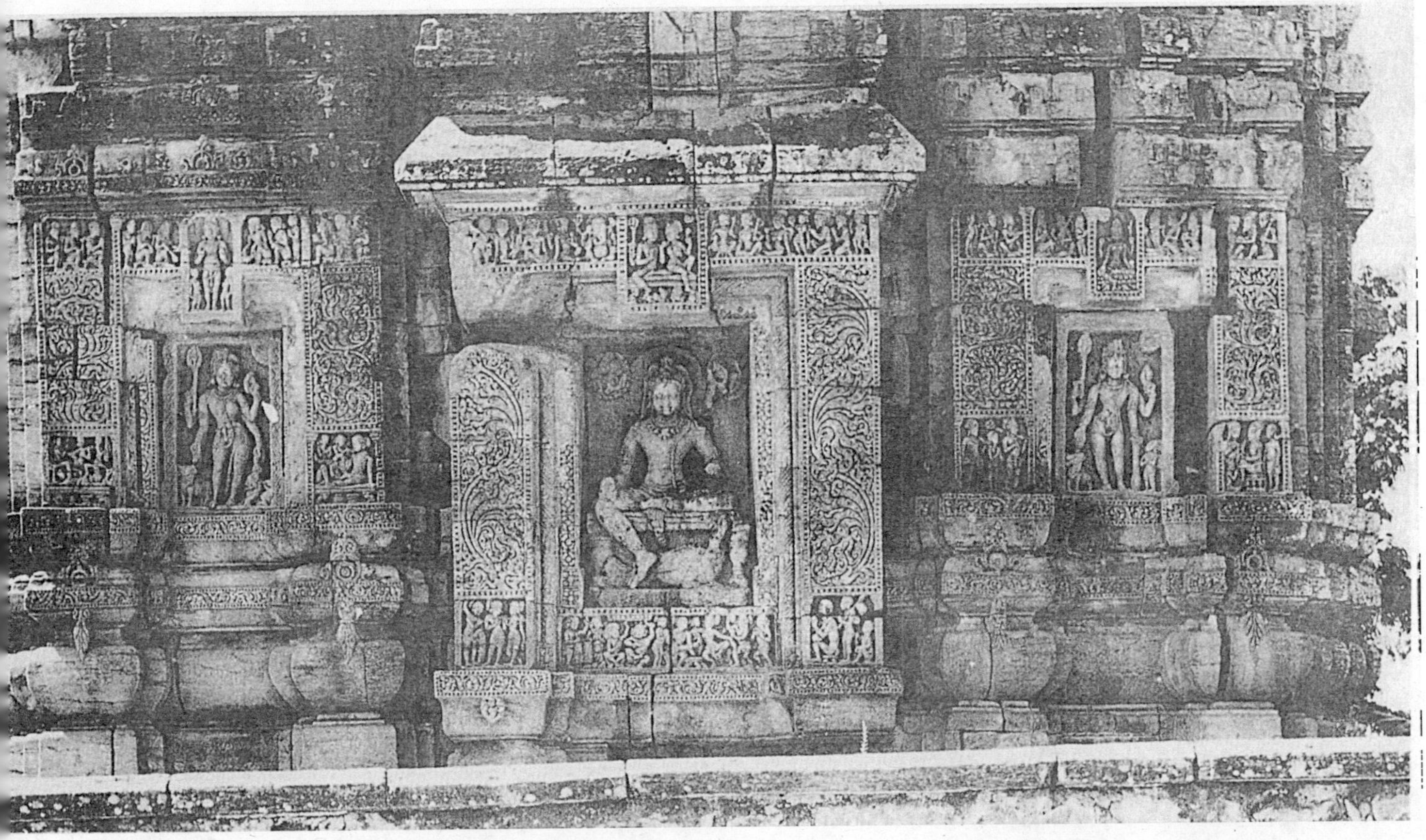

159. Someśvara temple, lower walls, from north (AIIS).

160. Baidyanath, Kośalesvara temple, porch.

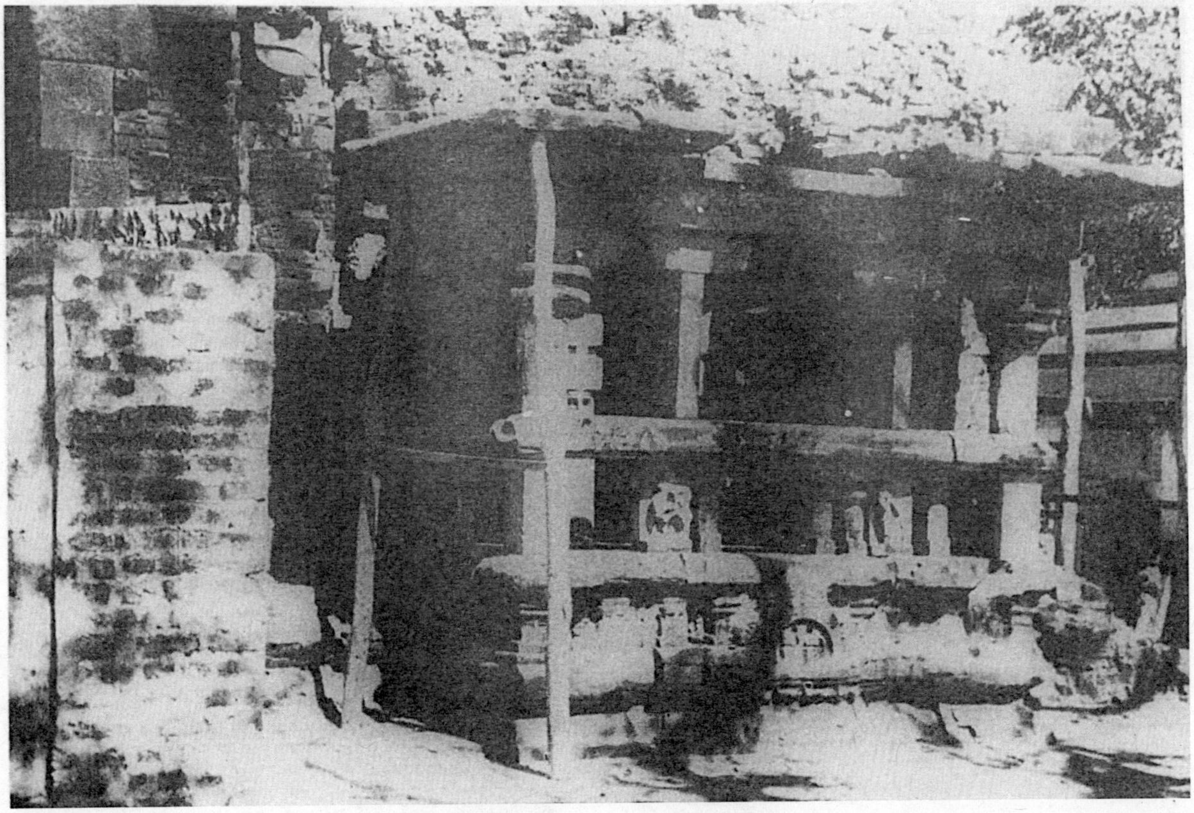

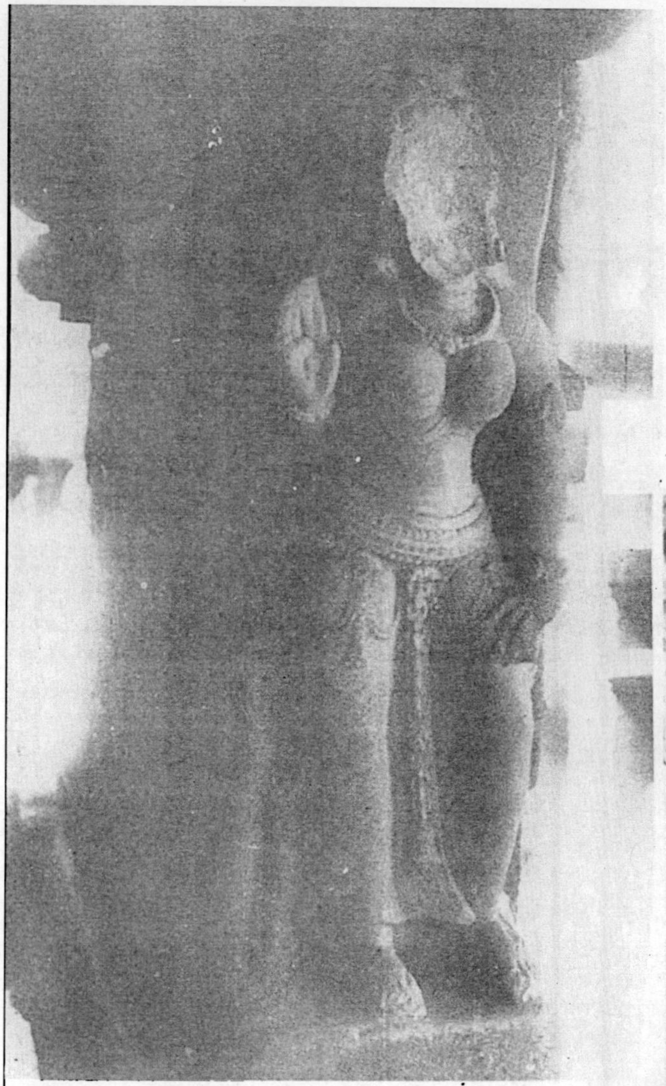

161. Kosaleśvara temple, interior, female figure on column.

162. Çharda, Kapileśvara temple. (AIIS).

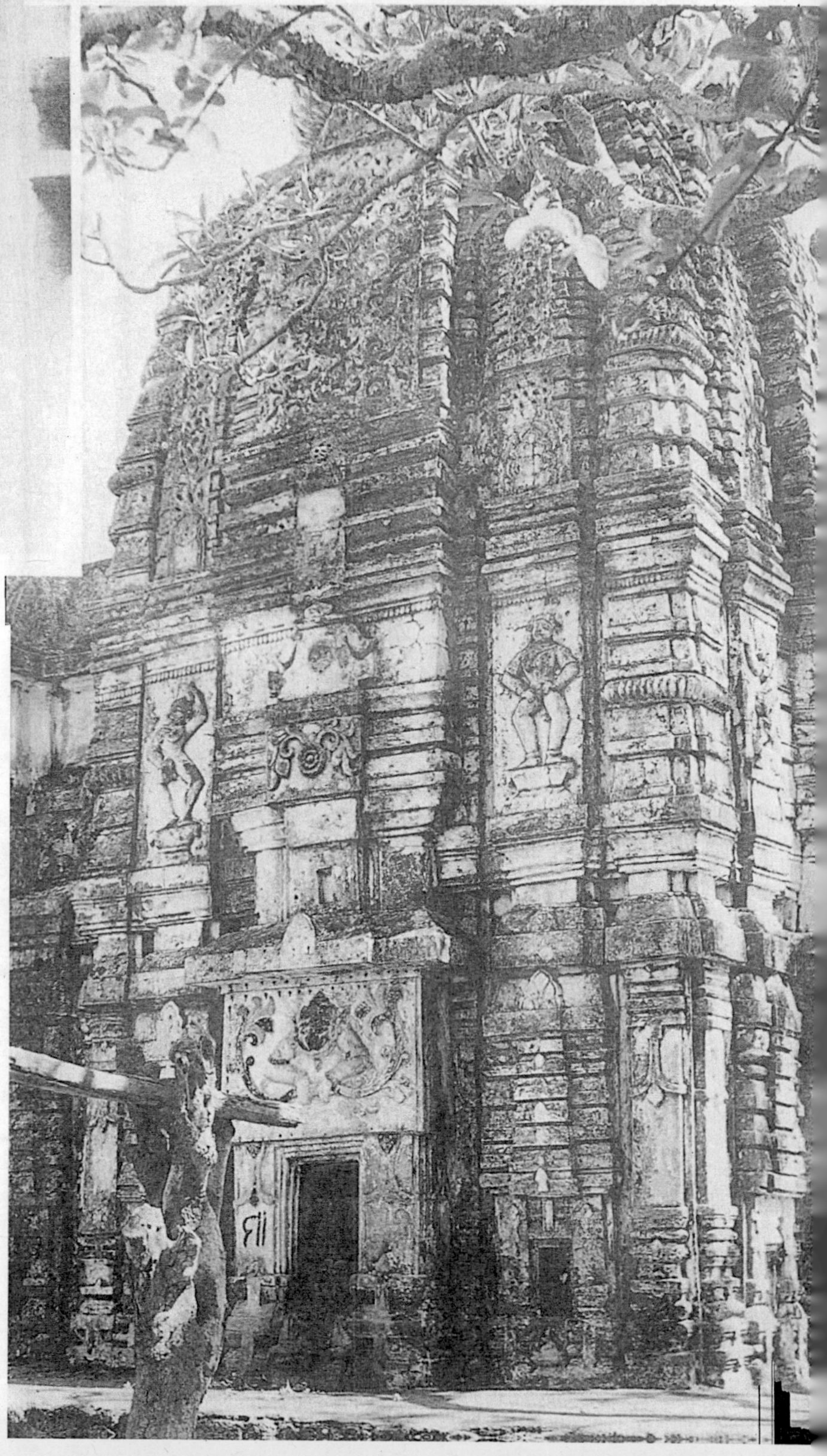

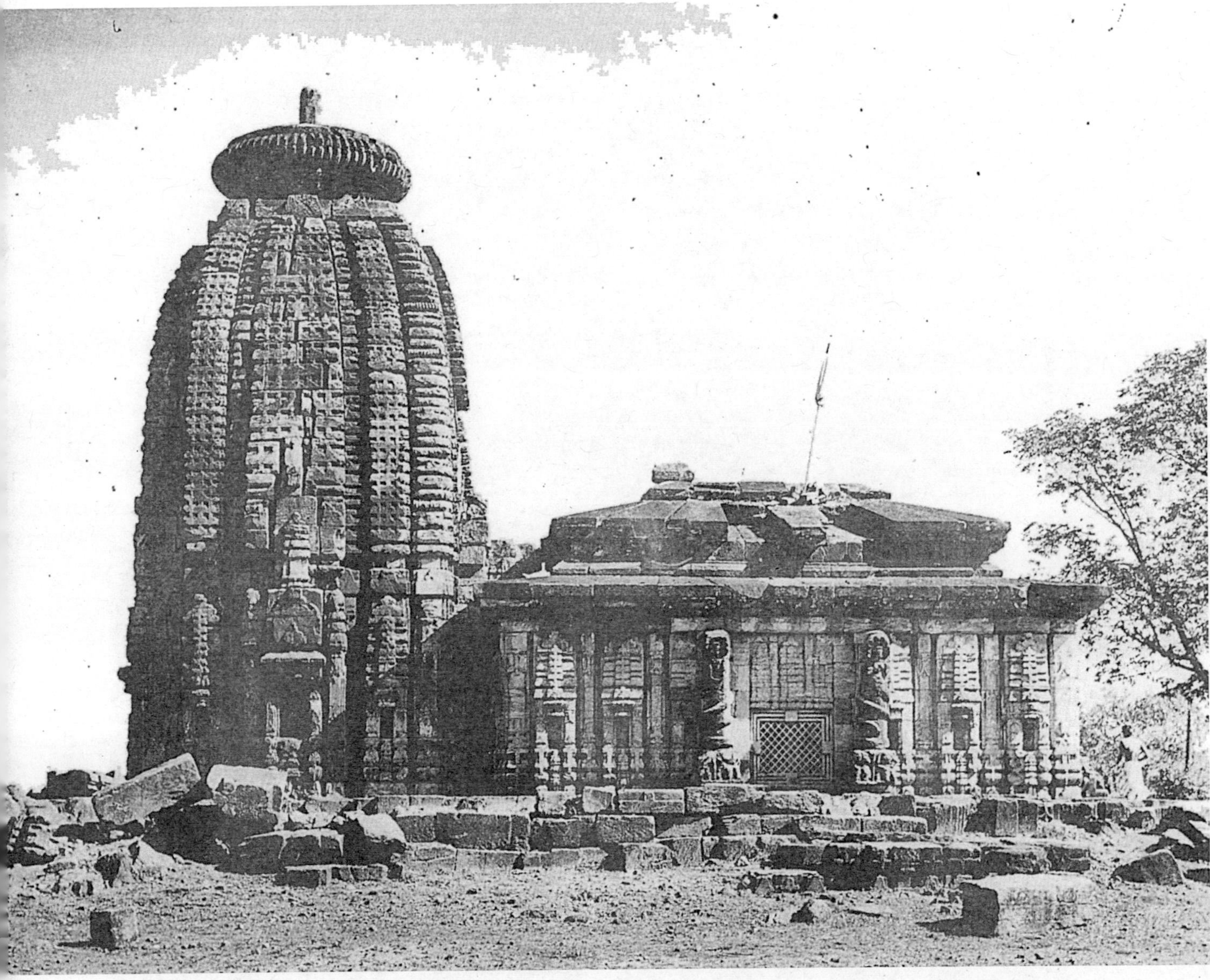

163. Gandharadi, Siddheśvara temple. (AIIS).

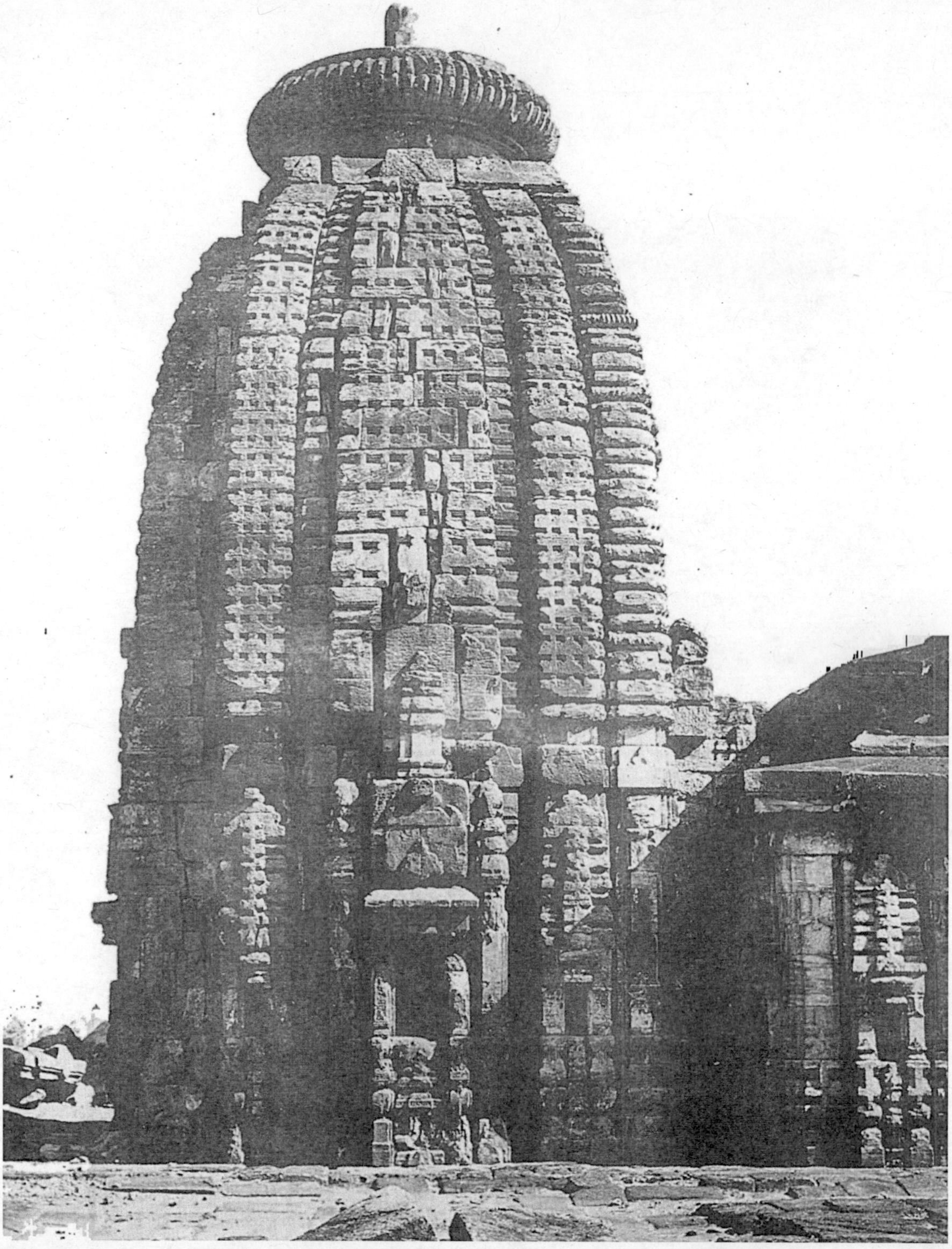

164. Siddheśvara temple, *prāsāda*. (AIIS).

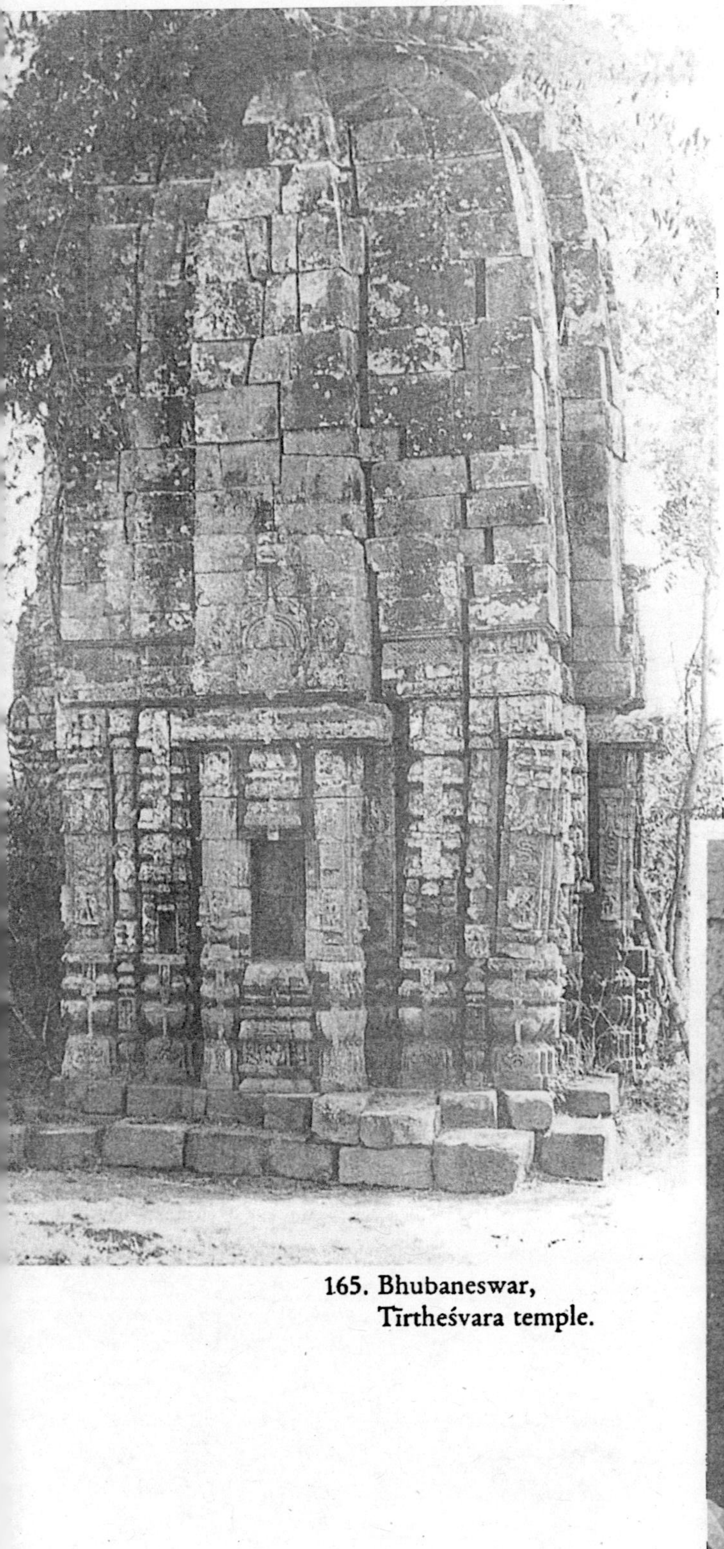

165. Bhubaneswar,
Tīrtheśvara temple.

166. Tīrtheśvara temple, detail,
base moulding.

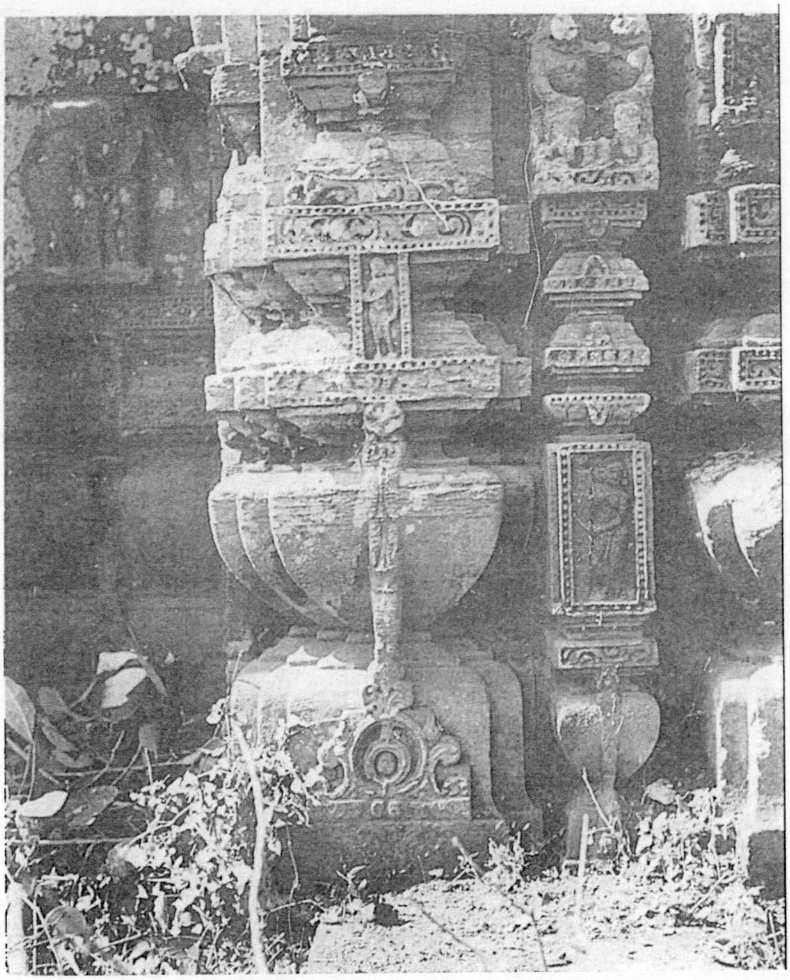

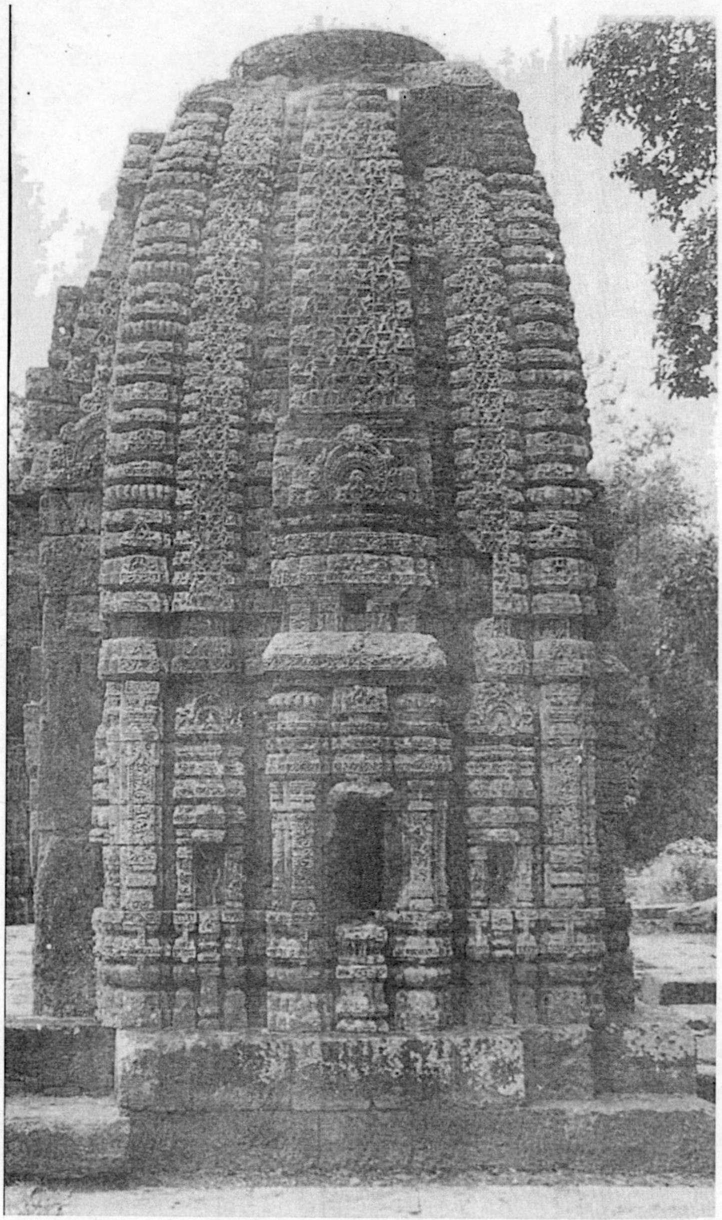

167. Ganeswarpur, Pañcayatana Viṣṇu temple, corner shrine.

168. Mankheda, Madhya Pradesh. Sun temple. (AIIS).

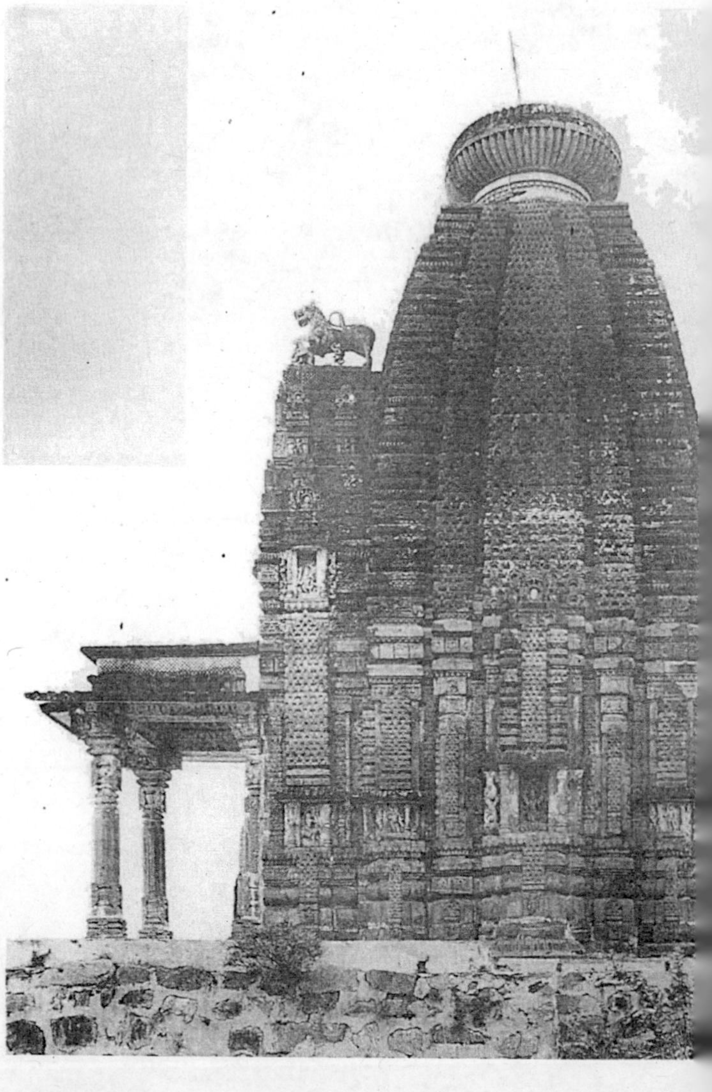

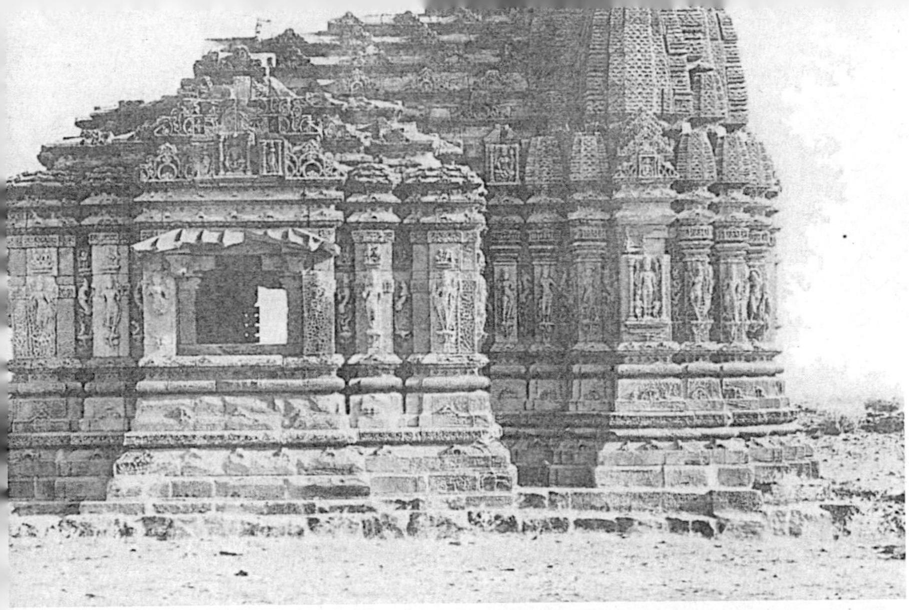

169. Kotai, Gujarat, Śiva temple. (AIIS).

170. Bhubaneswar. Gaurī temple. (AIIS).

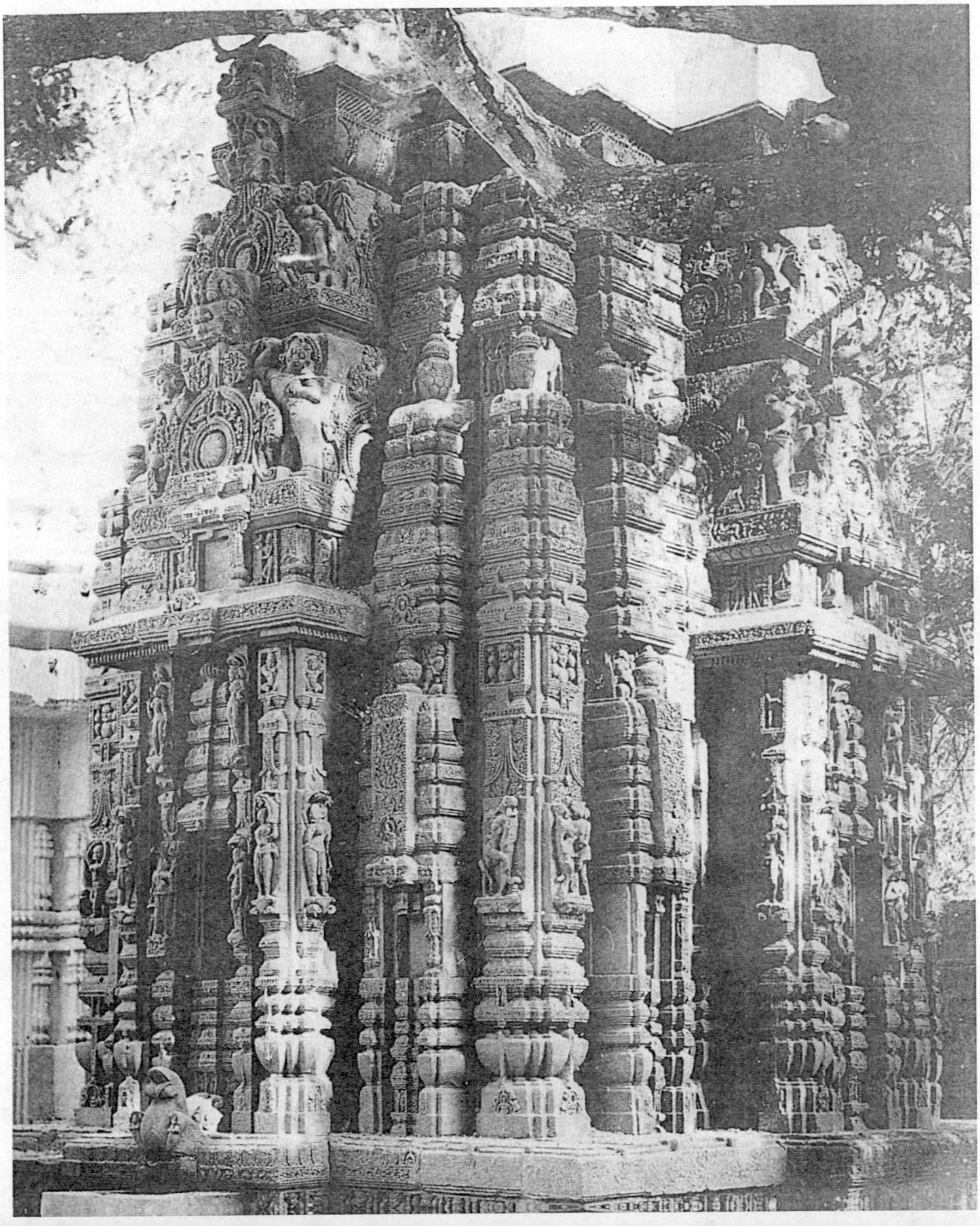

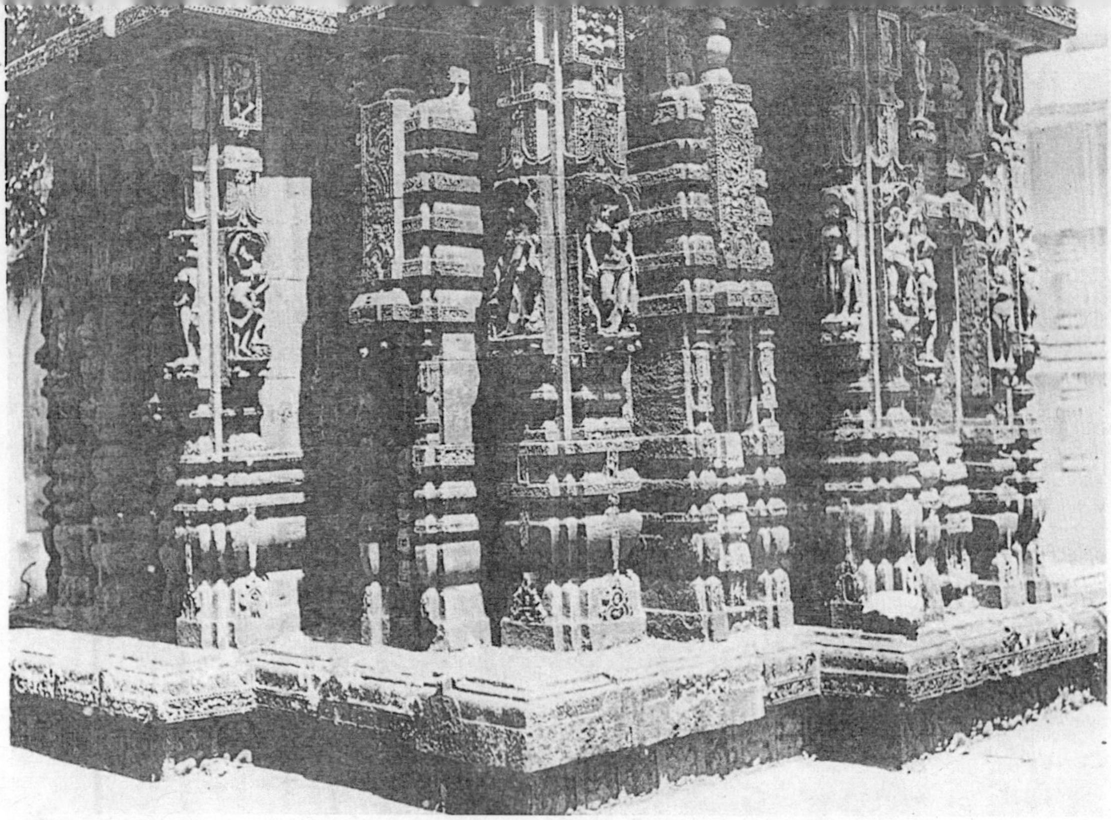

171. Gaurī temple, lower walls,
from southwest. (AIIS).

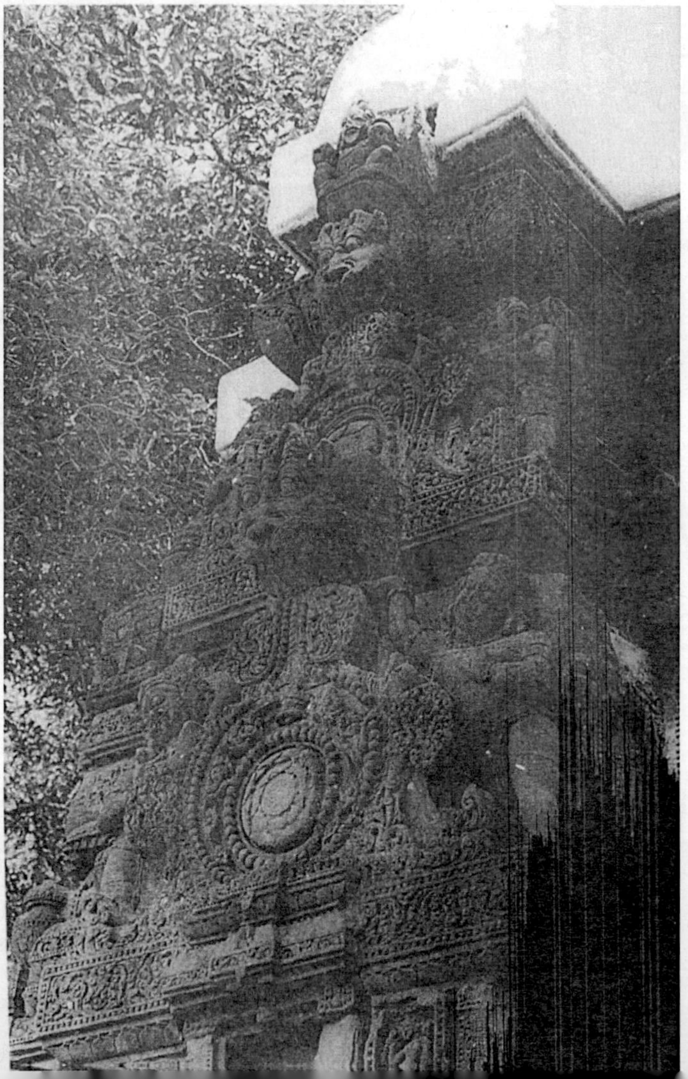

172. Gaurī temple, detail of *śikhara*.

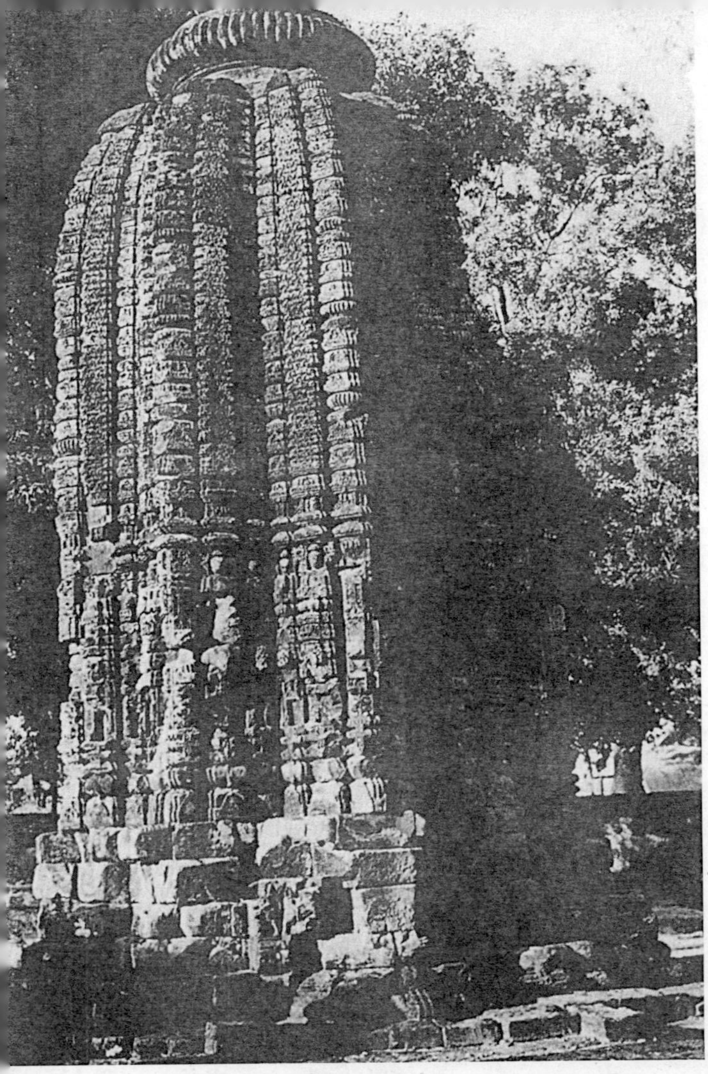

173. Baudh, Śiva temple. (AIIS).

174. Śiva temple, base mouldings and lower wall.

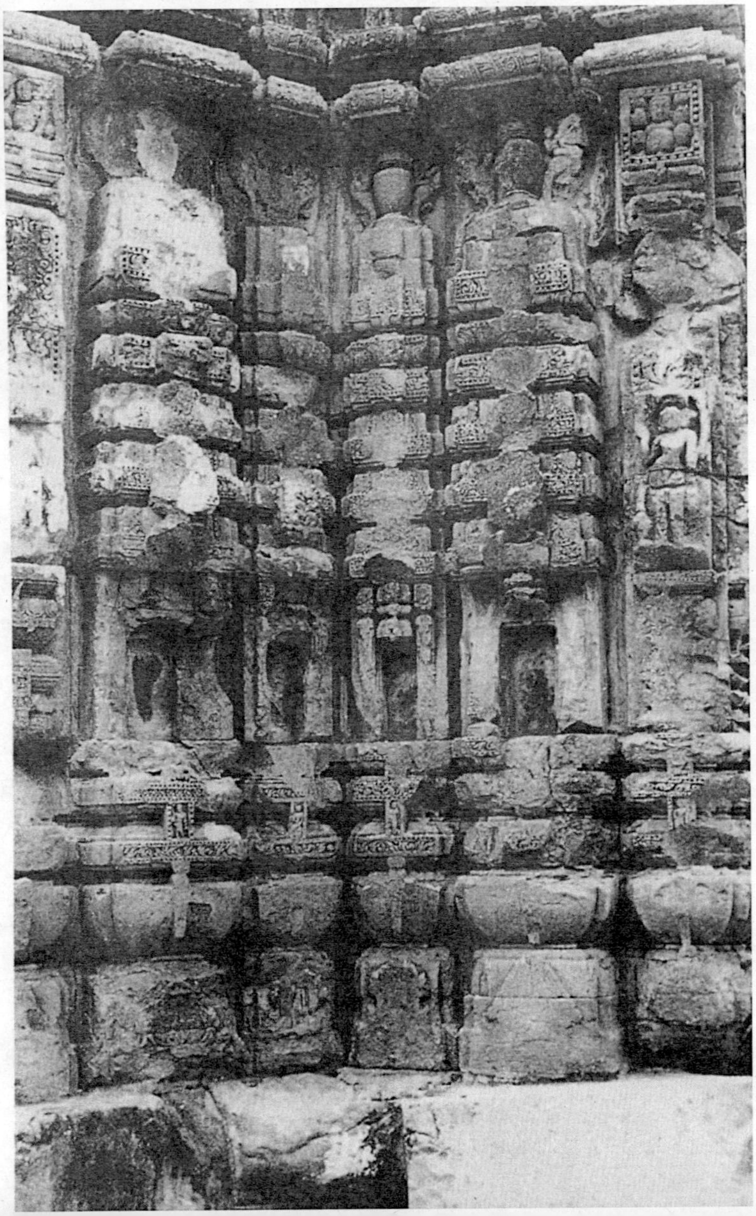

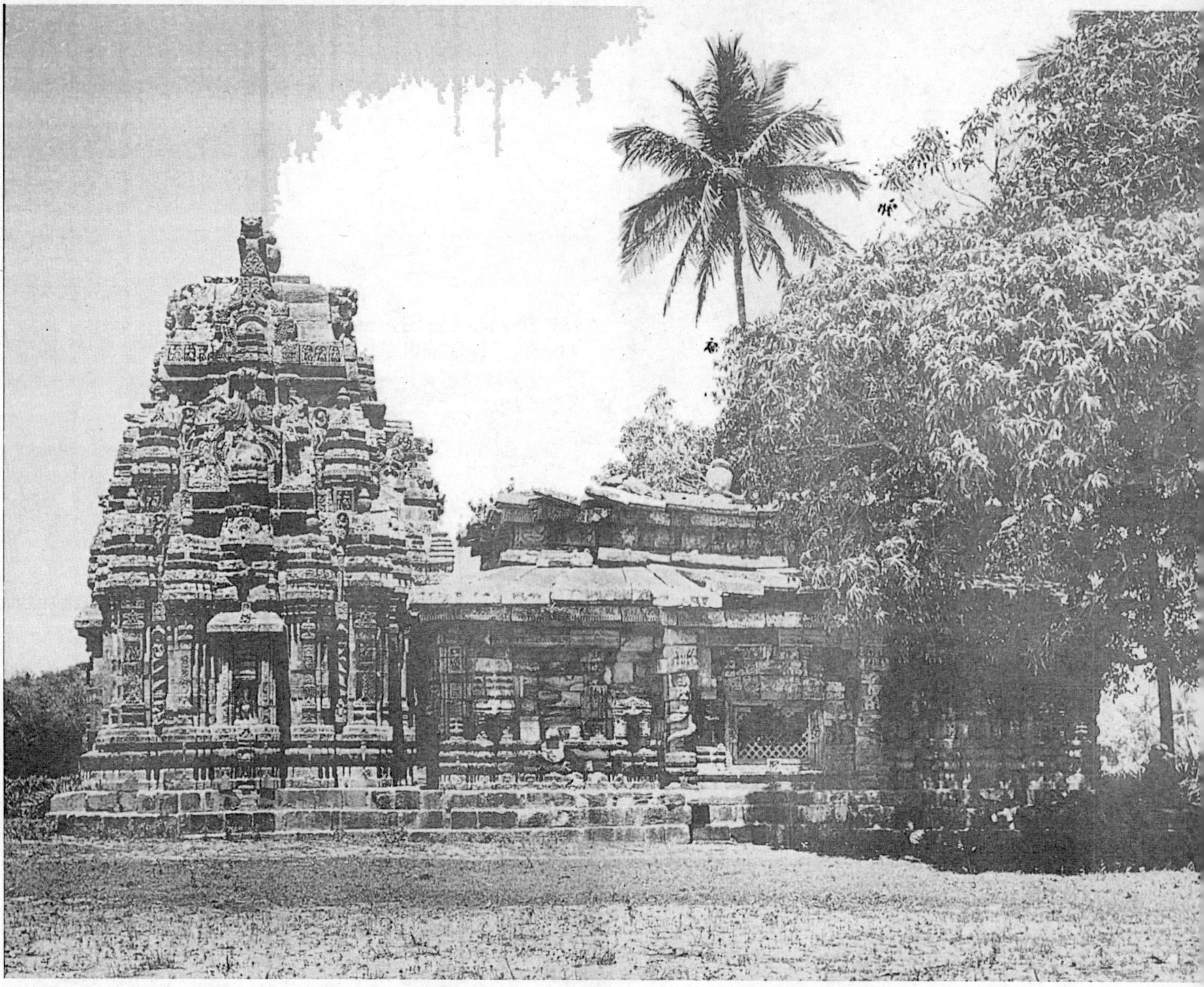

175. Chaurasi, Vārāhī temple. (AIIS).

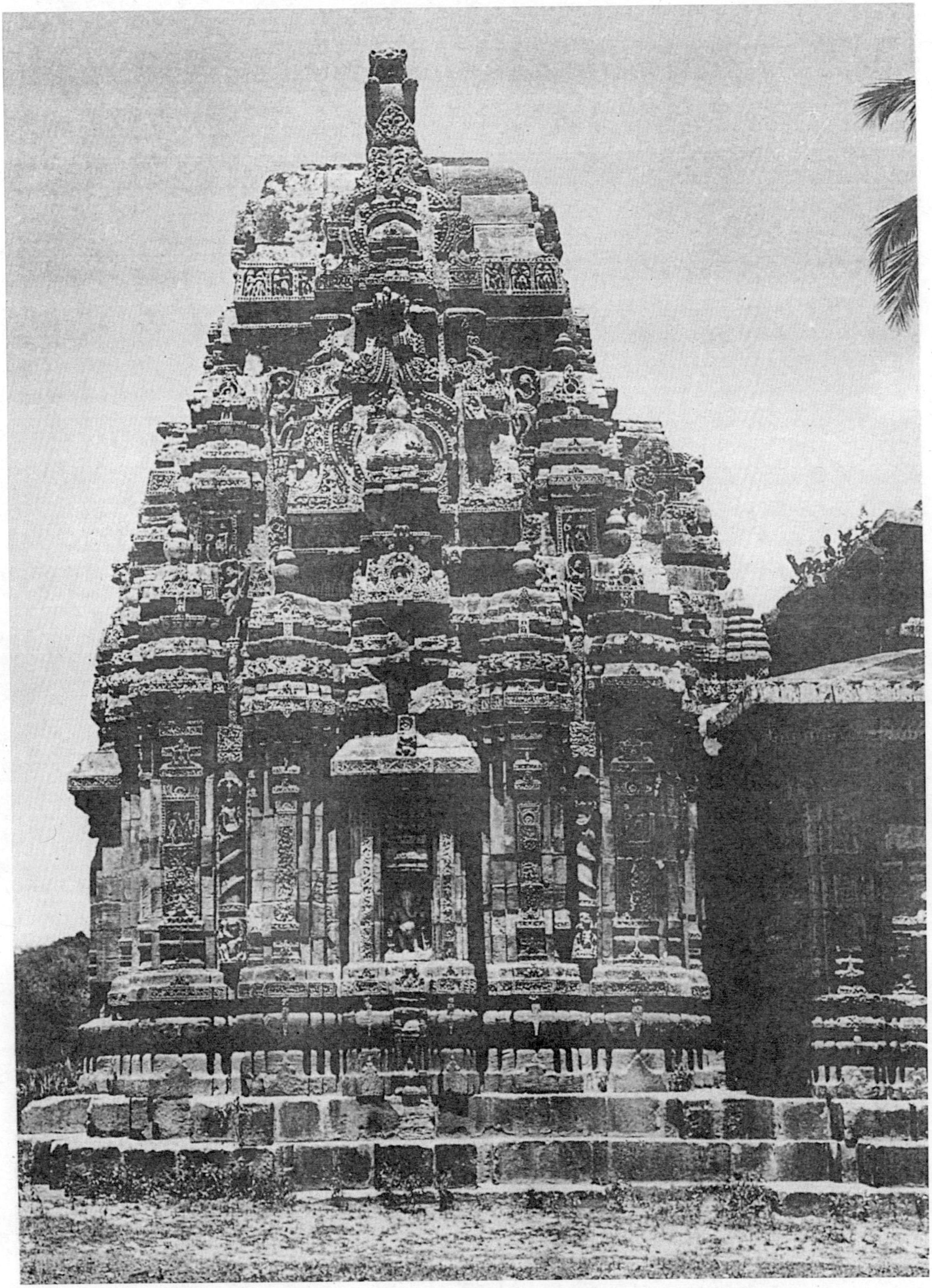

176: Vārāhī temple, *prāsāda*. (AIIS).

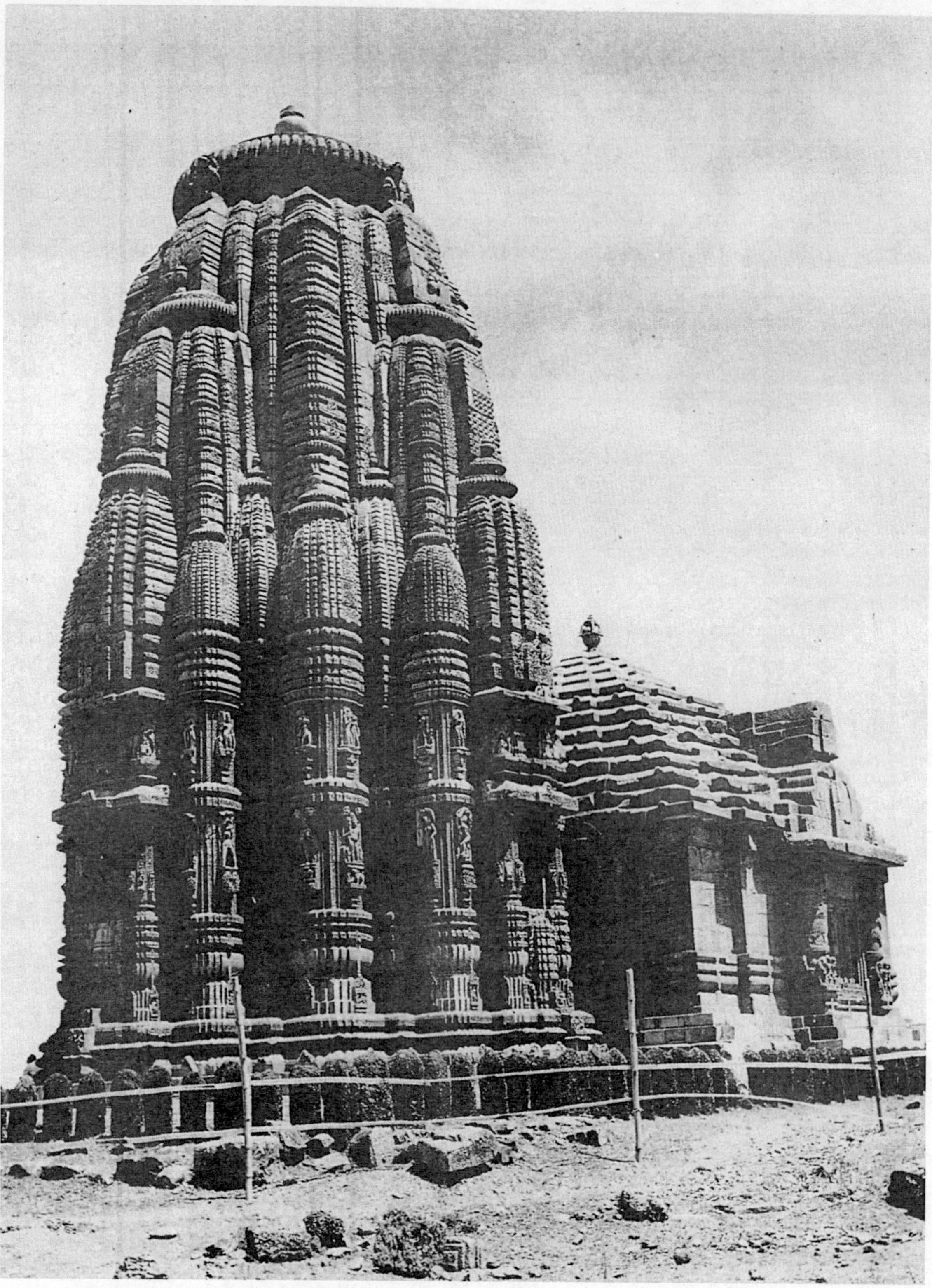

177. Bhubaneswar. Rājarāni temple. (AIIS).

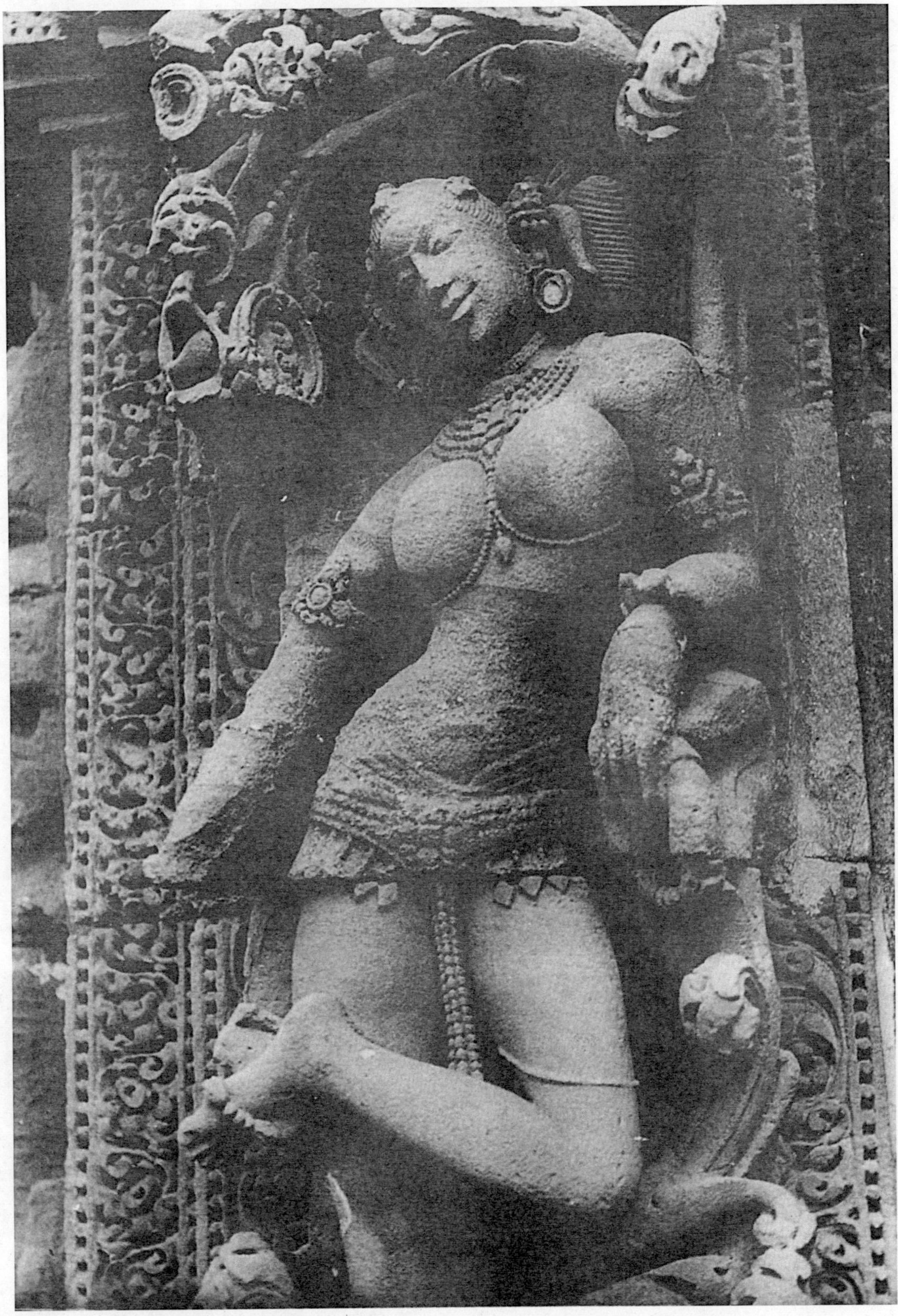

178. Rājarāni temple, female figure. (ASI).

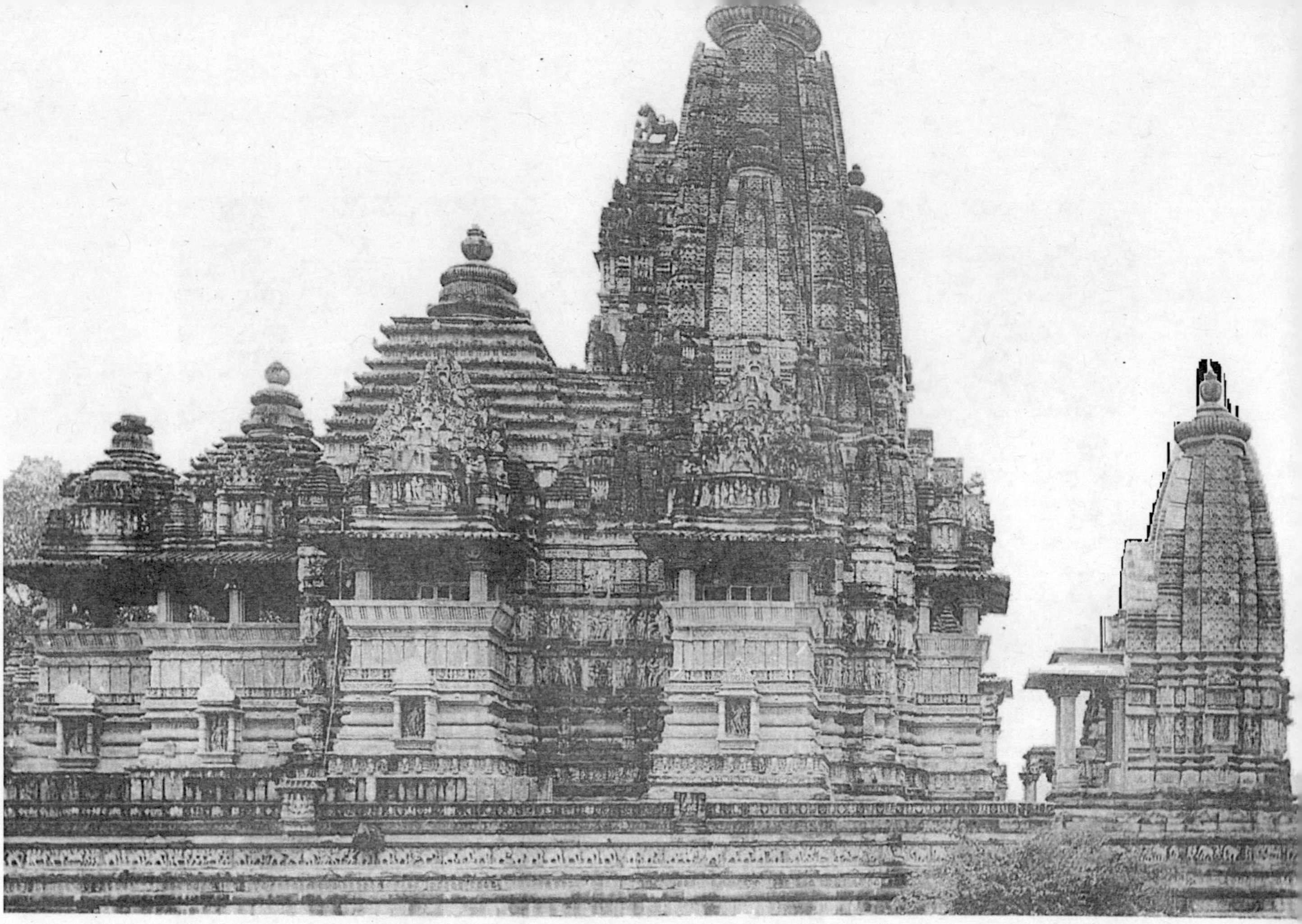

179. Khajuraho, Lakṣmaṇa temple. (AIIS).

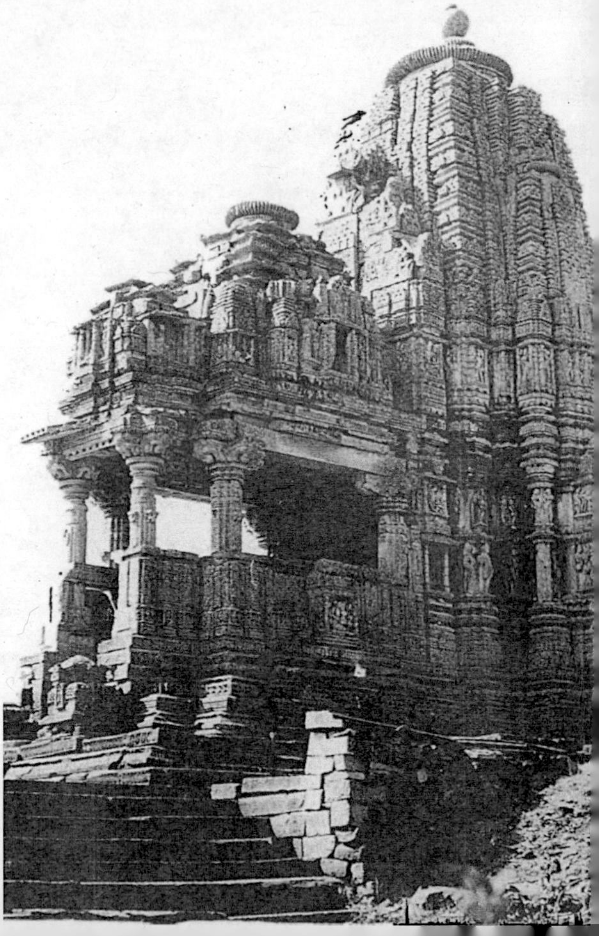

180. Kadwaha, Madhya Pradesh, Toteśvara temple. (AIIS).

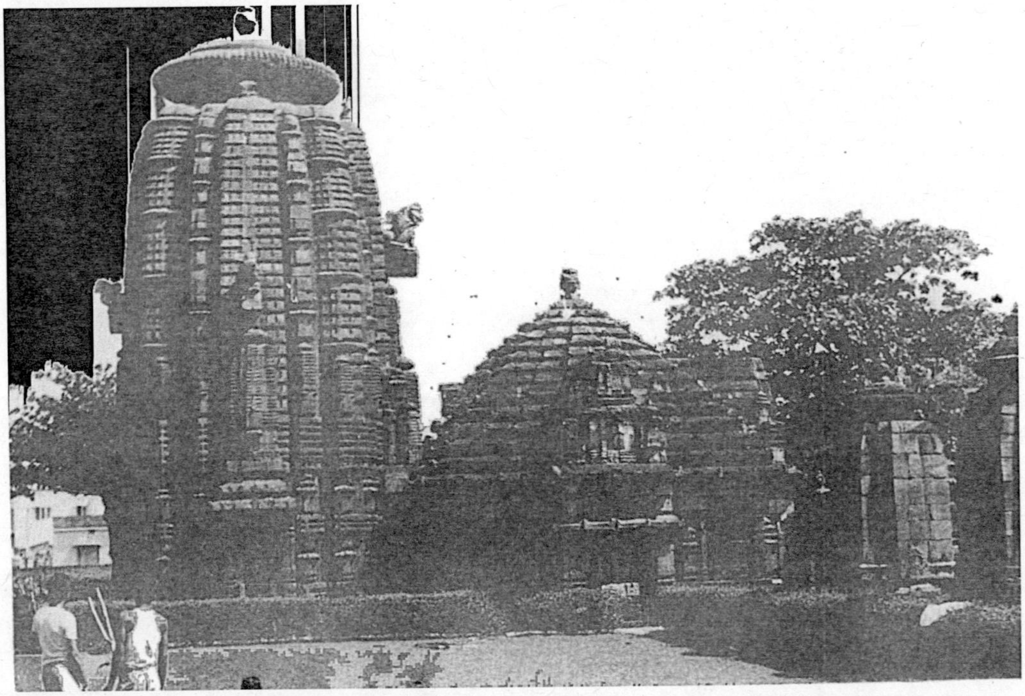

181. Bhubaneswar, Siddheśvara temple.

182. Bhubaneswar, Brahmeśvara temple. (AIIS).

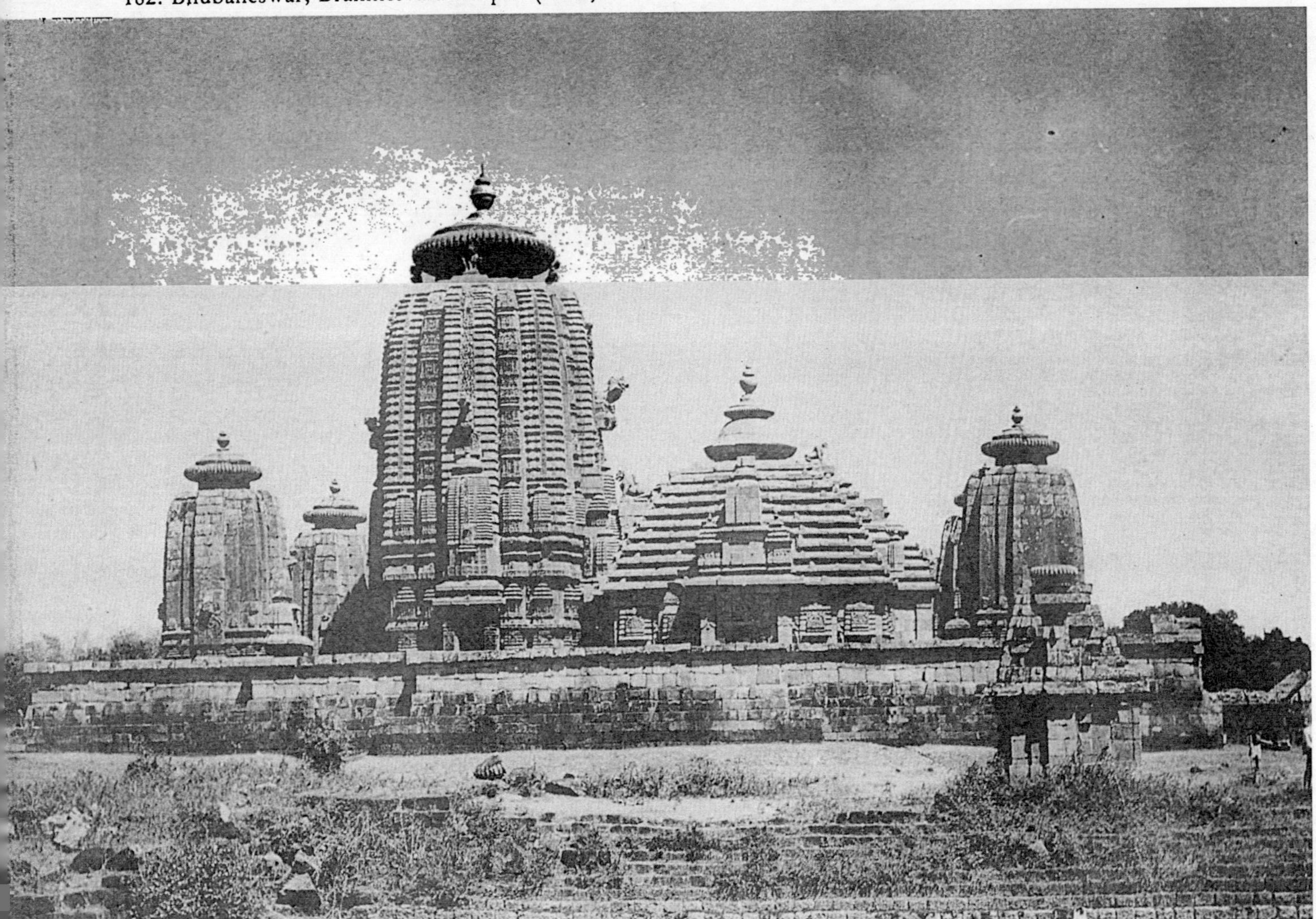

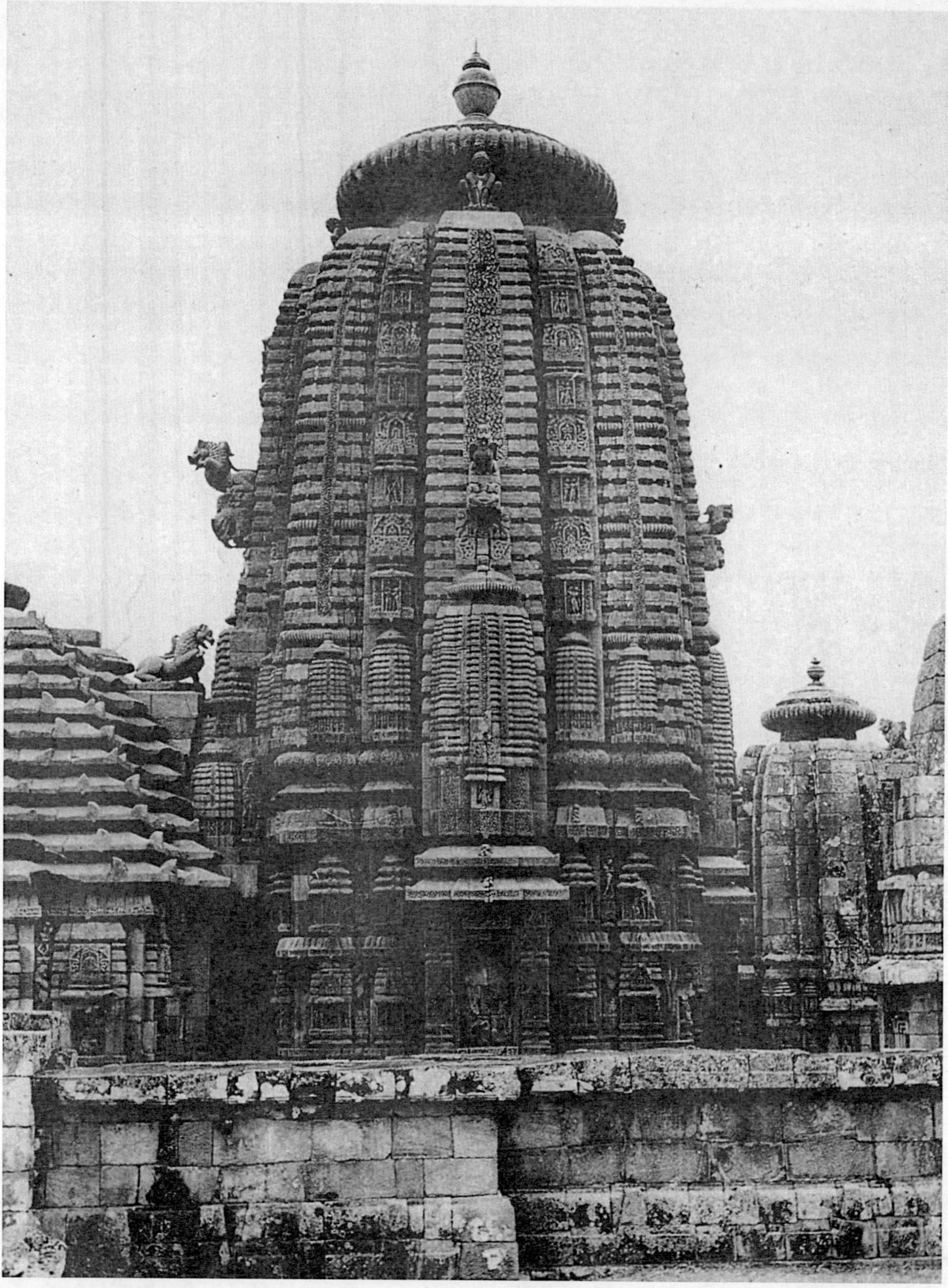

183. Brahmeśvara temple, *śikhara*. (AIIS).

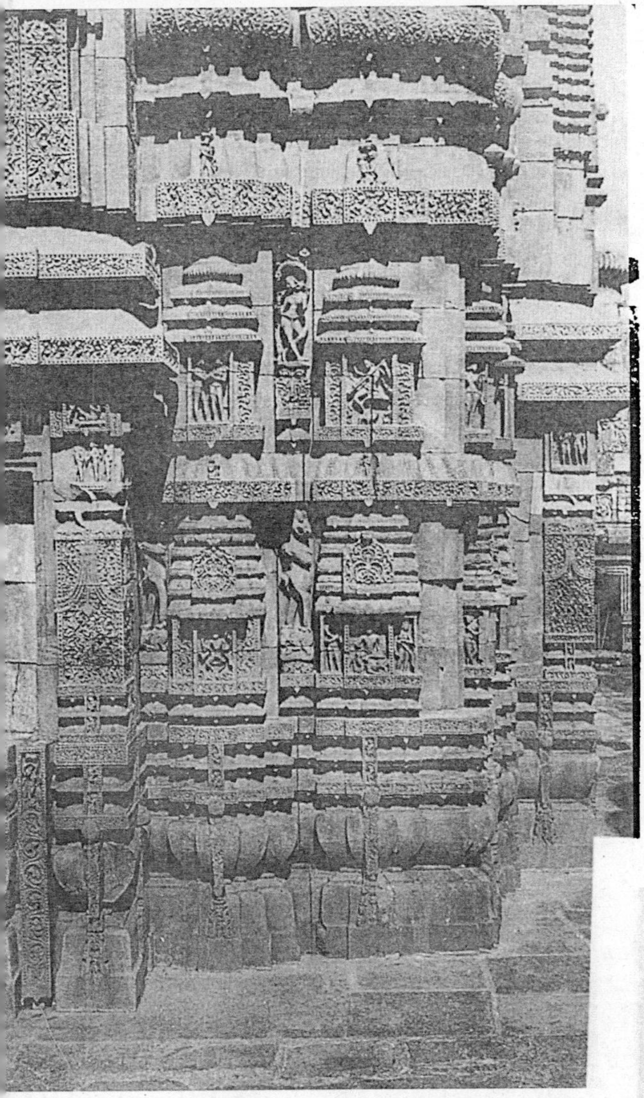

184. Brahmeśvara temple, detail, lower walls. (AIIS).

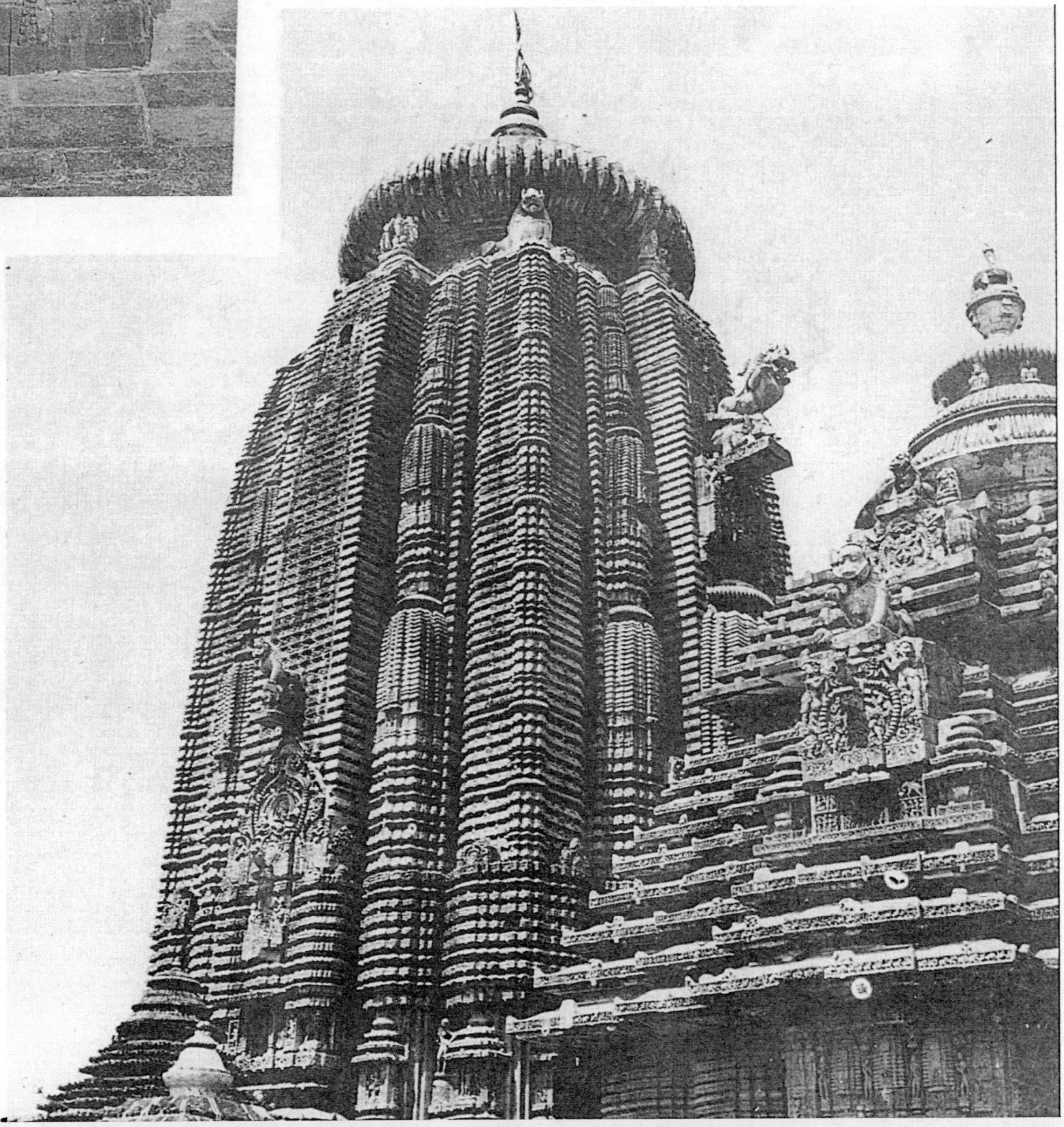

185. Bhubaneswar, Liṅgarāja temple. (AIIS).

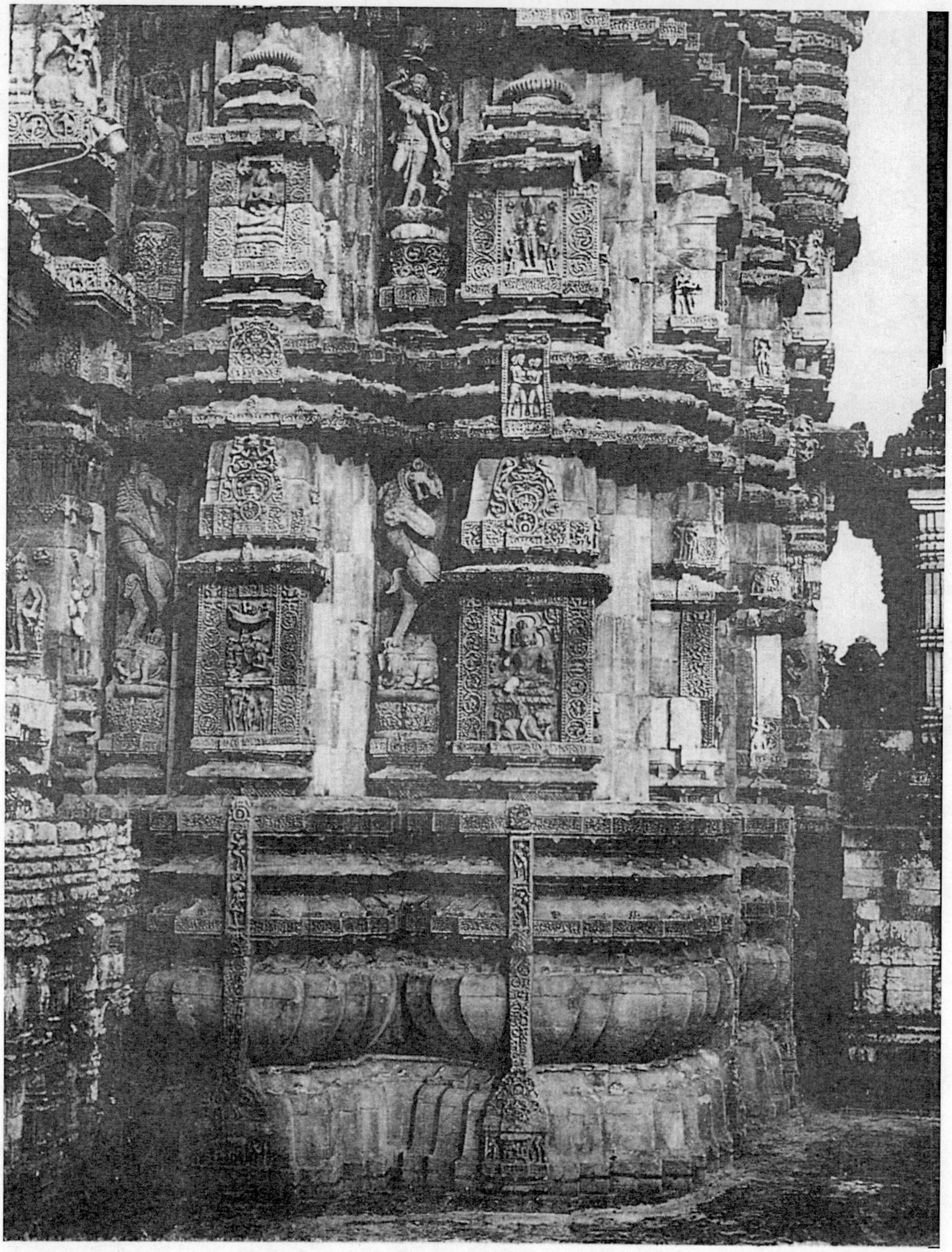

186. Liṅgarāja temple, detail of lower walls. (AIIS).